SPEECH

.8
7
56   4   14

.13.3
30)4.000   4F   .467
         L3   30)14.000
                    120
                    200

47

SPEECH

A Basic Text
THIRD EDITION

ROBERT C. JEFFREY
The University of Texas at Austin

OWEN PETERSON
Louisiana State University

1817
HARPER & ROW, PUBLISHERS, New York
Cambridge, Philadelphia, San Francisco,
London, Mexico City, São Paulo, Singapore, Sydney

Sponsoring Editor: Barbara Cinquegrani
Project Editor: Lenore Bonnie Biller
Text Design: Eileen Burke
Cover Design: Infield Design
Text Art: Vantage Art, Inc.
Photo Research: Mira Schachne
Production Manager: Jeanie Berke
Production Assistant: Paula Roppollo
Compositor: ComCom Division of Haddon Craftsmen, Inc.
Printer and Binder: R. R. Donnelley & Sons Co.
Cover Printer: Phoenix Color Corp.

Speech: A Basic Text, Third Edition

Library of Congress Cataloging in Publication Data

Jeffrey, Robert Campbell, 1927–
    Speech: a basic text.

    Includes bibliographies and index.
    1. Public speaking.   I. Peterson, Owen.   II. Title.
PN4121.J338   1989   808.5′1   88-24338

ISBN 0-06-043282-9

88 89 90 91 9 8 7 6 5 4 3 2 1

CONTENTS

PREFACE

The basic objective of *Speech: A Basic Text* is to present the principles and basic skills of effective speaking and to provide an appreciation of the nature, values, and uses of spoken communication. The ideas, principles, and practices discussed in this book apply to almost all forms of spoken discourse, including conversation, discussion, report giving, interviews, speeches for special occasions, debate, and reading aloud. The basic principles of effective communication that have developed over the past 2000 years still apply to most situations and vary only in detail. While our book is based on these 2000-year-old principles, it recognizes, too, the most recent theories and concepts of effective communication.

The authors have extensively revised this third edition of the text. We are grateful to our readers' insightful suggestions for improvement, and where applicable, we have incorporated their recommendations in this edition of *Speech: A Basic Text.* In response to those suggestions, we have, for example, eliminated the chapter on small groups and introduced a new chapter on listening.

In addition to updating the examples and illustrations in this edition, we have included portions of the adapted readings that appear in our other book, *Speech: A Text with Adapted Readings.* A significant feature of this book, these readings are designed to augment the textual material. We have tried to select readings that are contemporary and relate to contemporary problems confronting today's college and university students. Also included in this edition are models of student speeches and speeches with various rhetorical techniques identified in the margins. Another important feature of *Speech: A Basic Text* is the material in Chapter 17 on the legal and ethical responsibilities of the speaker.

We have provided many examples from speeches to demonstrate the principles of effective speech communication. Other materials seek to clarify difficult or complex concepts. Additionally, to aid the reader, each chapter begins with an outline of its contents and ends with study questions and exercises. For those interested in pursuing further any of the principles, additional readings are suggested.

Although the chapters in this edition have been rearranged in response to suggestions by its readers, we recognize that there is no single way to organize a textbook. Although we would probably use the book in the order published, experienced teachers may choose to assign chapters in a variety of ways.

We extend our appreciation to the publishers and authors of materials used in the book and to the many persons who assisted in reading, proofreading, and typing the manuscript. We wish to thank the following reviewers for their help: Halina Ablamowicz, SUNY Fredonia; Thompson Biggers, University of Miami; Sam Geonetta, University of Missouri at Rolla; Jim Jasinski, Southern Illinois University; Edith LeFevre, California State University, Sacramento; Norman Watson, University of South Dakota. Finally, we are particularly indebted to the following colleagues at Harper & Row who have contributed significantly to the project: Barbara Cinquegrani, sponsoring editor; Bonnie Biller, project editor; and Mira Schachne, photo researcher. Thanks also go to Zoe Kharpertion, copy editor.

Robert C. Jeffrey
Owen Peterson

CHAPTER 1

PRINCIPLES OF EFFECTIVE COMMUNICATION

Communication is probably more important today than it has been at any other time in history. With nuclear weapons capable of total destruction, population growth, the exploration of space, widespread poverty and famine, and amazing advances in science and technology, the world is beset with a welter of political, social, and economic problems. Most of these problems can be solved only through the development of mutual understanding and cooperation based on effective communication.

The advent of radio, television, and communication satellites has greatly enhanced the possibilities for effective communication. A speaker can now be heard instantaneously throughout the country and indeed most of the world. Television newscasts, documentaries, and programs such as "60 Minutes," "Meet the Press," and "20/20" help form Americans' perceptions of national and international affairs. Telecasts of the Watergate hearings in 1973 provided millions of citizens with an intimate glimpse of their government in action and contributed to the downfall of a president. Debates between candidates for political office from the local to the national level provide voters with information that influences their choices. Estimates of the audiences for debates between presidential candidates in several elections have ranged from 85 to more than 100 million.

Globally, almost half of the world's population heard Neil Armstrong's first words as he set foot on the moon. Famine in Africa, airplane hijackings, summit conferences, rock concerts, natural disasters, and other events can be viewed on television throughout most of the world. As the communications industry reaches even more remote countries, ever larger numbers of people—many unable to read or write—are brought into direct contact with the rest of the world. Because of these developments, the influence of the spoken word on peoples all over the globe is destined to become even more important in the future.

In this age of mass communication, however, it is still possible for individuals and small groups to exert an influence. Battling one of the largest corporations in the country, Ralph Nader used lectures and testimony before congressional committees to force manufacturers to produce safer automobiles and provided the incentive for a national consumer movement. The speeches of countless women, most unknown beyond their local communities, have focused attention on the status of women in our society. Likewise, the ecology movement has been largely the work of relatively unknown individuals interested in improving the environment in which we live. These examples and others attest to the importance of the individual in bringing about change.

While spoken communication affects everyone because of its impact on broad national and international issues, for most of us effective communication is important because of the ways it influences and affects our daily lives. Persons who communicate effectively usually find this ability makes their lives easier in terms of obtaining what they want, getting along with others, avoiding misunderstanding, making decisions, and leading better lives.

Considering how much talking a person does and the variety of ways speech is used in daily life, it is surprising how little attention most of us give to the way we speak. Even people in jobs and professions in which success depends on the ability to communicate with others often have little understanding of the speech process. Perhaps most people have spoken so much since they first learned to talk that they simply accept the fact that they *can* speak and only rarely stop to think about how, why, and when they do it. Sometimes this unconcern can keep a person from recognizing the true causes of speech communication difficulties. If things go wrong, people tend to blame others, when in fact it may be their own communication inadequacies that have caused or contributed to the problem. To improve communication and reduce the likelihood of communication breakdowns, speakers need to understand the speech process.

IMPORTANCE OF EFFECTIVE SPEECH COMMUNICATION

A first step toward better communication is to develop an appreciation of the importance of speech in one's daily activity. Speech communication does not refer only to public addresses such as lectures, sermons, and political talks. Although such speaking is important, the average person spends much more time communicating in less formal situations.

During a typical week, the average person is likely to engage in spoken communication with family, friends, coworkers, supervisors, employees, waiters, receptionists, salespersons, professional consultants such as doctors, lawyers, dentists, and educators, and others. The communication may consist of making a telephone call, ordering lunch, arranging a business transaction, making a purchase, visiting a doctor, giving directions or advice, asking for information, explaining a problem, participating in a class discussion, or conversing at a party, to mention a few examples.

To regard these situations as events of little significance is a mistake. Breakdowns in communication in these situations can result in bitterness, argument, confusion, mistakes, misunderstanding, or some other frustrating or disappointing experience.

The production and distribution of information is a major occupation, one that approached half the total United States output in 1985. The government and economy of this country can no longer be understood without appreciating the ever-expanding role of what is called "the knowledge indus-

In the United States there are more than twenty thousand different ways of earning a living and effective speech is essential to every one.

ANDREW WEAVER

try." A rapidly changing society needs to be able to organize the vast flood of information that is essential to our lives and environment.

Organizing and disseminating this information requires an appreciation of the importance of communication in person-to-person encounters. Saul Alinsky emphasizes:

> One can lack any of the qualities of an organizer—with one exception— and still be effective and successful. That exception is the art of communication. It does not matter what you know about anything if you cannot communicate to your people. In that event you are not even a failure. You're just not there.
>
> Communication with others takes place when they understand what you're trying to get across to them. If they don't understand then you are not communicating, regardless of words, pictures, or anything else.

FUNCTIONS OF SPEECH COMMUNICATION

Speech communication fulfills many functions and purposes. Probably its most important use is to influence others. In almost all spoken discourse, the speaker—consciously or unconsciously—seeks to affect the listener in some way: to provide information; to modify or change attitudes, beliefs, or conduct; to entertain or amuse; to attract; to strengthen conviction; to conciliate or antagonize; or to win respect, friendship, or support. At times we may speak with total spontaneity—as when we hit our thumb with a hammer or another car recklessly swerves in front of us. However, except for these infrequent exceptions, all speech communication is purposive. Because speech is purposive, it is important in fulfilling our needs and in understanding and responding to the objectives of others.

From a psychological point of view, speech communication is important to the individual in the realization of goals, in the expression of personality, and in the adjustment to society. One can imagine the frustration one would feel if one were unable to communicate to others, forced to be a silent observer, barely acknowledged, whose opinions were never sought. Speech communication contributes to social and psychological stability by enabling individuals to make known their ideas and feelings, to proclaim their existence, and to adjust and adapt to their surroundings.

From a broader perspective, speech communication is important in preserving one's heritage, transmitting cultural values, and maintaining social cohesion. To a large extent, it is through the spoken word that beliefs, traditions, customs, and our sense of identity are reinforced and passed from one generation to the next.

ESSENTIAL ELEMENTS OF SPEECH COMMUNICATION

From the time of ancient Greece to the present, scholars have attempted to explain the process of oral communication. Their approaches differ, and their terminology is not the same. The purpose of this textbook is not to review the different theories or to advance the merits of one approach over another but rather to provide basic information about the nature of oral communication.

Regardless of terminology, scholars agree that speech communication involves four essential elements: the speaker, the message, the channel, and the listener.

The Speaker

In spoken communication, the source of the message is a speaker, but it is possible to communicate without a speaker. Clocks, speedometers, traffic signals, thermometers, billboards, and class bells communicate, but these are not forms of speech and, of course, do not require a speaker. Newspapers, magazines, books, letters, blueprints, shorthand, sign language, Braille, and computers also communicate, but none requires a speaker.

Distinguishing between communication in which a speaker is the source of the message and other communication is essential to understanding the speech process.

The Message

The second necessary element of speech communication is a message. The message is the expression by the speaker of ideas through the use of symbols. A distinction should be made between the speaker's ideas and the message. As long as the speaker merely *thinks* ideas without actually uttering them, no message exists.

Only when the speaker takes deliberate action to communicate ideas audibly does a message come into being. The message can be said to consist of those disturbances, alterations, or disruptions of the physical environment set in motion by the speaker for the purpose of conveying an idea to someone else.

The Channel

The third essential element of speech communication, the channel, may be defined as the means, medium, or instruments used to convey or transmit the message. Conceivably, the source might choose to convey the message through smoke signals, sign language, a billboard, or any of several other channels, all capable of carrying a message, but in spoken communication the speaker depends on the verbal and nonverbal symbols of speech. The verbal symbols are the sounds the speaker makes by vibrating the vocal cords and manipulating the tongue, lips, teeth, palate, and breath supply. The nonverbal symbols include the speaker's facial expression, gestures, eye contact, movement, and other physical characteristics that affect the meaning of the words and sentences.

The Listener

The final element essential to spoken communication is a receiver of the message. While the receiver is often the listener or hearer, *receiver* is probably a more accurate term because the person to whom a message is directed does more than passively listen to or hear the message. The receiver also perceives the physical attributes of the speaker and influences the speaker by his or her reactions and responses.

CHARACTERISTICS OF SPEECH COMMUNICATION

Speech communication is unlike any other form of communication. Although it shares common characteristics with other modes of communication, several factors make it unique. Some of the important and unusual characteristics of speech communication are discussed next.

Speech Is Purposive

Almost every word that a person utters is said with a definite purpose in mind. From a simple request such as "Please pass the salt" to a classroom discussion, a conversation, a committee meeting, interview, sermon, or lecture, most speaking springs from a desire to obtain a specific response from the listener or listeners: to inform, to convince, to persuade, to inspire, or to entertain.

The speaker whose aim is to inform wants the listener to understand and remember what is said. In trying to convince, the speaker seeks to alter the beliefs or attitudes of the auditor. Persuasive speech goes a step further and seeks to influence the actions of the hearer. Inspirational speeches strengthen beliefs and attitudes already held by the listener. The speaker whose aim is to entertain seeks only to provide enjoyment.

Speech Involves Interaction

In most situations, speech communication is characterized by an interaction between two or more individuals: the speaker and listener or listeners. Exceptions to this statement would include broadcasts from a studio where no listeners are present, a closed-circuit television lecture, an announcement over a public address system in an office, school, or business, and other situations where there is no possibility of some form of response or feedback that could influence the speaker.

But the above exceptions are not representative of most spoken discourse. Speech communication usually occurs in face-to-face situations where the speaker can observe the auditors and vice versa. When the speaker and the listener face each other directly, the source-message-receiver relationship differs significantly from that of written communication. Written communication is largely a one-way process, whereas speech involves an interaction between the source and the receiver. In writing, the source has no way of knowing how the reader will respond. Once the message is committed to paper, a writer has no way of adapting to the reader's responses.

A speaker, on the other hand, has the distinct advantage of being able to see the receiver and to respond to cues from the auditor. The cue may be a yawn, smile, laugh, look of confusion, fidgeting, appearance of interest, shaking the head, inattention, note taking, interruptions, and other indications of the receiver's response. Cues may also include such overt responses as applause, booing, heckling, hisses, and cheers.

A speaker first lectures, then responds with a laugh, and finally listens. *(The Miami News)*

A question period provides an opportunity for interaction between the speaker and audience. (Teresa Zabala, NYT Pictures)

Such reactions provide speakers with information on how well they are communicating. Capable speakers respond to these cues and modify and adapt their messages to create interest and improve effectiveness.

This interaction, this flow of information back and forth between the source and the receiver in speech communication, is an important aid to the speaker in achieving effective communication.

Speech Is Transitory

Unlike a book, newspaper, magazine, or other printed document, speech is fleeting. Once a spoken message has been uttered, it is not likely to be repeated and cannot be reread or picked up at leisure for review or study.

Only the smallest fraction of all the oral communication that takes place in one day is recorded or reproduced in print. This means that to grasp and react to a speaker's meaning, the listener must respond at once. Auditors exercise little control over the conditions that affect reception of the speaker's message: they cannot choose a time when they are more alert; they cannot change the room temperature if they are uncomfortable; they are unable to look up the meaning of unfamiliar words; they possess no control over the rate at which the speaker speaks; they cannot review difficult passages; and they often can do nothing to eliminate distracting elements.

The listener's lack of control over the speaking situation forces the speaker to anticipate problems that may interfere with effective communication and to present the message in a manner that the auditor is able to understand and respond to at the time.

Speech Occurs in Specific Settings

Few people probably know where, when, and under what circumstances Ernest Hemingway wrote *A Farewell to Arms,* Mozart composed *Don Giovanni,* Rembrandt painted *The Night Watch,* David O. Selznick filmed *Gone with the Wind,* or Charles Schulz draws his "Peanuts" cartoons. Yet all these communicate messages and have provided countless persons with pleasure, inspiration, and ideas. As is true of much communication, an individual's response to these works is not dependent on the circumstances surrounding their creation.

A distinctive feature of speech communication, however, is that its effectiveness may be greatly influenced by the place, time, and conditions of its expression. Speech is both purposive and transitory. It is designed for a specific purpose and specific listeners at a specific time. Because of this, the result of any speech communication venture is affected by the setting in which it occurs.

Certain times, places, and occasions restrict a speaker's choice of messages and manner of presentation. Religious services, business meetings, funerals, retirement banquets, pep rallies, and inauguration ceremonies are occasions in which the expectations of the participants may render certain subjects and kinds of communication inappropriate. The place in which the communication occurs—a courtroom, office, church, fraternity house, home, auditorium, street corner, legislative chamber, or classroom—may also influence the type and manner of communication of a speaker. The size of the room, seating arrangements, acoustics, lighting, heating, and number of people present may affect the listeners' receptiveness to a speaker's message. Even the décor may contribute to a speaker's success or failure: a flag and red, white, and blue bunting; stained-glass windows and religious symbols; a dim, dark, run-down hall; or a brightly lit, colorful, and plushly furnished setting can create an atmosphere either conducive or detrimental to a speaker's purpose.

Time—time of day, time of year—can be important. Many people are not fully awake early in the morning, many are tired and drowsy late at night, and most tend to be somewhat lethargic following a meal. All these factors affect a listener's receptiveness and must be taken into account by the speaker. In addition, people's interests tend to vary according to the time of year. In the winter, people are more likely to be interested in skiing, Christmas, basketball, and snowmobiles than at other times of the year. Camping trips, vacations, baseball, picnics, yard care, and swimming are topics of more immediate interest to most people in the summer than at any other season. In the spring, thoughts turn to planting, outdoor activities, and plans for the summer. Fall for many people is the season for going back to school, raking leaves, football, and elections.

Particular events may affect the listener's interest at various times. Holidays such as Halloween, Thanksgiving, St. Patrick's Day, Easter, Passover, the Fourth of July, Mardi Gras, and Labor Day may heighten interest in a subject. Events such as the World Series, the Kentucky Derby, the Super Bowl, the Indianapolis 500, Wimbledon, and a championship boxing match may serve to focus attention on a sport. A crisis, scandal, or sensational trial; a hurricane, flood, or other natural disaster; and the death or assassination of a prominent figure may lead to a greater concern about these topics on the part of most people than they would otherwise feel.

Speech communication does not occur in a vacuum. Effective speech communication takes into account and adapts to the time, place, and circumstances of the speech setting.

Speech Is Influenced by the Fields of Experience of the Participants

Edgar Dale reports a conversation between a rabid baseball fan and an Englishman seeing a baseball game for the first time:

> The Englishman asked, "What is a pitcher?"
>
> "He's the man down there pitching the ball to the catcher."
>
> "But," said the Englishman, "all of the players pitch the ball and all of them catch the ball. There aren't just two persons who pitch and catch."
>
> Later the Englishman asked, "How many strikes do you get before you are out?"
>
> The baseball fan said, "Three."
>
> "But," replied the Englishman, "that man struck at the ball five times before he was out."

This conversation is an example of communication that ran into difficulty because the participants lacked a common field of experience. Neither one was actually wrong. Both agreed generally on what the words *pitch, catch,* and *strike* meant, but because of differences in their background and experience the terms did not have precisely the same meaning for the two of them.

Another example of lack of a common field of experience is found in the following excerpt from a London *Times* article on the retirement of an outstanding cricket player:

> Chosen as a *slow bowler,* he *sent down* 89 *overs* in the match. . . . He has scored 8032 *runs* and taken 235 *Test wickets* and 110 *Test catches.* He played an *inning* of 254. . . . He could equally well have *bowled* an *opening spell* with the *new ball* to strike terror into the hearts of the best *batsmen.* . . . He has been as likely to win a *Test match* with a breathtaking catch in the *leg trap* as with a brilliant throw from *cover point;* as likely to turn another with a spell of *orthodox, left arm spin* . . . as with a dozen *overs* of *chinamen* and *googlies* or a couple of *fast inswingers.*

Because words are symbols, language can produce understanding only if the words mean the same to both the source and the receiver of the message. When the speaker and listener attach different meanings to words, the result is a misunderstanding, even though the two parties may not realize it.

Words mean different things to different people because of differences in their fields of experience. In spite of tremendous advances in mass communications in recent years, persons whose field of experience consists of what they see on television and read cannot have the same understanding as others who are active participants.

For example, can a person who has never been in jail fully share an ex-convict's knowledge and feelings about prison? How well can a successful executive understand the concerns of a migrant worker? Does an increase in the cost of food mean the same thing to a well-to-do suburban family as it does to a family on welfare? Differences in experience not only determine each person's knowledge and understanding, but they also influence priorities and values.

Because one's understanding of the meaning of words is influenced by one's experiences, a speaker must be cognizant of and adapt to the listener's field of experience. Age, sex, education, religion, nationality, ethnic background, occupation, financial status, and social acceptance influence the understanding of a speaker's language and message.

Speech Lacks the Visual Cues of Writing

A reader can open this book to almost any page and find a variety of visible cues that help convey the authors' message. Capitalization and punctuation marks assist in comprehending the meanings of individual sentences. Indentations show new divisions or paragraphs. Italics and boldface type emphasize important ideas. Headings and subheadings assist in determining the writer's pattern of organization. Although these common writing devices are so familiar that a reader is hardly aware of them, they are of inestimable value to the writer. Lacking visual cues, the speaker must employ other devices to clarify his or her meaning and organization. These include vocal inflections, pauses, changes in rate and loudness of speaking, emphasis of important words, gestures, facial expressions, previews, transitions, internal summaries, and visual aids.

Speech Has a Distinctive Vocabulary

Most people have a reading vocabulary larger than their listening vocabulary. It is not uncommon for readers to understand printed words whose pronunciation they would not recognize. Because of the more limited vocabulary of the listener, a speaker usually should use simpler language than would a writer.

People today are accustomed to speech that is conversational and informal. Consequently, contractions a writer might avoid may actually prove helpful to the speaker. In a speech, *can't, shouldn't, aren't, I'm, we'll,* and *they're* may be more appropriate than a writer's *cannot, should not, are not, I am, we will,* and *they are.* Colloquial and regional words and expressions that might detract from a written work are usually readily accepted when appropriately used in speech.

Speech and writing differ not only in the words used but also in the way these words are put together into sentences. As experienced speakers who have prepared manuscript speeches know, some passages that read well simply do not sound right when spoken. They may be too complex, too lengthy, or tongue twisters almost impossible to say smoothly and meaningfully. To achieve a natural, conversational quality, most speakers find that short, simple sentences with few subordinate clauses are more effective than longer and more complex sentences.

Because of its vocabulary, speech cannot provide the same kind of communication as writing. To develop a natural oral quality, the speaker must give careful attention to word choice and sentence structure.

THE SPEECH COMMUNICATION PROCESS

Everything discussed so far has been included to help you understand the elements and distinctive characteristics of speech communication. Now it is time to examine the communication process itself.

Formulating the Message

Speech communication begins when someone decides to try to influence someone else. Many factors may motivate the speaker in reaching this decision. A desire to help, a sense of duty, a need for assistance, feelings of outrage or anger, a sense of justice, a respect for truth, a wish to impress, or a need for acceptance are a few of many possible motives that might prompt a person to wish to say something.

A variety of stimuli contribute to an individual's motivation to communicate. The stimuli are both internal and external.

INTERNAL STIMULI.   Internal stimuli are impulses received by the brain as a result of a person's physiological or psychological state. For example, fatigue, illness, hunger, thirst, good health, a full stomach, and relaxation affect a person's perception of a situation and the desire to do something about it. Psychologically, depression, shock, worry, happiness, enthusiasm, acceptance, or a feeling of insecurity might influence one's reaction to a given idea or condition.

EXTERNAL STIMULI.   In addition to these general states of physical and mental well-being or distress, the speaker receives other specific stimuli from sources outside the body. These external stimuli come to the individual through the senses—sight, hearing, smell, touch, and taste. The stimulus may be a single experience that has a profound effect on the individual or, more commonly, a series of stimuli that in combination lead to a particular response. For example, personal observation of a fatal automobile accident might prompt one to express concern for safe driving; on the other hand, this same impulse might be the result of reading newspaper stories about the increase in traffic fatalities, seeing television reports of automobile accidents, and listening to a lecture on the causes of automobile accidents.

External factors often are less obvious. The unpleasant smell of cigarette smoke, the disagreeable taste of cafeteria food, or the boring drone of a dull teacher might influence one's attitudes toward smoking regulations, the university food service, or the quality of education. Some stimuli affect people only at the unconscious level. For example, students' attitudes toward a particular course may be influenced by a windowless classroom, poor lighting, the drab color of the walls, the seating arrangement, the hum of outside traffic, and other covert stimuli of which they are not consciously aware and that, in reality, have little or nothing to do with the value of the course.

External stimuli affecting attitudes and the drive to communicate may be immediate or remote. A specific, immediate act, event, or statement may serve to motivate a person's wish to retort or respond. Although a specific event may trigger a response, more often the way a person reacts to any situation is determined by past training and experiences.

Because of the differences in the experiences of individuals, a single stimulus may evoke a variety of communication responses. What is accepted without a second thought by one person may arouse the indignation of another. Not only do individuals differ in how they react to a stimulus, they also differ in the kinds of stimuli they consciously perceive. For example, ask a group of people to glance out a window for a few moments and then to list what they recall having seen. Some will list items that others have overlooked. It is almost certain that no two lists will be identical. This can be explained by what is known as *selectivity* or *discrimination* in perceiving stimuli. At any given moment, everyone is bombarded by a variety of stimuli, and each individual will select or consciously perceive only a limited number of the stimuli. Thus, until someone says, "I hear a faucet dripping," "I wish they would turn down their stereo," "I wish that dog would stop barking," or "Why doesn't he quit tapping his fingers?" you may not notice these distractions.

The stimuli of which a person is consciously aware are constantly changing. These changes are based on the immediacy or importance of the stimuli to the individual. While we perceive many stimuli—at least unconsciously—at any given moment we allow only the more important ones to enter our consciousness.

Encoding the Message

Encoding is the process of translating thought into verbal symbols (spoken language) and nonverbal symbols (such as facial expression, gestures, and movement) of speech. It is highly unlikely that any two people will select exactly the same symbols to express the same idea. The words a speaker chooses to present a message and the manner in which the speaker expresses that message will differ according to the individual's perceptions, experiences, values, and facility with language. In addition, the context in which the communication takes place may alter the speaker's language and physical expression.

A speaker who is aware of the importance of adapting a message to the listener and the occasion will encode ideas into language suited to the auditor as well as the time, place, and purpose.

Transmitting the Message

The third step in the speech communication process is the transmission of signals destined for the listener. This is the stage of the process when the speaker actually utters the ideas. In some situations, the formulation and encoding of an idea may occur almost instantaneously, as when a person replies to a question or is prompted to respond immediately to something that has just been said. In prepared speeches, however, the speaker can carefully think through the ideas and the best way to present them in advance of their actual transmission. Regardless of the amount of time and thought given to the formulation and preparation of the message, communication begins only when the speaker actually states the message.

Transmission of the message consists of disturbing the airwaves with audible sounds (spoken language) and the light waves with physical movements (gestures, eye contact, facial expressions). These disturbances are then perceived by the receiver or listener.

Decoding the Message

Once the message reaches the receiver, decoding begins. At this point, the listeners begin to play a role in the speech communication process. Depending on what they have seen and heard (they may have missed an important word or misunderstood a key sentence because of distracting noises, poor acoustics, inattention, or any of several other reasons) and how they interpret what they have observed (determined by their past experiences, knowledge, and attitudes), the listeners will then proceed to decode the message.

It is at this stage that breakdowns in communication most often occur. The speaker may be at fault for misjudging the listener's field of experience, knowledge, vocabulary, or attitudes. The listener may be at fault because of inattention or prejudice. But regardless of who is to blame, when a receiver understands a message differently from the way the speaker intended it to be understood, effective communication has broken down.

At the decoding stage, communication may break down for any of several reasons. It may be that the listener is unfamiliar with the symbols employed by the speaker. For example, if the message were communicated in a language the receiver didn't speak, the symbols would mean nothing. Even when the source and the receiver speak a common language, the listener may be unable to decode the signals correctly because of abstract language, technical terminology, or jargon. At times the receiver may understand each word but misinterpret the message because of sentence structure, ambiguous words, or confusion caused by an inappropriate gesture, facial expression, or inflection. A communication breakdown may occur simply because the receiver has difficulty hearing what the speaker is saying.

Interpreting the Message

As they decode the signals transmitted by the source, the auditors determine what they think the speaker's symbols mean and send this understanding to its final destination, the brain. If for any reason the speaker's signals are decoded inaccurately, the auditor will *interpret* the message incorrectly. Differences in the fields of experience of the source and receiver may also lead to an incorrect interpretation of the message; a listener may understand exactly what the speaker has said but fail to respond in the way the speaker desires because he or she does not share with the speaker a common understanding of the message. For example, people who have never experienced poverty, starvation, discrimination, a physical handicap, fame, or wealth will have a different understanding of these conditions and respond in a different manner from those who have experienced such conditions. Although they may think that they understand the speaker's ideas, they may transmit to the brain a message quite different from what the source intended.

Interference

While effective communication is to a large extent dependent on the knowledge, experiences, and values of the participants, its success may also be affected by factors beyond the control of either the source or the receiver. These extraneous factors are known as *interference.* Most people are probably familiar with the interference caused by "snow" and floating pictures on the television screen, and the buzzing, clicking, and hum of a poor telephone connection, but interference is not restricted to mechanical or technical difficulties.

Interference may take many forms. One of the most common types of interference is noise: the noise of people talking, whispering, clearing their throats, coughing, shuffling their feet, or shifting position; the noise of equipment such as radiators, air conditioners, fluorescent lighting, piped-in music, typewriters, or office machines; and the noise of outside traffic, honking horns, airplanes passing overhead, an ambulance siren, or a sound truck. Even the weather may provide interference in the form of rain, thunder, and gusts of wind.

At other times the interference may be visual: a light shining in one's eyes, reflections of the sun, or poor lighting. The décor of a room may prove distracting if it includes unusual posters, signs, or furnishings. Even the dress or appearance of a speaker could be distracting and interfere with effective communication.

The conditions under which the communication occurs may interfere. Cold, heat, poor ventilation, the smell of smoke or gas, or an unpleasant odor may cause interference. Disrupting activities such as people coming and going, the interruption of a telephone call, and the seating of latecomers are other sources of interference.

Interference may even result from a pleasing or fascinating distraction. The presence of a celebrity or important person, the splendor or historic significance of the setting, or the tempting aroma of food emanating from a nearby room might very easily distract listeners and interfere with the communication process.

In addition to these distractions, interference may result from a faulty microphone or amplifier; difficulty in seeing the speaker; the seating arrangement; audience interruptions such as heckling, cheering, booing, and applause; or the activity of reporters and television technicians.

Occasionally, a momentous event preoccupies listeners' minds to such a degree that it interferes with normal communication. For example, the assassination of President John F. Kennedy, the landing of American astronauts on the moon, the Watergate scandal, and the Iranian hostage crisis could have evoked emotions that interfered with calm, lucid communication. Sometimes the interference may result from a more local incident, such as the Mount St. Helens volcanic explosion, the Three Mile Island nuclear plant accident, or a hurricane, flood, or tornado.

Whatever the cause, interference may keep the auditor from hearing the message and interpreting it in the way desired by the source.

Interaction

In addition to problems caused by interference, the effectiveness of speech communication is dependent on the interaction between the speaker and the hearer. Unlike the source in most other communication situations, a speaker usually enjoys the advantage of receiving immediate, on-the-spot indications of how well the message has been transmitted and received. Except in situations where a speech has been prerecorded and broadcast, the speaker is able to observe face-to-face the listeners' reactions to the message. This is an important advantage because the speaker does not have to guess the response but instead can see and adapt and adjust to it.

Unlike most other forms of communication, speech involves give-and-take, action and reaction. It is never static but always moving, changing, and dynamic.

SUMMARY

Understanding speech communication is vital to everyone. Effective communication is no less important to people whose lives and work require little formal speaking than it is to others who must frequently speak in public. Speech is essential to everyone in the conduct of day-to-day activity. Speech is the medium by which people seek to influence others—to inform, to convince, to persuade, to inspire, and to entertain.

Speech communication requires a speaker or source, a message, a channel, and a listener or receiver. The principal characteristics that distinguish speech from other forms of communication are: (1) it is purposive, (2) it involves interaction, (3) it is transitory, (4) it occurs in specific settings, (5) it is influenced by the fields of experience of the participants, (6) it lacks the visual cues of writing, and (7) it has a distinctive vocabulary.

The speech communication process begins with the formulation of a message by the would-be communicator, the speaker, who then encodes ideas into language transmitted by audible and visible symbols to the receiver. As these light and sound waves reach the receiver, the receiver decodes them and may then either physically or verbally respond to the speaker, who, if perceptive, will modify the message or manner of delivery to accommodate the hearer's reactions.

The speech communication process involves two additional factors that affect the speech act. These are interference and differences in the fields of experience of the participants, either of which can be the cause of a misunderstanding between the speaker and the listener.

STUDY QUESTIONS

1. How does speech communication differ from written communication?
2. What are some kinds of nonverbal communication?
3. What are the four essential elements of the speech communication situation?
4. What are the audible and visible symbols of speech?
5. Is speech the only form of communication that is purposive? Explain your answer.
6. What is feedback? Give several examples. Why is it important in speech communication?
7. How is the speaker influenced by internal stimuli in the formulation of a message? How influenced by external stimuli?
8. What is meant by selectivity or discrimination in perceiving stimuli?
9. What is interference? What are some examples of interference that may lead to a breakdown in communication?
10. How do differences in the fields of experience of the source and the receiver influence the effectiveness of speech communication?

EXERCISES

1. Make a list of everyone you have spoken or listened to over the last three days. Indicate with the following numbers which were important to you: 1 for important; 2 for somewhat important; and 3 for unimportant.
2. Cite an example of a breakdown in communication (a disagreement or misunderstanding) that you have observed recently. Analyze the situation and, to the best of your ability, explain why it occurred.
3. Make a list of speech topics (other than those listed in the text) that would be inappropriate or difficult to discuss in (a) winter, (b) spring, (c) summer, and (d) fall.

FURTHER READINGS

Burgoon, Michael, and Michael Ruffner, *Human Communication* (New York: Holt, Rinehart and Winston, 1978), sec. 1, "The Variables in the Communication Process."

Ehninger, Douglas, Bruce E. Gronbeck, Ray E. McKerrow, and Alan H. Monroe, *Principles and Types of Speech Communication,* 10th ed. (Glenview, IL: Scott, Foresman, 1986), chap. 1, "The Public Person and the Speechmaking Process."

Lucas, Stephen E., *The Art of Public Speaking* (New York: Random House, 1986), chap. 2, "Speaking in Public."

Mudd, Charles S., and Malcolm O. Sillars, *Speech: Content and Communication* (New York: Crowell, 1975), chap. 1, "The Process of Communication."

Osborn, Michael, *Speaking in Public* (Boston: Houghton Mifflin, 1982), chap. 1, "Speaking in Public: An Opening View."

Ross, Raymond S., *Speech Communication: Fundamentals and Practice,* 7th ed. (Englewood Cliffs, NJ: Prentice-Hall, 1986), chap. 1, "The Communication Process."

CHAPTER 2

LISTENING

Because speech involves interaction between a speaker and one or more listeners, effective communication is unlikely to take place if the listeners fail to provide meaningful feedback to the speaker. To do this, the listener must actually be listening to—and not just hearing—the message.

Listening and hearing are not the same. We hear television commercials, for example, but most of us do not really listen to them. We hear the words but don't analyze or evaluate their content. Actually, the sponsor doesn't really want us to listen carefully; he just hopes we will remember the name of the product. Television shows seldom require the viewer to listen. About as subtle as a bulldozer, most television shows demand little attention to follow their plots, action, and dialogue. In fact, the producer-directors probably don't want us to listen too carefully or critically.

Conditioned by viewing television, many people not surprisingly have never learned how to listen. They hear but have little skill in analyzing a message, determining its purpose or central thought, breaking down its structure, evaluating its content, perceiving what is important and what is not, remembering key ideas and information, and detecting nuances and shades of meaning.

IMPORTANCE OF LISTENING

Learning how to listen is important. Most people spend a great amount of time listening to others. Ralph G. Nichols, an authority on listening, estimates that 60 percent or more of our waking time is spent listening—more time than we spend talking, reading, or writing. Where does all of this listening take place? It occurs in the classroom, on the job, in professional activities, at lectures and seminars, in business meetings, at scholarly and scientific conferences, in ordinary, everyday transactions, and in a variety of other situations.

In view of its importance, what can be done to improve listening? Both speakers and listeners must actively work at this task.

The speaker has a responsibility to promote good listening by understanding the speech communication process and those factors that both interfere with and contribute to good listening. The speaker needs to:

1. Analyze in advance the audience and the occasion in order to anticipate potential problems, attitudes, and possible areas of confusion or disagreement. How much background, knowledge, and understanding of the subject do the listeners possess? Will they have difficulty understanding the language or following the explanations?

2. Be alert to listener responses. The speaker must pay very careful attention to how the listeners are reacting. Do they seem bored, confused, amused, interested, puzzled?

3. Be skilled in interpreting listener responses. *Why* did they giggle at something intended to be taken seriously? *Why* do they seem lethargic? *Why* are some reading newspapers, staring into space, or whispering with

each other? Are these negative responses the fault of the speaker or are other factors present that make it difficult for the listeners to pay close attention?

4. Be careful not to let inappropriate listener responses distract, irritate, or anger. This is not always easy to do. The speaker who is convinced of the importance or seriousness of what he or she is discussing may find it difficult to ignore seemingly frivolous or uninterested behavior. In truth, the response of a few individuals in the audience may have nothing to do with what is being said. They may simply be amused or distracted by something that happened earlier and, given time, will settle down and pay attention.

5. Recognize that the auditor's interest, enthusiasm, or concern may not be as great as the speaker's, especially if the convictions expressed are deep. If the initial response is somewhat bland, don't give up. Try to find new ways to create interest.

6. Seek ways to involve the listeners. Rhetorical questions can stimulate thought. Questions involving a show of hands or some other kind of action may create interest. Handouts—such as charts, recipes, diagrams, and questionnaires—may pique the listener's curiosity and enhance interest. Sometimes a visual aid can make the listener want to know more and, because of this, listen more carefully. For example, student speeches that have effectively involved the class and improved listening have included talks by speakers who showed brass rubbings they had made from Old English tombstones, an aquarium of unusual tropical fish, baseball cards collected by the speaker, and stained-glass objects made by the student.

LISTENING SKILLS

For effective communication to occur, the auditor also has obligations. As a listener—whether the situation is a one-on-one talk, a speech, a lecture, an interview, or a discussion—there are several ways that a person can improve listening skills and increase the likelihood of meaningful speech communication. Some of these ways are:

1. Prepare in advance
2. Eliminate distractions
3. Make a deliberate effort to concentrate
4. Adopt a positive attitude
5. Make an effort to understand
6. Find ways to remember
7. Encourage the speaker in his effort to communicate
8. Listen analytically and critically
9. Review and reevaluate the speaker's message before making a decision
10. Take advantage of opportunities to ask questions

Prepare in Advance

To listen effectively, one must be both physically and intellectually prepared. Physical conditions such as sleepiness, hunger, exhaustion, a headache, or illness can impair a person's ability to concentrate, comprehend, evaluate, and respond intelligently to the ideas of another person. The listener has a responsibility to come to the communication situation physically well prepared. While there is little that one can do about suddenly becoming ill, it usually is possible to prevent hunger, tiredness, headaches, and minor discomforts from interfering with understanding the speaker's message.

To listen intelligently, an auditor should try to determine the purpose of the meeting, study the agenda if available, gather background material on the subject to be considered, and read any literature or instructions distributed in advance. If the communication is to take place in a classroom or seminar, participants should complete any recommended readings or advance assignments. They should determine in advance what they want to learn and what they hope to get from the communication situation. It also may be helpful to learn what they can about the backgrounds, beliefs, and attitudes of the speaker and/or the other participants.

Eliminate Distractions

While it is not always possible to eliminate potentially distracting elements that may interfere with effective communication, every effort should be made to do so.

Effective listening can be impaired by physical distractions such as noise, uncomfortable clothing, room temperature, poor acoustics, the seating arrangement, glaring lights, or the background noise of piped-in music, a radio, or television.

Psychologically, it is difficult to concentrate if one is worried, irritated, angry, depressed, or overly excited. For example, illness, the death of someone close, an unpleasant argument, resentment over a rude remark, fear of failure, or overstimulation may make it difficult to listen calmly and analytically. Most students probably can recall a time when it was difficult to pay attention in class because something was bothering them.

Physical distractions often can be easily controlled. Psychological distractions may be more difficult to eliminate. Nevertheless, the listener has an obligation to try to put aside anything distracting in order to devote full attention to what is being said.

Try to Concentrate

Some people are poor listeners simply because they won't *try* to pay attention and understand. They deliberately sabotage communication by doing something designed to take their minds off what is being said, such as working on an assignment for a later class, reading a newspaper, writing a letter, or whispering to a neighbor.

Others are poor listeners because they pay attention to the wrong things: instead of trying to understand the message, they focus attention on the speaker's appearance or accent. Or they may spend the time surveying others who are present or thinking about later activities and events.

A good speaker will make a deliberate effort to arouse the interest of the auditors, but the listener, too, must make a conscious commitment to try to understand what the speaker is saying.

Adopt a Positive Attitude

Good listening is more likely to occur if the listener approaches the situation expecting the best—anticipating that it will be possible to learn, benefit, or be helped by understanding the message. One should listen with an open mind, putting aside preconceived ideas, attitudes, and biases. Stereotyping speakers and their messages because of appearance, age, profession, or other factors can make it difficult to listen objectively.

Encourage the Speaker

Most people communicate best when they feel the listeners are interested in what they have to say. Some speakers lose their composure and communicate poorly if the listeners show signs of boredom, lack of interest, or antagonism. Listeners can assist speakers by showing their interest, thereby aiding not only the speaker but themselves as well, because the speaker in turn will communicate better.

Listeners who give their undivided attention, appear alert and interested, take notes, respond to humor, ask questions if the situation permits, and in other ways indicate their involvement contribute greatly to the potential success of the communication process.

Listen Analytically and Critically

Effective listeners do more than merely attempt to understand a speaker's ideas; they also exercise their critical faculties in order to analyze and evaluate the message. To help evaluate a speaker's ideas, the listener might ask the following questions:

1. What is the speaker's purpose? What does the speaker hope to accomplish? Does the speaker have hidden goals or objectives?
2. Is the reasoning sound? Is the supporting evidence adequate? Are the facts correct?
3. Has the speaker omitted or overlooked important facts, other considerations, or conflicting evidence and arguments?

Speech involves interaction: the expressions of these listeners clearly indicate
that they are interested in what the speaker is saying. (Matheny, *Christian Science
Monitor*)

4. Are examples, illustrations, and specific instances fair and representative?
5. Is the language clear and precise?
6. Does the speaker employ emotionally loaded, vague, or ambiguous
   words intended to prejudice, confuse, or distract the listener?

Good listeners should never hesitate to say to themselves, "I don't understand that," or ask, "What does that prove?"

Review and Reevaluate

If the speaker's purpose is to convince or to persuade, listeners should take
their time in coming to a decision. They should avoid being pressured into
making on-the-spot judgments and commitments they may later regret. In

deciding whether to make a purchase, contribute to a fund, sign a petition, participate in a demonstration, join an organization, and in making similar decisions, the wise listener will not rush in but will take time to reflect and reexamine the pros and cons at length. Such a delay gives the listener an opportunity to separate emotional appeals from the facts and to verify the speaker's evidence and arguments.

SUMMARY

Because communication is a two-way process, the student of speech needs to develop skill in listening as well as speaking. Listening is not the same as hearing. It is easy to hear, but one must learn to listen.

Both the speaker and hearer can contribute to good listening and effective communication. The speaker needs to analyze the audience and occasion in advance to anticipate listening problems, to be alert to audience responses and skilled in interpreting them, to avoid being distracted or annoyed by inappropriate reactions, to understand the auditors' degree of interest, and to seek to involve them.

The listener, also, must make a deliberate effort to ensure good communication through advance preparation, eliminating distractions, and developing positive listening skills.

By making a conscientious effort to develop good listening habits, both speakers and auditors can improve communication.

RELATED READING

Polarization, Social Facilitation, and Listening

Walter W. Stevens

The increasing volume of research which has been completed during the last decade in the area of listening is encouraging. Compared to the other communication skills, progress in the sophistication of listening theory has been remarkable, undoubtedly in part because the auditor has been so thoroughly ignored in the past. However, two psychological concepts, which are vitally linked with listening, have not as yet been sufficiently explored by those in speech. These concepts are polarization and social facilitation. . . .

Polarization is strong group cohesiveness, unity, "we feeling," human homogenization so that everyone present in an audience situation becomes an integral member of the group. There is a sympathetic relationship between speaker and listener because the physical and mental processes of the auditor are in tune with those of the speaker and extreme sensitivity exists between the two. Bryant and Wallace affirmed that "the greater the feeling of solidarity and oneness an audience has, the stronger and surer its favorable response is likely to be." Polarization, an old technique, is unfamiliar to many people, although it is a perfectly ethical but powerful psychological device used to advantage by both the principled orator and the demagogue. Every citizen should recognize and understand its implications. The speaker who wishes to polarize an audience will maneuver it into taking joint action. He may use humor to get his listeners to laugh together; he may ask for a show of hands; he may get them to sing or chant together; he may ask them to stand together, kneel together, pray together, rise together, sit together, or read together. These procedures are repeated again and again, for it takes time to polarize a group; but, as most skillful orators know, it is well worth the effort.

What happens to a listener when he becomes polarized? He tends to relinquish his own set of values and to adopt the values of the audience. Instead of many diverse, individual, reflective responses to a speech, we observe a unified group response. As the group reacts, so does each person conform. Independent critical appraisal of what is being said is reduced to a minimum because nonconformity in a polarized group is socially unacceptable, even if it is only silent mental disagreement. The auditor is reduced to a private in a military drill platoon. When the speaker says, "Right face," [the auditor] does so along with everybody else without asking himself, "Why should I do a right face?" He has become a victim of a type of group hypnosis. The critical listener resists polarization. He identifies polarizing devices for what they are—emotional and psychological straitjackets that rob him of his individualism. He is aware that his critical judgment is impaired when he is under their spell. In a polarized audience, said Wollbert, "It takes energy to oppose. Men have to be schooled to hesitate and to doubt. . . . The fixed tendency is to receive willingly and without opposition."

A phenomenon similar to polarization is social facilitation, the effect of the members of a group upon each other because of their physical proximity. Obviously, stimuli move from speaker to auditor and from auditor to speaker; but in addition, each listener tends to be stimulated more than he realizes by the reactions of other persons near him. As a member of an audience, one has heard at some time a very poor speech or has attended a poor play or recital. Perhaps the only reason that one did not get up and walk out of the hall was that such an action would have been embarrassing. At the conclusion of the performance one felt as if [one] wanted to throw a tomato, but instead . . . applauded. Why? It was clapping time; everybody was clapping. To take another example, we have all laughed heartily with a group as we turned to the person next to us and asked, "What did he say?" Why were we laughing? It was social facilitation. Allport defined social facilitation as "an increase of response merely from the sight or sound of others making the same movements." It is radiation of social influence which can be obvious but more often occurs subliminally. The larger the group and the more emotional the stimulation presented by the speaker, the greater the effect of social facilitation.

Clark said that "some emotions, especially fear and sorrow, are produced or intensified by witnessing in others the expressions of like emotions. . . . It is evident that we tend to interpret objects as our fellows interpret them, to consider as real what others, by their behavior, seem to recognize as real, and to accept as true the ideas which our companions appear to accept." Woolbert corroborated: "The sound of other persons laughing, the sight of men who look angry, the perception of handkerchiefs dabbing at red eyes, snuffling and sobbing muttered ejaculations, sounds that represent protest—all these add to the response which the individual gives to the speaker. . . ."

Gurnee discovered that in a *viva voce* "uncertain members tended to be influenced to vote in the direction of the most vigorous response," and Burnham emphasized that "the individual alone and the individual in a group are two different psychological beings. . . ."

There is no lack of interest and documentation as to the conforming nature of man's behavior. Lasswell said that "there are counties where no white man has ever voted a Republican ticket, and there are counties where a respectable Democrat is a contradiction in terms." Campbell, Gurin, and Miller corroborate that "if the group has high positive significance to the individual, he will tend to conform to what he perceives to be its standards." Berelson et al. reported from a case study that "a worker's voting behavior is influenced by the pressures of the environment in which he works; the extent to which he is influenced by such stimuli depends on the amount of his exposure to that environment, and the amount of such exposure depends upon his interaction with others in the environment. In this way an individual comes to learn what is considered 'appropriate' by the participants in the environment. Rather than direct communications from leaders to followers, this is an indirect process that might be called 'social absorption.' "

According to some of the best information we can get, man's herd behavior is not only common, it is a sign of health and stability. Bonner stated that "every normal individual wants acceptance, and he will strive to please others—that is, play the role of a friendly and accepting individual—because of the anticipated belongingness that will accrue from it." Johnson said that "what most clinical psychologists call social adjustment lies in part in the fundamentally negative skill of not making oneself too conspicuous. Good adjustment for any individual, therefore, is generally assumed by these clinical workers to depend more or less on his feeling, thinking, acting pretty much as other people do, or liking what they like, hating what they hate, believing what they believe—and not knowing why. . . ."

Asch conducted an experiment which investigated the effect of group pressure upon the individual member of a group. There were nine subjects employed, eight of whom were in league with the experimenter and one of whom was completely unaware of the structure of the experiment. The subjects were requested to match a straight line with three other straight lines of various lengths, one of which was exactly the same length as the given line. The eight cooperating subjects at specified times were previously instructed to agree on an erroneous decision. The purpose of the experiment was to see if group pressure would force the single test subject to lie in order to conform with the group. The correct answer was obvious and unavoidable if one trusted his own sense of sight. Yet, in spite of what he perceived, one out of three of the test subjects, of fifty tested, conformed with the majority when the latter made an incorrect choice. This experiment is an excellent illustration of the effects of social facilitation and of the type of study which can be made in the area.

The critical listener tries to maintain his intellectual free will. No matter what the audience thinks of the speaker, no matter how it reacts to his skill and charm, the reflective auditor attempts to make an individual judgment independent of others in terms of his own criteria, to make his response truly his and not one subliminally forced upon him by the group. But so often the reaction of the audience in part determines the individual listener's reaction to the speaker; that is, his response tends to be a compromise between his impressions and those of the group. And social facilitation operates most irresistibly when the audience is polarized. We like to think that we possess a high degree of rationality, but the psychological consequences of polarization and social facilitation are so subtle that usually we are unable to recognize and oppose them when they occur. After the occasion, we may still be at a loss to explain why we responded as we did.

From *Western Speech*, Summer 1961, pp. 168–170.

STUDY QUESTIONS

1. Why is the ability to listen important in communication?
2. What, if any, obligations does a speaker have to promote good listening?
3. How can a speaker anticipate potential problems in communication resulting from the audience's characteristics?
4. In what ways must a person prepare in advance to listen? Why is this necessary?
5. Who has the greater responsibility for promoting good listening and effective communication: the speaker or the listener? Why?

EXERCISES

1. What, in your opinion, is the main reason why effective listening often does not occur? In a paper of 500 words, defend your answer.
2. Review the classes you are now attending and decide which course is the least interesting. Then try to determine why it isn't more interesting. Analyze your reactions and responses, and in a paper of 500 words indicate what you and your instructor could do to improve interest and understanding.
3. Make a list of five speaking situations in which the speaker would find it very difficult to interest you in his or her topic. Why would it be difficult to interest you? What ways might be effective in creating interest?
4. Based on this chapter, are you a good listener? Taking the 10 criteria of a good listener listed in this chapter, indicate for each whether you believe you are a good, average, or poor listener.

FURTHER READINGS

Ross, Raymond S., *Speech Communication: Fundamentals and Practice* (Englewood Cliffs, NJ: Prentice-Hall, 1986).

Taylor, Anita, Arthur Meyer, Teresa Rosegrant, and B. Thomas Samples, *Communicating* (Englewood Cliffs, NJ: Prentice-Hall 1986).

Zannes, Estelle, and Gerald Goldhaber, *Stand Up, Speak Out: An Introduction to Public Speaking* (Reading, MA: Addison-Wesley, 1983).

Zolten, J. Jerome, and Gerald M. Phillips, *Speaking to an Audience: A Practical Method of Preparing and Performing* (Indianapolis: Bobbs-Merrill, 1985).

CHAPTER 3

THE SPEAKER'S PURPOSE AND ATTITUDE

THE SPEAKER'S PURPOSE

A distinctive characteristic of speech is that it is purposive. Unlike a poet, artist, or composer, who may create a work for no purpose other than self-expression, a speaker seeks to evoke a specific response. Whether addressing a large assembly, participating in a discussion, or only conversing, speakers hope to influence the understanding, feelings, or actions of others.

The speaker who regards speech in this practical, utilitarian way—as an activity designed to accomplish a specific purpose, rather than as a performance or adherence to a set of rules—will probably approach the speech situation with confidence and direction. The practical uses to which speech is put are many. For example, a lawyer may speak to obtain information from clients; to present information to the client, to another lawyer, or to the court; to confer; to give advice; to negotiate; to reach agreements; and to persuade. According to Charles Bunn, a lawyer and authority on the practice of law, a lawyer's work is not judged by its impact on history or by a comparison with Clarence Darrow's but by how successfully a specific purpose is accomplished. Bunn believes that

> whatever the lawyer's professional use of speech, the essential thing is that it reach, in the sense intended by the speaker, not only the eardrums of the hearer, but his mind. . . . However attained, to be understood as you intend is the main thing any lawyer ought to seek in speech. The same is true of speaking in other professions and situations.

Because speech is purposive in nature, the speaker's general goal in any speech is to create in the listeners the response he or she desires. The key word in this principle is *desires.* The speaker does not seek just any response. For example, the speaker who sets out to inform an audience fails if the listeners merely enjoy the speech but do not understand the subject or recall anything they have been told. The speaker who hopes to persuade members of the audience to take some action also is unsuccessful if the auditors understand the remarks but fail to act upon them in the way intended. In both of these instances, the speaker has obtained a response but has not accomplished the primary objective of the speech. Although speakers may have one goal in mind, this does not mean that they may not at times utilize materials usually employed to elicit other responses. For example, a speech intended to per-

> In speaking there is always some end proposed, or some effect which the speaker intends to produce in the hearer. The word eloquence, in its greatest latitude, denotes "that art or talent by which the discourse is adapted to its end."
>
> GEORGE CAMPBELL

suade often includes humor, information, and inspirational passages. But if the speaker's ultimate objective is to persuade, the inclusion of materials to entertain, inform, or inspire is justified only so long as they contribute to the realization of the main goal. The speaker who hopes to obtain the desired response must always keep the central purpose foremost in mind.

General Purposes

Speech purposes may be classified in various ways, but traditionally they have been divided into five general types: to inform, to entertain, to convince, to persuade, and to inspire.

TO INFORM.   Informative speaking seeks to teach, to enlighten, or to educate. The speaker aims to present the material so that the auditor will understand and remember. Once informed, the listener may elect to act upon the information and to put it to use in a certain way; however, in an informative speech the speaker does not seek to initiate action or influence the listener's behavior but aims only to produce comprehension and retention of ideas.

Informative speaking occurs in any teaching situation, whether in a classroom, office, plant, conference room, or club meeting. It consists of explanations, analyses, descriptions, demonstrations, definitions, and narratives. It may utilize specific instances or examples, statistics, comparisons and contrasts, and the opinions of experts.

Topics that lend themselves to informative speaking might include "Student Scholarships and Loans," "How to Choose a Wine," "The World Cup of Soccer," "Foreign Exchange Rates," and "How to Select a Gift."

TO ENTERTAIN.   Entertaining speech aims at nothing more than providing momentary enjoyment for the listeners. The speaker wants the audience to relax, forget their problems, and have a good time. There is no concern about whether they remember what is said or desire to influence their beliefs or actions.

Most often heard at banquets, dinner meetings, and functions primarily social in nature, entertaining speech is not necessarily humorous. The entertaining speaker may choose to utilize the quaint, the exotic, or the unusual. Material that is startling, exciting, surprising, suspenseful, bizarre, little known, or incredible may be employed, or the speech may describe, explain, narrate, analyze, or demonstrate.

Almost any subject may be entertaining, depending on how it is handled. Some topics that might be entertaining include "Blind Dates," "My Feud with Computers," "How to Cope with an Embarrassing Situation," "Why I Am Not in the Guinness Book of Records," "Great Hoaxes," "The Most Thrilling Sports Event I Have Ever Attended," and "If You Drink, Don't Drive; Even if You Don't Drink, Don't Drive in Mexico."

Speaking to entertain: David Letterman, a television
talk show host. (AP/Wide World)

TO CONVINCE.   The difference between convincing and persuading is
largely an academic one. The distinction grows out of the belief once held by
faculty psychologists that the mind can be divided into segments, with one
part controlling the will and another regulating the feelings. This belief has
long since been discarded, but the separation of speaking aimed to alter
listeners' convictions and that designed to influence their actions is perhaps
useful for our purposes.

Speech to convince is defined as speech that seeks to influence the listeners' beliefs on subjects for which action is not requested. For example, a
speaker might try to convince listeners that a particular individual was a great
writer, president, athlete, or composer, or that there has been a decline in
moral and ethical values.

Convincing speech, as defined, is usually delivered by individuals who
are interested in evaluating people or events, establishing values, resolving
factual disputes, and "keeping the record straight." This kind of speaking
may frequently be heard in almost any group or organization, and some of
the most heated debates revolve around such issues.

The speaker's supporting materials are the same as those used by the
persuasive speaker: specific instances and examples, statistics, comparisons
and contrasts, and expert testimony.

TO PERSUADE.   Speaking to persuade, like speaking to convince, aims
at changing the listener's convictions, but it goes a step beyond simply seek-

ing agreement and, explicitly or implicitly, urges the listener to pursue a course of action in accordance with the speaker's beliefs. Persuasive speakers who fail to motivate their listeners to act in the way they wish cannot regard the speech as wholly successful. For example, a speaker who urges regular medical examinations will not be satisfied if the listeners merely nod their heads in agreement and say, "That's a good idea" but continue to see their doctors only irregularly. To be completely successful in realizing a goal, the speaker must somehow motivate the listeners to perform the action suggested.

At times, persuasive speakers identify very specifically the exact steps they wish the audience to take. They may, for example, urge the listeners to vote for a certain candidate, to buy a particular product, to sign a petition, or to embark on a specific physical fitness program. At other times, they may be less explicit in outlining the steps they wish the audience to take. They may, for example, ask the auditors to exercise tolerance, to eat a well-balanced diet, or to drive safely, without giving detailed instructions on exactly how to carry out their recommendations. But regardless of whether the course of action is explicitly stated or merely implied, speech that urges listeners to behave in a certain manner can be classified as persuasive. Whenever a speaker's main idea contains the words *should* or *need to,* the purpose is persuasive.

Persuasive speech utilizes the same supporting materials as do other kinds of speech. However, the persuasive speaker selects and arranges these materials in such a way that they support a course of action. In addition, in an effort to influence the auditors' feelings and thereby impel them to take the steps urged, the persuasive speaker often makes extensive use of materials designed to arouse the listener's emotion.

Persuasive speaking can be heard in almost any situation when the listeners have a voice in determining policy. Some obvious places are political rallies, legislative bodies, club and organizational business meetings, radio and television commercials, and sales talks.

Examples of persuasive speech topics are "Just Say No to Drugs," "Quit Eating Junk Food," "Support Stricter Gun Controls," and "Elect Candidate X."

TO INSPIRE.   In inspirational speaking, the speaker seeks to increase the auditors' appreciation or respect for an individual, group, cause, or event toward which they are already favorably disposed. This type of speech also is referred to as speech to impress or to stimulate. In everyday conversation, the word *inspirational* is frequently used to describe anything that moves the feelings of the listener. Thus, members of a congregation may refer to a particularly moving sermon as being "inspiring." Actually, much speech that is called "inspiring" urges a course of action and is, in fact, persuasive rather than inspirational.

Inspirational speech, as here defined, requires that the audience be either neutral or already sympathetic to the speaker's point of view. The speaker's task then is to create favorable attitudes toward the subject among the neutral members of the audience and to enhance the favorable attitudes of those who already agree.

Speeches to inspire are appropriate when an audience has gathered to honor or to pay tribute or homage to some individual, group, organization, or event toward which they feel deep devotion, affection, or respect. For example, a ceremony honoring a fellow employee upon retirement, the end-of-the-season athletic awards banquet, an anniversary observance, and a Thanksgiving Day service are occasions that demand a speech to inspire. The unsympathetic, the cynical, and the hostile will either not be in attendance or will be in the minority. Most of those present will already admire, respect, or appreciate the person, event, or achievement being honored. Obviously, then, the speaker's task is simply to heighten or stimulate the audience's feelings.

Inspirational speeches include eulogies, speeches of commendation, speeches of commemoration, presentation and acceptance speeches, and welcoming and farewell speeches.

Specific Purposes

Once the speaker has decided what is to be the general goal, the next task is to determine the specific purpose of the speech. Suppose that the purpose is to inform the auditors about tape recording. To proceed meaningfully, the speaker must consider the question, "Inform them of *what* about tape recording?" There are several choices. The speech could be limited to the uses of a tape recorder, how to operate a tape recorder, how to edit tapes, how sound is recorded on tape, or several other aspects of this subject; the speaker could discuss any combination of these or could attempt to cover all of them.

The importance of determining a specific purpose early was emphasized by Harry Emerson Fosdick. This famous preacher pointed out that "an essayist may be content with the discussion of a subject, but a preacher can be content only with the attainment of an object. I mean not simply some overall aim—such as the presentation of Christian truth and the persuasion of men to accept it," he continued, "but for each sermon a specific intent. It may be the help of individuals in facing some personal problem, or the answering of

A speaker who exhausts the whole philsoophy of a question, who displays every grace of style, yet produces no effect on his audience, may be a great essayist, a great statesman, a great master of composition; but he is not an orator.

THOMAS BABINGTON MACAULAY

a puzzling question in theology, or the persuasion of tempted souls to abandon some popular sin, or the confrontation of some public evil with the Christian ethic, or the winning of wavering minds and consciences to a definite decision for Christ." He concluded, "I, for one, cannot start a sermon until I clearly see what I propose to get *done* on Sunday morning."

The speaker should consider several factors in determining the specific purpose. These include the amount of time available, the interests of the listeners in different aspects of the subject, the speaker's understanding of the topic, the relative importance of the possible alternatives, and the nature of the occasion.

In preparing formal speeches, the specific purpose should be put in the form of an explicit statement of exactly what the speaker hopes to accomplish. For example, if a speaker decides to give an informative speech on the use of the library, the general purpose would be *to inform.* The specific purpose might be *to inform the audience on the use of selected aids and facilities of the library.* In formulating a specific purpose, the speaker should decide exactly what it is that he or she wishes to cover in the speech. For example, a specific purpose of informing the audience on "how to use the library" probably is too general, unless the speaker actually intends to cover every aspect of library usage. If not, the specific purpose might be more accurately stated when worded in one of the following ways:

To inform the audience how to check out a book at the library.
To inform the audience how to use the card catalog and *Reader's Guide to Periodical Literature.*
To inform the audience of the special collections of the library.
To inform the audience how to conduct a computer search.

Speakers who proceed with the preparation of a speech without knowing exactly what they wish to accomplish are likely to be plagued with false starts, wasted time, and confusion.

Some examples of statements of specific purpose for different types of speeches are:

To inform the audience of the three main causes of forest fires.
To persuade the listeners to use automobile seat belts.
To inspire the audience to greater respect for Thomas Jefferson.
To convince the audience that the Vikings discovered America before Columbus did.
To entertain the listeners with an account of a summer vacation.

Immediate and Long-Range Goals

In determining the specific purpose, a speaker must consider the auditors' prior knowledge of the subject, their attitudes toward the ideas, and the time available for the speech.

When the listeners have little knowledge of the subject, the speaker often finds it necessary to present considerable background information, and if the time available is limited, the speaker may be unable to present enough material for the listeners to understand the topic. For example, if the speaker wishes to explain the use made of the 12-tone scale by different composers to an audience with little knowledge of music, it may be impossible in the amount of time allotted to present enough information to enable the listener to comprehend the topic. The speaker then has two choices: abandon the subject entirely or settle for a lesser objective. Using the same example, discussion might be limited to an explanation of the difference between the regular 8-tone scale and the 12-tone scale. This would be an immediate goal. The long-range goal, however, might be to help the auditors understand how various contemporary composers have used the 12-tone scale. This goal, of course, could be reached only if the speaker or an associate had the opportunity to address the audience on the same general topic at some future date.

In determining the immediate goal, a speaker must also take cognizance of the attitudes, opinions, and biases of the listeners. In a single public speech, speakers can rarely hope to convert someone from deep-seated opposition to wholehearted support of their point of view. This is especially true if the auditor is influenced by a personal or selfish interest in the outcome or if the speaker's position contradicts social customs, mores, or firmly established beliefs.

In such a situation, a speaker may wish temporarily to abandon the hope for acceptance of the entire program or point of view and focus instead on reducing hostility to the position or on gaining support for a limited portion of the proposal.

For example, a speaker who strongly favors the abolition of intercollegiate athletics may—through some strange circumstance—have an opportunity to present these views to the university's athletic boosters club. Aware of the preconceived attitudes and hostility of the members to his or her point of view, the speaker knows that one speech will not get them to support the long-range goal—the abolition of intercollegiate football and basketball. However, the speaker might well hope to persuade the listener of any of several short-range or immediate goals that would curtail some of the objectionable abuses. The speaker might choose to try to persuade the listener that

1. The faculty should exercise greater control over the school's athletic programs.
2. Athletes and fans should always remember that the student's education is more important than athletic success.
3. Many college student athletes are being exploited.
4. Intercollegiate athletics can do the participants harm as well as good.
5. The number of athletic scholarships offered by the school is excessive in comparison to the number of grants for academic achievement.

With careful preparation and presentation, the speaker might reasonably hope to persuade the listener to accept one of these points.

Hidden Goals

At times speakers may not wish to reveal their true goal or purpose. They may prefer to withhold their actual goals because they believe they can better accomplish their purpose by refraining from an open statement, because they feel the time is not right to reveal this objective, or because such a statement might be embarrassing or seem immodest.

The unstated or withheld objective may be called a hidden goal. Examples of speakers with hidden goals are plentiful. Active community leaders who take every opportunity offered to speak in support of the local symphony, charity drives, and philanthropic endeavors may covertly be trying to convince the audience of their interest in civic affairs in anticipation of a later candidacy for political office. Speakers who announce that they "just want to present the facts in an objective manner and let the audience decide for itself" may actually be seeking to disarm auditors before presenting a partisan approach. Politicians who urge support of a low-income housing project as a general welfare measure may be hiding the fact that they stand to profit personally from such proposals.

Hidden motives are not necessarily evil or unethical. In the examples cited, it is possible that the future candidate might make an excellent political leader, that the cause being espoused by the deceptively impartial speaker might be virtuous and noble, and that a low-income housing project might greatly benefit the public. Listeners, however, will wish to locate any hidden motives that a speaker may have in order to avoid being deceived or misled.

The Central Thought

In addition to determining a specific purpose, the speaker preparing a formal public address should also determine the central thought before attempting to proceed with the preparation of the speech. The central thought is also referred to as the main idea, the theme, or the thesis of the speech. It is a refinement of the speaker's specific purpose—a concise statement of exactly what the speaker plans to say. The central thought, like the specific purpose, indicates what the speaker hopes to accomplish. Both consist of a single declarative sentence. Some examples of typical statements of specific purpose and central thought are:

- *Specific purpose:* My purpose is to inform the audience of three principal causes of forest fires.
- *Central thought:* The principal causes of forest fires are lack of rainfall, public carelessness, and acts of nature.

- *Specific purpose:* The purpose of this speech is to persuade the audience to support a bond issue to build a city auditorium.
- *Central thought:* You should support a bond issue to build a city auditorium because our community has no satisfactory place to hold conventions, concerts, and large public meetings.

- *Specific purpose:* My purpose is to inspire respect and admiration for Professor Morse.
- *Central thought:* Professor Morse deserves our respect and admiration for his scholarly research into the history of our state and for his long and able leadership of the state historical society.

The formulation of the central thought is an important step in speech preparation because it requires speakers to crystallize their thinking on the subject. Of the many possible approaches and the several aspects of a topic that could be discussed, speakers must settle on those they feel are most important or most conducive to achieving the desired response. Until speakers formulate a central thought, they cannot proceed with the organization and development of the materials, for they do not know exactly what they want to say. Once the central thought has been determined, the speaker knows where he or she is going and will find the subsequent speech preparation easier and more systematic.

Stating the Purpose and Central Thought

A speaker will often find that an actual statement of the specific purpose or the central thought early in the speech will promote clarity and understanding. In announcing the purpose or main idea, letting the audience know in advance what is going to be discussed, the speaker encourages the auditors to listen more intelligently. For example, the speaker says, "Today, I would like to explain how sugarcane is harvested." The audience then knows the exact topic. They know that planting sugarcane, its cultivation, sugar refining, or marketing the finished product is not going to be discussed. They also know that the speaker is not going to attempt to persuade them of the nutritional value of sugar, the need for greater sugar imports, the superiority of cane sugar to beet sugar, or some other point of view. Having been told what to expect, they are better prepared to understand the speech.

Occasionally speakers withhold any statement of purpose or central thought until late in the speech. This occurs most often in talks on controversial subjects. Speakers trying to convince or persuade a hostile audience may alienate some listeners with an early statement of the thesis. Knowing the speaker supports a proposal with which they disagree, antagonistic auditors often close their minds and devote their entire attention to detecting flaws and shortcomings in the speaker's arguments. This is discussed in greater detail in Chapter 8.

THE SPEAKER'S ATTITUDE

The centipede was happy quite
Until a toad in fun
Said, "Pray, which leg goes after which?"
That worked her mind to such a pitch,
She lay distracted in a ditch,
Considering how to run.

MRS. EDWARD CRASTER

The perplexed state of mind of the centipede in the above quotation resembles the mental condition of many people when they are faced with having to give a speech. Although they talk every day without hesitation or fear, the thought of having to address an audience raises all kinds of doubts and questions in their minds. "What can I talk about?" "How should I begin?" and "What do I do next?" they ponder until, almost like the centipede, they begin to wonder, "Am I capable of doing this?"

This section seeks to quell some of these misgivings by considering the speaker's attitude, the nature and causes of nervous tension, and the purposes of public speaking.

A very important factor influencing success or failure of a speech is the attitude of the speaker. To perform competently and effectively, speakers should approach the speech situation with confidence, with a desire to communicate, and with the expectation of success. They should regard the occasion as a challenge, as an opportunity to accomplish an important and worthwhile objective.

Unfortunately, some speakers cannot generate any real desire to communicate or to develop confidence in their ability to command the interest and respect of their listeners because of speaking apprehension or excessive nervous tension. Some speakers become so nervous that they are able to complete their speeches only with the greatest effort. Others worry incessantly for hours or even days before the speech. In the most severe cases of speaking apprehension, the speaker may actually feel nauseous, experience a loss of appetite, or be unable to sleep. This inordinate fear of public speaking leads some people to avoid opportunities to speak. For example, Mirabeau B. Lamar, second president of the Republic of Texas, was so apprehensive about speaking that he could not deliver his inaugural address in 1838. The speech was read by his secretary. Edward Gibbon, eighteenth-century historian and author of *The Decline and Fall of the Roman Empire,* served in the British House of Commons for eight years and was so terrified of speaking that he never delivered his maiden speech.

While excessive nervousness is most common among beginning speakers, it is obviously not confined to them. A 1973 survey of over 2500 adults

A speaker with a desire to communicate. (Carey, The Image Works)

who were asked to pick items from a list representing situations in which they had some degree of fear revealed that 40.6 percent of these adults feared speaking before a group. Conducted periodically since 1973 by R. H. Bruskin Associates, the survey consistently proves that speaking in public is the number-one fear among adults. Even experienced public speakers sometimes become tense when confronted by a new, unusual, or particularly challenging speech situation.

Keir Hardie, a founder of the British Labor party, a member of Parliament, and a man who delivered speeches almost daily for years, described his own nervousness as follows:

> I almost envy those public speakers, but not always their audiences, who can mount a platform or face a meeting without a qualm or a doubt. It must be pleasant to have such unlimited confidence in their own power. . . . For myself, I usually begin a speech, literally, in fear and trembling. . . . Stepping onto the platform, especially if there is little show of enthusiasm, a wave of cold feeling works its way down from the brain to my toenails, often producing a shiver as if I had struck a chill. At the same time, away somewhere in the inner recesses of my subconscious being, . . . I shrink until I am a mere pygmy surrounded by a circle of big brawny giants, each armed with a club. But whatever form the feeling takes it always produces a sense of my own insignificance.
>
> When rising to speak the feeling subsides. . . . When the hall is good, and the audience indulgent, a genial thaw soon sets in, and as it makes its way through me I cease to be a separate person. I absorb and am absorbed by my audience. In spirit we seem to melt and fuse into one, and I am not speaking to them, but through them, and my thoughts are

not my thoughts but their thoughts, and we are on the most comfortable and confidential terms, one with the other. (*The Labor Leader,* London, February 28, 1903, pp. 114–115)

Distressing as such fright may be to the speaker, a degree of nervous tension probably serves a useful function in delivering a speech. It seems doubtful that speakers totally free from anxiety would be very interesting. If they simply did not care what the outcome might be, it is unlikely that effective talks would result. But when speakers' apprehension and nervousness become so great that they begin to interfere with the ability to communicate, the problem becomes a matter of concern. Thus, the speaker's aim should be to learn to control nervous tension rather than to eliminate it entirely.

In an effort to overcome the harmful effects of speaking apprehension, speakers must be familiar with its symptoms and causes, as well as its possible remedies.

Symptoms of Speaking Apprehension

Persons who suffer from speaking apprehension usually react both physiologically and psychologically. The physiological symptoms may include trembling of the hands or legs; increased perspiration, especially in the palms of the hands and under the arms; shortage of breath; accelerated heartbeat; a parched or dry mouth; voice tremors; and a tenseness throughout the body.

Psychologically, speakers may experience the desire to withdraw; they may fear that the listeners will notice their nervousness or their embarrassing difficulties in controlling their own voices. These symptoms, in turn, may lead them to avoid looking at the audience, to hide behind the lectern, or to speak more rapidly.

Causes of Speaking Apprehension

Interestingly, most of the physiological symptoms of speaking apprehension are almost identical to the body's reaction to a sudden threat or danger. For example, if unexpectedly confronted by an attacker, one's body responds automatically. In preparation for warding off the attack or threat, the heart beats more rapidly, more oxygen is required to supply the heart, the mouth becomes parched, the muscles of the body tense, and the individual begins to perspire. In the case of actual danger, the excess energy summoned to meet the emergency would soon be released through some physical exertion such as fighting off one's attacker, fleeing, or in some other way coping with the threat. If, however, one were to discover that no real danger existed, the tension and additional energy automatically provided by the body would not be released, and the individual would discover that he or she had all the physiological symptoms of stage fright.

The similarity between an individual's reaction to the threat of physical danger and to giving a speech suggests that one of the main causes of speaking apprehension may be that speakers regard the speech situation as a threat to their welfare. This attitude could stem from several factors. One cause could be the speakers' knowledge that the outcome of the speech is important to them; they would therefore regard it as a threat to their security. Shakespeare warned, "Mend your speech a little, lest you may mar your fortunes." Some speakers are afraid that this is exactly what may happen to them.

Another reason for fear may be the speakers' awareness that they are being judged, that listeners will form opinions regarding their personalities, character, and intelligence solely on the basis of their skill as speakers. The possibility of being judged inadequate on the basis of speaking ability alone haunts them. Similarly, musicians in a symphony orchestra often suffer much the same kind of stress. A study of members of the Vienna Symphony by a team of psychologists found that many experienced severe anxiety before a concert and suffered from fits of perspiration, trembling, and giddiness for fear of missing their cues. Soloists were found to experience the highest levels of stress because of the importance of their contributions to the success of the performance.

Speaking apprehension may also be an expression of chronic personal insecurity. Giving a speech merely brings this general insecurity to a peak. O. Hobart Mowrer, a research professor of psychology, points out that if a person is generally afraid of being "seen through," there is no more threatening situation than being before an audience, the object of all eyes.

Other possible causes of stage fright may result from the speaker's lack of knowledge concerning public speaking. The fear may stem in part from lack of experience. People who have seldom spoken to audiences may not know how they will fare. Speakers may also suffer from lack of knowledge of what an audience expects and what constitutes a good speech. Thus, inexperienced speakers may believe that the listeners will be disappointed with anything but a polished oration and that their lack of training will make it impossible to produce a speech that will satisfy audience expectations.

Nervousness may also be the result, in part, of inadequate preparation; one may be unfamiliar with the material, uncertain of whether he or she really understands the subject, or doubtful about remembering the planned speech.

Even experienced speakers with considerable confidence may at times be apprehensive. This could happen if they encounter a new and totally unfamiliar audience or occasion, if there has not been time to prepare carefully, or if the consequences of the speech are more important than usual. However, the experienced speaker probably would be able to exercise enough control over such nervousness that it would not interfere with the ability to communicate effectively.

Developing Confidence: General Principles

No simple formula has been found for overcoming speaking apprehension. However, several general principles can be recommended for reducing nervous tension and bringing it under control. These suggestions can be divided into a long-range program for reducing apprehension and specific techniques that may prove helpful in the immediate situation.

The first principle in developing confidence as a speaker is to gain experience before a variety of audiences. In almost any endeavor, the first attempt will be accompanied by tension and anxiety. The youngster making a first dive from the high board at the swimming pool, the learner driving an automobile for the first time, the beginning teacher meeting his or her first class, the student pilot making a first solo flight, and the athlete preparing for a first competition all experience nervous strain and uncertainty. But with repeated exposure to these situations or activities, all gain experience and self-assurance. In a like manner, beginning speakers can increase their self-confidence by speaking often and, since no two audiences are identical, by speaking before many different groups. As a young man, George Bernard Shaw, the playwright and lecturer, embarked on such a program to overcome his anxiety about speaking. Joining a variety of organizations ranging from the Browning and Shakespeare societies to socialist political groups, Shaw took advantage of every opportunity to address their members, eventually gaining such wide experience that he could face almost any audience with poise and assurance.

A second suggestion for overcoming apprehension is to put the speaking situation into its proper perspective. Although speeches are important, some speakers overemphasize their significance. Very seldom will a single speech determine future policy, settle a controversy, or greatly alter an individual's professional future. A poor speech is a disappointment to an audience, but it is not a disaster. Even the greatest speakers fail from time to time. If speakers keep in mind that the consequences of an unsatisfactory speech are likely to be no more than temporary embarrassment—that a poor speech will not result in shame, imprisonment, bodily harm, social ostracism, or some other outrageous effect—they probably can approach the speaking situation with less strain and nervous anxiety.

Third, speakers should rid themselves of misconceptions about the audience's expectations. When a speaker addresses a group, most listeners do not expect the talk to be the most moving experience of their lives or to herald the dawn of a new era. If the speaker is interesting and provides them with useful information, stimulating insights, or fresh ideas, most listeners are satisfied.

Fourth, speakers should develop a desire to communicate. Speakers who are talking about something that interests them and who feel that they are fulfilling a useful function by sharing ideas with the audience will have little time or attention to devote to worrying about nervousness. The speaker who approaches the speech situation with the attitude of being there to aid or help the listeners, rather than to be judged by them, is likely to speak with calm assurance.

A fifth recommendation for controlling apprehension is to learn about speech making by studying the theories and principles of effective speech, by reading about the techniques of great speakers of the past and present, and by thinking about speech problems and possible solutions to them. A course in speech, books about speaking, listening to speakers, reading speeches by skillful speakers, and participation in voluntary speech improvement groups such as Toastmasters clubs can all contribute to a better knowledge of what constitutes a good speech and how to prepare and deliver an effective address.

Sixth, if speakers wish to reduce nervous tension, they should be well prepared for every speech. They should speak on subjects with which they are familiar; they should have planned their talk carefully and have practiced it frequently so they know what they want to say and how they plan to say it. It would be the utmost folly for speakers who are afraid of becoming extremely nervous when they face an audience to compound those fears with worries about their knowledge of their subject and how they plan to develop the speech.

By gaining experience in speaking, putting the speech situation into proper perspective, ridding oneself of misconceptions about the audience's expectations, developing a desire to communicate, learning about speech, and being well prepared for each speech, the beginning speaker can eliminate some of the common causes of speaking apprehension. These steps will not reduce nervousness overnight, but in time they should lead to a positive and more confident attitude on the part of most speakers.

Controlling Nervousness: Specific Techniques

In addition to the long-range program described, some speakers find that various specific techniques are helpful in combating nervous tension. While these approaches do not attack the underlying causes of speaking apprehension, they may prove helpful in immediately reducing tension on a particular speaking occasion.

One technique used by some speakers is to pause briefly before beginning a speech to make sure that their notes are properly arranged, to review mentally the first few sentences of the introduction, and to calm themselves. Since fear of failure is one cause of excessive apprehension, speakers who start hastily and as a result become confused at the very outset will probably find that their anxieties are compounded. Taking time to make sure that everything is in order and to review quickly the opening lines of the speech often can prevent a bad beginning.

Another practice that some speakers believe helpful is to breathe deeply several times just before beginning the speech. Since shortness of breath is one symptom of nervousness, pausing to fill the lungs with air may alleviate this problem.

A third technique favored by some for reducing stress is the speaker's mental "pep talk." If, just before beginning, speakers remind themselves that talking is an everyday activity, that the audience consists of people much like themselves, and that no dire repercussions are likely to follow should they fail in their effort, they may be reassured.

Some speakers employ a fourth technique to allay nervousness. This consists of seeking a favorable response of some kind from the listeners at the very start of the speech. The speaker may tell a joke to get the audience to laugh or may ask for a show of hands on some question about their experiences or knowledge of the speech topic. Such overt responses may suggest that the audience is good-natured and cooperative and the speaker has no reason to fear them.

Still another method to overcome anxiety is to pick out seemingly friendly or interested listeners and address the early part of the speech to them, ignoring those who appear bored or hostile. Eventually the speaker's eye contact should encompass the entire audience, but speaking mainly to individuals who appear sympathetic at the outset may reassure the speaker.

A sixth technique employed to get rid of excessive nervousness is movement. Since the speaker has an excess of unreleased nervous energy, he or she simply uses up some of the energy by moving about on the platform, writing on the blackboard, displaying a model or visual aid, or demonstrating something. While all speeches and situations do not lend themselves to this kind of physical activity, at times it may be an effective way to release nervous energy.

A few suggestions should also be made about things a speaker should avoid.

First, speakers should not talk about their nervousness during the speech. Remarks such as "I'm so nervous I don't know if I can go on" or "I hope you can't see my knees shaking" serve no useful function. They merely distract the audience from the speaker's subject and call attention to something that may not have been noticed. Many speakers suffering intense stress appear completely calm, cool, and poised to their listeners. To call attention to one's tension not only interjects an irrelevant thought in the listener's mind but may also diminish confidence in the speaker.

A second cautionary suggestion is that speakers should not plunge ahead heedlessly if they have become badly confused because of nervousness. It is much better to pause, even for a rather long time if necessary, to try to regain control of the situation, to go over the notes or mentally review the speech, to find the place, to call to mind what they want to say next, and then to resume speaking.

Third, speakers should not indirectly advertise their nervousness. Notes or visual aids on flimsy, thin sheets of paper that clearly and sometimes noisily shake embarrass the speaker by calling the audience's attention to his or her trembling. Demonstrations requiring a calm or steady hand (threading a needle, loading certain types of cameras, or other acts demanding precision) should be avoided by tense speakers, for in all probability they not only will experience difficulty in carrying out the demonstration but will also focus the audience's attention on their nervousness.

Finally, a speaker who experiences severe apprehension should not stop abruptly in the middle of the speech. If a pause to review notes and regain self-control fails, the speaker who is hopelessly lost should attempt some kind of summary, review, or conclusion before giving up. The reason for this recommendation is that at times one finds that speakers who feel that their speech has been a total failure have actually performed fairly well and have made progress toward achieving their goal.

While some of these dos and don'ts for coping with speaking apprehension may prove helpful on particular occasions, nervous tension can in the long run be more effectively reduced by gaining experience in speaking, by learning about speech, and by approaching the speech situation in the right frame of mind.

SUMMARY

People speak because they have a specific purpose that they hope to accomplish. The speaker's general purpose may be to inform, to entertain, to convince, to persuade, or to inspire an audience. The effectiveness of his or her speaking is determined by how well the speaker succeeds in obtaining the desired response from the listeners. The speech to inform seeks audience understanding and retention. The entertaining speech aims only to provide relaxation and enjoyment. The speaker whose goal is to convince hopes to alter the beliefs or attitudes of the listener. The persuader goes one step further, attempting to influence the conduct of the audience as well as their beliefs. The speech to inspire aims at heightening the auditors' admiration for an already respected person, group, cause, institution, or event.

If speakers are to obtain the response they wish, it is essential that they know specifically what they hope to accomplish. At times, because of the nature of the audience or the occasion, the speaker may elect to work for a short-range, immediate goal, with a view toward ultimately accomplishing a broader and more long-range objective. At other times, a speaker may find it inexpedient to reveal the true goal and so will conceal it.

The speaker's central thought consists of a single, declarative sentence summarizing the speech in its entirety. The formulation of the central thought—whether actually stated or not—is important because it forces speakers to determine exactly what they hope to communicate. In most speeches, stating the central thought or purpose early in the speech helps the audience to understand the speaker's ideas. However, at times the speaker may elect to withhold any statement of the main purpose or idea until later in the speech in order to improve the chances of obtaining the desired response from the audience.

The speaker's attitude is important in determining the success or failure of the speech. While speakers should be concerned with how well they do, inordinate fear and tension can interfere with effective communication. Among the causes of speaking apprehension are insecurity, inexperience, lack of knowledge of the audience and of what constitutes a good speech, and inadequate preparation. To develop confidence, speakers should gain experience before many different kinds of audiences. They should put the speaking situation into its proper perspective, rid themselves of misconceptions about the audience's expectations, and develop a desire to communicate. The study of speeches and speakers and careful preparation can increase their knowledge of speech making and contribute to the development of their confidence.

STUDY QUESTIONS

1. Could a speech that does not obtain the response desired by the speaker ever be called successful? Why or why not?
2. Is it always essential for a speaker to have formulated a specific purpose and central thought before preparing the rest of the speech? Explain your answer.
3. Under what circumstances might hidden motives or goals be considered unethical? When would they be ethical?
4. When should a speaker usually state the purpose or central thought? Why? Under what circumstances might he or she wish to withhold a statement of purpose or the central thought?
5. What are some reasons why speakers experience speaking apprehension? In what ways does giving a speech differ from "just talking" in a small group? Are these differences great enough to explain why speakers who converse easily often are frightened at the prospect of giving a speech?
6. To what degree should the speaker feel at ease while delivering a speech? Justify your answer.
7. Of the six steps recommended for controlling nervous tension, which ones do you think are most essential? Why?

EXERCISES

1. Read a speech in *Vital Speeches* or *Representative American Speeches*. Indicate (a) the speaker's general purpose, (b) specific purpose, and (c) if stated, central thought. If the central thought is not specifically stated, frame a statement of the central thought.
2. Taking the general subject Education, frame a specific purpose for a speech (a) to inform, (b) to convince, (c) to persuade, (d) to inspire, and (e) to entertain.
3. Using the topic Television, frame a central thought for a speech (a) to inform, (b) to convince, (c) to persuade, (d) to inspire, and (e) to entertain.
4. Find three subjects on which a speaker might not wish to reveal his or her specific

purpose or central thought to an audience early in the speech. In a paragraph discussing each topic, explain the reasons why it might be advisable for the speaker to withhold the statement of purpose or central thought until later.

5. What usually is the general purpose of each of the following kinds of speeches? After writing down the most frequent general purpose for each, list exceptions (occasions when the speaker might have a different general purpose).
   a. Sermons
   b. Campaign speeches
   c. Classroom lectures
   d. Funeral eulogies
   e. Television commercials
   f. Talks at pep rallies
   g. Debate speeches
   h. Announcements at club meetings

FURTHER READINGS

Ehninger, Douglas, Alan H. Monroe, and Bruce E. Gronbeck, *Principles and Types of Speech Communication,* 8th ed. (Glenview, IL: Scott, Foresman, 1978), chap. 4, "Choosing Speech Subjects and Purposes."

McCroskey, James C., "Oral Communication Apprehension: A Summary of Recent Theory and Research," *Human Communication Research* 4 (Fall 1977), 78–96.

Myers, Gail E., and Michele Tolela Myers, *Communicating When We Speak,* 2d ed. (New York: McGraw-Hill, 1978), chap. 6, "Speech Subjects and Types."

Ross, Raymond S., *Speech Communication: Fundamentals and Practice,* 7th ed. (Englewood Cliffs, NJ: Prentice-Hall, 1986), chap. 7, "Purpose and Delivery," and chap. 6, "Emotion and Confidence."

Taylor, Anita, Arthur Meyer, Teresa Rosegrant, and B. Thomas Samples, *Communicating,* 4th ed. (Englewood Cliffs, NJ: Prentice-Hall, 1986), chap. 11, "Preparing Speeches: Organizing Thoughts," and chap. 13, "Public Speaking: Using Voice and Body."

Zannes, Estelle, and Gerald Goldhaber, *Stand Up, Speak Out* (Reading, MA: Addison-Wesley, 1983), chap. 1, "Preparing for the Event."

CHAPTER 4

ANALYZING AUDIENCES AND OCCASIONS

Abraham Lincoln reputedly wrote his most memorable address by jotting notes on the back of an envelope while en route to Gettysburg. More recent presidents, on the other hand, have employed staffs of speech writers who may labor for weeks on a single speech. These extremes demonstrate that there is no single correct method for preparing a speech.

Nevertheless, as in most activities, a systematic approach to planning and presenting a speech is preferable to a random, haphazard preparation. While under some circumstances the speaker might wish to alter the order of preparation, for most occasions the speech can be developed most efficiently by following the plan outlined below.

THE PREPARATION OF A SPEECH

1. *Analysis of the audience and the occasion* to determine the background, interests, and attitudes of the listeners and the nature of the speaking occasion.
2. *Selection of a subject* suitable to the audience and occasion, and narrowing of the topic so that it can be covered in the time available.
3. *Determination of the speaker's purpose,* including general purpose, specific purpose, and central thought.
4. *Gathering of materials for the speech* from the speaker's own knowledge and understanding of the topic and from other sources.
5. *Evaluation and selection of materials* for inclusion in the speech.
6. *Organization of the materials of the speech* and the preparation of an outline and speaker's notes.
7. *Wording of the speech* through the preparation of a written text for manuscript and memorized speeches or through oral practice for extemporaneous addresses.
8. *Practice in delivery* of the speech, giving attention to both the verbal and nonverbal aspects of presentation.

The chapters in this book examine each of these steps. This chapter deals with the first step, analyzing the audience and the occasion.

THE AUDIENCE

Often members of an audience do not share common attitudes, beliefs, drives, or expectations; they are heterogeneous in this respect. Some audiences, however, are more homogeneous than others. A professor, for example, who presents a classroom lecture to 30 sophomores in a psychology class faces a more homogeneous audience than when addressing 300 people in a public lecture. Single-interest audiences, such as a group of farmers who march on Washington to demonstrate for legislation to save the family farm, represent audiences that, at least for the moment, probably have the same attitudes, beliefs, desires, and expectations and on these occasions represent highly polarized homogeneous groups. It is essential for a speaker to understand and

Governor Mario Cuomo of New York is well known
for his care in preparing speeches. (DeLucia, NYT
Pictures)

adapt to the attitudes, beliefs, desires, and expectations of the audience in
order to be effective.

Determining the specific audience for a speech is sometimes difficult. For
example, a president of the United States who makes a policy speech on
television knows in advance that the audience is not confined to persons in
the studio, nor even to the groups of people gathered around television sets
to listen to the live presentation. The audience extends to the members of the
press who will print the remarks for millions of other people to read the
following day; to the radio and television news agencies that will later re-
broadcast portions of the speech for still others to hear; to the millions of
people around the world who will hear the same speech live via satellite or
from tape recordings; and to others around the world who will read the
speech translated into their native languages. The audience is composed of
the whole civilized world.

Other leaders may have similar broad exposure. However, for the great
majority of speeches, the audiences are more easily defined. The student
speaker in the classroom knows that the audience is composed of 18 to 25
other students. The minister is aware that the audience on Sunday morning

will probably consist of the same people who attended the previous Sunday and perhaps for years of Sundays before. The commencement speaker should know that the audience will be composed of the graduates, their families, and their friends. To determine the degree of homogeneity, the speaker should seek to discover the audience's *knowledge, interest,* and *attitudes* toward the *subject,* the *speaker,* and the *occasion* early in the preparation of the speech. To discover these, the speaker must examine the composition of the audience and its reason for assembling.

Audience Composition

In analyzing the audience, for most talks, the speaker should give attention to the following factors that may influence the preparation, presentation, and effectiveness of the speech.

AGE.   The speaker must know the age level of the audience in order to adapt explanations, examples, language, and other speech components to the listeners. It is rather obvious that some subjects and illustrative materials that might be readily perceived by an adult audience would not be intelligible to a teenage audience. Language and materials appropriate to a youthful audience might, for example, be unclear to an adult audience. On the other hand, historical allusion to a period through which an adult has lived may make sense to the older person who recalls this era but be meaningless to a younger person. Speaking at commencement exercises at Emory University in 1983, Terry Sanford, then president of Duke University, referred to this factor of analysis:

> Communicating with college students is always somewhat of a challenge. It is not that I have too much difficulty understanding your changing expressions and attitudes. It is that I forget what you never saw. I recently read in a church magazine that when preparing a sermon, one should remember to assume that 10 is the age at which an event creates an impression, which means that of today's 200 million Americans:
>
> 86 percent cannot recall Charles Lindbergh's solo flight to Paris;
> 68 percent cannot recollect Hitler;
> 65 percent cannot remember life without television;
> 58 percent cannot remember Senator Joe McCarthy (so listen when I mention him later);
> 53 percent cannot remember a Studebaker or think it is a German pudding.
>
> And 64,345,092 people don't know what a church key is; they started life with Coca-Cola's pop-top cans.

When audiences are composed of people in the same general age-group, adaptation is relatively easy. Of course, when the audience consists of people of various ages, adaptation taxes the speaker's ability. Some speakers may prefer to select subject matter, materials, and language that will be generally interesting and meaningful.

SEX.   Often speakers are called upon to address audiences that are all or predominantly male, such as the Rotary Club, the Lions Club, and the Junior Chamber of Commerce; or they are called upon to address primarily female gatherings, such as meetings of the League of Women Voters, the Business and Professional Women's Club, the National Organization for Women (NOW), and women's church groups. Topics and materials for speeches to audiences composed mainly or exclusively of members of one sex should be carefully selected. If, for example, the speaker is interested in talking about auto racing and is qualified to discuss this subject, the chances are very good that a speech on the dangers and thrills of this sport would go over well with a male audience but might be considerably less effective with a predominantly female group, since auto racing today is still largely a man's sport. A speech on the special problems that affect the lives of the wives of auto racers and their attitudes and fears might be more suitable for a female audience.

In the choice of subject supporting materials and language, a speaker should always be aware of differences in interests, attitudes, and motivations of males and females.

RELIGION.   Because members of the various religions found throughout the world differ in their beliefs on many subjects, it is essential that speakers analyze this factor in planning a speech. Some religious convictions are so personal and so deeply felt that the individuals are unable to tolerate or even discuss contrary beliefs.

Because of religious differences on matters such as war, birth control, abortion, gambling, observance of the Sabbath, and the consumption of alcoholic beverages or other stimulants—to name just a few examples—it would be foolish to approach a group on a subject related to these questions without first knowing the predisposition of the audience. The wise speaker will adapt his or her approach to the audience. For example, a speaker favoring birth control as a means of curbing overpopulation would vary the approach when

To study persuasion intensively is to study human nature minutely.

CHARLES WOOLBERT

speaking to a Catholic audience from that used with a group of Unitarians. The speaker should not change his or her convictions to those of the differing audiences but certainly should adapt them to the values and doctrinal differences of the groups. On many subjects, the religion of the auditors will have no bearing on the success or failure of the speaker—for example, if the subject is photography, gardening, inflation, or the World Series. In treating other subjects that involve moral or doctrinal differences, it is extremely important that the speaker know something about the audience's religious beliefs.

Failure to recognize differences in religious beliefs and attitudes could result in the embarrassing situation of the Baptist minister who, when his church burned down, received a call from the Jewish rabbi. The rabbi, in the best ecumenical tradition, offered the use of his synagogue to the Baptists until the church could be rebuilt. Accepting the invitation, the minister expressed his appreciation by saying, "That is very Christian of you." Teaching the minister a lesson in audience adaptation, the rabbi responded "It is very Jewish, too." Good taste and a personal sensitivity to the religious attitudes and beliefs of the audience are essential to the effectiveness of a speech.

POLITICS.   How often have you heard the statement, "There is no sense in arguing about religion and politics"? Although it is inherently false, for both subjects are so vital that they should be discussed often, the statement serves as a warning to speakers.

Political affiliation takes on a religious fervor for some people. For them it is difficult to argue rationally, or even to discuss intelligently, problems within these two realms. Political belief, like religious conviction, is to a large degree based on faith and often permits little intellectual examination. To abuse the political sensibilities of an audience could be disastrous for a speaker. The good speaker will adapt materials to the political attitudes of the audience, not by becoming fraudulent or dishonest in the development of arguments but by avoiding useless antagonism and by capitalizing on those arguments that relate positively to the auditors' political convictions.

Although political differences are often deeply ingrained and may sharply divide groups on many questions, the speaker should not overlook the common bonds that unite most people regardless of political affiliation. People of all political faiths tend to agree in their love of country; in their belief in liberty, justice, and freedom; and in their desire to have a satisfactory standard of living, to help others, and to promote the general welfare of the community. Their means of attaining these goals may differ, but regardless of party loyalty, most people share many common aspirations and values.

RACE.   It is important for a speaker to know in advance both the racial characteristics of the audience and their attitudes toward racial differences. To avoid injuring the cause, the speaker should eschew any reference that might cause racial antagonism. It might seem harmless to tell an ethnic or racial joke, but it could also prove disastrous. The attitude of the audience toward speaker and subject and the atmosphere of the occasion will determine the propriety of racial references.

Information about the racial characteristics of the audience provides the speaker with insight into cultural orientation and reveals something of their attitudes toward various programs, policies, and institutions. For example, white Americans often assume that all black Americans share the same goals. This belief is often unfounded. White Americans may look to Ronald Reagan, Ralph Nader, and Lee Iacocca, for example, as leaders in their fields deserving of admiration and emulation, while black Americans may find inspiration in the lives of Martin Luther King, Jr., Lena Horne, Jesse Jackson, and O. J. Simpson. American Indians have heroes and aspirations that differ from those of both blacks and whites. While most white Americans are granted their rights to a decent job, satisfactory housing, and a good education for their children, many blacks, Indians, and members of other racial minorities are still struggling to obtain these opportunities. The speaker who recognizes and adapts to these differences has a better chance of securing the desired response from the audience than the speaker who ignores them.

On the other hand, the speaker should not make the mistake of stereotyping racial groups and assuming that all blacks are underprivileged, all whites have good jobs and nice homes, or all Orientals run laundries. Within any racial group there are many shades of opinion, conflicting attitudes, and differing aspirations. Furthermore, within each racial or ethnic group there is usually a large segment whose goals and values are the same as those of the general population. Much misunderstanding could be avoided by resisting the tendency to classify all members of a group as psychologically and philosophically identical simply because of the color of their skin.

NATIONALITY.   The considerations that apply to the racial sensitivities of an audience also apply to nationality groups. Ethnic references need not be avoided, but they should be selected with care, for if members of an audience feel that their race or nationality is being derided, the speaker will probably lose the respect of the listeners and jeopardize the cause for which he or she speaks.

Ethnic groups often differ in their attitudes, beliefs, customs, and interests—the Amish in Pennsylvania, Scandinavian Americans in Minnesota, Cajuns in Louisiana, Hispanics in the Southwest, Japanese Americans in California, and those of Italian, Puerto Rican, and Irish descent in New York frequently observe holidays and customs of their ancestral countries. The speaker should know the degree of ethnic identification felt by the members of the audience in order to avoid offending them or to win their approval. Perhaps no one is more aware of the significance of such sensitivities than a mayor of New York City, where the acceptability of any policy depends on its appeal to various ethnic groups.

The presence of international students on college campuses offers excellent opportunities for the student speakers to test their abilities to adapt to listeners of different nationalities. Persuading Israelis and Jordanians to accept a common point of view toward Middle East problems would indeed be challenging. Or imagine the obstacles in convincing students from Formosa to accept our recognition of the People's Republic of China. Yet the public speaker is often faced with just such challenges.

OCCUPATION.   Vocations of audience members often serve as an index to the listeners' economic status and attitudes. Physicians, for example, are financially better off than nurses; college administrators are better paid than elementary school teachers. Physicians and cab drivers probably differ in their attitudes toward medicare; factory workers and corporation executives rarely agree on unionization; farmers and businesspeople have contrasting views on agricultural subsidies. Not only do various occupational groups hold different attitudes toward many topics, but because of their vocations they may have a special knowledge about certain subjects. The speaker should be aware of the occupations represented in the audience.

If the audience is composed of people from a single vocation or profession (machinists, professors, secretaries, dentists, nurses), adaptation of language and topic may be less difficult for the speaker. The language of such groups is often specialized, and the speaker can use their jargon freely. In addition, interests are likely to be similar, which makes the task of selecting a topic and supporting materials easier. If, however, the audience is composed of persons from diverse occupations, speakers have a more difficult problem. They must select a topic of general appeal, use supporting materials appropriate to the various occupations represented, and avoid professional jargon.

ECONOMIC STATUS.   Economic status, of course, is closely related to occupation or profession, although the relationship is becoming less rigid as members of traditionally "lower-income" occupations begin to share more equitably in the national wealth. It is important for the speaker to know the economic status of an audience, however, since people's interests and attitudes are often governed by their pocketbooks. The poor, for example, are rarely interested in such topics as investing in the stock market, international travel, yachting, and debutante balls. The rich, on the other hand, are generally not interested in shopping bargains, job hunting, or buying on the installment plan.

Knowledge of the economic status of the audience is particularly important if a speaker is urging support of a referendum or piece of legislation that will require an increase in the expenditure of public monies. A speaker who hopes to win support for such proposals must know and adapt to the audience's attitudes toward higher taxes. One's approach to an audience of businesspeople should differ considerably from that employed with an audience of migrant laborers. Since most social and political issues have economic implications, the wise speaker will seek to determine and adapt to the economic status of the auditors.

SOCIAL STATUS.   Social status is more important to many people than income or wealth. Some professional groups, such as educators, have social prestige unrelated to their incomes. The authority and prestige that accompany social position is sometimes sufficient to cause persons to abandon high-income positions and accept low-paying jobs with greater social prestige. Examples of this are business executives, lawyers, and others who give up lucrative business or professional careers to accept cabinet posts and ambassadorships. Poets, scholars, literary critics, and scientists, whose incomes may not be particularly high, often enjoy considerable social status.

Social status differs greatly from one group to another. Rock stars, professional boxers, and talk show hosts—no matter how well-to-do or well known—may enjoy little social prestige among scholars, artists, scientists, and other groups. Motion picture and television performers may command considerable respect in some circles but be dismissed as socially questionable in others. Professional athletes rank high on the social ladder with some and low with others. The speaker who knows in advance the social status of the listeners and their attitudes toward other social groups will have a better understanding of their values, interests, and opinion of the subject and the speaker.

EDUCATION.   The knowledge a person possesses is not directly related to the number of years of formal education attained or the number of degrees earned. Eric Hoffer, for example, author of several books that have brought him international fame for his incisive examination of contemporary society, failed to finish high school and spent most of his adult life as a common laborer. Although Hoffer is an exceptional case, no speaker should make the mistake of inferring that people lacking a formal education are uneducated.

There is a difference, of course, between the *type* or *kind* of education and the *amount* of education. A person with an advanced degree may be totally ignorant in areas well understood by high school dropouts. Thus someone who has a Ph.D in biology or music may know nothing about repairing an automobile, baking bread, or playing football. The person with a Ph.D in biology and one with a Ph.D in music may be unable to talk to each other about anything technical in their respective fields. Therefore, the speaker should not make unwarranted assumptions about the audience members' knowledge of a specific topic. The speaker should discover the amount of formal education attained by the majority of the audience but should also include in the evaluation the extent of their nonformal learning. The responsibility, then, is to adapt the language and illustrative materials of the speech to their particular kind and range of knowledge.

SIZE.   The size of the audience will help determine the speaker's approach to the listeners. A general rule of thumb can be used: the larger the audience, the more formal the presentation. Although it does not always hold true, experienced speakers testify that it is difficult to be informal with a large group and often awkward to be formal with a small one.

The size of the audience may also influence the degree of difficulty a speaker has in stimulating the emotions of listeners, in employing visual aids, and in obtaining audience participation. Individuals in small groups, for example, tend to be less subject to emotional appeals than people in large crowds, for people in small groups establish an intimacy with the speaker and with other members of the audience that produces inhibitions not found in large gatherings. Thus, the fewer present, the more inhibited the audience and the more rational the response. Also, a large assemblage may preclude the use of some types of visual aids or at least place different demands on the speaker who wishes to employ them. The size of the audience also influences the amount and type of audience participation during a speech. Small groups may become involved in active discussion with the speaker, whereas audience participation by members of large audiences is usually restricted to asking questions at the end of the speech.

HOMOGENEITY.   Polarization or "one-mindedness" of an audience is partially achieved when the members are of the same profession or occupation, have the same interests, or share similar social, political, or religious attitudes. Since the speaker seeks to polarize the thinking of the audience, it is obvious that the greater the similarity of characteristics shared by the listeners, the easier it is to accomplish this goal. For example, the speaker's task is greatly simplified if an audience is composed entirely of elementary school teachers, Young Democrats, accountants, or liberal arts majors.

Audience homogeneity may consist of similarity in any of a number of characteristics such as sex, religion, politics, race, occupation, nationality, or combinations of these. Usually, the greater the number of shared interests and attitudes, the simpler the task for the speaker, who can select materials aimed at stimulating those shared interests.

Many audiences, however, are not highly homogeneous; members may come from a variety of occupations, professions, social levels, and income groups. Often members have different values. Such groups test the imagination of the speaker, who must attempt to find areas of common belief. In discussing questions where the listeners' interests, needs, and attitudes differ sharply, a speaker should seek areas of shared understanding and aspiration. For example, in spite of differences in opinion on many issues, most Americans share a belief in such values as fair play, justice, equality, and freedom and such goals as the right to a satisfactory job, decent housing, an education, and the opportunity to advance. A speaker can always find shared interests among the members of a heterogeneous audience, although sometimes they are obscure and the speaker must search hard to find them.

Audience Expectations

When people take the time to hear someone else speak, they do so with certain expectations that the speaker must fulfill if the speech is to be effective. The speaker must discover those expectations and attempt to satisfy them.

Not long ago, the coordinator of an intercollegiate student conference made a series of announcements to the assembled participants. Although not planned, his remarks were humorous. The next day, at a meeting of the same group, the director was again called upon to make some announcements. Knowing that the audience anticipated an amusing effort similar to that of the previous day, the speaker deliberately employed humor to satisfy those expectations. The audience forms an image of a speaker that must be satisfied in future speaking performances. Audience expectations are not limited to the manner of presentation but extend to the ideas the speaker will talk about, the arguments used, the language employed, and the attitudes exhibited toward the audience.

The television newscaster must adapt to a heterogeneous audience. (Mike Keza, NYT Pictures)

> You persuade a man only in as far as you can talk his language, by speech, gesture, tonality, order, image, attitude, idea, identifying your ways with him.
>
> KENNETH BURKE

Reason for Assembling

Speakers also are limited by the nature of the occasion and the audience's expectations for that particular occasion. For example, a sports banquet demands a speech on athletics, a testimonial dinner calls for a speech on the honoree's accomplishments, and a religious meeting requires discussion of some moral or theological question. The speaker who delivers a partisan political address to a Parent-Teachers Association group expecting to hear a talk on education risks rejection and failure, as does the speaker who addresses the Garden Club on drug abuse or aerobics.

To be effective, the speaker must determine the expectations of the audience and attempt to satisfy them by selecting appropriate subject matter.

An audience does not just happen; people usually gather for a reason. Occasionally the group may be simply a collection of passersby who congregate out of curiosity to hear someone on a soapbox at the campus free-speech area or in Central Park. But most audiences are formed of people who have planned to be present at a particular event or to hear a person speak. Such audiences may be divided into three major categories: (1) coerced or captive, (2) voluntary, and (3) organizational.

COERCED.   Perhaps the best example of a coerced audience is that of college students in a classroom. Once students are assigned to a course, they are required to attend all the lecture sessions. This is one type of coerced audience, but not the only one.

Coercion also exists when the sales staff is called together for a meeting with the manager, when a group of junior executives are ordered to a session with the president of the company, or when an athletic team is assembled for a meeting with their coach. In these instances, a common interest is shared by those being coerced; a desire for self-improvement or advancement in the organization provides interest and incentive for them to be attentive.

A third type of coerced audience is the one that has gathered voluntarily to hear one speaker and then finds itself the victim of another, unexpected speaker. Often people attend a meeting to hear a United States senator or distinguished scholar and find themselves forced to sit through the harangues of a battery of warm-up speakers they may not care to hear. Chairpersons of meetings sometimes use these occasions to make speeches of their own, taking advantage of an audience gathered for another reason. This is seldom advantageous to the speaker.

Arousing the interest of a coerced audience often is difficult. A particularly challenging assignment is to lecture to a college class. Many students exhibit the attitude "O.K. I've paid my fee; I dare you to teach me." Some members of the audience may be openly belligerent if the course is a required one. Others are often apathetic. Even eager students feel coerced when on a particular day they believe their time might be better spent elsewhere but they are forced to attend the lecture for fear of forfeiting a grade advantage. The lecturer has a built-in hostility to overcome. The same is true of the speaker who intrudes on the time of the audience when he or she is not scheduled on the program. In such situations, the speaker must convince the auditors of the value or significance of the subject and must constantly strive to maintain interest through the use of vivid, striking, and memorable material.

VOLUNTARY.   A voluntary audience is one that gathers of free will in order to hear a speaker. Its voluntary nature makes preparation no less important, for often these "volunteers" may be hostile to the topic, the speaker, or the organization the speaker represents.

On most controversial issues, a speaker whose views are well known will find that the audience—even though voluntary—includes not only supporters but detractors determined to heckle, disrupt, and discredit the speaker.

Having a voluntary audience, however, whether favorable or antagonistic, has advantages, for the members are not apathetic or indifferent. Regardless of their position, they approach the speech with an interest in the speaker, the subject, or both.

ORGANIZATIONAL MEMBERSHIP.   At times speakers are invited to talk to audiences composed of members of a particular organization, such as a business, service, charitable, philanthropic, or professional group. The interests of the members of such audiences usually are rather well defined. Although the members may differ in a variety of ways, the speaker knows they share the interests of the group to which they belong. For example, a national project for Lions International is the procurement of seeing-eye dogs for the blind. Other organizations have other objectives. The speaker should discover these goals and projects.

Obtaining Information About the Audience

Little progress has been made if the speaker knows what information is needed to find out about a prospective audience but does not know where to obtain it. Usually the person who arranged the speaking engagement will be able to provide information about the more mechanical aspects of the audience, such as the size, sex composition, race, and age. If the program organizer cannot provide answers to questions concerning the religious, social, political, and other characteristics of the audience, the speaker has several alternatives. The speaker might seek out other officers of the organization, talk to individual members in advance of the program, or consult someone who has previously appeared before the group. From these sources the speaker should try to obtain information concerning the predisposition of the audience toward the issues he or she plans to talk about.

Another source of information is printed material. A speaker who has accepted an invitation to address the B'nai B'rith Society and knows nothing about the organization might turn to an encyclopedia or a book about the society for general information regarding its history, membership, and aims. Newspaper accounts of recent activities of the group and publications of the association may be helpful. Most labor unions, religious groups, businesses or corporations, civic and service clubs, and fraternities and sororities publish magazines or "house organs" containing information about issues vital to the group and can provide a general understanding of the group's activities.

The speaker should investigate all the suggested sources of information before preparing a speech. The more one knows about the audience before beginning preparations, the more effective one's effort will be.

THE OCCASION

Not long ago, an experienced speaker was asked to deliver his first high school commencement address. He was determined to be original and break with the traditional patterns of commencement speeches. Consequently, he prepared his speech exclusively for the graduating seniors, without regard for the families and friends who would attend the exercises. It was a good idea, and a good speech.

Upon arriving at the auditorium he discovered, to his consternation, that the audience was separated; the graduating seniors were on the stage of the auditorium, the families and friends in the seats out front. The speaker's rostrum stood between the groups, facing the guests. What a predicament! He had a speech for the graduates, but he was to face the guests. What should he do?

Alternatives ran through his mind. "I can change the speech a bit and adapt it to the general public," he thought. But that was contrary to his intention when he accepted the assignment. "I can speak to the graduates even though they are behind me." But then he would be facing one group and addressing another. "I can turn the rostrum around and ignore the parents and friends." But that might be considered rude. The speaker had to solve the dilemma. With explanations and an apology, he turned the rostrum to face the graduates, leaving the larger part of the audience to gape at his back.

This awkward and embarrassing situation could have been avoided had the speaker analyzed his audience in advance; by doing so he would have discovered the seating arrangement and planned accordingly.

The setting for a speech is just as important to the speaker's preparation as knowledge of the audience. To realize the significance of the occasion, consider the speaker who prepares a 45-minute speech, as requested by the program planner, only to find that he or she is the sixth speaker on a program that begins at 9 PM. If all five preceding speakers have prepared speeches of the same length, it will be after midnight when our speaker begins, by which time the audience either will have disappeared completely or dwindled to those who lack the strength to leave. All of the preparation was for naught. What to do? The more significant question is: Why didn't the speaker discover the situation in advance? To avoid the embarrassment and wasted effort suffered by this speaker, five aspects of a speaking situation should be investigated early in the preparation stage: (1) the length of the meeting, (2) the time of day, (3) the size of the room and the anticipated number of listeners, (4) the facilities available to the speaker, and (5) the nature of the meeting.

The Length of the Meeting

It is important for the speaker to know the length of the meeting, for even if 30 to 40 minutes are available, the speaker may want to pare down the time if the meeting begins late or a business session precedes the speech. The good audience analyst takes into consideration the audience fatigue factor. Although the listeners might tolerate a longer time limit for a given speech, their receptivity diminishes rapidly with time. If a preceding speaker has spoken at great length and with some tedium, it might be wise to limit the length of one's speech. Often the audience will appreciate the speaker's consideration in remaining brief and will therefore listen with greater interest and retention.

The Time of Day

As all college students and professors know, and as low enrollments reveal, it is more difficult to listen attentively to a 7:30 AM lecture than a 9:30 AM lecture, regardless of the speaker. The professor knows that it is more challenging to deliver the earlier lecture than the later one. One of the authors recalls that he registered for a course in music appreciation when in college

General Alexander Smith, a tedious speaker in Congress, observed: "You sir, speak for the present generation; but I speak for posterity." "Yes," replied Henry Clay, "and you seem resolved to speak until the arrival of your audience."

and was assigned to a 1:30 PM class. Three times a week he attended the class. Three times a week he went to sleep listening to Beethoven, Brahms, or Bach. A full stomach combined with soothing music defeated his will to stay awake. He dropped the course after two weeks and took it in a subsequent semester at a more appropriate time.

A speaker should adjust to the time of day and when planning the speech take into consideration such universally shared physical states as early morning sleepiness, early afternoon listlessness, late afternoon fatigue, and late evening grogginess. The speaker should discover his or her own periods of high and low alertness and adjust to them. It may be necessary to make an extra effort during particular parts of the day.

The Size of the Room and Audience

The degree of formality of a speech is dictated in part by the size and shape of the room and the number of people present. The comfort of both the speaker and the members of the audience is also affected by these two aspects of the situation.

Few things are more disconcerting to a speaker than to address an audience of 25 persons in a room that seats 300. The audience, too, is embarrassed. Jerry Bruno, who was the "advance man" in charge of making all arrangements for the speeches of two recent presidents and for other prominent political figures, stresses the importance of scheduling the speeches in halls that can be filled. He contends that if one attends a rally or meeting where seats are at a premium, the listener has the feeling that it is an important occasion. On the other hand, if surrounded by a vast expanse of empty seats, the auditor has the feeling of "being had." The program organizer should anticipate the number of listeners and select a room that seats approximately that number. If there is little information upon which to base an estimate of attendance, it is better to schedule a room that is too small for the audience than one that is too large. The optimum ratio of seats to people is one-to-one, but it is better for the speaker's morale to have people standing or turned away than to have a few listeners surrounded by a sea of empty chairs.

The speaker's manner of delivery certainly will be modified according to the size of the room and the number of people present; people will normally speak more softly and use less expansive gestures in a small room than in a large auditorium.

The Facilities

It is always a good idea for speakers to visit the room in which a speech is to be given, not only to determine the dimensions but also to inspect the facilities so they may request any additional needed items. A speaker may want a lectern if it is a large room, or a public address system if the auditorium has poor acoustics, or the speaker may request that an existing public address system be removed.

A speaker who plans to use photographic slides to illustrate a speech should make sure that the room can be darkened (some cannot), be certain that a screen and projector will be provided, know where the light switches are located, and plan to have the lights dimmed or turned off at the appropriate time in the course of the speech. And if the lighting in the room is not adequate for exhibiting prepared visual aids, the speaker should request additional lighting or modify the talk to exclude the visual aids.

The speaker should also learn in advance whether there is a stage, raised dais, or other kind of platform, for special challenges confront the speaker raised physically above the audience. The situation of the commencement speaker described earlier in this chapter would not have occurred had the speaker discovered in advance that he was to speak from a stage where part of his audience would be seated. For the best rapport with listeners, the speakers should be on the same level as the audience and as close to them as possible. The higher and farther removed in distance a speaker is from the listeners, the greater is the psychological distance between him and them. It is important, then, that the speaker be familiar with the facilities and total environment of the speaking situation.

The Nature of the Meeting

As stressed earlier, people gather to hear a speech for some particular reason. It may be a regularly scheduled meeting of a group or a special occasion. It may be a special gathering of a group that meets regularly. The speaker should ask three basic questions concerning the nature of the meeting: Is it a regular meeting? Is it a special occasion? and What is the nature of the program?

1. *Is it a regular meeting?* Groups that meet on a regular basis often are starved for programs and invite guests to speak with little or no long-range planning. It is the responsibility of the speaker to determine the interests of the members, discover what previous speakers have talked about in order to avoid repetition, and adapt to those speeches. Normally such situations require a relatively short speech and, if the speech follows a meal, it should probably entertain as well as enlighten or persuade.

2. *Is it a special occasion?* Many groups hold meetings to commemorate special events in the history of the country or their own organizations. Universities celebrate Founders Day, and different organizations observe anniversaries and holidays such as the Fourth of July, Lincoln's birthday, Memorial Day, St. Patrick's Day, and Labor Day, whereas others commemorate events such as Boy Scouts Day, Martin Luther King's birthday, and Registration Day (celebrated by the League of Women Voters). Special occasions would also include

luncheons and banquets arranged for purposes such as political fund-raising, support of a charitable organization, and the presentation of an award. If asked to speak to a group gathered to celebrate a special event, one should be familiar with the event and the relationship of the event to the organization and then, of course, adapt the speech to that special occasion.

3. *What is the nature of the program?* Is there other entertainment? Are there to be other speakers? If so, what are their topics? Am I to be the main speaker or a supplementary one? All these questions should be answered by the speaker before beginning preparation.

It is distressing for a speaker to appear at an occasion expecting to be the principal speaker only to discover that three other people share the program. Distress turns into panic when one further learns that an earlier speaker is talking on the same topic. What to do now? Perhaps the best solution would be to feign illness and make a strategic exit, but that would be the coward's way out. The average speaker would stumble through the prepared text with a nervous preface to the effect that he or she "didn't have much to add to the remarks of the previous speaker," and might then proceed to prove the preface remarkably accurate. Such situations are not only embarrassing to the speaker but cruel to the audience as well. Yet because of poor planning, the situation occurs frequently.

A good program planner will avoid this embarrassment by fully informing the participating speakers of the entire program and their role in it. But many programs are planned by inexperienced chairpersons. (One program organizer telephoned a speech department and asked them to present a debate but to be sure it wasn't controversial.) Capable speakers will avoid embarrassment by requesting this information should it not be supplied. They can then adapt their remarks to those of the other speakers.

SUMMARY

Preparing a speech is a task that requires a systematic method. The first step a speaker should take in preparing for a speech is analyzing the audience and occasion. When analyzing the audience, the speaker should investigate its composition—age, sex, religion, politics, race, nationality, occupation, economic status, social status, education, size, and homogeneity—in order to select a topic and supporting materials that will be of interest. The speaker should also discover the audience's expectations and their reason for assembling and select a topic and supporting materials consistent with the occasion as well. The speaker's preparation should include learning as much as possible about the length of the meeting, the time of day, the size of the group, the facilities, and whether the audience is captive or voluntary. With this kind of information about the audience and occasion, the speaker is prepared to select a topic and to begin gathering materials for the speech.

STUDY QUESTIONS

1. What is polarization? Why is knowledge of this concept important to a speaker?
2. In what ways does the size of the audience affect the speaker's delivery, rapport with listeners, and audience participation?
3. How do audience expectations influence the speaker's choice of subject and selection of supporting materials?
4. In what ways can a speaker adapt to a coerced audience, a voluntary audience, and an organizational audience?
5. If you were asked to give a speech to each of the following organizations, where might you obtain information about your prospective audiences: (a) the Junior League, (b) the Speech Communication Association, (c) the local chapter of the American Civil Liberties Union, (d) your state historical society?
6. What is meant by the "occasion" for a speech? Do all speeches have occasions? What kinds of information does a speaker need to obtain about the speech occasion?

EXERCISES

1. Prepare an outline for a speech for a classroom audience on some subject about which you are well informed. Then prepare a second outline adapting the same materials for a speech to a business luncheon meeting.
2. Attend a speech and analyze the speaker's use of materials to interest or adapt to the audience. Did the speaker use any special appeals or techniques to account for (a) the composition of the audience, (b) the expectations of the listeners, and (c) the nature of the occasion? Write a paper summarizing your analysis.
3. In outline form, prepare an analysis of the class as an audience. In what ways are they much alike? In what ways do they differ?
4. Prepare a list of five topics that most of your classroom audience would be interested in. Prepare another list of five topics on which most of the class members would be in agreement. Prepare a third list of subjects on which there probably would be differing attitudes among the class members.
5. Read a speech in *Vital Speeches* or *Representative American Speeches*. In a paper, indicate the ways that the speaker seemed to be trying to adapt to the interests, attitudes, or characteristics of his or her audience. How necessary, in your opinion, was audience adaptation in this situation? Indicate your opinion of the speaker's effectiveness in adapting to listeners.
6. Select a teacher and analyze his or her effectiveness in adapting to an audience of students. Prepare a 3- to 4-minute report in which you analyze both the strong and weak points of the audience adaptation of this teacher. You need not name the teacher in your report. Deliver the report to the class.

FURTHER READINGS

Ehninger, Douglas, Bruce E. Gronbeck, Ray E. McKerrow, and Alan Monroe, *Principles and Types of Speech Communication,* 10th ed. (Glenview, IL: Scott, Foresman, 1986), chap. 4, "Choosing Speech Subjects and Purpose," chap. 5, "Analyzing the Audience and Occasion," and chap. 6, "Determining the Basic Appeals."

Lucas, Stephen E., *The Art of Public Speaking* (New York: Random House, 1986), chap. 4, "Analyzing the Audience."

Mudd, Charles S., and Malcolm O. Sillars, *Speech: Content and Communication* (New York: Crowell, 1975), chap. 4, "Analyzing the Audience," and chap. 5, "Attention Factors."

Osborn, Michael, *Speaking in Public* (Boston: Houghton Mifflin, 1982), chap. 7, "Adaptation to an Audience: Situational and Psychological Factors."

Ross, Raymond S., *Speech Communication: Fundamentals and Practice,* 7th ed. (Englewood Cliffs, NJ: Prentice-Hall, 1986), chap. 5, "Audience Psychology."

Vasile, Albert J., and Harold K. Mintz, *Speak With Confidence: A Practical Guide,* 4th ed. (Boston: Little, Brown, 1986), chap. 9, "Know Your Listeners and Speak Their Language."

Zannes, Estelle, and Gerald Goldhaber, *Stand Up, Speak Out,* 2nd ed. (Reading, MA: Addison-Wesley, 1983), chap. 1, "Preparing for the Event."

CHAPTER 5

FINDING SUBJECTS

George Bernard Shaw, the British lecturer and playwright, claimed that the most popular speech he ever delivered was at the invitation of "the superior persons at Toynbee Hall who step condescendingly down from the universities to improve the poor." Informed that his audience would consist entirely of poor people, he chose as his topic "That the poor are useless, dangerous, and ought to be abolished." Shaw relates, "I had my poor audience, and they were delighted. They cheered me to the echo: that was what they wanted to have said."

Although Shaw's selection of topic at first seems preposterous, upon reflection it becomes apparent that it was a shrewd choice. Extensive reading in economics and years of study of the social conditions in Britain had given Shaw an understanding of poverty and its causes; he appreciated that to the members of his audience nothing was more vital than their day-to-day struggle for existence and that the nature of the meeting was ideal for a discussion of their problems. The subject was right for the speaker, the audience, and the occasion.

In situations other than public speaking, the speaker often will find that the subject is predetermined. For example, when two executives get together to conclude a deal, when a committee meets to resolve a problem, when a personnel manager interviews a job applicant, when a supervisor explains a new method or program to employees, or when a client consults a lawyer, the purpose of the meeting dictates the general topic.

In much interpersonal communication, such as conversations, a student-teacher consultation, and social discourse, the participants may touch on a wide range of subjects that grow out of the interactions of the persons involved in the communication.

In public speaking situations, however, the speaker often must determine what the subject will be, and not all speakers will find the choice as easy as did George Bernard Shaw. For many, this first step in the preparation of a speech may be an arduous and soul-searching endeavor. The choice of a subject, of course, presents no problem if the speaker is asked to speak on a specific topic that he or she is qualified to discuss. More commonly, however, speakers are invited to address groups without a particular topic being specified. The speaker may be asked to deliver a talk on some general subject with which he or she is familiar; for example, a college president might be invited to discuss education, or a public official might be asked to speak on some aspect of government. At other times, not even a general topic is suggested. In either circumstance, the speaker has a wide range of possible subjects and so must compile a list of potential topics, examine each, and select one well suited to the requirements of the situation.

Student speakers often face a uniquely difficult task in that they must address the same audience of classmates regularly and at short intervals of time. They may choose the first two or three subjects with little difficulty, but thereafter they will probably find it increasingly difficult to choose topics for speaking assignments.

FINDING TOPICS

For a variety of reasons, speakers frequently find it difficult to select subjects. Often the prime reason is the speaker's feeling of inadequacy, which results in indecision. Speakers may select one topic and begin preparation of a speech only to decide that another topic will be more interesting. So they start to work on a second subject. After a while they begin to doubt their competency to discuss that topic and choose still another. And on and on. Aside from the time wasted in these false starts, such speakers are also plagued by doubts, fears, and general insecurity and feel that their ideas and experiences are not important enough to interest others.

Another reason speakers may experience difficulty in selecting speech topics is lack of self-knowledge. Speakers may not have taken the time to compile an inventory of those subjects on which they are well-informed. So when the time comes to select a speech topic, they must begin the painstaking task of trying to sort out from the many things in which they are more or less interested a topic suitable for the requested speech.

A third reason speakers have trouble choosing topics is that they do not know other people. They are unable to place themselves in the position of their expected listeners and to understand these listeners' attitudes, interests, knowledge, and experiences. A topic that seems commonplace to the speaker may be one in which the audience would be highly interested. For example, one student who was having trouble locating speech topics revealed to his instructor that he had been raised on a remote island off the Louisiana coast, that he had been tutored at home by his mother until he reached high school age, and that upon entering high school he could speak only French. From this unusual background, the student could have chosen from among many speech topics of interest to his audience, but he had overlooked those possibilities because to him his experiences seemed commonplace.

To overcome these difficulties in selecting speech subjects, speakers should recognize that everyone is an "expert" on some subject, take inventory of their own interests, and study and know the audience and the nature of the speaking occasion. The speaker who has nothing worthwhile to talk about probably does not exist. Aside from specialized information acquired on the job, in the classroom, and through reading, travel, and various other pursuits, almost everyone has a store of general knowledge, opinions, and observations

Blessed is the man who, having nothing to say, abstains from giving in words evidence of the fact.

GEORGE ELIOT

based on personal experiences. Each individual is the best possible expert—actually the only expert—on his or her personal reactions to the people, places, and activities with which he or she has come into contact. A few examples of effective student speeches based on "ordinary" experiences include talks based on summer jobs (in a pizza parlor, on an offshore oil rig, as a state legislator's page, and as an encyclopedia salesperson); editing a high school yearbook; backpacking; a concert; Jewish holidays; and a canoe trip.

Admittedly, some people have led more exciting lives than others, their experiences are more varied, and their knowledge is more extensive. But there is nothing to prevent the speaker whose life has been unduly sheltered or prosaic from broadening his or her scope of knowledge and experiences through reading, conversation, hobbies, sports, television, and other activities. There is no excuse for an individual's having nothing worthwhile to talk about.

Rather than having nothing to discuss, speakers who have difficulty finding speech topics have probably simply failed to take careful inventory of their interests. One should examine both the present and the past and, as sources for possible topics, consider personal experiences and observations; reading and study; radio, television, lectures, and conversations; jobs; the organizations to which one belongs; special research and investigations that one has conducted; leisure activities; travels; and other related items. Specifically one might consider:

1. Sports
2. Hobbies
3. Skills
4. Jobs
5. Travels
6. School
7. Food
8. Social activities
9. Clubs, organizations
10. Personal beliefs
11. Music
12. Health
13. Personal conduct
14. Customs, traditions, holidays
15. Art
16. Home, family, and friends
17. Goals and ambitions
18. Unusual experiences
19. Nature
20. Animals and pets
21. Clothing and grooming
22. Etiquette
23. Creative activities
24. Words, language
25. Politics
26. Personality traits
27. Books, literature, reading
28. Subject matter areas:
   a. Mathematics
   b. Science
   c. Architecture
   d. History
   e. Geography
   f. Anthropology
   g. Government
   h. Law
   i. Medicine
   j. Agriculture
   k. Forestry
   l. Geology
   m. Economics
   n. Sociology
   o. Psychology
   p. Home economics
   q. Communication
   r. Computer science

As the preceding list suggests, the number of areas that a speaker might examine in searching for speech topics is large. However, it is possible to extend even further the number of potential topics. Specific aspects or sub-topics of various areas might serve as subjects for speeches, as shown below:

Music
1. How to play the guitar
2. How to buy a good guitar
3. The guitar in country-western music
4. How to listen to country-western music
5. Why country-western music has become popular
6. The country-western recording industry in Nashville
7. The Grand Old Opry
8. Great country-western performers
9. Care and storing of records
10. A basic country-western record library

Tennis
1. Tennis terminology and scoring
2. Rules in tennis
3. How to serve
4. How to develop a good backhand
5. Care of a tennis court
6. Great tennis players of the past and present
7. The Davis Cup competition
8. The status of amateur and professional players
9. How to buy the right racquet
10. The great tennis tournaments

London
1. The Houses of Parliament
2. Westminster Abbey
3. London's parks
4. London as a theater center
5. Free entertainment in London
6. The Tower of London
7. Pomp and circumstance: ceremony and the royal family
8. Eating in Britain
9. Differences between American and British speech
10. London's pubs

After the speaker has completed an inventory of potential speech topics, it should be filed for future use. In addition, the speaker may want to start the kind of speaker's scrapbook or file of clippings discussed in Chapter 6.

SELECTING THE SUBJECT

After taking inventory of possible topics for discussion, the speaker is now ready to begin the process of finally selecting a subject. To ensure a wise choice, the speaker should apply four tests to the subjects being considered: (1) Is the topic suitable for the speaker? (2) Is the subject suitable for the audience? (3) Is it appropriate to the occasion? and (4) Is the subject suited to the time available?

Is the Topic Suitable for the Speaker?

The most important test for a speech topic is whether it is appropriate for the speaker. To determine this, the speaker should consider the following questions.

1. *Am I truly interested in this subject?* Any speaker will find it difficult to interest an audience in a topic he or she cares little about. To speak with enthusiasm and conviction requires a subject in which one has a lively and continuing interest. A speaker should be especially cautious about choosing to talk on something that may have caught the fancy or aroused curiosity momentarily but in which the speaker has never before felt any interest. Magazine and newspaper articles about exotic places, odd occurrences, bizarre customs, and strange coincidences often pique one's curiosity, but they are risky choices as possible speech subjects. The danger is that the speaker's interest may wane so rapidly that by the time of the speech he or she no longer cares about the subject. Speakers would be much better advised to choose a topic in which they have been interested for some time. A reliable guide to our true interests usually can be found in the regularity or frequency with which we turn our attention to certain subjects. The parts of a newspaper we usually read first, the kinds of books we choose, the sports that we follow or in which we participate, hobbies we pursue, occasions that we anticipate with pleasure, and subjects we like to discuss in conversation all are indicators of our true interests. Speakers who choose subjects in which they have long been interested run fewer risks than those who decide to discuss something that only recently has caught their attention.

2. *Is the subject important to me?* In choosing a topic, the speaker not only

There never was in any man so great eloquence as would not begin to stumble and hesitate so soon as his words ran counter to his inmost thoughts.

QUINTILIAN

needs to feel a deep interest in it but also should regard the topic as significant. Most people have some interests that they know are not very important. They may enjoy reading the comics, doing crossword puzzles, soaking in the tub, reading their horoscopes, feeding the sparrows, or drinking beer. While these may be enjoyable pastimes, they probably would not make good subjects for speeches. Most speakers recognize these activities for what they are—mere diversions—and probably would find it difficult to sustain any real desire to communicate on such topics.

Norman Thomas, who spoke to an almost endless number of audiences under a wide variety of circumstances in his many years as leader of the Socialist party, emphasized that interest is contagious. He believed that "to arouse interest in his speech, a speaker must be interested in it himself. His interest, moreover, must be in what he is saying and its importance, not in his own sufferings while he is speaking."

3. *Do I know enough about the subject?* In addition to being interested in the subject and feeling that it is worthwhile, the speaker should be well-informed on the topic. Controversial legislation, a sensational trial, scandal, or a remarkable discovery may arouse interest and a desire to communicate, but unless the speaker thoroughly understands the subject, the speaker should avoid such topics. How much should the speaker know? Certainly the speaker should know more than most of the listeners. A speaker who is not as knowledgeable as the audience not only will find it difficult to hold their attention but will also run the risk of losing their confidence. An inaccurate piece of information, a confusing explanation, uncertainty about details, or omission of a key point or step can trigger suspicion that the speaker does not really understand the subject. Still another reason to be better informed than listeners is that in many speaking situations questioning by the audience is permitted. Speakers who cannot handle listeners' queries will command little respect. However, while they should be well-informed, speakers should not hesitate to speak on a particular topic simply because a few listeners may be true experts on that subject. Ideally, the speaker will be as well-informed on the subject as time and the information available permit.

4. *Can I secure additional information on the subject?* Most speakers, no matter how well-informed, supplement their own general knowledge on a subject with information and ideas from others. They do so to refresh their understanding of the subject, to verify facts, to obtain the most recent data, to get other viewpoints, and to reevaluate their thinking. For

> To know when one's self is interested is the first condition of interesting other people.
>
> WALTER PATER

these reasons, in selecting a topic the speaker should determine whether any additional information is available. Books, magazines, newspapers, encyclopedias, interviews, broadcasts, pamphlets, government documents, atlases, indexes, yearbooks, and bibliographies are sources of supplementary information.

Is the Subject Suitable for the Audience?

A recent presidential candidate made the mistake of failing to analyze his audiences' interests and attitudes in his selection of subjects for several major campaign speeches. In a region that had prospered because of the Tennessee Valley Authority, he spoke disparagingly of government power programs; facing an audience of elderly persons concerned about his position on social security, he totally avoided this topic and discussed law and order instead; addressing audiences in poverty-stricken Appalachia, which had one of the highest unemployment rates in the country, he attacked government programs to relieve poverty-stricken areas; and in a large city badly underrepresented in its state legislature, he opposed reapportionment. Unquestionably, his poor judgment in the choice of issues to discuss with each of these groups did little to help his political campaign.

The errors of judgment just described suggest the second consideration in selecting a speech topic: the subject should be appropriate to the audience. In determining the suitability of a topic to listeners, speakers should consider whether they can develop the subject in such a way that the audience will be interested and will understand what is said. Specifically, the speaker should ask:

1. *Can I interest this audience in this subject?* If a speaker has been asked to address a group on a particular subject, it most likely is because the audience is interested in that topic. In this instance, the speaker's task consists simply of determining which aspects of the subject should be discussed. In situations in which the choice of topic is left to the speaker's discretion, the task is more complicated. However, in either case, the speaker should give careful attention to the interests of the listeners and select a topic in which the audience has already expressed interest or a subject that is unfamiliar but of potential interest to them. The speaker should ask, "Is the audience interested in this subject and, if not, can I arouse their interest in it?" The listeners need not be interested at the outset, but they must become interested early in the presentation.

The speaker should also consider the timeliness of the subject. It is a good idea to examine the ways in which the topic is related to the listeners' needs and desires and to determine whether the topic is fresh and original. A good example of a timely topic was a speech by newspaper columnist Jack Anderson to a college audience at a time when a *New York Times* reporter had been jailed for refusing to reveal his sources for several articles related to a prominent trial. Anderson wisely chose to discuss freedom of speech and the importance of confidentiality for reporters.

2. *Can my listeners understand this subject?* In addition to gauging listeners' potential interest in the subject, the speaker should also give attention to their background and education. Some audiences may not have the general knowledge or specialized training necessary to understand the topic on which someone would like to speak. To determine whether he or she is likely to be able to develop the subject in a meaningful and comprehensible manner, the speaker should consider the listeners' formal education, personal experiences, and specialized knowledge. The speaker must be discriminating in trying to determine exactly what kinds of knowledge the auditors possess: whether it is general or specific, practical or theoretical, outdated or recent. No speaker should make the mistake of assuming that the degree of expertise and type of knowledge are the same for generals and war veterans, for executives and recent business school graduates, for architects and carpenters, for dieticians and cooks.

If an audience lacks the knowledge necessary to understand the topic, the speaker has three choices. First, the speaker might try to provide the audience with the requisite background information in the course of the speech, through definitions, explanations, examples, and comparisons to other more familiar matters. If, however, the audience's ignorance on this topic is so great that the speaker cannot hope to provide the necessary background in the time available, he or she may decide to aim at a lesser goal. Instead of seeking to develop the subject as planned, the speaker may find that by focusing on one part of it, on a few basic principles, or on another aspect of the same general topic, he or she can present a speech that the audience will understand. Or, finally, the speaker may be forced to abandon the subject and seek another.

Is the Topic Appropriate to the Occasion?

Emily Kimbrough reports having been discomfited to learn that she was scheduled to deliver a humorous lecture on Hollywood and motion pictures in a church. To her, the topic seemed inappropriate for an audience assembled in a place of worship.

Another speaker, invited to deliver the main address at a banquet commemorating the founding of a college, was dismayed as the master of ceremonies introduced alumnus after alumnus, most of whom embarked on reminiscences about their undergraduate days at the school. By the time the speaker was introduced, just before 11 PM, the audience was worn out and too tired to pay attention to the speech he had prepared.

A prominent educator was asked to speak at an awards dinner held annually by a university's department of speech and theater. Unaware of the unusual nature of the event, the speaker prepared a serious talk on communication. After skits satirizing the faculty, the presentation of several facetious awards, and some clever musical numbers, he realized that the occasion called for a humorous talk and that the audience was in no mood for his serious discourse.

In each of the above instances, the speaker had chosen a topic supposedly well suited both to himself or herself and to the audience but had overlooked some important element of the speaking occasion. The occasion can be defined as the situation and surrounding circumstances in which the speech is given. The occasion includes the physical surroundings, the nature of the meeting, and the pertinent events occurring both before and during the speech. Some addresses are given on special occasions such as anniversaries, testimonial meetings, holidays, and other similar events, but every speech is delivered under a unique set of circumstances. These circumstances constitute the occasion and include such factors as:

1. The place where the speech is given:
   a. Is it indoors or outdoors?
   b. Is the hall large or small?
   c. What is its shape, arrangement, and seating capacity?
   d. If indoors, what kind of room is it: classroom, auditorium, theater, church, gymnasium, living room, club room, banquet room?
   e. What facilities are provided for the speaker? Does the room have a lectern, a stage, a public address system, a blackboard, a projector, a record player? Can it be darkened if necessary?
   f. Is it properly cooled, heated, and ventilated?
   g. What are its acoustical properties?
2. The time when the speech is to be given:
   a. What time of year?
   b. What time of day?
   c. At what time or place on the program?
3. The reason for assembling:
   a. Did the audience come voluntarily?
   b. Were the listeners required to attend?
   c. Is this a regular meeting?
   d. Has the audience come for a special reason?
4. Events transpiring before the speech:
   a. Has some event that occurred outside the meeting place altered the nature of the occasion?
   b. How has the length of the program, a change in procedure, or the tone or audience reaction to an earlier speaker's remarks altered the situation?

In choosing a subject, the speaker must give attention to all these elements of the speech occasion. The place is important. Certain subjects may be inappropriate if the speech is to be given in a church or synagogue. Inadequate equipment or an outdoor setting might prevent the use of visual aids essential to the development of a particular topic. The ability of the audience to see and hear might also influence the speaker's choice of subject. Whether the surroundings are intimate and cozy or large and uncomfortable may also have some bearing on what the speaker chooses to discuss.

The time is important. The interests and activities of most people vary from season to season. Most people are more interested in vacations, baseball, travel, picnicking, camping, fishing, and swimming in the summer than during other times of the year. Other sports, activities, and holidays are associated with other seasons. Speakers should keep this in mind in selecting a topic. The hour of the day and place on the program may also influence the speaker's choice of subject. To prevent duplication, repetition, and possible embarrassment, speakers should consider the personality, speech topic, and point of view of anyone else scheduled to address the group either before or after his or her own appearance.

The speaker's choice of topic may also be influenced by the audience's reason for assembling. Has the meeting been called to observe an anniversary, commemorate an event, learn about a certain subject, or resolve a particular issue? If so, the speaker would wish to select a topic appropriate to the particular purpose of that occasion. Is the speech to be given at a regular meeting of the group? If this is the case, the speaker will want to know what type of topic the audience expects to hear. Is the audience—perhaps a group of students or military personnel—required to attend the meeting? All these factors assist the speaker in finding a suitable topic.

Is the Subject Suited to the Time Available?

Whether deserved or not, Edmund Burke, the British political philosopher, earned a reputation as a "dinner bell" because of his long speeches to the House of Commons. For many members, Burke's rising to speak became the signal to retire for a meal. It was said, "He went on refining and thought of convincing while they thought of dining."

It is doubtful if there is a human being on the face of the earth who has not been forced to sit through a too-long speech. Many otherwise impressive speakers have failed simply because they didn't know when to stop. Some speakers, in situations in which time limits are strictly enforced, find that they

Don't speak unless you have something to say. Don't be tempted to go on after you have said it.

JOHN BRIGHT

literally are unable to complete their talks. In both such circumstances, the speaker has failed to consider the fourth test of a good speech topic: Is it suitable to the time available?

In most speech situations, a time limit is suggested. The speaker may be asked to talk for "about twenty minutes" or "half an hour." In some situations, however, such as a radio or television broadcast, a debate, or a professional meeting or convention, time limits are set and rigidly enforced. One civic club had a rule that any member who felt it necessary to return to business after the regular luncheon meeting was free to do so at 1:30 PM. Guest speakers who ignored this warning and exceeded their allotted time were frequently embarrassed by a mass exodus at the specified time. Radio and television are merciless in their enforcement of time limits.

If time limitations are strictly enforced, speakers owe it to themselves to choose a topic that can be covered in the time available. If time limits have only been suggested, the speaker owes it to the audience, as a matter of courtesy, to adhere closely to that request. Even when no limitations on time have been indicated, good judgment will tell the speaker that the interest span of the audience is not limitless and that the speech should be completed in a reasonable length of time.

NARROWING THE SUBJECT

Contrary to the beliefs of many students, a short speech is usually more demanding on a speaker than a long address. In a long talk, a speaker may approach the subject in several different ways, digress a bit now and then, and occasionally repeat material without serious damage to the speech. However, in a short talk, the speaker must select from a wide range of available information and ideas only those facts that are most essential and vital. The approach must be direct and the language clear and concise.

In choosing a speech topic, the speaker should recognize that some topics are so limited that they cannot possibly be expanded into a speech of the length requested. A more common problem, however, is the topic that is too broad to be covered in the specified speaking time. Faced with a subject that seems too broad for the time available, the speaker has three choices: abandon the topic and seek another; attempt to condense the subject; or limit the speech to just one part, aspect, or facet of the more general topic. The principal danger in trying to compress a broad subject into a limited amount of time is that the speaker may be forced to omit details and explanations essential to the audience's understanding or acceptance of a speech. Another risk in this approach is that the speech may become so general—so lacking in examples, illustrations, and concrete facts—that the auditors will lose interest. At times, the speaker may find that the subject can be condensed without any serious loss; in fact, by making it more concise and direct the speaker may

FIGURE 5.1

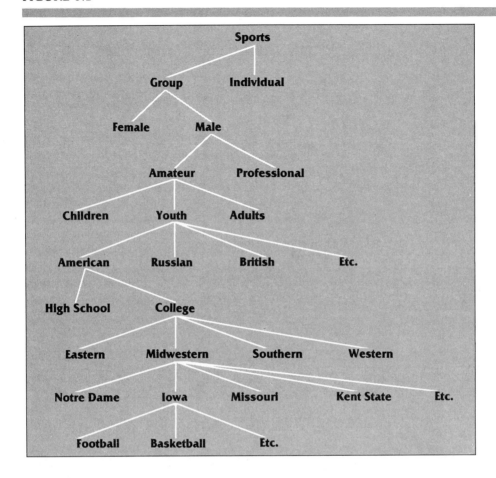

actually improve it. But in general, it is probably better to restrict the topic to one part of the broader subject, to eliminate some arguments, or to focus on the most important aspect of the topic.

In narrowing subjects that are too broad, a helpful procedure is to select a general area suited to the speaker's knowledge and interests, as well as to the audience and occasion, and then systematically divide the subject into increasingly limited subtopics. The process is graphically illustrated in Figure 5.1. This procedure guides the speaker to several specific topics that might be appropriate for the situation. It narrows the subject so that it can be covered in the time available for the speech.

Taking the general subject of "sports" as an example, a speaker might, by successive steps, limit it in the manner shown in Figure 5.1.

Specific subjects might be:

The Prospects of the Iowa Football Team for the Coming Season
Iowa's Use of the Q Formation
Iowa Fans Should Support the Football Team
Great Moments in Iowa Football History
Football Is Overemphasized at Iowa

SUMMARY

The beginning speaker's first step in selecting subjects is largely psychological: the speaker must recognize that he or she has knowledge and experiences that others will find interesting and worthwhile. In order to discover areas of interest that may yield speech topics, the speaker should undertake an exhaustive self-examination of personal skills, hobbies, experiences, and knowledge, searching for subjects that can be discussed with authority and that others will find stimulating and useful.

Having compiled an inventory of potential topics, the speaker is ready to choose a specific subject for a particular speech occasion. In the final selection of a topic, the speaker should apply four tests: (1) Is the topic suitable for me, the speaker? (2) Is it appropriate to this audience? (3) Does it fit the occasion? and (4) Can I develop it in the available speaking time? When the speaker is convinced that a subject passes all four of these tests, he or she is ready to begin actual preparation of the speech.

STUDY QUESTIONS

1. What are some reasons why speakers experience difficulty in locating speech topics?
2. What are four tests of a good speech subject?
3. How does the speaker determine whether a topic is well suited to himself or herself?
4. In deciding whether a speech subject is appropriate for the audience, what should the speaker consider?
5. Should a speaker reject a possible subject because the audience has shown no interest in the topic *before* the speech? Why or why not?
6. If a speaker decides that a topic is too broad to be covered in the time available, what alternatives are available?

EXERCISES

1. Prepare an inventory of your interests and experiences that may serve as future speech topics.
2. From your inventory of speech subjects (above exercise), select the general topic that you feel best qualified to discuss. List four or five specific aspects of that subject that might serve as speech topics.
3. From your inventory of speech subjects, find topics for a speech to inform, a speech to entertain, a speech to convince, a speech to persuade, and a speech to inspire. For each, write out a specific purpose and a central thought.

4. Select one of the following subjects and graphically narrow it by steps as illustrated in Figure 5.1 (page 82): books, school, clothing, occupations.
5. For each of the following situations, select a subject that you could discuss with enthusiasm and knowledge. Justify the appropriateness of your selection for each audience.
   a. A speech to this year's senior class at your former high school.
   b. A 10-minute speech to a group of German business executives touring your state.
   c. A 20-minute speech to a social club of retired persons.
   d. A 20-minute speech to a class of police officers studying law enforcement.
6. Choose a subject that is suited to your interests and background, to the members of the class, and to the occasion. Prepare a 4-minute informative speech to present to the class. After each speech, the class members and instructor will evaluate the speaker's choice of topic.

FURTHER READINGS

Lucas, Stephen E., *The Art of Public Speaking* (New York: Random House, 1986), chap. 3, "Selecting a Topic and Purpose."

Mudd, Charles S., and Malcolm O. Sillars, *Speech: Content and Communication* (New York: Crowell, 1975), chap. 2, "The Subject and Purpose of the Speech."

Osborn, Michael, *Speaking in Public* (Boston: Houghton Mifflin, 1982), chap. 5, "Selecting and Analyzing a Speech Topic."

Vasile, Albert J., and Harold K. Mintz, *Speak With Confidence: A Practical Guide,* 4th ed. (Boston: Little, Brown, 1986), chap. 6, "Selecting a Topic and Doing Research."

Verderber, Rudolph F., *The Challenge of Effective Speaking,* 6th ed. (Belmont, CA: Wadsworth, 1985), chap. 3, "Selecting Topics and Finding Material."

CHAPTER 6

GATHERING MATERIALS

Winston Churchill, upon leaving the chamber of the House of Commons after delivering a classic rebuttal to an opponent's argument, was asked, "Mr. Prime Minister, how long did you prepare for that speech?" "For forty years," Churchill responded. In a sense, a speaker spends his or her entire life preparing a speech. Everything we have learned and experienced, as well as the attitudes we have developed, shapes and influences our speech.

A responsible speaker will not, however, rely solely on general background in developing the subject. It pays to know what others have said, the most recent information, and the materials that will be particularly effective in obtaining the desired response from the groups. By obtaining a broad understanding of the subject and a wide range of information, the speaker can be selective in choosing those facts, reasons, and illustrations best suited to a particular audience on a specific speech occasion. Speakers who can exhaust their knowledge of a subject in the time allowed for a speech have failed to prepare properly. The speaker is obligated to know considerably more about the topic than can be related in one speech.

When searching for quality materials, the speaker sometimes wonders whether analysis precedes investigation or investigation precedes analysis. The answer is not always clear, but in most cases analysis is not possible without a thorough understanding, and this requires information. Where does one locate such information?

As suggested in the preceding chapter, in this hurried and harassed world, people too seldom sit down to meditate or reflect. Yet this is the first step in finding material for a speech. One should review one's present knowledge of the subject and then, for supplementary materials, turn to other sources—books, interviews, lectures, speeches, personal surveys, and experiments.

REVIEW ONE'S OWN KNOWLEDGE OF THE SUBJECT

Reflection

Every speech should be distinct and creative. The creative element is not to be found in books or interviews but in the imagination of the speaker. Creativity is the result of the artistic responses of the author to the materials of the speech and of the personalization of those materials. Many people have spoken on such diverse subjects as preparing for a job or profession, physical fitness, the economy, drug abuse, preventing nuclear war, and other similar topics. But each speech has been an individual creation. Each speaker has had something personal to contribute, whether it was an experience, a discriminating choice of materials, the arrangement of the ideas, or emphasis of the materials selected. This kind of creativity is attained only by reflection.

Reflection is difficult when distractions are present. A roommate playing the guitar or loud recordings, conversation by others, people walking by in a library reading room, or a television set blaring in the corner all contribute to muscular tension that inhibits reflection. The speaker should get away from distractions to gain the most from reflection.

A clergyman of the authors' acquaintance has had a small closet in his main office fitted with a desk and bookshelves. He secludes himself in that room, even though his main office is well removed from traffic and outside sounds. He reports that he must feel confined physically in order to open his mind to conscious thought. Each speaker, indeed each person, should discover the means by which to feel sufficiently alone to examine his or her thoughts.

The accumulation of ideas and knowledge is a lifelong process. Learning begins at birth. The human mind serves as a catalog in which experience is recorded. Too seldom, however, is the catalog opened. Sears, Roebuck and Co. does a better job of making the contents of its catalog readily available than do most people: the catalog is indexed. And that is the purpose of reflection—to find the index to experience. Almost every person has been in a situation that is seemingly new but that appears to mirror an earlier experience; a landscape is so familiar that we feel we have observed it before, even though we have not previously passed that way; we hear a newly composed piece of music that we recognize as something old; we meet a person for the first time but sense that we have met previously. For a fleeting moment, experiences are in the present. But rather than reach into our minds for the source of the experience, we dismiss it as some kind of supernatural phenomenon. The human brain is a mysterious and marvelous mechanism; it should be used more often. The good speaker is conscious of its use.

Once the subject has been selected, the speaker should reflect on what is known about the topic and then write down thoughts as they come to

---

The mind of the orator grows and expands with his subject. Without ample materials no splendid oration was ever yet produced.

TACITUS

He looked upon a subject like a man standing on an eminence taking a large and rounded view of it on every side, contemplating each of its parts under a vast variety of relations, and these relations often extremely complex and remote.

Description of Edmund Burke by
CHAUNCEY A. GOODRICH

mind. After all one knows about the subject has been extracted from the memory, the reflections should be organized; order should be created from the free flow of thought. Reflection, when systematized, may provide the speaker with an outline for the speech and certainly will suggest those areas of the topic that need further research.

Personal Files

Either before reflection (in order to jog one's memory) or after (in order to supplement one's existing knowledge of the subject), the speaker should turn to personal files of materials. A good speaker maintains a collection of notes, for even someone who reads widely and experiences much in life cannot remember everything, and no one should rely on memory alone to record events that might be helpful in the future. Consequently the speaker should keep notes on experiences, collect clippings, and record bibliographical listings on subjects of interest.

NOTES.   A good speaker should have a broad understanding of the times and the people, for it is people who make up the audiences and whom the speaker attempts to motivate. The more speakers know about people, the better equipped they are to influence them. Perhaps the best way to learn about people is to observe them consciously, to analyze them and their actions. The speaker should take notes concerning individual physical and intellectual responses to certain stimuli by observing how people react to action situations—automobile accidents, football games, weddings, funerals, barking dogs, and so forth. The notes made by an observer at such times may serve to illustrate an idea to be used in the future. The speaker should record observations about events, statements overheard, thoughts expressed in conversations over coffee, or ideas dimly perceived in the twilight period between consciousness and slumber. Many sound ideas born in the middle of the night are forgotten by morning. If such an idea strikes, get out of bed and make a record of it before it fades.

CLIPPINGS.   How often a speaker thinks, "I wish I could remember where I read that." If a collection of clippings is kept, the speaker can go to the file and pull out the exact reference. Speakers should collect a file of materials on subjects that interest them. Into that file should go clippings

From contemplation one may become wise but knowledge comes only from study.

A. EDWARD NEWTON

from newspapers (everyone should read at least one responsible newspaper daily), magazines, special publications, pamphlets, and brochures. The file should be organized in a meaningful way, classified according to general subjects. Folders containing topics of special interest can be color-coded by using different-colored identification tabs. Such a file might have the following designations, for instance:

Agriculture	Foreign affairs	Quotations
Art	Health	Religion
Broadcasting	Literature	Science
Celebrities	Movies	Space
Communication	Music	Sports
Crime	Politics	Travel
Education	Pollution	Women

Although this is not an exhaustive list of possible folder classifications, it is an example of a workable file. General areas are easily identified, and special-interest areas are represented. The general classifications can also be subdivided into more specific categories. For example, Communication may include the subcategories of Communication Technologies, International Communication, Interpersonal Communication, Nonverbal Communication, and Satellite Communication, to list a few.

The subjects on which a person collects clippings and the categories within the file will, of course, vary, reflecting individual interests and concerns. Unquestionably, a football coach who speaks frequently will have many categories related to sports but probably will also have sections devoted to such topics as competition, youth, personality, character, success, cooperation, and physical fitness.

BIBLIOGRAPHIC LISTINGS.   A more detailed discussion of bibliographies appears later in this chapter, but it should be mentioned here that bibliographic clippings are valuable references. When one is reading the *New York Review of Books,* for example, and discovers a review of several books on poverty, drug abuse, or education, one should clip that item and file it for later use.

SUPPLEMENTING KNOWLEDGE

After reflecting on and organizing experiential knowledge, the speaker can begin to supplement that information from outside sources. Many business executives and government administrators employ outside sources in the form of ghostwriters. The ideal arrangement would demand that the prospective speaker and the "ghost" sit down together to discuss the ideas the speaker wishes to include. In practice, there is rarely time even for this brief

Genius lights its own fire, but it is constantly collecting materials to keep alive the flame.

WILMOTT

meeting. Responsible speakers, however, will contribute to both the content and the style of the speech.

Available to all speakers are four major sources for collecting supplementary materials: (1) reading; (2) interviewing; (3) lectures, radio and television programs, and films; and (4) personal surveys and experiments.

Gathering information for a speech. (Southwick, Stock, Boston)

Reading

PREPARING A BIBLIOGRAPHY.   Frequently, so much has been written on a selected topic that the sheer volume of it becomes intimidating. At
other times, little appears to be in print. In either instance, the speaker's first
step should be to prepare a bibliography. The next best thing to having the
information is knowing where to find it. That is the key to research for
speaking or writing. The speaker should prepare a bibliography of material
specifically related to the topic, read extensively, but also investigate intensively selected areas of the problem in order to reinforce existing knowledge
and gain new insights. Although most students are familiar with the card or
computerized catalogs of libraries, some are not aware that numerous special
indexes are published to help the investigator. The following is a list of
sources to which a speaker might turn to prepare a bibliography. Although
the list is not exhaustive, the sources are available in most libraries and are
representative of other materials.

For General Information
Encyclopedia Americana
Encyclopaedia Britannica
Political Handbook of the World: Parliaments, Parties and Press
Statesman's Yearbook: Statistical and Historical Annual of the States of the World
Statistical Abstract of the United States
United Nations Yearbook
World Almanac

For Specialized Information on People and Disciplines
Alexander, Carter, and Arvid J. Burke, *How to Locate Educational Information and
        Data*
Black, Henry Campbell, *Black's Law Dictionary, Containing Definitions of the Terms
        and Phrases of American English Jurisprudence, Ancient and Modern*
Cambridge History of American Literature (15 volumes)
Contemporary Authors
Current Biography: Who's New and Why
Dictionary of American Biography (22 volumes)
Dictionary of American History (5 volumes)
Dictionary of American Scholars
Dictionary of Education
Dictionary of National Biography (British; 66 volumes)
Encyclopedia of Educational Research
Encyclopedia of the Social Sciences (15 volumes)
Harriman, Philip Lawrence, *New Dictionary of Psychology*
Literary History of the United States (3 volumes)
Oxford Classical Dictionary
Who's Who: An Annual Biographical Dictionary (British)

Who's Who in America: A Biographical Dictionary of Notable Living Men and Women of the United States

For Information About Available Books
Art Index
Biography Index
Educational Index
International Index to Periodicals
Psychological Index
Reader's Guide to Periodical Literature
Vertical File Index (of current pamphlets and booklets)

For Information in Newspapers
Chicago Tribune
Christian Science Monitor
Directory of Newspapers and Periodicals
New York Times Index
Times (London) *Official Index*
Washington Post

For Information in Public Documents
Monthly Catalogue of United States Public Documents

Also available in many libraries are computer on-line data bases for quick and thorough searches for information. New data bases are introduced frequently. The following is a representative sample of those already available.

ABI-Inform	(Management, Business, Marketing. 610 journals indexed.)
America: History and Life	(History, Humanities, Social Sciences, Current Affairs for United States and Canada. More than 2000 journals indexed.)
ERIC: CIJE	(Current Index to Journals in Education)
ERIC: RIE	(Education. Index to Reports and Documents in Education.)
LEXIS	(Law. Largest on-line, full text data base of legal information.)
Modern Language Association International Bibliography	(Literature, Language, and Linguistics)
National Newspaper Index	(General reference, news, current affairs. Indexes *New York Times, Wall Street Journal, Christian Science Monitor, Los Angeles Times,* and *Washington Post.*)
NEXIS	(General News and Business. Full text with over 100 newspapers, magazines, wire services, etc. Indexed.)

Psychinfo	(Psychology, Mental Health and Biomedicine. 1300 journals indexed.)
Social Scisearch	(Social Sciences. 1500 leading journals indexed.)
Trade and Industry	(Business and Industry. 300 trade-specific and general business journals indexed.)

Not included in this list are such commonly used publications as the *Congressional Record* and *Public Affairs Pamphlets.* Bibliographies of bibliographies, such as Besterman's *World Bibliography of Bibliographies,* are not included. But the list does provide a workable base from which to gather materials. A speaker studying a specific topic might well locate a more specialized list of sources in that subject area.

When investigating potential materials to read, it is wise for the speaker to prepare two lists, one for general background and one for specific information on the subject.

How does a speaker use the bibliographical sources once located? Let us cite an example. Suppose a speaker has elected to prepare an informative speech on poverty in the cities of the United States and has limited the subject to "Some Aspects of Poverty in Chicago's Inner City." After significant investigation, further narrowing will be possible. First, the speaker reflects on the topic and makes notes of recollections. The speaker then arranges these

Using an on-line data base. (Louisiana State University)

thoughts in some meaningful way, thereby defining the extent of his or her understanding and limitations and hence the need for further discovery.

Next, the speaker might turn to the *Book Review Digest* to locate recent books on the subject of poverty and to the *Reader's Guide to Periodical Literature* and *Poole's Index* for articles appearing in periodicals. The *Vertical File Index* lists pamphlets and booklets on the subject, and the *New York Times Index* notes recent newspaper articles of relevance. Use of the Social Scisearch data base will yield a bibliography of journal articles on the subject. If the speaker wants to know what the federal government has published concerning the poverty problem, the *Monthly Catalogue of United States Public Documents* can be

Using the card catalog. (Louisiana State University)

Main reading room of the Library of Congress. (Teresa Zabala, NYT Pictures)

consulted. Of course, the speaker's congressional representative is a good source for government publications. After collecting a bibliography of books and articles, the speaker should investigate the credentials of the authors. If some of them are unfamiliar, their backgrounds can be discovered by referring to *Who's Who in America* or *Dictionary of American Scholars.* The credibility of an author will help the speaker select significant and authoritative reading material.

Should the speaker desire statistical data, that information is in the *Statistical Abstract of the United States.*

SECURING LITERATURE FROM INTERESTED PARTIES.   Still other sources of reading materials are available. Special-interest groups, representing various positions on almost every issue imaginable, abound in the United States. These groups will usually provide printed material to any interested person upon request. For literature about women's rights, for instance, the speaker might request materials from the National Organization for Women; for data on the conservation of natural resources, the Audubon Society or the Sierra Club can be contacted; for information about freedom of speech, the American Civil Liberties Union or the Speech Communication Association should be solicited. The number of interest groups grows almost daily. For a list of special-interest associations and societies and their mailing addresses, the speaker should consult the *Encyclopedia of Associations* in the reference room of most libraries. Should the speaker not have access to the *Encyclopedia of Associations,* many addresses can be located in the *World Almanac.*

Speakers run a risk in using materials supplied by special-interest groups. These organizations are by nature propaganda agencies whose purpose is to persuade the readers, sometimes with exaggerated claims and manipulated statistics, to accept their position on an issue. The use of slogans is also popular with such groups. The National Rifle Association, for example, attempts to persuade the public with, "When guns are outlawed, only outlaws will have guns." The absurd logic of this appeal is apparent, but a listener who does not weigh the message carefully might be influenced by it. If the speaker is aware of the biases and limitations of information supplied by special interests, these groups can provide valuable assistance in gathering materials for a speech.

Government bureaus such as Action, the Small Business Administration, the Federal Aviation Administration, and the Work-Study Program are other sources for materials. The Bureau of Labor Statistics might prove helpful in providing specialized statistical information about employment, population, food production, and so forth. Perhaps the best way for speakers to obtain this information is to request their congressional representative to supply pertinent government documents. If the correct address is not known, write to the representative in care of House Office Building, Washington, DC 20515.

Armed with a substantial bibliography of books and articles written by responsible authorities, materials supplied by interest groups and government agencies, and statistical information, the speaker is well prepared for meaningful reading.

NOTE TAKING.   Obviously, speakers cannot read everything published about an area of concern, unless, of course, they are established authorities and only need to keep abreast of the new literature in the field. Most speakers must be selective in what they read. The larger the bibliography, the greater the need for discriminating among the materials. Some general materials should be read for background purposes. But to conserve time and effort, speakers should select those books and articles that appear to be most directly related to the specific subject and purpose and concentrate to assimilate what is read and relate it to what they already know about the topic. Speakers should read with a purpose, discriminating between items vaguely relevant and those directly related to the topic, and constantly be aware of the purpose of reading and not waste time on interesting but relatively useless materials. For example, while searching for historical data in an old newspaper, it is so easy to become absorbed in advertisements for beef at 6 cents a pound and for hoopskirts that the speaker may end up being locked out of the library at closing time without the purpose having been accomplished. Read purposively; use leisure time for reading for pleasure.

All speakers, being human, suffer the agonies of lost memory at some time or other in their speaking careers. Most people too often depend on their memory. When something significant is discovered while reading, do not say, "I'll have to remember that," but jot it down on a note card.

Two basic kinds of notes can be taken: *direct quotations* and *summaries*. If the speaker finds a statement he or she wishes to quote directly, the statement should be copied accurately and in full, with source, date, and circumstances in which it was made (i.e., an answer to a question asked in an interview with Sam Smith). Related to the direct quotation is the paraphrase. If a direct statement is too lengthy or contains irrelevant material, a paraphrase of the statement may suffice. It is vital, however, that the speaker rephrase the quotation with integrity, making certain that the sense of the original has not been altered.

A second kind of note is the summary. After reading an article or book, the speaker might wish to record the general nature of the work and list the main ideas and forms of support. Again, the note taker must summarize the gist of the article honestly and with integrity, avoiding any alteration of the author's arguments or purposes. Should you wish to evaluate the article or book, do so on the note card. Such commentary may be helpful later when you select ideas for the speech.

If the notes are to be used effectively, the speaker should organize them. Although no standard form is required, a few simple but important rules can be suggested. First, use note cards. Cards can be filed much more effectively than papers and can be reused without damage. Second, keep only one piece of information on each card. If the speaker tries to save space by putting several quotations or summaries on one card, the job of organizing references becomes almost impossible. Third, identify each card with a heading indicating its subject matter, such as "Ghostwriting," "Beaujolais Wine," "Gambling," "Religious Cults" (Fig. 6.1). Fourth, place the source of each piece of information on the card. This includes (1) the author's name; (2) the title of the article; (3) the name of the newspaper, periodical, or book from which the information was taken; (4) the publication date; and (5) the page number (Fig. 6.2; see p. 99). If this information is clearly placed on the card, it will be easy to locate the article for future use. Fifth, when copying a direct quotation, always set it off with quotation marks for, after a lapse of time, it is not always possible to determine what is quoted directly and what is quoted indirectly if the marks are omitted. Additionally, take pains to ensure accu-

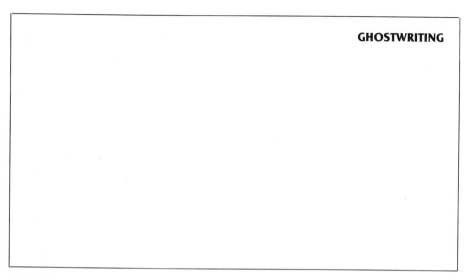

GHOSTWRITING

FIGURE 6.1

racy of content and meaning when extractions of materials are noted. The sense of the quotation should not differ from its original meaning within the context of the entire article. When parts of a longer quotation are copied, an ellipsis (. . .) should be used to remind the speaker that some words or thoughts have been omitted (Fig. 6.3).

Interviews

A second way for the speaker to broaden understanding of a subject is by interviewing people who have special knowledge of it. The type of interview that probably is most familiar is the one used by the employees of George Gallup, Louis Harris, and Elmo Roper during political campaigns. Advertising firms also frequently use interviews to test the market for new products. These market analyses provide information that helps the companies determine the desired image for the product and the best methods for creating that image. These two forms of interviews are not unlike the type a speaker might use to collect information. The same general principles of good interviewing apply.

Lectures, Television, Film

Along with reading and interviewing, the speaker may find supporting materials for the topic by attending lectures, watching television, and viewing films. A university is a unique community where literally hundreds of lectures are given annually on a wide variety of topics. All the student need do is examine the calendar of events for the day in the student newspaper in order to obtain times and places for lectures of special interest. Often students

GHOSTWRITING

Bormann, Ernest G., "Ethics of Ghostwritten Speeches,"
Quarterly Journal of Speech, **October 1961, pp. 262–267.**

GHOSTWRITING

Bormann, Ernest G., "Ethics of Ghostwritten Speeches,"
Quarterly Journal of Speech, **October 1961, pp. 262–267.**

Prof. Bormann considers the ghostwritten speech to be a deception and argues that double standards are applied when students are not allowed to have speeches written for them, but presidents are. He concludes, "If we impose an ethical standard on our students and on ourselves ... we must impose ethical standards upon ... the president of the United States, upon the president of our college or university, upon our governor ... upon everyone who presents himself and his ideas to an audience for its acceptance.

FIGURES 6.2 and 6.3

will be able to find a lecture on a topic directly related to a speech subject they have selected for classroom presentation.

Many television programs provide information for the speaker. Documentaries, interviews, presidential addresses, panel discussions, special topical programs, investigative reporting (such as "60 Minutes"), and other television shows may provide speakers with important materials for their speeches. The growing popularity of public television (PBS) is significant, for the programs on that "Fourth Network" are particularly designed to enlighten its viewers.

Films often deal with complex social problems—race, poverty, drug addiction, sexual mores, and the computerized society. Even science fiction films may offer insight into the complexities of an increasingly scientific civilization.

Occasionally, purely entertaining programs on television and in films may provide materials for elaboration in the form of illustrations, examples, topical references, and humor.

Again, the speaker should not trust to memory but should jot down notes and file them for future reference.

Personal Surveys and Experiments

Although most speakers have neither the training nor the resources to conduct a scientific poll, the student speaker may find it helpful in dealing with some topics to conduct a personal poll on campus or among members of a church group or other organization. This type of survey should be identified for what it is, and, in most instances, great reliance should not be placed on it. The results of such informal polls, however, may provide the speaker with personal insights and could add to the ethical appeal, as well as to the substance, of the argument. Student newspapers frequently poll students on campus topics and report the results.

When seeking support for a proposition, a speaker might also conduct an experiment that can be done without extensive statistical analysis. Recently a student teacher designed an experiment to collect information about the effects of social pressure on individuals in a group. On the first day of class, the student teacher went into his beginning speech class and, using a German accent throughout, gave a lecture appropriate for a class in nineteenth-century German history. Even though the students knew that this was supposed to be a speech class, not one raised a hand to question the student teacher about the course. Each apparently felt pressured into remaining silent rather than expressing what the others might interpret as irresponsible questions. Some students even took notes! Without having to quantify a mass of information and produce a statistical analysis, this student teacher had conducted an experiment that could be used as supportive material in a speech he was preparing on group social pressure. With some imagination and a desire to obtain supporting information, any speaker can conduct such experiments.

A final admonition should be given. After speakers have collected information from reading, interviews, lectures, television, films, personal surveys, and experiments, they should contribute some originality in fitting the supporting materials together. Synthesize the materials and summarize them when full disclosure of the information would be excessively time-consuming. Compare and contrast the various materials collected, and then interpret the information accurately, drawing only those conclusions that are justified by the available information.

SUMMARY

The success of a speech depends largely on the selection of the materials for a particular audience and occasion. The gathering of materials for a speech begins with a review of one's own knowledge of the subject and can be supplemented by reading, obtaining literature from special-interest groups, note taking, interviewing, attending lectures, viewing television and films, and taking personal surveys and conducting experiments. Probably the greatest aid to the speaker in collecting materials for a speech is an effective note-taking and filing method. In addition to books and periodicals, the speaker can often obtain reading materials from special-interest groups and government agencies. Be aware, however, of the prejudices and purposes of special-interest groups, for it is likely that the materials supplied by such organizations will be characterized by a bias, sometimes to the extent of exaggerated claims and inaccurate information. In general, the speaker should use all available sources, taking care to weigh the relevance of the material and the objectivity and accuracy of the sources.

STUDY QUESTIONS

1. What are the advantages of beginning the process of gathering materials for a speech by reflection?
2. Why is it important to keep an organized file of materials for speeches? What kinds of materials should be filed?
3. In what ways can a speaker supplement existing knowledge about a speech topic?
4. What is the difference between a direct quotation and a summary note?
5. What basic information should be included on a note card for inclusion in the speaker's file?
6. What are the five basic rules for filling out note cards for a speech? Why is each necessary?
7. Why is it important to make special arrangements with an interviewee in advance of the interview? Why is it important to prepare an outline of questions before the interview?

EXERCISES

1. To become familiar with the reference materials in the library and to gain practice in the correct ways of recording bibliographical material, prepare a bibliography of one piece of information from each of the special indexes listed in this chapter.
2. For your next speech, take an informal poll of students on campus or in your town to test general attitudes toward your topic. Use the survey results in the speech as introductory material or to substantiate your position on the subject.
3. Prepare and conduct an informal experiment to use in your next speech.
4. Interview an established authority who might reside in your community or teach at the university on the subject of your next speech. Follow the suggestions for interviewing found in this chapter.
5. Take any three topics listed below and locate at least two sources each for an informative speech on the subject:

a. Why we bury the dead
b. How a spectrograph is made
c. How a warm front develops
d. Esperanto
e. How records are pressed
f. Why the tower of Pisa leans
g. The author of the letters of Junius
h. Origins of Mardi Gras
i. How the British observe Guy Fawkes Day
j. How chewing gum is made
k. How fish see
l. The Davis Cup tennis competition
m. The making of Mount Rushmore
n. Paul Bunyan
o. How to play the bagpipe
p. Setting stones in rings
q. Dutch cheeses
r. How an igloo is built
s. How boots are made
t. The Fabian Society
u. How to become a professional clown
v. Stonehenge
w. Ntozake Shange
x. Urdu
y. The Loch Ness monster
z. Golan Heights

FURTHER READINGS

Ehninger, Douglas, Bruce E. Gronbeck, Ray E. McKerrow, and Alan Monroe, *Principles and Types of Speech Communication,* 10th ed. (Glenview, IL: Scott, Foresman, 1986), chap. 7, "Developing Your Ideas: Finding and Using Supporting Materials."

Lucas, Stephen E., *The Art of Public Speaking* (New York: Random House, 1986), chap. 5, "Gathering Materials."

Minnick, Wayne C., *Public Speaking* (Boston: Houghton Mifflin, 1979), chap. 3, "Finding Speech Materials."

Mudd, Charles S., and Malcolm O. Sillars, *Speech: Content and Communication* (New York: Crowell, 1975), chap. 7, "Supporting Materials: Sources."

Osborn, Michael, *Speaking in Public* (Boston: Houghton Mifflin, 1982), chap. 6, "Research for Speaking in Public."

Vasile, Albert J., and Harold K. Mintz, *Speak With Confidence: A Practical Guide,* 4th ed. (Boston: Little, Brown, 1986), chap. 6, "Selecting a Topic and Doing Research."

Verderber, Rudolph F., *The Challenge of Effective Speaking,* 6th ed. (Belmont, CA: Wadsworth, 1985), chap. 3, "Selecting Topics and Finding Material."

Zannes, Estelle, and Gerald Goldhaber, *Stand Up, Speak Out,* 2d ed. (Reading, MA: Addison-Wesley, 1983), chap. 2, "Doing Research."

CHAPTER 7

THE PARTS OF A SPEECH

The universe exists as an organized mass of elements. Order is maintained within societies by a system of organized rules, regulations, and codes of ethical conduct. Without a proper balance between the many facets of the universe and between persons, chaos would exist. Governmental bodies—city councils, legislatures, and school boards—are formed to evaluate and implement the proposals and policies of the citizens they represent. Such bodies are necessary to operate schools, build streets, provide essential services, enforce laws, and conduct elections. Without them, anarchy would prevail.

Just as groups of people cannot exist without community organization, neither can people think clearly without mental organization. Often people act irrationally, thoughtlessly, or on an emotional impulse. But when a person's conduct is based on rational thought, that person's actions are the result of a systematic pattern of analysis and reasoning. For instance, when we read a book or newspaper, we read from left to right and from top to bottom. If publishers printed books or other reading material at will, to be read from right to left and from bottom to top, no standard reading habits could be formed. The same is true in oral communication. A speaker must follow certain patterns of expression to be understood. This process is called organization. Organization refers to the way a speaker divides the speech, arranges ideas, and orders them for presentation. The process is also often referred to as *structure* or *arrangement.*

THE IMPORTANCE OF ORGANIZATION

Although well-structured communication is important in both writing and speaking, it takes on special significance for the speaker. Readers who complete a page of information in a book and realize that they have missed the central thought can go back and reread the page. This is not so with listeners. Once the words are spoken and the sound waves have passed the listening sensors of the auditor, the message is gone. Listeners must perceive the message upon first hearing it or be forever ignorant of its content. Consequently, the speaker must take special pains to make the purpose clear, to arrange material logically, and to relate one idea to another in such a way that the hearer perceives the relationship between the speaker's ideas and the central purpose.

A clear pattern of organization is more important in speaking than in writing because in written communication the reader has many visual clues to aid in determining how the subject has been divided. These include paragraph

> Order is the first law of heaven.
>
> JOSIAH ROYCE

indentations, main headings, subheadings, and different sizes and kinds of type. The reader has an additional advantage in that he or she is able to pace the communication act by proceeding as rapidly or slowly as desired, pausing to study difficult passages until they are fully understood. In the speech situation, however, the listener exercises almost no control over the delivery and has no visual clues, as does the reader, to assist in understanding the arrangement of the material. For these reasons, it is usually necessary for a speaker to be more obvious and explicit in organization than a writer need be.

The purposes of speaking are discussed at some length in Chapter 3. Before discussing specific forms of organization, let us look at the general organizational structure of speeches.

Someone once said that a speaker should first tell the audience what is going to be said, then say it, then tell them what has been said. Although often desirable, this is not always necessary. Some public speaking is relatively formless. These speeches usually occur when the speaker seeks only to stimulate the audience's emotions, such as a speech at a religious revival, a protest demonstration, or a rally of supporters or opponents of a controversial cause such as abortion, capital punishment, gay rights, and nuclear power. However, although emotion has its place in oral discourse, people are courting disaster when they act mainly on feelings and impulse without regard to rational thought. If logical decision making is to prevail, it will do so only in the form of a structured message with rational objectives. Consequently, the student of public speaking must be aware of the importance of organization and the methods for achieving a clear arrangement of the speech materials.

Generally, speakers should introduce a speech by telling the audience what they are going to talk about, then develop the ideas, and finally end the speech with a conclusion. We shall now turn our attention to the ingredients of these major divisions.

THE INTRODUCTION

Many speakers worry most about the beginning of a speech, and with good cause, for it is in the opening remarks that a speaker often wins or loses a favorable response. The introduction serves three main purposes. It should

> Every speech ought to be put together like a living creature, with a body of its own, so as to be neither without head nor without feet, but to have both a middle and extremities, described proportionately to each other and to the whole.
>
> PLATO

prepare the listener (1) to be interested in the speech topic, (2) to listen intelligently, and (3) to receive the speech with an amiable, or at least objective, attitude.

Arousing Interest

How important it is for the speaker to create interest in the topic will depend on the subject and the reasons that motivated the listeners to assemble. If the audience has come voluntarily, the speaker probably can assume that they are interested.

However, many speakers face audiences that are not so receptive. In such situations, the speaker's first concern is to create or intensify the audience's interest in the topic. Indeed, the speaker's very first sentences should be directed toward that end.

The speaker's method of arousing interest will depend on the subject and the audience. An effective technique for awakening interest is to present the subject as important to the hearers' personal welfare. Similarly, a speaker might stress the significance or urgency of the topic.

Other ways to create interest include asking questions, posing a problem, setting forth a dilemma, or referring to the bizarre, unusual, strange, or puzzling aspects of the subject. At times, a speaker can appeal to listeners by recounting a personal experience or making effective use of examples or illustrations. A striking or familiar quotation also can stimulate interest. Humor also can be effective in creating interest. Visual aids—photographs, charts, and diagrams—are also effective devices. At times a speaker might even risk irritating or challenging the audience in order to create interest, but this technique can backfire if it offends the listeners to the point that they will not listen to the rest of the speech with open minds.

Whatever approach speakers decide to utilize to arouse interest, they should make certain that it clearly is related to the subject—that it will not simply focus attention on the speaker or some irrelevant aspect of the speaking situation. Second, the attention-gaining device must be striking. A series of ordinary questions, a dull personal experience, or an uninspiring illustration will not arouse interest. Third, the speaker's approach should be in good taste. Anything vulgar, obscene, or even risqué may prove offensive to some in the audience. Fourth, the speaker should avoid startling or frightening listeners. A speaker who fires a gun to animate an audience will so stun them that they may remain distracted throughout the speech. And the speaker who removes a live snake from a box is apt to frighten so many listeners that their receptivity to the speaker's message will be minimal. If the speaker must use a frightening action, statement, or object, the audience should be assured of its harmlessness.

A speaker has, then, a variety of techniques available for creating interest in the subject.

HUMOR.   In a speech keynoting a three-day meeting of women may-ors of United States cities, Dianne Feinstein, the first woman mayor of San Francisco, began: "About thirty years ago, Senator Margaret Chase Smith was asked by *Time* magazine what she would do if one day she woke up in the White House. She replied that she would apologize to Bess Truman and leave immediately."

Senator Edward Kennedy delivered a speech at Liberty Baptist College in Lynchburg, Virginia, an institution founded by a political opponent, the Reverend Jerry Falwell. The audience was hostile, and Kennedy opened the speech with humor:

> Let me thank Dr. Jerry Falwell for that generous introduction. I never expected to hear such kind words from him. So, in return, I have an invitation of my own: on January 20, 1985, I hope Dr. Falwell will say a prayer—at the inauguration of the next Democratic president of the United States. Now, Dr. Falwell, I'm not sure exactly how you feel about that. You might not appreciate the president but the Democrats certainly would appreciate the prayer. (*Representative American Speeches, 1983–1984*, New York: H. W. Wilson Co., 1984, p. 54.)

Many people share the misconception that it is essential to begin a speech with a humorous story. This is an acceptable and sound practice so long as certain requisites are maintained. First, the humor should relate to the audience, the speaker, the speech, or the occasion. If the humor is unrelated to any of the four elements of the speaking situation, it fails to achieve the purpose of an introductory statement—to focus attention on the speaker's topic. In fact, if the humor is totally unrelated, the speaker may actually transfer interest to another subject.

In the following introduction, the speaker relates his humor to his subject and audience. He used this introduction for a speech entitled "How to Com-pose an Ancient, Undiscovered Folk Song":

> One of the more baffling phenomena on the music scene today is the folk song. It was only a few years ago that folksinging became popular. Today there is a serious shortage of new ones for the old ones have been gobbled up. There are no more genuine authentic folk songs, but only artificial authentic folk songs. To meet the demand, everyone is now writing them, and there is no reason why you shouldn't too.

QUOTATION.   A second method of creating interest is by use of quo-tations. The quotation should refer to the speech topic or to some element of the speaking situation. It should direct attention to the speaker's subject. It might also be used to paraphrase the speaker's theme. If the source is un-known to the audience, it should be identified.

In the following example, a student combined humor with a quotation to arouse interest in his speech on "The Bangkok Taxicab":

"About the most hazardous thing in Thailand is a ride in a Bangkok taxi. The driver will invariably take his hands from the steering wheel each time he passes a major Buddhist shrine, clasp them before his face in the traditional *Yai,* lower his eyes, and hold this ritual attitude of prayer until the taxi has hurtled—unguided by man—past the object of his devotion." A recent issue of *Reader's Digest* included this description of the hazards of riding in a Bangkok taxi. As a survivor of countless safaris in a Siamese taxi of Bangkok, I speak with a measure of authority when I say that an intracity trip in one of these kamikaze cabs is an experience one will never forget.

Another example of a speaker combining humor and a quotation in the introduction was Barbara Franklin's opening remarks to a Boston College audience:

As a federal regulator, I accept speaking engagements these days with more and more trepidation. The trepidation turns to outright fear as the day of the speech arrives and the experience of Winston Churchill comes to mind. On one of his trans-Atlantic tours, a student asked, "Mr. Churchill, doesn't it thrill you to know that every time you make a speech the hall is packed to overflowing?" Churchill pondered the question for a moment. Then he replied, "Of course, it is flattering. But always remember that if I were being hanged, the crowd would be twice as big."

QUESTION.   A speaker can often create interest in a subject by addressing listeners with questions that will stimulate their imaginations or pique their curiosity. The questions may be rhetorical and require no response or be designed to elicit some kind of audience action. Some examples of questions that might be used by a speaker in an introduction to create interest in the topic are:

Would you believe me if I told you I have seen a ghost?
If you were the defendant in a court trial, would you wish it to be televised for everyone to see?
In view of the fact that the UPI and AP polls frequently disagree on who is number one at the end of the season, shouldn't the National Collegiate Athletic Association establish a playoff to determine a national college football champion?

Note how the first two questions only suggest the issue or question to the auditors, while the third question attempts to sway the audience toward the speaker's point of view.

REFERENCE TO THE AUDIENCE OR OCCASION.   By referring to either the audience or the occasion in the opening remarks, the speaker can readily identify with listeners and enhance the significance of the subject. Although politicians frequently use this device, at times they seem less than sincere. References to the audience or to the occasion should be simple, direct, and sincere. Such was the case when Grayson Kirk used this technique in a convocation address celebrating the centennial of the University of Denver:

> It is a pleasure to be in Denver once more, to visit again this university where I taught one happy summer, and to have the opportunity to renew so many long-standing and precious friendships. Actually, I can, in retrospect, associate this institution with one of the major changes in the direction of my life. It is here that I enjoyed my last full-time teaching—though I did not know it at the time—because immediately after my return from the pleasant summer here I was invited to become the Provost of Columbia, a decision that, once made, brought my teaching days to a close. Now that I am here again, who knows but that when I go back to New York there might be a strong campus opinion developed in my absence in favor of my return to teaching. If this should be the case, then, I think I ought to come back here and start where I left off in 1949. (*Representative American Speeches, 1964–1965,* New York: H. W. Wilson Co., 1965.)

PERSONAL REFERENCE.   Opening remarks utilizing personal reference to create attention must be handled so that the speaker appears modest, humble, and sincere. Mention of one's experience, triumphs, or personal success in the field one plans to discuss may establish the speaker's qualifications as an authority, as well as enhance interest in the topic by reminding the audience of the speaker's expertise or broad background. However, the speaker must not appear to be boasting. An excellent example of a speaker citing his own qualifications as an authority on his topic is found in the following introduction of a speech delivered by Father Bruce Ritter, a Franciscan Roman Catholic priest, to a meeting of the United States Senate Caucus on the Family:

> Ladies and gentlemen of the Senate, my name is Father Bruce Ritter, a Franciscan priest from New York. I am delighted and privileged to have this opportunity to speak to you this morning about my concerns and those of my friends. Concerns based on more than fifteen years caring for some of the most desolate children in our society.

I am president of Covenant House, a child-care agency I founded almost fifteen years ago to care for street children. If I may take the liberty of speaking for a few moments about how our work began, I think you may find our early history somewhat entertaining, but it will also certainly provide you the context from within which you can understand the sort of problems, indeed the fearful suffering, faced by these children.

Within my order I was trained as an academician. I have an earned doctorate in late medieval history of dogma, and I taught that rather arcane subject for about ten years. I spent the last five years of the teaching part of my priesthood in New York City at Manhattan College, where I also became chaplain to the student body. (*Representative American Speeches, 1983–1984,* New York: H. W. Wilson Co., 1984, pp. 175–176.)

SIGNIFICANCE OF SUBJECT.   A speaker may create interest by stressing the importance of the subject or problem about to be discussed. If listeners are convinced that the way an issue is resolved will have a direct, significant, and lasting effect on their or their children's lives, they probably will pay close attention to what the speaker has to say.

Donald Kennedy, president of Stanford University and biologist, utilized this technique in a speech to over 100 scientists and media representatives:

There is a convention that applies to all so-called keynote speeches, and it requires that I begin by telling you how happy I am to be here. *Actually, I am not happy at all; ours is anything but a happy subject.* In the first place, the consequences of nuclear war are dire indeed, and it can be no great pleasure to assemble for the purpose of telling people that they are even more dire than they have been told. Furthermore, there is unfortunately no *simple* way out of the problem posed for us by the nuclear arms problem—though some people insist that there is. Instead, there is a continuing need to deal with danger, and to struggle with a national security policy that seems terribly refractory to rational design. It is against this depressing background that we meet to discuss the long-range biological consequences of nuclear war. (*Representative American Speeches, 1983–1984,* New York: H. W. Wilson Co., 1984, p. 66.)

PUZZLES AND PARADOXES.   At times a speaker may create interest in a topic through use of a puzzle or paradox that appeals to the curiosity of listeners. An example of this technique is:

A riddle is making the rounds that goes like this: A man and his young son were in an automobile accident. The father was killed and the son, who was critically injured, was rushed to a hospital. As attendants wheeled the unconscious boy into the emergency room, the doctor on duty looked down at him and said, "My God, it's my son!" What was the relationship of the doctor to the injured boy?

If the answer doesn't jump to your mind, another riddle that has been around a lot longer might help: The blind beggar had a brother. The blind beggar's brother died. The brother who died had no brother. What relation was the blind beggar to the blind beggar's brother?

As with all riddles, the answers are obvious once you see them: The doctor was the boy's mother and the beggar was her brother's sister.

The above riddles were used to introduce a discussion of stereotypes regarding the roles of men and women.

HYPOTHETICAL EXAMPLE.   Closely related to the appeal to curiosity to arouse interest is the hypothetical example. A student wishing to create interest in a speech in which he opposed abortion quoted the following example from an article he had read:

Two physicians are talking shop. "Doctor," says one, "I'd like your professional opinion. The question is, should the pregnancy have been terminated or not? The father was syphilitic. The mother was tuberculous. They had already had four children: the first was blind, the second died, the third was deaf and dumb, and the fourth was tuberculous. The woman was pregnant for the fifth time. As the attending physician, what would you have done?"

"I would have terminated the pregnancy."

"Then you would have murdered Beethoven."

This hypothetical example dramatically focuses attention on the problem a physician faces when deciding whether to recommend an abortion.

SOLVING A PROBLEM.   Many Americans regularly turn the pages of their daily newspaper to features such as "Dear Abby," "Ann Landers," "Heloise," "Miss Manners," "Action Please," and columns offering advice on investments, medical care, horoscopes, and physical fitness. Although much of the advice offered may be of questionable value, the popularity of the columns is an indication of a deep-felt need on the part of many for aid, assistance, and direction in solving personal problems. Recognizing this desire for help, speakers often may create interest in a subject in the introduction by indicating how they hope to aid the listeners. If the auditors believe they will benefit from the speech, they will listen with greater interest and closer attention.

COMPARISON.   At times a speaker may find using a comparison in the introduction helpful in creating interest in the subject. The comparison may be employed to relate something unfamiliar to the audience to something with which they are well acquainted. The speaker may compare something abstract or vague with something concrete, specific, and more easily comprehended.

An example of this technique for arousing interest is found in a banquet speech by Professor Glenn A. Crosby to members of an honors society at Washington State University. Dr. Crosby took an abstract concept, the modern university, and made it more vivid and concrete by comparing it to a concrete object, an ancient cathedral. Referring to what a favorite author had to say about the cathedral, the speaker related:

> He begins by describing that great monument of Byzantine culture, the Cathedral of St. Sophia. When viewed from afar, both physically and historically, the cathedral gives the impression of otherworldly perfection, but, upon close inspection, this impression quickly vanishes. Within its corpus the cathedral hides shoddy workmanship, hasty structural shortcuts, and poorly disguised inferior building blocks. Much of its history is laced with brutality and the worst manifestation of cultural rottenness. In short, it is a very human construction. Nonetheless, it has stood for over a thousand years.
>
> What struck me as I reread the book were some obvious parallels between the building of the Cathedral of St. Sophia and the development of the modern university, particularly those institutions, such as Washington State University, that have grown explosively during the last few decades. The cathedral was built in a hurry, a mere six years; little wonder that the workmen cut corners. It was dedicated to God but was quite clearly a personal triumph of the Emperor Justinian. The cathedral still stands, but everything is wavering, bulging, or askew. Most modern universities have a similar history. They have grown fast, too fast, and many corners have been cut. Although dedicated to education, scholarship, and research, they often developed in directions dictated by political, social, and economic pressures, directions sometimes perpendicular to the intended course. They stand, some of them quite well, but much is wavering, bulging, and askew. (*Representative American Speeches, 1976–1977,* New York: H. W. Wilson Co., 1977, pp. 157–158.)

Creating a Favorable Impression for the Speaker and the Topic

While most audiences tend to regard the speaker objectively, under some circumstances the speaker may feel it necessary to improve his or her image with the audience before proceeding to the body of the speech. If the speaker represents a cause or group unacceptable to the audience, or has been associated with any questionable or controversial program, organization, or act, or if the listeners have reason to question the speaker's motives in addressing them, they are likely to regard the speaker with hostility or, at best, skepticism. The audience may even consider a speaker suspect simply because they regard him or her as an "outsider"—someone of a different race, religion, nationality, class, age, vocation, or sex—or someone from another part of the country.

Since an audience that is skeptical of or lacks confidence in a speaker is unlikely to listen impartially, it is incumbent upon the speaker, early in the speech, to eliminate or minimize any misgivings the hearers may have. Several devices are available to the speaker for removing audience reservation:

1. Openly acknowledging disagreement with the audience or differences from them, but also stressing common goals, premises, and attitudes.
2. Pointing out experiences in one's past that are similar to those of the audience.
3. Expressing understanding of their problems and sympathizing with their goals.
4. Correcting misconceptions that they have by directly refuting unfavorable attacks and/or allegations.
5. Associating detractors with causes generally disliked by the audience.
6. Disclaiming any selfish or personal motives for his or her acts and beliefs.
7. Complimenting the audience on its goals and achievements.
8. Praising leaders, members of the group, or the community for their activities or accomplishments.
9. Deprecating personal achievements in order to demonstrate humility or modesty.
10. Poking fun at oneself, thereby lessening any impression of arrogance or conceit.
11. Relating a story or a joke to reveal a sense of humor.
12. Appealing to the audience's sense of fair play and imploring them to listen with an open mind.

While the above list by no means exhausts the possible approaches a speaker may take to achieve a favorable audience attitude, it suggests some of the methods one might pursue. Even a speaker who is highly respected and well liked may wish to employ some of these techniques.

Preparing the Audience to Listen Intelligently

After creating interest and establishing credibility, the speaker should be concerned with the third function of the introduction: preparing the audience to listen intelligently to the subject matter. If the auditors are to follow the speaker without difficulty, it is essential that by the time the body of the address is reached, they know the topic. For most speeches, they should also know either the specific purpose or the central thought.

At times, however, a speaker may decide to withhold the specific purpose if revealing it will jeopardize chances of obtaining the desired response. For example, in a speech to persuade on a highly controversial issue, revealing the main idea in the introduction may immediately alienate many persons in the audience. Instead, the speaker might first seek to win the goodwill of the listeners, provide them with essential background material, and lay a foundation of fact, so that when the main idea is presented, the audience will be more disposed to agree.

In addition to revealing the subject and purpose, the introduction may also include materials designed to assist the audience in understanding the remainder of the speech. Frequently, a preview of the main points of the speech or an outline of how the speaker plans to approach the topic will prove helpful. For example, in an informative speech to an audience of college students on how to save money on a summer trip to Europe, the speaker might preview the main recommendations as follows: "If you plan to go to Europe on a limited budget, let me make three recommendations: (1) consider purchasing a Eurailpass, (2) obtain a directory of low-cost hostels and hotels, and (3) investigate several new inexpensive airline fares." Previews effectively prepare the audience for what is to follow. With an outline of the main steps or parts, they know what to expect as the speech progresses.

The following excerpt from a speech by Caroline Stewart Dyer titled "The Costs of Freedom of the Press" and addressed to the Humanities Society of the University of Iowa is an effective illustration of how a speaker might state the central thought and preview the main ideas in the form of rhetorical questions:

> I selected this title for my lecture to permit me to decide what to talk about, as my research involves several issues that could fit the title. I have studied the costs of establishing newspapers on the frontier and the question whether it was really possible for anybody to start one to express his views as other historians claim. I have been interested in the emotional costs of the way the media cover rape on the victims. But I am going to talk about the meaning of freedom of the press and how the costs of litigation affect the meaning.
>
> The basic questions are, What does freedom of the press mean? What is its function in society? How does one determine what it means? (*Representative American Speeches, 1983–1984,* New York: H. W. Wilson Co., 1984, p. 141.)

Joseph Cardinal Bernardin, Archbishop of Chicago, stated his purpose and previewed his points as follows in a speech to the National Conference of Catholic Bishops:

> My purpose this evening is to analyze the relationship of the church to the fact of poverty in our time. I will examine where we stand as a

church, what we can bring to the struggle against poverty, and how we should proceed in this struggle precisely as the church. More specifically, I will address three questions: the nature of the problem we face, the role of the Church, and one aspect of the policy debate on poverty. (*Representative American Speeches, 1984–1985,* New York: H. W. Wilson Co., 1985, p. 175.)

Other information, including necessary background and pertinent historical data, may assist the audience in understanding. For example, a speaker might say:

Before I get into my discussion of what should be done regarding the Atchafalaya Basin, I think you should understand the complex nature of the question. The Atchafalaya Basin presently is a "wet wildlands area" which can be flooded at any time upon the order of the U.S. Corps of Engineers to take off the overflow from the Mississippi River should a flood endanger south Louisiana. It is partly privately owned and partly government owned. Private owners would like to fill in the land and convert it into agriculturally profitable space; ecologists would like to keep it in its natural state; and the Corps of Engineers would like to purchase the land so it can dredge and maintain the overflow areas.

Or the speaker might define a term in the introduction:

When I talk about "grade inflation," I am talking about the fact that college freshmen arrived on campuses last fall with the highest ever high school grade averages, while at the same time their scores on various entrance exams were much lower than those of entering freshmen 10 and 15 years ago.

Whether information in the above excerpts is included in the introduction or presented later will, of course, depend on the audience, the subject, and the judgment of the speaker. At times, such material is essential in the introduction if the audience is to listen to the rest of the speech intelligently. The speaker should remember that the major aim in preparing the audience for the speech is to make the content in the body of the speech easy to comprehend. An excellent example of preparing an audience for the subject was exhibited by Carl Rogers, Professor of Psychology and Psychiatry at the University of Wisconsin, in a speech delivered to a faculty and staff forum at the California Institute of Technology on a technical subject, "What We Know About Psychotherapy—Objectively and Subjectively":

In the field of psychotherapy considerable progress has been made in the last decade in measuring the outcomes of therapy in the personality and behavior of the client. In the last two or three years additional progress has been made in identifying the basic conditions in the therapeutic relationship which bring about therapy, which facilitate personal development in the direction of psychological maturity. Another way of saying this is that we have made progress in determining those ingredients in a relationship which promote personal growth.

Psychotherapy does not supply the motivation for such development of growth. This seems to be inherent in the organism, just as we find a similar tendency in the human animal to develop and mature physically, provided minimally satisfactory conditions are provided. But therapy does play an extremely important part in releasing and facilitating the tendency of the organism towards psychological development or maturity, when this tendency has been blocked.

I would like, in the first part of this talk, to summarize what we know of the conditions which facilitate psychological growth, and something of what we know of the process and characteristics of that psychological growth. Let me explain what I mean when I say that I am going to summarize what we "know." I mean that I will limit my statements to those for which we have objective empirical evidence. For example, I will talk about the conditions of psychological growth. For each statement one or more studies could be cited . . . when these conditions were present which did not occur in situations where these conditions were absent, or were present to a much lesser degree. . . .

I would like to give this knowledge which we have gained in the very briefest fashion, and in everyday language. (Carl R. Rogers, "What We Know About Psychotherapy—Objectively and Subjectively," in *On Becoming a Person,* Boston: Houghton Mifflin, 1961, pp. 60–61.)

THE BODY OF THE SPEECH

The most important part of a speech is the body, for it is here that the speaker develops propositions and arguments. In fact, the body *is* the speech, with the introduction and conclusion serving as appendages, albeit important ones.

Since methods for dividing the body of the speech are developed in Chapter 8, this chapter treats only four aspects of organization related to the body of the speech: (1) the number of main parts or divisions within the body of the speech, (2) maintaining order, (3) maintaining balance, and (4) maintaining cohesion.

The Number of Parts

When dividing the subject, the speaker should choose a limited number of main parts (or steps, arguments, contentions, points, or issues). The major divisions of the body should be few enough that the audience can easily remember them upon conclusion of the speech. If the speech is to have a lasting effect, the audience must also be able to recall the supporting materials.

The number of divisions a speech contains varies. In most instances, the speaker should develop probably no more than four major points, although, on occasion, one might conceivably stretch this to as many as five or even six points. Beyond that number, however, most listeners will have difficulty recalling all the principal ideas.

If a subject demands eight, nine, or more logical divisions or steps, the speaker should devise a new approach, combining several of the original points or developing an altogether different pattern of division. Reducing the number of main divisions may require some ingenuity, but it can usually be accomplished without much difficulty and almost always results in an improved speech. For example, let us suppose that a speaker plans to give an informative speech explaining how to build a birdhouse. After analyzing the subject, she decides that there are nine main steps involved in building a birdhouse. But since the audience probably would not be able to remember that many points, she might regroup the nine steps into four larger units: (1) planning the birdhouse, (2) assembling the necessary materials, (3) undertaking the actual construction, and (4) putting on the finishing touches. Or let us suppose that a speaker has decided to discuss the prospect of eight conference schools for winning the football championship in the forthcoming season. Instead of assessing each school individually, thereby requiring the audience to remember eight distinct points, he might combine the schools into groups such as: (1) the leading contenders, (2) the above-average teams, and (3) the also-rans.

The speaker should remember that the number of main points is restricted to aid the audience in recalling them and not because of any limits on speaking time; whether a speaker has 5 minutes or 50 minutes, most listeners experience difficulty in remembering a lengthy list of points, steps, or contentions.

The Order of the Points

If the audience is to grasp the main parts easily, the parts should be arranged systematically within the body of the speech. Of the several methods available for arranging the material (see Chapter 8), the speaker should be consistent in using whatever method is chosen. For example, if the speaker decides that a chronological method of arrangement best suits the subject matter, the chronological approach should be retained throughout. Or if a subject is to be divided topically, every major point should be another topical division.

Within the main divisions of the speech, the speaker should also adhere to a single method of subdividing. Thus, if he or she decides to subdivide the first major point spatially, all the subpoints under that first main heading should be part of the spatial pattern. The speaker may wish to subdivide the second point in another way—let us say, according to cause-and-effect method throughout the development of that point.

Not only should speakers adhere to a consistent method of division, but in speeches to convince and to persuade, they should give some thought to the strength or persuasiveness of the various arguments in developing a plan of organization. Should the strongest argument be presented first, second, or last? If one argument is noticeably weaker than the others, where should it be introduced? Although experimental studies of these questions have produced conflicting conclusions, the speaker should not wholly ignore such considerations. By carefully analyzing the mood and background of the audience, their knowledge of the topic, and their attitudes toward the stated position, the speaker may gain some insights to assist in determining the most effective order for presenting the arguments.

A Balanced Division

Another factor the speaker should consider while organizing the body of the address is whether the overall pattern of organization is well balanced. The term *balance* refers to the amount of development or time accorded each main division. The parts of a speech may be said to be well balanced if the amount of time devoted to each is roughly equal or at least not highly disproportionate.

For example, if a speaker has three main divisions and devotes 35 percent of the discussion to the first point, 30 percent to the second, and 35 percent to the third, the overall division could be regarded as unusually well balanced. Or if the speaker spends 40 percent of the time on the first point, 35 percent on the second, and 25 percent on the third, the speech will still be nicely balanced. However, a division in which 45 percent of the discussion is devoted to the first point, 45 percent to the second, and only 10 percent to the third lacks balance, as would an arrangement in which 70 percent of the discussion dealt with the first point and 15 percent with each of the other two divisions. In the latter two examples, so little time is devoted to the third point in one and to both the second and third points in the other that the audience would probably leave with the impression that these were of minor importance. If they are truly unimportant, the speaker should probably omit them. If, on the other hand, they are regarded as significant, the speaker needs to devote more attention to them.

A Cohesive Division

After breaking the subject down into various divisions and subdivisions and arranging these in an orderly pattern for development, the speaker should fit the parts together in such a way that the relationship of the various divisions and subdivisions to one another and to the speaker's central thought will be clear to the audience. To achieve a cohesive organization, the speaker can draw on six organizational techniques: (1) transitions, (2) signposts, (3) internal previews, (4) internal summaries, (5) interjections, and (6) special devices.

TRANSITIONS.   Transitions are words, phrases, and sentences that serve as bridges between two ideas or thoughts to indicate to the listener that the speaker has completed the discussion of one point and is proceeding to another part of the speech. Transitions are also important to the speaker in the development of the organizational pattern, for they serve as a means of testing the relationship of one idea to the next. Ideas should flow logically, and if it is impossible to construct a logical transition between one idea and the next, the speaker should realize that the relationship between the two ideas is not correct. Some examples of transitional words and phrases are: *next, in addition to, another aspect is, we must also consider, still another reason is, also, let us now examine another,* and *I will now turn to.*

Just as bridges come to rest on both sides of the body of water they span, the best transitions also clearly indicate the place they are leaving and the area they are approaching. A few examples of transitions of this kind are listed below:

In addition to giving attention to our diet, we also need to be concerned with proper exercise.
Not only is a proper diet important, but so also is exercise.
After examining the importance of a proper diet, next we should look at the need for regular exercise.

In connecting two ideas, a transition may establish either a horizontal or a subordinate relationship between them. For example, if the speaker has decided to develop three major points in a talk, to show that the second idea is as important as the first he or she might decide on a simple transitional statement: "Not only should we seek disarmament because . . . , but we seek such a policy for still another reason, namely . . ." This effectively ties the second idea to the first on a horizontal or equal status. If, on the other hand, the speaker wanted to show the subordinate status of an idea, one might say, "To support this idea I offer the example of . . ." This indicates that the example to follow is in support of, or subordinate to, the idea just presented. In a speech to delegates attending an energy conference, Senator Mark Hatfield moved from a general discussion of his topic to more specific considerations with the following transitional statement: "In order to nail down the points I have been trying to make, I would like to discuss some particular details."

Transitions can take many forms. They may be as simple as the phrase "Let's take, for example," or they may be sufficiently detailed so as to constitute an internal summary. Rhetorical questions can also act as effective transitions, as in this usage: "What are the benefits of such a policy?"

Since oral communication lacks the visual clues such as paragraph indentations, main headings, and subheadings found in written messages to indicate a new topic, idea, or subdivision, the speaker should generously employ clear and explicit transitions to connect ideas.

SIGNPOSTS.   Signposts are similar to transitions and serve the same function of identifying for the listener the introduction of a new idea or point. Usually, they are simply numbers—*first, my second argument is, third, the fourth step is*—although words such as *finally, the last point,* and *last* may also be regarded as signposts. Charles R. Stoffel, a director of the Federation for American Immigration Reform, provides this example of a signpost from a speech he delivered to the California Roundtable in San Francisco:

> What we have to ask as a nation are three basic questions:
>
> *First,* how many people will we admit to this country for permanent residency?
> *Two,* who will get the slots? Who, of the 600 million people around the world who want to migrate, most of them to the United States, will be allowed entrance to our country?
> And, *three,* how are we going to enforce the rules of our immigration policy? (*Representative American Speeches, 1983–1984,* New York: H. W. Wilson Co., 1984, p. 202.)

Signposts have one advantage over transitions as organizational devices in that, unlike the transition, they indicate exactly where the speaker is at that moment in the speech. In other words, when a signpost is used, the listener knows that the speaker is now on the *third* point or has just introduced the *second* argument. While the numbering of one's ideas with signposts may seem overly explicit and mechanical to some, this technique effectively reinforces understanding and is rarely obvious to the audience.

INTERNAL PREVIEWS.   In discussing introductions earlier in this chapter, the preview or outline of one's main ideas was recommended as a method the speaker might use to prepare the audience to listen intelligently to the remainder of the speech. The preview may also be employed effectively within the body of the speech to prepare the audience for a particularly complex, difficult, or lengthy discussion of some aspect of one's subject. Thus, after introducing a new point or subdivision, the speaker might indicate exactly how he or she intends to divide the discussion of this particular part of the speech. In a speech referred to earlier, Carolyn Dyer employs an internal preview: "I come now to the basic questions I want to address here: What are the costs of freedom of the press? What is the cost of First Amendment litigation? What are the costs of exercising uninhibited freedom of the press? What are the costs to the general public and to people with ideas to communicate an economically determined meaning of freedom of the press?"

INTERNAL SUMMARIES.   Just as internal previews may be necessary to prepare an audience for an understanding of the development of a difficult point, so internal summaries or reviews may be required to clarify the speaker's remarks when concluding a discussion of a highly important, complex, technical, or abstract idea. Instead of merely moving to the next subtopic, the speaker stops to repeat or emphasize the key parts of this aspect of the present topic, hoping thereby to insure audience comprehension.

In addition to being an effective device for restating in simple form the idea just discussed, the internal summary may also serve a transitional function in permitting the speaker to complete one idea and advance to the next. An internal summary might take the following form:

> We have just examined four examples in history to prove that armament leads to greater armament and eventually to war; now let us consider some of the problems in past attempts at disarmament.

INTERJECTIONS.   Used as a device to emphasize key points or important ideas, the interjection can be a valuable organizational tool for the speaker. An interjection is simply a declarative statement that draws attention to an idea, such as, "Now this is important," "Now this is central to understanding the remainder of the speech," or simply, "Get this." These statements focus attention on key ideas the speaker does not want listeners to miss.

SPECIAL DEVICES.   Special devices to assist the memory of the audience should be considered by the speaker. It is often possible for persons to remember what they hear longer if a visual image is associated with the ideas. For instance, to explain the three major ingredients of the speaking situation—speaker, speech, and audience—a speaker may say, "If one views the speaking situation as a triangle and locates at each of the points of the triangle one of the major ingredients—speaker, speech, and audience—one can perhaps comprehend better the interrelationships of the three and the concept that without any one of these, the triangle is incomplete."

For additional examples of special devices, see pages 143–144, Chapter 8.

THE CONCLUSION

The conclusion of a speech has two major functions. The first is to reinforce the purpose of the speech and the second is to bring the speech psychologically to a conclusion for speaker and audience. If, for instance, the general purpose has been to instruct or inform, the speaker may want to conclude simply with a summary of the ideas presented in the body of the speech. If, on the other hand, the speaker's general purpose was to evoke a change of attitude or to precipitate action, the speaker may wish to suggest a course of action for implementing the ideas. It is important to remember that audiences do not retain all the ideas the speaker presents in the course of a speech. Consequently, speakers should summarize the most important and compelling ones.

The second function of the conclusion, that of psychologically ending the speech, is vital to a favorable final impression. Most people have experienced a long-winded speaker who seems to conclude one speech but instead begins another. This is frustrating and distracting for those in the audience, and the speaker loses respect and attention. On the other hand, the speaker who talks without hint of concluding and then suddenly stops gives listeners an abrupt and jolting experience, again evoking a negative audience attitude. The concluding statements in the speech should be selected carefully to achieve a cathartic effect.

SUMMARY.   Many speakers believe that a summary is essential to the conclusion of a speech. If, however, the speech is a very short one—a one-idea speech—it may not be necessary to summarize. If the speech is complex, containing several important ideas, a summary conclusion is not only appropriate but probably necessary. In summarizing, the speaker may review the main points in the order that they were presented or follow an inverse arrangement. The latter practice assumes that people will forget the ideas presented early in the speech and better retain those presented later. By reversing the order in the summary, the speaker reinforces the ideas discussed early in the body of the speech.

Whether the speaker summarizes in natural or inverse order will depend on an analysis of audience attitudes toward the subject and the approach the speaker thinks is best suited to achieve the objectives. If the strongest idea was presented early in the speech, it might be wise for the speaker to leave the platform with the strongest idea last in the minds of the audience. On the other hand, the speaker who has selected a climactic ordering of ideas in the body of the speech may wish to summarize ideas in the same order. Avoid the trite phrases *In conclusion* and *In summary* when preparing the concluding portion of a speech. Not only are they stylistically barren, but they also cue the audience to stop listening. Most members of an audience will interpret those words as meaning that the speaker has said all that he or she is going to say and is now merely repeating material.

REFERRING TO INTRODUCTORY MATERIAL.   Frequently a speaker will conclude by referring to the ideas introduced in the opening portion of a speech. A speaker may want to restate the purpose of the speech as a concluding technique. If, for example, the introduction opened with a quotation, the speaker might wish to conclude with the same quotation. In the excerpt from Glenn Crosby's speech quoted on page 112, the speaker began by comparing the contemporary university to the Cathedral of St. Sophia. In conclusion he returned to this comparison, saying:

> The Cathedral of St. Sophia became a museum. People still frequent her halls and chambers, but more to satisfy curiosity than historical interest, and certainly not for religious edification. Decades from now, WSU [Washington State University] will still stand. A flight over the Palouse hills will reveal her walls gleaming in the sunlight. Will she have realized her potential as a university, or will she be a hollow mockery? The hour of decision is at hand and you, her faculty, illustrious students, and eventual alumni must help her make the right choice. Help her make use of adversity.

If the speech began with a narrative or an anecdote, the speaker might wish to remind the audience of it in the conclusion.

RHETORICAL QUESTION.   An effective method of concluding a speech, particularly if the speaker is suggesting action that is to be taken by the audience, is the rhetorical question. Jenkin Lloyd Jones concluded his speech titled "Who Is Tampering with the Soul of America?" with this technique. Speaking to a group of newspaper editors, he argued that the press had a responsibility to interpret and elevate the morals of America through newspapers. He concluded with these words: "And there, gentlemen, is where you come in. You have typewriters, presses, and a huge audience. How about raising hell?"

PLEA FOR BELIEF OR ACTION.   In a speech to convince or persuade, the speaker may wish to leave the audience with an appeal for belief or action. Daniel Boorstin concluded a speech on "Dissent, Dissension, and the News" with this type of appeal. After pleading for greater responsibility in the press at a meeting of the Associated Press Managing Editors Association in Chicago, Dr. Boorstin implored:

> Finally, it is possible for our newspapers—without becoming Pollyannas or chauvinists or superpatriots or Good Humor salesmen—to find new ways of expressing and affirming, dramatizing and illuminating, what people agree upon. This is your challenge. The future of American society in no small measure depends on whether and how you answer it. (Daniel Boorstin, "Dissent, Dissension, and the News," in *The Decline of Radicalism,* New York: Random House, 1970.)

In a more direct appeal for action, Senator Daniel Patrick Moynihan, speaking to the annual convention of the American Newspaper Publishers Association, concluded his speech opposing the Reagan administration's attacks on freedom of speech with the following request for action:

> The president won't reply to me. Nor, probably should he. He will respond to you. But I don't think he has heard from you, nor has Congress. This is truly a menacing atmosphere gathering in Washington. And it is not all confined to the executive branch. Freedom of the press, freedom of information is under attack.
>
> It is time you tigers roared. (*Representative American Speeches, 1983–1984,* New York: H. W. Wilson Co., 1984, p. 140.)

PERSONAL REFERENCE.   If the occasion and subject warrant, the speaker may end with a personal reference. Such a situation occurred during the "Farewell to the Cadets" speech of General Douglas MacArthur, delivered to the United States Military Academy at West Point. In concluding this ceremonial speech, General MacArthur spoke the following words:

> The shadows are lengthening for me. The twilight is here. My days of old have vanished—tone and tints. They have gone glimmering through the dreams of things that were. Their memory is one of wondrous beauty watered by tears and coaxed and caressed by the smiles of yesterday. I listen vainly, but with thirsty ear, for the witching melody of faint bugles blowing reveille, of far drums beating the long roll.
>
> In my dreams I hear again the crash of guns, the rattle of musketry, the strange, mournful mutter of the battlefield. But in the evening of my memory always I come back to West Point. Always there echoes and reechoes: Duty, honor, country.
>
> Today marks my final roll call with you. But I want you to know that when I cross the river, my last conscious thoughts will be of the corps, and the corps, and the corps. (Wil A. Linkugel, R. R. Allen, and Richard L. Johannesen, eds., *Contemporary American Speeches,* Belmont, CA: Wadsworth, 1972, pp. 288–289.)

SOME FINAL WORDS ON THE CONCLUSION.   The speaker should not introduce new material in the conclusion of a speech, for the purpose of the conclusion is to close or to summarize. The introduction of new material in the conclusion only confuses or distracts the listeners.

A final admonition is to avoid the use of the phrase "Thank you" or "Thank you for your attention" in closing a speech. In most instances, it is not necessary to thank the audience for listening, and in some cases it may be detrimental. If a speaker has provided the listeners with useful information, with a clearer understanding of a question, or with valuable insight into how to solve a complex problem, logically the audience should thank the speaker. The phrases imply that the speaker has imposed on the audience. The speaker should end on a positive rather than an apologetic note. Another reason for avoiding these phrases is that they may become crutches for a speaker; instead of ending with an effective closing statement, the speaker uses "thank you" as a way of telling the listeners that the speech is finished. "Thank you" can never substitute for an effective conclusion.

Occasionally, however, it may be appropriate to thank the audience at the end of a speech. If the speaker actually has imposed on the listeners, been given time normally reserved for other business, or has asked for and been granted permission to interfere with a regularly scheduled activity, then the speaker probably should thank the audience for having listened.

SUMMARY

Organizing material is one of the speaker's more important tasks. In arranging subject matter, the speaker should keep in mind the fleeting nature of oral communication. To a great extent, organization will be determined by the speaker's purpose and the audience's attitudes and understanding of the topic. Most speeches have three main parts: the introduction, the body of the speech, and the conclusion. The function of the introduction is to prepare the audience to listen with interest, understanding, and a favorable disposition. The body of the speech is best organized around a limited number of main ideas or divisions. Within the body, the speaker should order the main points in a consistent and psychologically meaningful manner. The divisions should be well balanced and the various parts bridges with frequent transitions, signposts, previews, and summaries. The conclusion serves to summarize or review the speaker's main ideas. In addition, it may include an exhortation to belief or action.

MODEL INTRODUCTIONS

Below are two sample introductions that effectively illustrate some of the methods of preparing an audience to listen to a speech with interest, intelligence, and goodwill.

Dissent, Dissension, and the News

Daniel J. Boorstin

To understand and fully appreciate the first introduction, the reader needs to know that the speech was given in the late 1960s, a time of great dissent and disagreement in this country. In the following excerpt from his speech, "Dissent, Dissension, and the News," note how historian Daniel J. Boorstin seeks to associate himself with his listeners, members of the Associated Press Managing Editors Association, and to win their goodwill. Observe also how Professor Boorstin's introduction states his subject and his central thought and includes a definition of the terms *dissent* and *disagreement* as he plans to use them in his speech.

Speaker demonstrates friendliness and modesty.

Gentlemen, it's a great pleasure and privilege to be allowed to take part in your meeting. It is especially a pleasure to come and have such a flattering introduction, the most flattering part of which was to be called a person who wrote like a newspaperman.

Speaker compliments his listeners.

Speaker associates historians with journalists.

Humor ————→

The historians, you know, sometimes try to return that compliment by saying that the best newspapermen write like historians, but I'm not sure how many of the people present would consider that a compliment.

This afternoon I would like to talk briefly about the problems we share, we historians and newspapermen, and that we all share as Americans.

Speaker associates historians and himself with journalists.

Twain statement praises Associated Press.

Newspaperman's statement adds humor.

Transition links Twain and newspaperman's comments to speaker's statement of his subject.

Speaker stresses importance of topic.

Speaker inserts definition of two key terms for clear understanding.

About sixty years ago Mark Twain, who was an expert on such matters, said there are only two forces that carry light to all corners of the globe, the sun in the heaven and the Associated Press. This is, of course, not the only view of your role. Another newspaperman once said it's the duty of newspaper to comfort the afflicted and afflict the comfortable.

If there ever was a time when the light and the comfort which you can give us was needed, it's today. And I would like to focus on one problem. It seems to me that dissent is the great problem of America today. It overshadows all others. It's a symptom, an expression, a consequence and a cause of all others.

I say *dissent* and not *disagreement*. And it is the distinction between dissent and disagreement which I really want to make. Disagreement produces debate but dissent produces dissension. Dissent, which comes from the Latin, means originally to feel apart from others. People who disagree have an argument, but people who dissent have a quarrel. People may disagree but may both count themselves in the majority, but a person who dissents is by definition in a minority. A liberal society thrives on disagreement but is killed by dissension. Disagreement is the life blood of democracy, dissension is its cancer.

A debate is an orderly exploration of a common problem that presupposes that the debaters are worried by the same question. It brings to life new facts and new arguments which make possible a better solution. But dissension means discord. As the dictionary tells us, dissension is marked by a break in friendly relations. It is an expression not of common concern but of hostile feelings. And this distinction is crucial. Disagreement is specific and programmatic, dissent is formless and unfocused. Disagreement is concerned with policy, dissenters are concerned with identity, which usually means themselves. Disagreers ask, What about the war in Vietnam? Dissenters ask, What about me? Disagreers seek solutions to common problems, dissenters seek power for themselves.

The speaker emphasizes the seriousness of his subject.

The spirit of dissent stalks our land. It seeks the dignity and privilege of disagreement, but it is entitled to neither. All over the country on more and more subjects we hear more and more people quarreling and fewer and fewer people

Rhetorical
questions are used
to indicate the
speaker's specific
topic.

debating. How has this happened? What can and should we do about it? This is
my question this afternoon.

(*Source:* Daniel Boorstin, *The Decline of Radicalism,* New York: Vintage Paperbacks,
Random House, 1970, pp. 97–106.)

Address to the U.S. Congress

Winston S. Churchill

In December 1941, British Prime Minister Winston S. Churchill addressed
a joint session of the United States Senate and House of Representatives.
The introduction of the address effectively illustrates the use of humor,
praise, and references to shared beliefs and attitudes in an apparent effort
to create goodwill.

I feel greatly honored that you should have thus invited me to enter the
United States Senate chamber and address the representatives of both branches
of Congress. The fact that my American forebears have for so many generations
played their part in the life of the United States and that here I am, an
Englishman, welcomed in your midst, makes this experience one of the most
moving and thrilling in my life, which is already long and has not been entirely
uneventful. I wish indeed that my mother, whose memory I cherish across the
vale of years, could have been here to see. By the way, I cannot help reflecting
that if my father had been American and my mother British, instead of the other
way around, I might have got here on my own. In that case, this would not have
been the first time you would have heard my voice. In that case, I should not
have needed any invitation, but if I had it is hardly likely that it would have been
unanimous. So perhaps things are better as they are.

I may confess, however, that I do not feel quite like a fish out of water in a
legislative assembly where English is spoken. I am a child of the House of
Commons. I was brought up in my father's house to believe in democracy: trust
the people, that was his message. I used to see him cheered at meetings and in
the streets by crowds of workingmen way back in those aristocratic, Victorian
days, when as Disraeli said, the world was for the few and for the very few.
Therefore, I have been in full harmony all my life with the tides which have
flowed on both sides of the Atlantic against privilege and monopoly, and I have
steered confidently towards the Gettysburg ideal of government of the people, by
the people, and for the people.

I owe my advancement entirely to the House of Commons, whose servant I
am. In my country as in yours public men are proud to be the servants of the
state, and would be ashamed to be its masters. On any day, if they thought the
people wanted it, the House of Commons could by a simple vote remove me
from my office, but I am not worrying about it at all. As a matter of fact, I am sure
they will approve very highly of my journey here, for which I obtained the King's
permission, in order to meet the President of the United States, and to arrange

with him for all that mapping out of our military plans and for all those intimate meetings of the high officers of the armed services of both countries which are indispensable to the successful prosecution of the war.

STUDY QUESTIONS

1. What are the purposes or functions of the introduction? the body? the conclusion?
2. In what ways can a speaker arouse interest among the members of the audience? Are there reasons for choosing one method over another for a particular speech or occasion?
3. Under what circumstances does it become particularly important for a speaker to create a favorable impression in the introduction of the speech? How might he or she go about accomplishing this?
4. Why is it important for an audience to know a speaker's topic before the body of the speech is reached? Under what conditions should a speaker not reveal the purpose or central thought early in the speech?
5. What methods are available to a speaker for concluding a speech? What are the values of each?

EXERCISES

1. Prepare three conclusions for a speech. Explain the values of each one and discuss the possible responses of the audience to each conclusion.
2. Listen to a speech, or read one in *Vital Speeches, Representative American Speeches,* or an anthology, and write a criticism of the effectiveness of the organizational techniques used by the speaker in the introduction, body, and conclusion. When writing your criticism, remain aware of the speaker's relationship to the audience and the occasion.
3. Prepare an outline for a 4- to 5-minute speech to inform. Then plan an introduction for the speech. Practice the introductory portion and deliver it to the class, stopping just before reaching the body of the speech. The class and instructor will then evaluate the introduction and make suggestions for improvement.
4. Incorporating the suggestions of the class and instructor, revise the introduction presented in exercise 3. Present the improved introduction again in class, this time continuing with the remainder of the speech.
5. Write out three separate introductions for a speech to inform, using a different attention-gaining device or method in each. Choose the best introduction, and in 100 words indicate the reasons for your choice.

FURTHER READINGS

Ehninger, Douglas, Bruce E. Gronbeck, Ray E. McKerrow, and Alan Monroe, *Principles and Types of Speech Communication,* 10th ed. (Glenview, IL: Scott, Foresman, 1986), chap. 10, "Beginning and Ending the Speech."

Lucas, Stephen E., *The Art of Public Speaking* (New York: Random House, 1986), chap. 8, "Beginning and Ending the Speech."

Ross, Raymond S., *Speech Communication: Fundamentals and Practice,* 7th ed. (Englewood Cliffs, NJ: Prentice-Hall, 1986), chap. 8, "Preparing and Organizing the Message."

Taylor, Anita, *Speaking in Public* (Englewood Cliffs, NJ: Prentice-Hall, 1979), chap. 7, "Beginning and Ending: More Important than You Think."

Vasile, Albert J., and Harold K. Mintz, *Speak With Confidence: A Practical Guide,* 4th ed. (Boston: Little, Brown, 1986), chap. 7, "Putting It All Together."

Verderber, Rudolph F., *The Challenge of Effective Speaking,* 6th ed. (Belmont, CA: Wadsworth, 1985), chap. 4, "Organizing Speech Material."

Walter, Otis M., and Robert L. Scott, *Thinking and Speaking* (New York: Macmillan, 1979), chap. 5, "Making Introductions, Conclusions, and Outlines."

Zannes, Estelle, and Gerald Goldhaber, *Stand Up, Speak Out,* 2d ed. (Reading, MA: Addison-Wesley, 1983), chap. 6, "Starting and Stopping."

CHAPTER 8

METHODS OF DIVISION

After the National and American football leagues agreed to merge in 1968, one of the most difficult problems they faced was deciding how to organize the new conference. Since it would be impossible for each of the 26 teams to play every other club in one season, the owners had to decide how to divide the league into smaller units and to assign teams to each subdivision.

On the question of how to divide the league, the owners had several alternatives: to keep intact the old conference alignments of 16 teams in one division and 10 in the other; to create 2 new divisions of 13 teams each; or to establish 4 to 6 subdivisions of unequal size. Once this was settled, officials faced the delicate task of deciding which clubs would be assigned to each division. Proposals for realignment were almost as numerous as fourth-down punts. Some owners favored a strictly geographical division. Others suggested an arrangement along the lines of the old leagues' memberships. Some advocated plans that would keep together traditional rivals. An important feature of several proposals was the drawing power of various teams. The prestige of playing against well-established clubs, the strength of the competition within each division, and perennial financial considerations were other factors motivating owners to choose one plan over another. After much controversy, the league finally worked out a satisfactory method of division.

The league's reorganization difficulties illustrate the variety of methods available and the many factors involved in dividing a subject—in this case, a conference of 26 football teams. The public speaker faces a similar task in dividing a speech topic. The speaker must decide not only how many subdivisions to have but also how best to subdivide the subject matter. Several methods of division will be available, and many factors will influence the choice of the approach best suited to achieve the goal.

Two major influences, the audience's attitudes toward the subject and the subject matter of the speech, affect the speaking situation and help the speaker to select the best method for dividing material. In most speeches, the subject matter lends itself to division by one of six methods: chronological, geographical, topical, causal, problem-solution, or pro-and-con arrangement.

INFLUENCE OF AUDIENCE ON THE DIVISION OF MATERIALS

Based on their attitude toward a topic, audiences may be classified as friendly, hostile, or neutral. The hostile and friendly audiences have special characteristics important to the persuasive speaker, because they may influence the speaker's division of materials.

The Hostile Audience

In most speeches to persuade, the speaker faces an audience that is at least partially hostile, doubtful, or apathetic toward the speaker's ideas. Indeed, if no one in the audience disagreed, the speaker would have no need to try to convince or persuade. Some examples of speakers facing extremely hostile audiences might include officials trying to reassure angry and frightened local residents after events such as the nuclear accident at Three Mile Island, the toxic water pollution at Love Canal, and the Miami riots of 1980. Under these circumstances, the emotions of the audience may be so great that communication is almost impossible. And to greet hostility with defiance certainly will not create an atmosphere conducive to mutual understanding. If, however, speakers are determined to be heard and the audience is willing to give them a chance, adroit speakers can at times arrange materials in such a way that listeners' antagonism can be overcome. Basic to this approach is the speaker's emphasis on areas of agreement and common interest with the audience. The speaker might demonstrate fairness, honesty, and objectivity and display friendliness and goodwill toward the audience. By locating and developing areas of common ground, the speaker not only can build a bridge permitting communication with the audience but may also win the respect of the hearers. Gaining the listeners' respect is important, because normally the audience will transfer its hostility toward the speaker's ideas to the speaker. Therefore, arranging materials so that they build confidence and respect is important to the speaker in persuading hostile groups.

After introducing material to gain personal acceptance and to establish common ground with auditors, the speaker is ready to begin developing the theme. With audiences opposed to the central thought, the speaker should organize the speech inductively. In the inductive approach, the speaker refrains from stating the main idea at the outset. This approach permits the speaker to introduce ideas and factual information acceptable to the audience, to develop areas of agreement, and to lead the listeners toward acceptance of the speaker's proposal. Use of this method of organizing prevents immediate rejection of the speaker's proposal by the listeners.

To illustrate the inductive method of organization, take a hypothetical speaker who believes that local taxes should be increased to improve the public schools. No one favors higher taxes, so the speaker knows that he has an unpopular theme. However, rather than announcing his position early in the speech, thereby creating a negative attitude toward his proposal, the speaker might instead first develop arguments on which he and his audience could agree. For example, he might begin by suggesting that one of the most important responsibilities of the community is to educate its youth—something all his listeners would probably accept. He might then stress the advantages of a good education to the community and to the young people. From there, the speaker could proceed to his second contention, that the local school system is not providing its students with the best education. Although the audience may be hesitant to accept this argument, if the speaker can demonstrate that the local schools are inferior—perhaps by comparisons to other schools, by statistics revealing substandard teacher salaries, by data from educational tests, and by specific information on the lack of equipment and facilities—he can probably convince his auditors that something needs to be done.

He is then ready to move to his third point, that improving the school system will cost money. Although the audience may not like the idea of having to spend more on its schools, they would undoubtedly understand that the improvements outlined by the speaker could not be made without additional funds. But in the backs of their minds, the listeners probably entertain the hope that *they* will not have to provide the money. So the speaker's next step is to show that alternative sources are not available. Admitting that the state and federal governments might provide limited financial assistance, the speaker must demonstrate that outside funds alone would not be sufficient to effect the needed improvements.

He is now ready to introduce his main idea: that only a tax increase can provide the funds necessary to improve the schools. Having prepared the audience logically and psychologically by developing the importance of the problem, by removing doubts and objections, and by eliminating alternatives, the speaker has a better chance of winning acceptance of his proposal than he would had he opened with a blunt statement saying that he favored higher taxes to aid the schools.

A speaker who organizes materials so areas of common interest and concern are developed first, followed by an inductive method leading to the conclusion, may still fail to win the desired response from a hostile audience. However, this approach usually improves the speaker's chance of obtaining at least a fair hearing and may reduce or even eliminate the hostility of the auditors.

The Friendly Audience

A friendly audience is one already interested in and favorably disposed toward the speaker's central thought. Because the friendly audience is already inclined to agree, the speaker need not be concerned with what method of organization is best suited to persuading the auditors.

Unlike the speech delivered to a hostile group, an address to a friendly audience probably does not require an inductive approach. Instead, the topic can be developed deductively, with the main idea or conclusions stated at the outset, followed by whatever supporting material is needed. Since the audience is favorably predisposed, stating one's position clearly at the beginning establishes immediate rapport with the auditors.

INFLUENCE OF SUBJECT MATTER ON THE DIVISION OF MATERIALS

Six main methods are available for arranging materials in the body of a speech. Selecting the proper method is important in obtaining the desired response from the audience. This is the function of organization. The six methods are discussed below.

Chronological Sequence

The chronological method of arrangement of materials is simply a division based on *when* events occurred. Materials or events may be arranged in their chronological order from beginning to end, and from end to beginning, or by some other plan (such as past, present, and future). A speaker who wishes to talk about our desire to explore the moon might decide that the most effective method of division would be chronological, beginning with early attempts to reach the moon, proceeding to the team effort to achieve that goal in the 1960s, and, finally, describing the first moon landing. Travelogues are frequently divided into time sequences from the beginning of the trip to the end.

One should not assume, however, that a simple chronological enumeration of events is sufficient to produce a stimulating speech. Each step of the process should be amplified and developed with interesting and descriptive material. Nothing is quite so boring as spending an evening in a friend's home watching slides of a vacation with no elaboration on the events that took place at each location. Therefore, the speaker who decides to use the chronological method in describing attempts to reach the moon will have to do more than simply list the flights taken in the Mercury, Gemini, and Apollo missions and will want to identify the types of information gleaned from various flights, describe the specific missions, and discuss the significance of each mission.

The chronological pattern is generally used for presenting historical materials, describing a process or procedure, or relating a personal experience.

The following passage from Mark Twain's *A Tramp Abroad* is a simple example of time or chronological arrangement.

> To make this excellent breakfast dish, proceed as follows: Take a sufficiency of water and a sufficiency of flour, and construct a bullet-proof dough. Work this into the form of a disk, with the edges turned up some three-fourths of an inch. Toughen and kiln-dry it a couple of days in a mild but unvarying temperature. Construct a cover for this redoubt in the same way and of the same material. Fill with stewed dried apples: aggravate with cloves, lemon-peel, and slabs of citron, and two portions of New Orleans sugar, then solder on the lid and set in a safe place till it petrifies. Serve cold at breakfast and invite your enemy. (Mark Twain, *A Tramp Abroad,* vol. II, New York: Harper & Row, Publishers, Inc., 1907, p. 241.)

Spatial Division

A spatial or geographical relationship is the positioning of an object in relation to the location of another object. A spatial development can create a visual appreciation for the subject matter of a speech as well as providing a logical and orderly process of division (see Figure 8.1). Most television weather reports are arranged spatially, with the announcer showing where the warm and cold fronts and high- and low-pressure areas are located and then proceeding to explain to viewers how these factors will affect the

FIGURE 8.1   Spatial division: A cruise ship. (Eastern Steamship Lines)

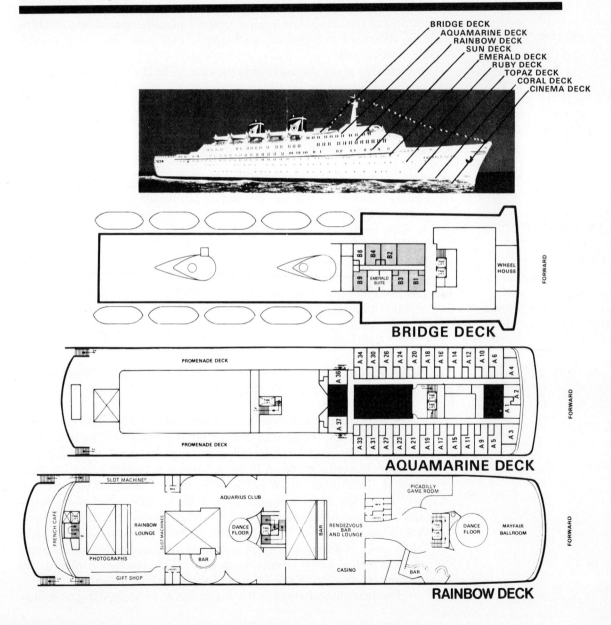

weather in various regions of the country—the East, the South, the Midwest, the Southwest, and the Pacific Coast, for example. The announcer usually then elaborates on the weather in a more limited spatial area, the state and local community.

To illustrate the various approaches available when the speaker divides a subject spatially, let us consider the description of the décor of a room. The speaker would begin at some logical point and then explain the location and arrangement of the various objects in the room and on the walls relative to the position of that central or original point. Normally, spatial relationships could be described in terms of north-south, east-west, up-down, inside-outside, and around.

In a spatially divided speech, as in the case of the chronologically divided speech, the subject matter should include elaboration and clarification of the relationships of one spatial item to another. A simple listing of the relationship of various objects or places without elaboration will result in a sterile presentation.

The following is an example of a spatially divided speech in outline form:

The Economy of South Dakota Varies from Region to Region
  I. Eastern South Dakota (from the eastern border to the Missouri River) is primarily agricultural.
      A. Rich farmland
      B. Some small industry related to agriculture
 II. West central South Dakota (from the Missouri River to the Badlands) is primarily cattle-raising ranch country.
III. The far western part of the state is a popular tourist area because of:
      A. The Black Hills
      B. Mount Rushmore
      C. The Badlands

The following description of the battlefield of Waterloo by Victor Hugo provides an unusual illustration of spatial division or development:

Those who would get a clear idea of the battle of Waterloo have only to lay down upon the ground in their mind a capital A. The left stroke of the A is the road from Nivelles, the right stroke is the road from Genappe, the cross of the A is the sunken road from Chain to Braine-l'Alleud. The top of the A is Mont St. Jean, Wellington is there; the left-hand lower point is Hougomont, Reille is there with Jerome Bonaparte; the right-hand lower point is La Belle Alliance, Napoleon is there. A little below the point where the cross of the A meets, and cuts the right stroke, is La Haie Sainte. At the middle of this cross is the precise point where the final battle word was spoken. There the lion is placed, the involuntary symbol of the supreme heroism of the imperial guard.

The triangle contained at the top of the A, between the two strokes and the cross, is the plateau of Mont St. Jean. The struggle for this plateau was the whole of the battle.

The wings of the two armies extended to the right and left of the two roads from Genappe and from Nivelles; D'Erlon being opposite Picton, Reille opposite Hill.

Behind the point of the A, behind the plateau of Mont St. Jean, is the forest of the Soignes.

As to the plain itself, we must imagine a vast, undulating country; each wave commands the next and these undulations, rising toward Mont St. Jean, are there bounded by the forest. . . . (Victor Hugo, *Les Miserables,* New York: Dodd, Mead & Co., Inc., 1925, pp. 114–115.)

Other topics that might lend themselves to a spatial arrangement include a description of a college campus; a discussion of the geological formations underlying a particular area; an analysis of election results by regions of the country; a guide to a museum, library, or art gallery; and an explanation of the physical layout of a ship, park, or airport.

Topical Division

Topical division of speech materials involves the selection and development of categories of a subject. For instance, if one were to describe a recent trip around the world, rather than approach the subject chronologically, one might divide it by topics as follows:

I. Modes of transportation during the trip
II. Religious ceremonies observed
III. Architecture of different places
IV. Costs of living in various locations

By using a topical division, the speaker easily avoids the common fault of simply narrating, in order, the nations or cities visited without elaboration on the subject. Topical arrangement also provides for an extensive number of subtopics and makes selection of materials for a particular audience relatively simple.

Political speakers often arrange their ideas by topics, considering such factors as the political, economic, social, and psychological effects of various issues on their constituents. The topical arrangement is excellent for logical consideration of controversial subjects.

The topic "A Visit to the British House of Commons" might be arranged topically. For example:

A Visit to the British House of Commons
I. Officials
II. Ceremonies

III. Regular business
IV. Special debates
    A. Adjournment debate
    B. Question period

Often a subject may be treated topically in several different ways. For example, if a speaker were to divide a college population into topical subdivisions, he or she might choose from any of the following categories:

Class
    I. Freshmen
    II. Sophomores
    III. Juniors
    IV. Seniors

Sex
    I. Male
    II. Female

Major
    I. History
    II. Art
    III. English
    IV. Chemistry
    V. Engineering
    VI. Others

Scholarship
    I. Superior students
    II. Average students
    III. Below-average students

Residence
    I. In-state students
    II. Out-of-state students
    III. Foreign students

Housing
    I. Dormitory students
    II. Members living in fraternities and sororities
    III. Off-campus students

Religion
    I. Catholic students
    II. Protestant students

   III. Jewish students
   IV. Others

Type
    I. Party boys and girls
   II. Politicians
  III. Bookworms and grinds
  IV. Potential dropouts
   V. Jocks

Causal Division

The cause-effect division of materials is most frequently used in the development of a speech of advocacy or persuasion. It is, however, also useful in describing events with an instructional purpose. In a causal division, the speaker's material may be arranged either from cause to effect or from effect to cause. For example, a speaker may decide that present conditions provide a clear understanding of a particular problem and so may wish to begin with a description of those conditions and move from there to the causes of them. On the other hand, if the speaker desires to show the possible outcome of certain acts or proposals, he or she may decide to move from the act as the cause to the potential effects.

A speaker might decide to use the causal method of dividing a speech to show the potential dangers or advantages of a particular piece of legislation being considered by a state or national legislature. In this case, the speaker would be moving from cause to possible effect. On the other hand, a person speaking on conservation might begin by describing the unsightly litter existing in our national parks or the pollution of our streams and air and, after illuminating the problem, examine the causes, possibly concluding with a plea for action to eliminate those causes.

An advocate of a program to fight urban decay might argue causally from the following outline:

   I. The principal causes of urban decay are three:
     A. Poor planning by city officials.
     B. The movement of middle- and upper-class families to the suburbs.
     C. The lack of state and federal concern and financial assistance.
  II. The effects of the present state of urban decay create additional problems:
     A. Poor housing, slums, and ghettos contribute to crime and delinquency.
     B. As more middle- and upper-class families move to the suburbs, needed taxes for urban renewal are lost.
     C. The lack of urban renewal, slums, and crime further accelerate the movement to the suburbs.

Problem-Solution Division

One of the most frequently used methods of speech division is the problem-solution pattern. This method is a logical way for individuals and groups to solve problems, and consequently it is also a logical pattern to follow in a speech presenting problem-solution arguments. Based on John Dewey's method of reflective thought, this approach systematically leads the audience through a definition and analysis of the problem, a consideration of the suggested solutions, the determination of the best solution, and, finally, a suggested course of action. The pattern of collegiate debates follows the problem-solution order in that the affirmative presents a need, representing the problem, and a plan, representing the solution.

A problem-solution order is used in the following example:

I. There is a need to improve the quality of American television programming.
   A. Because the commercial networks are entirely dependent on advertising revenue, they cater to the lowest common denominator—the least well informed viewer.
   B. Because of this, they devote almost all their time to mass-appeal situation comedies, soap operas, sports, and cops-and-robbers series.
   C. The networks almost totally ignore millions of Americans whose interests and needs are not those of the majority.
II. To solve this problem, the United States should:
   A. Establish an independent, government-financed network comparable to the British Broadcasting Corporation to present programs to viewers not presently served by commercial television.
   B. Give greater support to PBS stations.
   C. Require commercial broadcasters to devote substantially more air time to documentaries, music, educational programs, and other types of telecasts designed to appeal to viewers with an interest in programs other than those that interest the "average" American.

Or a speaker might wish to follow each step of John Dewey's formula for problem solving in the following manner:

Election Campaign Financing
   I. What is meant by "election campaign financing"?
      A. The funds used by candidates and their election committees to promote election campaigns
      B. Excluded from consideration are funds necessary to conduct the election.
   II. In approaching this problem, what goals or guidelines should be considered?

    A. The solution should provide equal access to communication channels.

    B. The solution should encourage all those who wish to seek public office regardless of their personal wealth.

    C. The solution should resolve the problems inherent in the present system of financing elections.

III. How serious is the problem?

    A. How does the problem manifest itself?

        1. Persons of wealth use the present system to their advantage.

        2. Persons in positions of power in government and industry use the present system for personal gain.

    B. What are the causes of the problem?

        1. Unlimited financing

        2. Unenforced legislative restrictions on spending

        3. Loopholes in the legislation governing spending

        4. A desire by some persons for power

        5. The widespread development of Political Action Committees (PACs) with unregulated spending in campaigns

    C. What are the effects of the present system of financing elections?

        1. Access to public office is often denied to persons with little financial means.

        2. It has bred contempt for the voter.

        3. It has led to personal accumulations of wealth at the expense of the taxpayer.

IV. What possible solutions might be considered?

    A. Retain the present system.

    B. Legislate more severe penalties for violators of the law on election financing.

    C. More rigid enforcement of the laws on election financing

    D. Reduce the limits of spending on campaigns, including limitations on PACs.

    E. Finance campaigns equally for all candidates by initiating a special tax to pay campaign and election expenses.

    F. Permit free and equal access to radio and television networks.

    G. A combination of these suggested solutions is a possible remedy.

V. In view of the goals set earlier, the best solution is _____.

VI. The solution could be implemented and would work as follows: (Here the speaker would present the details of the plan.)

Pro-and-Con Division

In the pro-and-con method of division, the speaker presents both sides of a question or examines all possible solutions to a problem before identifying the best position or remedy. For example, a speaker might discuss the arguments for and against a piece of legislation before taking a position on it or elaborate on three or four suggested remedies to a problem before indicating a proposed solution. The wisdom of presenting opposing points of view before outlining one's own conclusions has been questioned, for the speaker may inadvertently raise objections or create doubts in the auditors' minds that were not there before. But if the speaker presents the opposing points of view and then convincingly minimizes their value, desirability, or benefits by showing their weaknesses, shortcomings, or inconsistencies, the audience can be led to accept the speaker's point of view as the best or only answer to the question.

Such an approach is often effective in removing objections to the speaker's position and in pointing out weaknesses of other positions perhaps overlooked by the listener. The repudiation of other proposals is almost essential when the speaker is advocating a proposition about which many auditors have serious reservations or objections. To ignore alternative contentions and proposals that are well known or widely held will leave listeners with unresolved questions and doubts. Refutation of alternative approaches may lead them to abandon their original position and agree with the speaker. The speaker, of course, must avoid antagonizing members of the audience who hold the opposing points of view while attempting to lead them to accept the desired position.

An outline of this type of division might look something like this:

Dishonesty and Exploitation in Intercollegiate Athletics
I. One solution to end the abuse and exploitation of college athletes would be to abolish all intercollegiate athletics.
   A. Advantages
   B. Disadvantages
   C. The disadvantages are greater than the advantages.
II. Another possible solution is to abolish all athletic scholarships.
   A. Advantages
   B. Disadvantages
   C. The disadvantages outweigh the advantages.
III. A third possibility is more stringent control of the athletic programs and practices at colleges and universities and more severe penalties for violation of rules and regulations.
   A. Advantages
   B. Disadvantages
   C. Advantages are greater than disadvantages and, therefore, should be adopted.

The speaker should be aware of the methods of division available and then select those best suited to the subject matter of the speech and to the audience.

OTHER INFLUENCES ON THE DIVISION OF MATERIALS

For most speeches, the speaker will probably find one of the methods of division already discussed to be the most satisfactory plan for developing the topic. However, at times one may feel that a special approach is needed or would prove beneficial. Two such methods are discussed below.

Adaptation to Another Speaker

In one of the great debates in the British House of Commons during the eighteenth century, Charles James Fox arose and announced that he would like to speak at that time because the issues discussed by the previous speaker had been raised in the manner he wanted to discuss them. He then took his opponent's arguments, starting with the last contention, and, in reverse order, developed his position on each major issue raised by his opponent. His plan was determined in part by his analysis of the subject as the prior speaker had divided it but was also related to the emotional and mental condition of the listeners at that point in the debate. By taking the last argument first, he began with something still fresh in the members' minds. Then, by working through the remainder of the issues in reverse order, he systematically discredited the views of his adversary.

At times one may be moved by such considerations to adopt a method of division that one might not otherwise have chosen. A speaker need not take the issues in reverse order as Fox did. However, there may be something about the arguments raised by another speaker, by the inclusion or exclusion of a particular contention, or by the order in which each idea was discussed that will lead a speaker to adapt the arrangement of materials to what the previous speaker has said or to the frame of mind of the audience at that moment.

Applying a Formula

Most persons rely on at least one or two formulas or gimmicks to recall information they might not otherwise readily remember. "Never eat oysters in months without an *r*" and "Thirty days hath September, April, June, and November . . ." are two examples of such aids to memory. A similar type of formula to assist recall is the "Survey Q3R" method for studying. If you can recall the name of the method, you can remember the method itself, which consists of survey, (Q) question, (3R) read, review, and recall. At times a speaker may decide that listeners will more readily remember what is said or that ideas will be more vivid and memorable if some type of formula is provided for the audience.

Thus, a speaker who hopes to impress upon listeners the varied duties performed by law enforcement officers might develop a plan of arrangement similar to the following one.

Police Perform a Variety of Important and Useful Services

P   Protection. The police protect citizens and property.

O   Order. The police maintain order in the community.

L   Law enforcement. The police enforce the laws enacted by the people through their representatives.

I   Investigation. The police perform an important function by investigating complaints, accidents, and alleged violations of the law.

C   Crime control. The police act to apprehend violators of the law.

E   Emergency aid. Police provide aid in emergencies such as floods, hurricanes, blizzards, fires, and similar disasters.

Slogans lend themselves easily to this type of formula. For example, a speaker might organize recommendations for maintaining international law and order around the letters P-E-A-C-E as follows:

P   We must take a Practical approach.

E   We must consider the Emotions of the parties involved.

A   We must Act promptly in international disputes.

C   We must secure the Cooperation of all nations.

E   We must Enforce international law.

While many topics do not lend themselves to division according to some formula, a speaker may at times find this approach particularly appropriate to the topic and helpful to the audience in recalling ideas.

SUMMARY

Speakers may divide the materials of the body of the speech in a number of ways. The main methods available are chronological or time sequence, spatial, topical, causal, problem-solution, and pro-and-con. The method selected by the speaker for a specific occasion is influenced primarily by the subject matter of the speech. Some subjects, such as accounts of travels and explanations of the operation of mechanical devices, logically lend themselves to a chronological division; other topics, such as descriptions of objects or places, may be developed more effectively by a spatial or geographical arrangement. Topical division involves the arrangement of materials according to the categories, parts, or facets of a subject and the development of each subtopic. Causal, problem-solution, and pro-and-con methods of division are often well suited to speeches to convince or to persuade.

Audience attitudes in a persuasive setting are important to the speaker and may influence the speaker's division of materials. For a hostile audience, one may wish to adopt an inductive approach, delaying the statement of the proposition until late in the speech or until one has established common ground and areas of agreement with the listeners. In organizing a speech for a friendly audience, the inductive approach usually is not necessary, and the speaker can state the position in a clear and straightforward manner at the outset.

While not common, occasionally a speaker's method of division may be influenced by factors other than the audience and the subject matter. For example, a speaker might wish to divide a speech in a manner used by a previous speaker or devise a formula for the arrangement of materials in order to aid the audience in remembering the ideas.

STUDY QUESTIONS

1. What are the major influences on the selection of a method of dividing the body of a speech? In what ways do they influence the selection?
2. What types of subjects are most adaptable to chronological division? to spatial division? to topical division?
3. What is the difference between the problem-solution division and the pro-and-con division? Under what conditions might a speaker select one of these over the other?
4. It is possible to arrange materials from cause to effect or from effect to cause. Is it possible to arrange the same materials by either method? Under what conditions might the speaker select one method over the other?
5. What is the relationship between John Dewey's reflective thought process and the problem-solution method of dividing speech materials?
6. What is the danger in using the pro-and-con division in a speech of advocacy? How can a speaker overcome it? What is the value of this method of division?
7. How does the attitude of the audience affect the division of materials?
8. Under what conditions might a speaker decide not to reveal the purpose or central thought early in the speech?
9. How might a speaker overcome hostility among members of an audience?

EXERCISES

1. Prepare two outlines for an informative speech using a different method of dividing the materials for each. Explain the advantages of each method.
2. Read a speech in *Vital Speeches, Representative American Speeches,* or another anthology and determine the method of division used by the speaker for the main ideas. Did the speaker use other patterns for developing each idea? Was the method chosen the best for presenting the subject, in your opinion? Could the speaker have employed an alternate method advantageously? Write a short paper summarizing your evaluation.
3. Select a speech topic that would lend itself to chronological division and prepare a short outline of the three or four main points for the body of a speech. Do the same for spatial division and causal division.
4. Select a topic for a persuasive speech that lends itself to the problem-solution division. Prepare a short outline indicating the main points of the body of the speech.

5. Select a topic that might be developed by a pro-and-con division. Briefly outline the main points of the body of the speech. What would be the advantages of using a pro-and-con division for this subject? What would be the dangers?

6. Prepare a 4-minute informative speech. Choose the most appropriate method for dividing your subject. Prepare an outline of the speech to be presented to the instructor just before giving the speech. Deliver the speech in class.

FURTHER READINGS

Ehninger, Douglas, Bruce E. Gronbeck, Ray E. McKerrow, and Alan Monroe, *Principles and Types of Speech Communication,* 10th ed. (Glenview, IL: Scott, Foresman, 1986), chap. 9, "Adapting the Speech Structure to Audiences: Traditional Patterns of Organization."

Lucas, Stephen E., *The Art of Public Speaking* (New York: Random House, 1986), chap. 7, "Organizing the Body of the Speech."

Minnick, Wayne C., *Public Speaking* (Boston: Houghton Mifflin, 1979), chap. 4, "Organization."

Reid, Loren, *Speaking Well* (New York: McGraw-Hill, 1977), chap. 10, "Organizing Messages."

Ross, Raymond S., *Speech Communication: Fundamentals and Practice,* 7th ed. (Englewood Cliffs, NJ: Prentice-Hall, 1986), chap. 8, "Preparing and Organizing the Message."

Zannes, Estelle, and Gerald Goldhaber, *Stand Up, Speak Out,* 2d ed. (Reading, MA: Addison-Wesley, 1983), chap. 5, "Organizing the Message."

CHAPTER 9

OUTLINING

"Order and simplification are the first steps toward the mastery of a subject." Applied to the composition of a speech, this observation by Thomas Mann provides a compelling reason for the speaker to prepare an outline of ideas. An outline contributes both to simplification and order: it simplifies because it reduces the content of the speech to its essentials; it provides order because it necessitates arranging materials logically and systematically. Just as an architect prepares a blueprint, a lawyer constructs a brief, a professor devises a syllabus, and a traveler makes an itinerary, so too should a speaker evolve a plan to provide an overview of what he or she seeks to accomplish and to give direction in achieving that goal.

IMPORTANCE AND VALUES

Outlining permits the speaker to examine the speech visually and to test it for balance and thoroughness. The outline helps the speaker to discover whether everything necessary has been included to achieve the purpose, to determine whether the ideas are adequately supported, and to decide whether all the material contributes to the attainment of the goal. It shows the logical relationships between ideas and reveals flaws of imbalance or inconsistency, lack of order, and potential weaknesses in adapting the speech to the audience. The outline further serves as a memory aid for the speaker who can visualize and thereby better remember the major ideas and supporting materials.

When preparing a speech, it is much easier to rearrange ideas in outline form than in a written manuscript, just as it is simpler to study the bone structure of an animal by examining the skeleton rather than the fleshed-out form. For that reason, preparation of an outline is usually done *after* the speaker has chosen the topic, determined the purpose, analyzed the audience and subject, and gathered and selected supporting materials, but *before* the preparation of a manuscript or speaker's notes.

PRINCIPLES OF OUTLINING

Order in Preparation of a Speech

Since a speech follows the sequence of introduction, body, and conclusion, it may seem natural to prepare the outline of a speech in that order. Such is not the case. Since the speaker does not know exactly what is to be introduced until the main part of the speech has been planned, it is more reasonable to prepare an introduction after the body of the speech has been outlined. Otherwise, the speaker might develop an introduction that—after supporting materials in the body have been rearranged, revised, and altered—introduces the wrong speech. It is profitable to prepare the conclusion last so that the speaker may incorporate and summarize materials from the introduction, as well as from the body of the speech, in the closing remarks.

Speech preparation includes writing out an outline,
notes, or manuscript. (Cynara, DPI)

Use of Symbols

The organization of this book is outlined by means of main heads, second-level heads, and third-level heads. These headings in the chapters identify major ideas, their coordinate ideas, and subordinate ideas. Major ideas or points in the speech situation are steps, events, parts, aspects, reasons, or arguments the speaker wishes the audience to understand or accept. Ideas or points that have equal value in the mind of the speaker are called coordinate, whereas those materials that serve to amplify, explain, or support the main ideas are considered to be subordinate. In an outline of a speech, the major ideas, coordinates, and subordinates are identified by using a symbolic system. Normally, the Roman numeral *I* is used first, followed by the capital letter *A,* then the Arabic numeral *1,* and then the lowercase letter *a* to identify an order of subordination. In outline form, it would look like this:

I.
   A.
      1.
         a.
         b.
      2.

      B.
        1.
        2.
  II.
    A.
        1.
        2.
              a.
              b.
      B.
        1.
        2.
      C.
        1.
        2.
              a.
              b.
      D.
        1.
        2.
  III.
    A.
        1.
        2.
      B.

In this example *A* and *B* are coordinates or equals, and Arabic numerals *1* and *2* are subordinate to A and B. In this typical outline form, the Roman numerals might indicate the introduction, body, and conclusion.

To understand better the concept of coordination and subordination, consider the cluster of statements that follows. Among the statements are two major ideas and two subordinate ideas for each main idea. These assertions support the central idea that labor unions have promoted the general welfare of the United States.

1. Strikes have become less destructive.
2. Collective bargaining has become more widespread.
3. Strikes have become less disruptive.
4. Strikes have become less frequent.
5. The method of collective bargaining has become stronger.
6. Collective bargaining has become more efficient.

After analyzing each of the statements for levels of importance, it should be apparent that statements 3 and 5 reflect the two main points; that statements

1 and 4 are subordinate to statement 3; and that statements 2 and 6 are subordinate to statement 5. They are subordinate because they help to support more specifically the generally stated main points. Consequently, in proper outline form, the statements should be organized and set down in this way:

I. Strikes have become less disruptive. (main idea)
   A. Strikes have become less destructive. (subordinate idea)
   B. Strikes have become less frequent. (subordinate idea to I but coordinate with A)
II. The method of collective bargaining has become stronger. (main idea and coordinate with I)
   A. Collective bargaining has become more widespread. (subordinate idea)
   B. Collective bargaining has become more efficient. (subordinate to II but coordinate with A)

It is important that each of the symbols in the outline represent only one idea. If more than one idea is included, the basic advantage to outlining is lost, for the symbolic system in outlining is used to establish relationships between ideas. Also, the speaker should observe that if an idea is subdivided, it is subdivided into at least two subordinate ideas. If there seems to be just one idea subordinate to another, think again—it is probably either coordinate with the main idea or identical to it.

Indentation

In the preceding examples, each of the symbols has been indented, reflecting its proper relationship of subordination to other symbols. The indentation is essential to show visually proper coordination and subordination of ideas. Note the loss of visual usefulness in the following outline, even though appropriate symbols are used.

The President Should Be Elected by a Direct Vote of the People
   I. Electoral votes are unrealistically apportioned according to the decennial census.
 A. Based on the census, each state receives the same number of votes as it has congressional representatives, plus two.
 B. Because of shifting population, many people are not fairly represented.
 1. In 1984 several hundred thousand new California and Texas residents were not reflected in the electoral vote.
 2. States that have lost population will be overrepresented in the electoral vote.
 3. This imbalance is inherent in the electoral college.
 II. The electoral college does not reflect the popular vote.

A. The "unit rule" gives all the electoral votes of a state to the winner regardless of plurality.
B. Thus, the electoral college can declare the candidate with the fewest popular votes the winner.
C. Electors are not bound to vote for their state's winner.
III. Direct election of the president is in the best interests of America.
A. Direct election would be consistent with the Supreme Court's "One-person–one-vote" ruling.
B. The vote of every American should carry equal weight.

In contrast to this outline, visual identification of equal and subsidiary ideas is found much more easily in the following outline of the same material.

The President Should Be Elected by a Direct Vote of the People
  I. Electoral votes are unrealistically apportioned according to the decennial census.
     A. Based on the census, each state receives the same number of votes as it has congressional representatives, plus two.
     B. Because of shifting population, many people are not fairly represented.
        1. In 1984 several hundred thousand new California and Texas residents were not reflected in the electoral vote.
        2. States that have lost population will be overrepresented in the electoral vote.
        3. This imbalance is inherent in the electoral college.
 II. The electoral college does not reflect the popular vote.
     A. The "unit rule" gives all the electoral votes of a state to the winner regardless of plurality.
     B. Thus, the electoral college can declare the candidate with the fewest popular votes the winner.
     C. Electors are not bound to vote for their state's winner.
III. Direct election of the president is in the best interests of America.
     A. Direct election would be consistent with the Supreme Court's "One-person–one-vote" ruling.
     B. The vote of every American should carry equal weight.

It is important to note that in the proper visual form of subordination and indentation, if the statement of an idea takes more than one line, the second line should not begin any farther toward the left-hand margin than the beginning of the first line. To extend the second line farther left would destroy the basic principle of the outline—that is, to show visually the proper relationships of ideas.

TYPES OF OUTLINES

The two major types of outlining are the *complete-sentence* outline and the *topic* or *key-word* and *key-phrase* outline.

Complete-Sentence Outline

The complete-sentence outline is used for the purpose of writing out in outline form the full content of the speech to be delivered. This type of outlining takes a great deal of discipline and time but is essential for complex speeches or for speeches designed to meet difficult audience situations. Many people write speeches in their entirety without ever preparing an outline. However, outlining the speech is preferable to writing it out because the sentence outline is almost as complete as a written text and yet provides a much clearer guide to the relationships and order of

Sir Winston Churchill combined a variety of methods of delivery—the outline, the manuscript, and last-minute impromptu additions—in the preparation and delivery of his speeches. (Wide World)

the speech materials. In an outline, the arrangement of ideas and the need for transitions is more easily recognizable to the speaker. Consider the following complete-sentence outline, which includes a statement of general purpose, central thought, and desired response. Also note the written introduction and conclusion.

- *General purpose:* To inform
- *Central thought:* The central theme of this speech is how the master plan was developed for a regional emergency medical services (EMS) VHF communications system, and how the system functions.
- *Desired audience response:* The desired response is for the audience to understand how this system functions within a three-county radius.
- *Introduction:* As a result of an extensive survey of public safety communications relating to Emergency Medical System Operations within the three counties constituting the Texoma Region, a master plan for regional emergency medical services communications system was developed.

I. The Master Plan offers a unified approach to the EMS requirements of each county in the Texoma Region by upgrading existing facilities and utilizing VHF communications resources within the region.
   A. This master plan should be implemented over a two-year period and can be incorporated with future VHF systems to provide command control communications and additional reliability through redundancy.
   B. The survey's conclusions give valuable insight into the human aspects and the local constraints that must be considered in developing a unified approach to emergency medical services in the region.
      1. Every county in the region has a public safety dispatcher on duty 24 hours a day.
      2. Needs exist for mobile VHF ambulance equipment and VHF hospital base stations.
      3. Paging operations could be expanded to other hospitals and included in other EMS systems in the region.
      4. The VHF equipment installed in the region is reliable and directly applicable to the project.
      5. As a general guide, it is not advisable to utilize radio communications for routine hospital-to-hospital communications if telephone service is available.
      6. Law enforcement dispatch and assistance are an integral part of health-care delivery systems.
      7. The impact of highly developed EMS systems in the Dallas area is significant.
II. A classification system for EMS operations is defined with specific relevance to the Texoma region to denote the qualification levels of operating

personnel, the emergency care provided, and the communications required for effective operations in each class.

  A. Class B concerns first aid and transportation, with volunteer personnel.

  B. Class A concerns basic life support with volunteer personnel.

  C. Class AA concerns basic life support with paraprofessional personnel.

  D. Class AAA concerns advanced life support with paraprofessional personnel.

III. This master plan is designed to provide effective EMS command and control communications in each county in the region.

  A. The system provides communication links for public access by telephone to central dispatching points, dispatch to ambulance, ambulance to hospital, hospital to hospital, mobile to mobile, mobile to base, paging, physician access, and interagency interface.

  B. Communications equipment for the VHF base station consists of a single transmitter with a two-frequency transmit capability and two receivers.

  C. The remote control station is an electronic unit that operates the base station in transmit, receive, and paging modes.

  D. The paging receivers will be carried by EMS physicians and hospital staff.

  E. Ambulances in all counties in the region should be equipped with VHF transreceivers similar to those installed in law enforcement vehicles.

  F. Portable transreceivers indicated in the scheme of its master plan should have at least a two-channel capability.

  G. A helicopter is frequently used as an airborne ambulance.

■ *Conclusion:* Disasters can come at any time, and it is reassuring to know that there are plans to take care of all the aspects of an emergency.

One danger of preparing a complete-sentence outline is that the speaker may follow it too closely in actually delivering the speech, resulting in a reading of a written manuscript. This usually is not desirable nor is it the purpose of the outline. The specific wording of the speech rises out of the speaker's understanding of the topic. The sentence outline should be used only in the planning stages for the purpose of determining the order, balance, and completeness of the analysis of the topic.

Topic Outline

The topic outline is simply a miniature of the complete-sentence outline. All the rules of outlining are followed as in the complete-sentence outline, but the language is reduced to key words or key phrases. With a simple subject and a speaking situation posing no particular problems of audience adaptation, a speaker may at times dispense with the preparation of a complete-sentence outline and substitute a topic outline. However, in most argumentative speeches and informative addresses of any complexity or degree of technicality, the speaker probably should prepare both a complete-sentence and a topic outline. The topic outline is particularly useful as a memory device when the speaker is practicing the speech to develop familiarity and an extemporaneous method of presentation. Once the logic and the arrangement of the speech materials have been tested in the complete-sentence outline, the speaker can then reduce the outline to one of key words and phrases for practice and rehearsal.

The following outline is a condensation of a more complete outline given earlier:

I. Electoral votes unrealistically apportioned
   A. Each state same number of votes
   B. Not fairly representative
      1. 1984 new California and Texas residents not represented
      2. Some states overrepresented
      3. Imbalance is inherent
II. Popular vote not reflected
   A. Unit rule
   B. Candidate with fewest votes can be elected
   C. Electors not bound
III. Direct election is in best interest
   A. "One-person–one-vote" ruling
   B. Equal weight

Speaker's Notes

Once the topic outline has been used for rehearsal, the speaker can further reduce the outline to an abbreviation of the original complete-sentence outline. These are the notes the speaker probably will wish to use during the actual presentation of the speech, and they will contain even fewer cues than the key word or phrase outline. The value of speaking from notes rather than from a manuscript or detailed outline is recognized by many speakers. Speakers who rely only on notes usually feel that this permits them greater flexibility in adapting to the audience's reactions and that it also contributes to spontaneity of expression.

Speakers vary in their type and use of notes. However, many speakers find it helpful to record them on 3" × 5" cards so that they can be held in the hand in the event that no speaker's stand is available. This also permits greater freedom of movement and more animated physical delivery during the speech. By the time the speaker has rehearsed the speech several times using the topic outline, he or she can determine what notes are needed. Figure 9.1, photographs of Winston Churchill's speaking notes, illustrates one type.

FIGURE 9.1   Speech notes of Winston Churchill.

Secret Session.   House of Commons.

My reliance on it as an instrument for waging
                                              war.

More active and direct part for its Members
    L.D.V.

All this in accordance with past history.

This S.S. a model of discretion.

My view always Govt. strengthened by S.S.

~~Quite ready to have others~~

Agree with idea S.S. shd be quite a normal par
        of our procedure,
            not associated with any crisis.

Relief to be able to talk without enemy readin

Quite ready to have other S.Ss.,
        especially on precise subjects.

But I hope not press Ministers engaged in
    conduct of war too hard.
                        this war!

    epushed by
    Mood of the House.
            Cool and robust.

Speeches most informative.   *confidence from*
    Difficult to betray any secrets disclosed
                                        today

Moore-Brab (Wallesey)   Praise.

He was sorry I mentioned expert advisers
    favoured fighting on.

Politicians and Generals, -

In last war and this.

Not put too much on the politicians:
    even they may err.

Goering.   How do you class him?
    He was an airman turned politician.

I like him better as an airman.
    Not very much anyway.

Moore-Brab tells us of his wonderful brain,
    and the vast dictatorial powers and plans.

Anyhow he did not produce the best pilots
    or the best machines,
        or perhaps, as we may see presently,
            the best Science.

M.B. said 250 nights in the year
    when no defence against night bombing.

I hope it is not so

This is one of those things you can only tell
        by finding out.

The speaker who uses direct quotations may wish to write or type these on separate cards and actually read them when the time comes. The speaker who is well prepared, however, may use no notes at all; if notes are used, they will be as brief as possible, providing only the barest guide to the information the speaker needs to lead him or her through the speech.

The following is an example of a speaker's-notes outline of the same speech outlined earlier:

I. Unrealistically apportioned
  A. Same number
  B. Not fair
    1. California and Texas 1984
    2. Overrepresented
    3. Imbalance
II. Popular vote
  A. Unit rule
  B. Fewest votes
    1. 1824
    2. 1876
  C. Electors
III. Best interest
  A. One-person–one-vote
  B. Equal

Combination of Types

It is possible to combine the types of outlines, for instance, by combining a topic outline with a complete-sentence outline. A "notes-manuscript" combination was used by James G. Traynham, Dean of the Graduate School of Louisiana State University, when he spoke at a convocation at Reinhardt College, Waleska, Georgia, on October 1, 1975. It is reproduced here to illustrate the possibility of combining types. Note, for instance, the penciled-in, last-minute additions and reminders. Comments on the sides of the pages call attention to the speaker's techniques of organization and audience adaptation. The speaker's overall method of organization is topical in that he presents a list of recommendations to his auditors on how they may benefit from their college educational experiences.

Speaker identifies with listeners.

INTRODUCTION. Now at large university, but I began college in a small junior college
    Long time ago—now middle-aged
    Characterization of middle age

Speaker uses humor to create goodwill.

The time in life when you know all the answers—but no one asks you any questions!

Speaker announces topic and theme. Speaker adapts to audience. Speaker uses humor to create goodwill.	**ADVICE.** What to do until the diploma comes; how to succeed in college. Some of the advice may sound as though it is for freshmen only—but that part is the advice I find it necessary to give most frequently to graduate students now. The whole advice can best be summed up, perhaps, by a quotation from an eminent, contemporary philosopher, Snoopy: "It's hard to win at chess with a checkers mentality."
Contrast introduced, which later will be used to clarify and vivify analysis. Humor contributes to the speaker's goodwill. Develops checkers-chess contrast.	**CONTRAST CHECKERS AND CHESS.** Checkers—zigzag; only a crowned checker has any sweep to its moves. Now skill is required to win at checkers—it's not just a dull game, at least not until you have played chess. Chess—variety of moves—some straight ahead one space at a time, others in a powerful L-shaped move; some sweep diagonally, others nondiagonally; the queen is the most powerful piece, the king one of the least so—(a potent social commentary that could be the basis for a different discussion, don't you think?)—but even the plodding pawns can, in the hands of a knowledgeable chess player, frustrate the moves of the powerful pieces. Such variety—but definite restrictions! And you are sure to lose at chess if you keep trying to play checkers. The possibilities and the restrictions are different.
States thesis with an analogy utilizing his checkers-chess contrast.	College is to high school as chess is to checkers. And you can't win at chess with a checkers mentality.
Rhetorical question used as a transition. Signpost: "The *first . . .*"	**NOW WHAT ARE THE CHESS MOVES I RECOMMEND TO YOU?** The first move might be called the Dean's Gambit, because it is seldom, if ever, used by a faculty member; much to the consternation of deans and students alike: Read the catalog. From time to time we see listings of the great books that one selector or another has decided are the ones for a college student to read. Pity the shortsightedness that omits the college catalog from the list. Read the catalog—you will learn what ought to be going on. In the Graduate School Office at LSU, I have put up a sign at the counter to which students come first, illustrated with a picture of Snoopy and asserting "The catalog can be a student's
Reviews first main point.	best friend." Ask your faculty what the academic rules are, if you like, but check their answers in the catalog before you bank on them.
Transition: *"Next move . . ."* Note special device of *3 R's* to help his auditors remember. Repeats point.	**NEXT MOVE WE MIGHT CALL THE GROUP DEFENSE.** Pick a major. When you pick a major, you give yourself direction. You focus on a particular set of 3 R's; requirements, restrictions, and recognition. Change next term—or next month—if you wish. In fact, I hope that your horizon is broadened enough so that you will seriously consider changing your choice. But don't delay too long benefiting from the sense of direction, the sense of belonging—Pick a major.
Note last minute addition of a personal experience. The speaker has no transition here and apparently hopes that blunt, short	*Question about my picking chemistry.* **COUNT THE HOURS IN A WEEK.** I spend a large proportion of each registration period dealing with student requests for overloads. I begin the discussion by pointing out that the week

admonition will
indicate a new idea.

contains only 168 hours—and no matter how eager, conscientious, or intelligent
you are, you can't change that number. I enthusiastically approve of the idea of
making all the hours count—but I refuse to approve a schedule which requires a
student to neglect some obligation—employment or academic schedule or
bathing. Count the hours in the week, so you can make the hours count.

Repeats idea in
summary.

STUDY.

Statement of next
point, rhetorical
question, and then
restatement of the
idea to emphasize.
Associates himself
with his listeners
through a
comparison of his
and their situations.

Surprised? Yes, study. If you aren't surprised by the advice, you may be by
the rationale behind it. Election is coming up in Baton Rouge a month from today,
and I know you have elections in Georgia, too. Hardly any election gets by
without talk about misappropriation of public funds—and I am willing to bet that
you are against misappropriation of funds. Now you or parents or someone pay
dearly for your enrollment at Reinhardt—but you don't pay the full cost of your
education. Many of you are likely to go to a public university after graduation
here—and the difference between your costs and the real costs is even greater
there—usually over $2000 a year. If you don't study, you are guilty of
misappropriation of funds—as guilty as the office-holder thief or the
record-manipulating bank clerk. There is a substantial investment in your being
here—don't misappropriate the money by not studying.

Repeats idea.

TALK TO THE FACULTY.

No transition into
this thought, but
the speaker makes
clear that this is a
new
recommendation in
second sentence.
Speaker probably
enhances goodwill
by poking fun at
the faculty.
Last-minute
addition of an
anecdote about a
family member.
Speaker emphasizes
the importance of
his next point. He
is saying. *"Now get
this!"*
Reminds listeners
of checkers-chess
contrast.

Even to the administrators. In spite of what you may have been told by
students who preceded you, the faculty welcome your conversations, just as
though they really were people themselves. But, in small college or large
university, the choice is really yours. You can actually get through without ever
conversing with a faculty member, and you can converse with them daily.

Story about sister Alice at chemistry meeting

In write-ups of chess games, some move is so astute that the notation for it is
followed by an exclamation point. This next move is such a one.

TAKE ADVANTAGE OF THE COLLEGE!

There's more here than even you sophomores have yet discovered, I am
sure. Concerts, theater, art—and I strongly recommend that you take a foolish
course every year—at least one. A course that has no relationship to that major
you picked. Just to sample a new facet of life. College at its best might even be
characterized as the time and place in life when sampling new facets of life is
most convenient and least expensive. Don't miss the chance—take advantage.

LEARN ENGLISH.

Read it, write it, speak it—use it and appreciate it. One of the better ways to
learn English is to study a foreign language—and today that may be the best
justification for foreign language study for most students. Don't be misled by the
many who counsel that language is alive and changing and therefore care in its

use is wasted attention. Language is alive, and vital, and both powerful and fragile at the same time. Learn to use it with and for precision. Language and thought are so intimately connected that sloppiness in one indicates rather convincingly sloppiness in the other.

Learn to be comfortable with the elegance and precision of words longer than four letters

BE PREPARED.

Note that I did not say "get prepared." College is often looked upon as getting prepared for life. But this is life now—be prepared now. Plan, organize, schedule, select—be prepared, but be prepared, too, for surprises—and hope that they come. Many scientists write research papers as though they were involved in the dullest work: "It was not unexpected . . ." Thank heavens it really isn't that way at all. The president of Ohio State University recently used the simile of a Cooks tour and a Lewis and Clark expedition. You know about a Cooks tour: every detail plotted out and everything on schedule. "If this is Tuesday, this must be Belgium." Contrast with the Journals of Lewis and Clark. A definite goal, an unswerving commitment—but every bend in the river was an adventure. Be prepared—for a Lewis and Clark adventure, not a Cooks tour of life.

FINALLY, *HAVE FUN.*

In a way, that's what all the other recommended moves have been aiming at. Have fun. Lest you think too little of this advice, let me illustrate what I mean. Nearly all of society's problems about which we are presently concerned will be solved by scientists if they are solved at all—food, fuel, health. And scientists are interested in solving those problems, and they rejoice at any partial solution. But if you hear a scientist say that solving society's problems is his motivation for those long hours of work, much of it tedious and repetitious, don't believe him. The reason scientists are scientists—and artists are artists—and faculty are faculty—and, I dearly hope, students are students—is that it is fun.

Last month a young woman student named Heather spoke to me in the hallway as I was on my way to class. Heather has red hair, fair countenance, and charm. She was not a student in my section last year, when she took organic chemistry on her way to med school, but like every other chemistry faculty member—we are trained observers—I knew she was there. You have a picture of Heather? When she spoke to me last month, she was bubbling with excitement as she proclaimed: "Organic Chemistry is the greatest thing that has ever happened to me in my entire life." And she changed her major. She had discovered fun, and being an organic chemist, I understood. Andrew, on the other hand, had always been a chemistry major—but I had seldom seen him so genuinely enthusiastic as he was last week when he told me about his first Shakespeare course that he was then on his way to. Maybe organic chemistry or Shakespeare won't do it for you, but I hope something does.

Another last-minute addition to adapt to listeners.

Although, once again, the speaker has no translation, he goes out of his way to explain what is his next idea.

Repeats idea "Be prepared."

Finally can be regarded as either a signpost or a transition.

He repeats idea.

The speaker repeats idea.

The speaker's two examples drawn from personal experience should have earned him goodwill and respect, because they display an interest in and concern for students.

Here, the speaker has taken an ordinary and unimportant encounter to illustrate his main idea and to suggest, indirectly, that although he is a dean he understands students.

College is a time for change. The essence of that aspect was illustrated for me years ago by a freshman who came timidly to my open office door during preregistration period. He asked: "Can you tell me the way to the boy's—uh, I mean the men's room?"

Final summary.

Change from your checkers mentality when you begin to play chess. Read the catalog—take advantage—have fun—checkmate!

SUMMARY

In preparing a speech, an outline helps the speaker to determine whether all the ideas necessary to achieve the purpose have been used and permits the speaker to determine visually the balance of the speech and decide on the most effective arrangement of coordinate and subordinate ideas. In outlining, one should prepare the body of the speech first, followed by the introduction, and, finally, the conclusion. Using a consistent symbolic system in outlining and employing a method of indentation provide further visual aid in examining the balance and subordination of ideas. The three types of outlines are the complete-sentence outline used in the early preparation stages, the key-word or key-phrase outline used in the rehearsal stages, and the speaker's-notes outline to be used in the actual presentation. The speaker may wish to combine two or all of these types for the presentation. The speaker who uses discipline to follow these procedures in outlining will be assured of a much better prepared and consequently much better received presentation.

STUDY QUESTIONS

1. Why is outlining important in the preparation of a speech?
2. What principles of outlining should the speaker follow? Why is each important?
3. What is meant by coordinate and subordinate ideas in outlining?
4. What is the difference between a complete-sentence outline and a key-word or key-phrase outline? What practical functions do each serve? How do they differ from the speaker's notes?

EXERCISES

1. Arrange the following subtopics in a topical outline with the central thought that *H-Bar-C Ranch offers vacationing guests a wide range of activities and accommodations.*

Air-conditioned rooms   On Beau-catcher Mountain
Square dancing   Sailing
Activities   Souvenirs
Swimming   Snack bar
At Lake Tippecanoe   Bridge and other card games
Outdoor activities   Waterskiing
Accommodations   Restaurant
Fishing   Indoor activities

trail rides   weekly talent shows
Hiking

Trail rides   Weekly talent shows
Hiking

2. Select a speech from *Vital Speeches, Representative American Speeches,* or another anthology and reduce it to a complete-sentence outline using the principles of proper outlining. Identify the coordinate and subordinate ideas.

3. Prepare a complete-sentence outline for your next speech. Reduce it to a key-word or key-phrase outline. Further reduce it to speaker's notes. Submit all three to your instructor after you have given the speech.

FURTHER READINGS

Ehninger, Douglas, Bruce E. Gronbeck, Ray E. McKerrow, and Alan Monroe, *Principles and Types of Speech Communication,* 10th ed. (Glenview, IL: Scott, Foresman, 1986), chap. 3, "Outlining the Speech."

Lucas, Stephen E., *The Art of Public Speaking* (New York: Random House, 1986), chap. 9, "Outlining the Speech."

Mudd, Charles S., and Malcolm O. Sillars, *Speech: Content and Communication* (New York: Crowell, 1975), chap. 2, "Outlining."

Osborn, Michael, *Speaking in Public* (Boston: Houghton Mifflin, 1982), chap. 10, "Outlining the Informative Speech," and chap. 13, "Developing, Outlining, and Wording the Persuasive Speech."

Ross, Raymond S., *Speech Communication: Fundamentals and Practice,* 7th ed. (Englewood Cliffs, NJ: Prentice-Hall, 1986), chap. 8, "Preparing and Organizing the Message."

CHAPTER 10

DELIVERY: NONVERBAL COMMUNICATION

The nationally televised debates between John F. Kennedy and Richard M. Nixon during the 1960 election campaign convincingly demonstrated the importance of the physical or visible elements of a speaker's delivery. Surveys after the first debate showed that people who had listened on the radio felt the speakers were evenly matched, with Nixon perhaps more effective. Television viewers, however, gave Kennedy the victory by a considerable margin. The only difference in the two media—that those watching television *saw* the speakers—clearly indicates that the physical attributes of delivery were significant in the viewer's reactions.

On television, Kennedy projected an image of vigor, confidence, and maturity, which contrasted sharply with Nixon's tired, worn look. Theodore White described Nixon's appearance as "tense, almost frightened, at times glowering and, occasionally, haggard-looking to the point of sickness." The difference in the responses of radio and television audiences in this instance emphasizes the importance of the two separate elements of delivery—the audible factors and the visible characteristics. Vocally Nixon was Kennedy's equal, but visibly Kennedy was superior. An important lesson was learned from these debates, and since then advisers to political figures and other prominent persons have paid careful attention to their speakers' physical and vocal presentation.

Chapters 10 and 11 deal with these two facets of delivery. This chapter discusses methods of delivery and the speaker's nonverbal communication. The next chapter treats the speaker's vocal usage.

WHAT IS DELIVERY?

It is important to understand the difference between the delivery and the content of a speech.

Delivery refers to the actual presentation of the speech. It consists of what is heard—the speaker's voice quality, pitch, rate, volume, articulation, and pronunciation—and what is seen—the speaker's posture, movement, gesture, eye contact, and facial expression.

Speech content consists of *what* the speaker has to say, while delivery refers to *how* he or she says it. From a printed transcript a reader may learn *what* the speaker said. Such accounts frequently are published in newspapers, the *Congressional Record,* and collections of speeches. If they have not been subsequently edited or revised, these texts provide an accurate report of the content of the speech—the ideas, supporting materials, organization, and language. These versions, however, provide an incomplete representation of the speech because they do not include *how* it was presented. A written transcript contains no record of the speaker's voice quality, rate of speaking, inflection, loudness, and other vocal characteristics that may have been important in influencing those who heard it. It also gives no indication of the speaker's gestures, posture, facial expression, and other physical attributes.

The vocal and physical elements of speech that cannot be recorded in writing constitute the speaker's delivery. Delivery is no less important than content in determining the response to any spoken communication.

METHODS OF DELIVERY

Many, perhaps most, beginning speakers do not know how to go about preparing and delivering a speech. Some write it out and then read it to the audience. Others prepare a manuscript and attempt to memorize it. Some deliver the speech from an outline or a set of notes. A few make no advance preparation and hope the inspiration of the moment will see them through. Finally, some speakers combine these approaches, memorizing portions, reading other parts, and extemporizing or speaking impromptu here and there.

In choosing a method of preparation and presentation, no single approach is better than another. One method may be appropriate to a particular situation but poorly suited to another. The choice of method will be dictated by the speaker's abilities, the nature of the situation, and the type and length of the speech.

Speakers thus have a choice of four methods of delivery: manuscript, memory, extemporaneous, and impromptu. At times, these methods may be combined. Each has advantages and disadvantages.

Manuscript

Delivery from manuscript consists of reading the speech from a complete, prepared text.

This method has several advantages, the most important probably being that it permits speakers to determine in advance exactly what they wish to say. They are able to select words with care, to revise and to polish so that the final version represents their most careful effort. Another advantage is that in presentation speakers need not worry about forgetting or becoming lost, for they have the complete text before them all the time. Still another desirable feature is that a speaker who reads from a manuscript need never fumble or search for the precise language wanted.

This method is useful in several speaking situations. If a speech is important and the speaker wishes to make certain that it will not be misunderstood, a manuscript is almost essential. For example, the president of the United States delivering a major address would not want to risk speaking extemporaneously because a careless or incorrect word or phrase might have national or international repercussions. A scientist reporting technical data might also wish to avoid being misunderstood by following a carefully prepared text. A manuscript is also useful if the speaker must adhere to enforced time limits. Radio and television rarely permit a speaker to exceed a scheduled time limit. Speakers who do not want their concluding remarks replaced by a commercial may decide to speak from a carefully prepared and timed manuscript.

Despite these values, the manuscript method has many drawbacks. First, many speakers do not read well. Instead of appearing natural and spontaneous, they stumble over words, pause at awkward places, read too fast or too slowly, and sound monotonous. A second disadvantage is that many speakers find it difficult to maintain eye contact with their listeners when reading from text. A third weakness is that the use of a manuscript restricts movement. The speaker must either remain at the lectern or pick up the sheets of paper, often obtrusively, and carry them while moving about. The use of a manuscript also seems to inhibit gestures. Perhaps the most serious drawback, however, is that with a manuscript, speakers find it difficult to make on-the-spot adjustments to fit the reactions of the listeners. The insertion of new materials may make it difficult to devise a smooth transition back to the text. If remarks of a prior speaker or some unforeseen development suggest that the speech should be altered, a speaker may find it difficult to make such changes at the last minute.

Although the manuscript poses some problems, these difficulties can be overcome. With practice, speakers using a manuscript can learn to read conversationally, to maintain direct eye contact, to move and gesture, to communicate, and to develop skill in last-minute adaptations.

A speaker who plans to use a manuscript should keep in mind the following suggestions:

1. *In writing the manuscript, the speaker should remember that the speech will be said aloud,* not be read silently. The speaker should read aloud each sentence to make sure it can be spoken easily and meaningfully. The manuscript should contain direct reference to the audience *(you, we, our, your).* The organization should be clear and easy for a listening audience to grasp. Obvious literary phrases such as "the above" and "in the last paragraph" should be avoided.

2. *The speech should be practiced aloud.* Practice should be oral rather than silent for two reasons. First, because most persons read silently much faster than they read aloud, if the speech is not practiced aloud the speaker will not have an accurate estimate of its length. Second, only by reading the speech aloud can the speaker identify tongue twisters or awkward, "unsayable" sentences and phrases that should be eliminated.

3. *The speaker should give attention to vocal usage, eye contact, facial expression, gestures, and movement while practicing.* To avoid stumbling over words, becoming lost, and encountering reading problems, the speaker needs to be familiar with the manuscript so that a glance at the first words of a sentence will be enough to remind him or her of the entire sentence. This familiarity can be acquired only through extensive practice. Recording and playing back, practicing before a mirror, or delivering the speech to a friend may be helpful in preparing the speech.

4. *The manuscript should be easy to read.* The speaker should use a typewritten manuscript, preferably outsize type, that has been triple-spaced. The manuscript should be neat and free of spelling and punctuation errors. It should be typed on paper that can be handled easily. Pages should be carefully numbered. To facilitate reading while turning the pages, the speaker may include the beginning words of the next page at the bottom of each sheet or

the last words of the preceding page at the top of each sheet. This enables the speaker to look ahead and to begin turning a page before actually completing what is written on it.

5. *Avoid overrehearsal.* While extensive practice is desirable, frequent practices for short periods of time are better than a few prolonged practice sessions. Lengthy sessions produce carelessness, so that after the first 10 minutes the speaker may be reinforcing bad habits by continued rehearsal.

6. *Indicate in the manuscript the interpretation of key words or sentences.* While practicing the speech, some speakers find it helpful to mark words and phrases in the manuscript that are to be emphasized. This may be done by underlining, using colored pencils, and other devices. While such devices may help some, for others they often are distracting and of little help.

Memory

The memory method of delivery consists of preparing a manuscript and then simply memorizing the entire speech.

The memorized speech has most of the advantages of the manuscript speech, such as careful timing, precise choice of language, polishing, and, if properly memorized, a smooth, effortless presentation.

The memory method is best suited to short addresses in which the speaker wishes to appear sincere and spontaneous while paying careful attention to the composition of the speech. Speeches of presentation and acceptance of awards, eulogies, and commendations, speeches of welcome and farewell, and other short ceremonial and occasional addresses are often given from memory.

The disadvantages of speaking from memory are several. The chief drawback is the time required to memorize the speech. If a speech is short, memorizing is not a serious problem. But for most people, memorization of a speech of 30 minutes or longer is extremely time-consuming. And for a speaker who must speak frequently—such as a candidate for political office or a classroom lecturer—the time required is prohibitive.

A second shortcoming is that many people do not speak naturally when reciting from memory. They tend to talk too fast, to develop inflection patterns, or to drone on in a monotonous manner.

They also suffer memory lapses. The speaker who has committed the entire talk to memory often finds it difficult to resume the speech after momentarily forgetting one phrase or sentence.

Like the manuscript speech, the speech delivered from memory also hinders audience adaptation. The speaker who inserts new material at the last minute is likely to lose the train of thought and experience difficulty in resuming the memorized presentation. However, unlike the manuscript speech, the memorized address does facilitate direct eye contact and permit freedom of movement.

In preparing the speech to be delivered from memory, the speaker should keep in mind several of the recommendations for preparing a manuscript speech:

1. Remember that the speech is to be presented orally and make certain that the language is conversational rather than written.
2. Practice aloud.
3. In practicing, give attention to the vocal and physical aspects of delivery.
4. Practice for several short rather than a few long periods of time.

In addition the speaker should:

1. *Memorize the speech thoroughly.* A speaker who commits a manuscript to memory at the last minute or who approaches the speaking situation with a speech poorly memorized is inviting difficulty. Unless one is confident that the speech is so well memorized that one cannot forget, undue nervousness will undoubtedly occur. Furthermore, if the speech is not thoroughly memorized, the speaker will be required to devote attention almost entirely to remembering the text, thereby neglecting other aspects of delivery.

2. *Concentrate on the meaning of the speech.* A speaker who is thinking about what he or she is saying is not only much more likely to avoid memory lapses but able to speak more convincingly.

3. *Avoid panic if a memory lapse occurs.* A pause to review what has been said and to pick up the thread of the speech will not disturb the audience. The speaker should not apologize for the lapse and above all should not try to proceed until what comes next has been recalled.

Extemporaneous

The extemporaneous method of delivery consists of extensive advance study, careful organization, preparation of an outline or notes, practice, and presentation with the speaker relying only on the outline or set of notes. In preparing an extemporaneous address, some speakers write out the speech in its entirety but when presenting it rely only on an outline or notes, making no effort to adhere to the manuscript. Some speakers use note cards to which they refer when necessary, whereas others prefer to memorize the outline and use no notes at all.

For most speaking situations, this method probably has more advantages and fewer disadvantages than other types of delivery. Its chief advantage is its flexibility. It permits the speaker to make on-the-spot changes in response to the reactions of the audience. It also encourages spontaneity.

Furthermore, eye contact is easily maintained, and movement and gestures are in no way inhibited, as they may be in the manuscript speech. Memory is no problem either, because the speaker has notes and does not attempt to present a speech word for word.

The extemporaneous method is well suited to most speech situations.

Except when an extremely precise statement is imperative, when a time limit is rigidly enforced, or when reference to notes suggests insincerity, the extemporaneous method is appropriate.

The principal handicap of speaking extemporaneously is that it sometimes results in pedestrian language. The speaker who lacks a good vocabulary or is inexperienced speaking extemporaneously may detract from the speech with awkward sentences, vague and ambiguous language, nonfluencies, and vocalized pauses. Even skilled speakers, when speaking extemporaneously, often are unable to summon the well-turned phrase required to transform a good speech into a truly eloquent address.

People with limited experience speaking extemporaneously may encounter other difficulties. The lack of a manuscript or memorization of the speech may lead the novice speaker to feel insecure. They may also develop the habit of referring to their notes almost constantly, even though they do not really need them. With practice, these handicaps can be overcome.

In preparing an extemporaneous talk, the speaker should:

1. *Prepare thoroughly.* The speaker who has not decided exactly what to say is likely to digress or to omit important supporting material.

2. *Keep notes or outline simple and brief.* Each speaker must determine what kind of notes are most helpful. Some will prefer to memorize the main headings of their outline and rely on no written notes whatever. Some use an outline, whereas others rely on a list of key words or phrases as a reminder. Only by experimenting with different methods can each individual determine which is most helpful.

Whatever type of notes a speaker uses, they should be kept simple. Sentence outlines usually are unnecessary. The notes should be sufficiently clear that a single glance will remind the speaker of what to say. The notes should be legible—preferably typewritten—and brief.

3. *If notes are used, place them on small cards.* Although the speaker should not try to hide the fact that he or she is using notes, they should be unobtrusive and not interfere with the presentation of a speech. Notes on small cards (3" × 5") are more easily handled than those in a notebook or on a sheet of paper. They also can be picked up by the speaker who wishes to move around, and they do not interfere with gestures.

4. *Practice the speech often and aloud.* Although the speech will never be given in exactly the same way, practicing aloud permits the speaker to become familiar with the material, to time the speech, and to give attention to vocal and physical aspects of delivery.

Impromptu

Impromptu delivery consists of speaking without any advance preparation. It is completely off-the-cuff.

The only advantage of this method is that it does guarantee spontaneity.

The disadvantages are many: it precludes careful consideration of the subject, ideas, supporting materials, organization, style, and delivery, and it permits no practice.

If a speaker has received any advance notice whatsoever—even a few minutes—the time should be used to jot down a few notes.

While no one likes to have to speak impromptu, there are times when it is necessary. A person may unexpectedly be asked to provide information or an opinion at a meeting or may decide, on the spur of the moment, to take part in a discussion or debate—in other words, to speak impromptu.

If you must speak impromptu, some suggestions are:

1. *Don't panic.* Remember that the audience understands that the speaker has had no time to prepare the remarks and doesn't expect a Gettysburg address.
2. *Stick to the subject.* Avoid digressions.
3. *Be brief.* Without advance preparation, the speaker cannot treat a subject thoroughly.
4. *Try to organize the ideas you wish to present.* Develop an introduction, body, and conclusion.

Combining Methods of Delivery

Skillful speakers usually use more than one method of delivery within a speech. The speaker may follow notes for portions of the speech and then, responding to the reactions of the listeners, may insert completely impromptu remarks. The speaker may memorize parts of the speech that need to be presented in a particular way or may rely on a manuscript for portions of the speech. Political campaigners often are adept at combining several methods of delivery. They frequently deliver most of a speech extemporaneously because of the natural conversational quality of that method, but may interject impromptu material in response to the audience's reactions; they may recall from memory portions of the speech they have delivered several times before; and they may read from manuscript passages on which they do not want to be misunderstood or misquoted.

PRINCIPLES OF EFFECTIVE NONVERBAL COMMUNICATION

The concept of delivery embraces both visible and audible elements. The visible aspects of delivery include appearance, posture, movement, gestures, facial expression, and eye contact of the speaker. Neglect of the physical aspects of delivery can be damaging, for what the audience sees may influence them as much as what they hear.

At this point, it should be stressed that no single manner of delivery is best. One need list only a few recent prominent speakers to illustrate the wide disparity in delivery among effective orators. The speeches of Billy Graham and Jesse Jackson might be described as dynamic and forceful; Dick Cavett and Barbara Walters would probably be called suave and sophisticated; Jimmy Carter and Gerald Ford might be described as calm and restrained; Johnny Carson and Ronald Reagan would be classified as conversational; Howard Cosell and Jeane Kirkpatrick could be described as aggressive; Dan Rather and Phil Donahue could be called direct; whereas David Letterman's delivery might be characterized as understated tongue-in-cheek. Yet all these speakers have demonstrated an ability to influence listeners. Since no one manner of presentation is superior to others, student speakers should avoid copying the delivery of someone else and instead strive to develop a manner of presentation suited their own personality and temperament.

In developing good delivery, the beginning speaker should be aware that effective nonverbal communication is characterized by four qualities: (1) it is unobtrusive, (2) it reinforces the speaker's idea, (3) it appears natural and spontaneous, and (4) it is appropriate to the audience and occasion.

Unobtrusiveness

A speaker's nonverbal communication should never distract the listeners. If the speaker is to obtain a specific response, this purpose can be achieved only if the listener's attention is focused on what the speaker is saying. Whenever the listeners start paying attention to a speaker's gestures, movements, appearance, or some other aspect of physical delivery, they no longer are concentrating on the subject. Flamboyant dress, eccentric gestures, peculiar mannerisms, constant pacing, fidgeting with notes or adjusting clothing, scratching, and similar physical activities are likely to distract the listeners from what is being said.

Reinforcement of Ideas

Good nonverbal communication should reinforce the speaker's ideas. It is not enough to eliminate distracting action. Effective nonverbal communication should actually contribute to communicativeness. If the subject is serious, the speaker's posture, gestures, and countenance should add to the impression of seriousness. When relating an exciting experience, the speaker should appear enthusiastic; when telling a humorous story, the speaker should seem relaxed and at ease; and when praising the auditors, the speaker's stance, expression, and appearance should reflect honesty and sincerity.

Naturalness

Effective nonverbal communication appears natural and unplanned. Ideally the speaker's physical activity will be spontaneous, arising from a desire to communicate, enthusiasm for the topic, and a positive response to the audience and occasion. However, in actuality this is often not the case. The speaker may be tired, self-conscious, uninspired, and not inclined to gesture, move about, or react physically. Under such circumstances, the speaker may find it necessary to simulate interest, to force him or herself to incorporate gestures, movement, and facial expression, and to feign enthusiasm. If this is necessary, the speaker should try to avoid appearing artificial, forced, or rehearsed. It probably is better for the speaker to employ no gestures or movement than to engage in physical activity that calls attention to itself. However, often a speaker who begins by forcing gestures and an appearance of interest will find that physical activity will begin to occur spontaneously as the speech progresses.

Occasionally speakers develop idiosyncratic mannerisms, unusual facial expressions, gestures, and awkward movements that, although natural to them, appear strange to the listeners. Should this occur, the speaker will need to make a conscious effort to avoid the distracting mannerism.

Appropriateness

Effective speakers always adapt their delivery to the occasion. A small audience in relaxed, informal surroundings dictates a quiet, restrained delivery; the requirements of addressing 1000 people in a large auditorium differ significantly from those of talking to a small group. The occasion, too, may suggest modifications in one's nonverbal communication. A television speech, which in fact is a talk to small groups of people, an address to a rally where the audience expects to be aroused, a classroom lecture where the listeners are accustomed to a dignified presentation, and an after-dinner talk where the audience may be lethargic after consuming a meal are situations that demand different kinds of physical activity.

SPECIFIC ELEMENTS OF NONVERBAL COMMUNICATION

While the four general principles discussed above—unobtrusiveness, reinforcement of ideas, naturalness, and appropriateness—should aid speakers in achieving effective nonverbal communication, some specific techniques that at times cause problems for beginning speakers are discussed below in detail.

Much of delivery is the natural and unconscious bodily expression of the emotions.

PHILODEMUS

Appearance

A speaker's appearance can affect the effectiveness of a speech. Although little can be done to alter the features one is born with, speakers should present themselves in the best possible light. A simple rule of thumb is: speakers should be groomed and dressed in a manner suitable to the audience and the occasion. Their appearance should in no way distract the audience. The cocktail gown may be the height of fashion, the plaid vest may be a hit at the racetrack, and the miniskirt may be provocative, but these may be inappropriate to many speaking situations. In other situations, jogging clothes, shorts, dirty jeans, and sneakers might be unacceptable. The speaker should remember that every moment spent in admiration, awe, shock, or disgust because of the speaker's appearance is time when the listener is not giving full attention to what is being said. While people have the right to dress in any way they wish, speakers should be aware that extremes in clothing and grooming not only distract but may actually alienate some auditors.

Right or wrong, many people do react negatively to speakers on the basis of unconventional dress and grooming. Conversely, a conservatively dressed and groomed speaker might be handicapped in influencing listeners with more unconventional tastes. Prejudice against speakers who dress unconventionally is not new. In the nineteenth century, British statesman Benjamin Disraeli was criticized for his flamboyant dress and hairstyle, as was Oscar Wilde during an American lecture tour.

Each speaker must decide whether individuality in dress and grooming is more important than a possible negative effect on the audience. However, it would seem sensible in most situations to accommodate one's appearance to the audience's expectations. Samuel Butler's observation might serve as a rule of thumb: "The more unpopular an opinion is, the more necessary is it that the holder should be somewhat punctilious in his observance of conventionalities generally."

The Speaker's Approach and Departure

The approach to the platform, podium, or stand is important, for at that time the audience forms its first impression of the speaker. If one appears bored or indifferent, seems frightened, has difficulty in locating notes or assembling materials before proceeding to the platform, one probably will make a poor initial impression. To make sure that the audience is ready to listen, the speaker should not begin the speech until the speaker's stand is reached. The speaker should not stop to greet friends, shake hands, or otherwise delay approaching the lectern. Upon arriving at the stand, the speaker should pause for a moment, survey notes or materials, mentally review the opening remarks, and then, when the audience is quiet and prepared to listen, begin.

Upon completing the speech, the speaker should pause before leaving the platform. If notes, books, visual aids, or other materials were used, the speaker should not begin to gather up these items until the entire speech is completed.

Speaking Position

The physical arrangement of the auditorium stage, platform, or dais may determine where a speaker must stand. Given a choice, the speaker should select a position that enables the speaker and audience to see each other with the least difficulty.

To establish close rapport with the audience, speakers should avoid elevating themselves and should place as few barriers as possible between themselves and their audience. Although there may be occasions when speakers actually wish to create such distance, in most instances they will probably seek to establish the closest possible rapport by speaking from a position on level with their listeners and with few if any barriers between them.

Posture

While delivering the speech, a speaker's posture should be erect but at ease—neither rigid and tense nor slovenly or ill at ease.

Beginning speakers sometimes wonder what they should do with their hands. They may have been told "Don't put your hands in your pockets," "Don't clasp your hands behind your back," or "Don't fold your hands in front of you." Although generally good advice, students should not be overly concerned with the placement of their hands.

Speakers should be physically comfortable enough in front of an audience to be able to concentrate on what they have to say. Hands in pockets or clasped behind one's back may inhibit gestures and an appearance of spontaneity, but there is nothing "wrong" with these gestures. However, the speaker should be careful not to distract listeners by jingling pocketed keys or coins.

Occasionally a speaker is required to address listeners from a sitting position, such as in a roundtable discussion or a television interview. Under such circumstances, the speaker's posture should be erect, but not stiff.

Some speakers, especially in the classroom, like to talk while seated on the edge of a desk. While this practice lends greater informality to the occasion, it probably should be discouraged in most instances, for the audience is better able to see a speaker who stands, and a speaker is more likely to achieve a dynamic, energetic presentation if he or she is not too relaxed.

Movement

In most situations, speakers should move freely about the platform. Movement not only relaxes a speaker but may also contribute to the audience's interest.

The speaker's movement should not interfere with communication. Constant pacing can distract; noisy walking on a creaky platform can make it difficult for listeners to hear; abrupt or meaningless movement can confuse an audience. Under certain circumstances, movement is virtually prohibited. If the speaker is using a public address system, any movement away from the microphone may result in inaudibility.

Gestures

When interested or excited by what they are talking about, most people "talk with their hands"—they reinforce what they are saying with spontaneous gestures. Gesturing when speaking is normal and natural.

However, inexperienced speakers sometimes are self-conscious about gesturing. Each hand seems to weigh 50 pounds, and the speaker feels that lifting a finger will cause every eye in the audience to focus on it. To overcome this self-consciousness, speakers may have to *force* themselves to include a few gestures early in the speech. For example, a speaker might raise two fingers while saying, "My second reason . . .", point to some object, or use both hands to describe the size or shape of something. These planned gestures may help the speaker to relax, overcome self-consciousness, and begin to gesture spontaneously. The speaker who is deeply immersed in communicating with the audience will not be concerned with gestures. They will occur naturally and spontaneously. Speakers should also strive for variety in gestures. One or two gestures used too often can distract the audience.

A university president gestures expressively in reinforcing his ideas. (Drake Hokanson, the *Spectator*)

Use of Notes

The way in which a speaker prepares and uses notes or a manuscript can greatly influence the effectiveness of the delivery. While it is not necessary to pretend that notes or a manuscript are not being followed, they should be used unobtrusively. So as not to attract undue attention, the notes should be legible and easy to handle. The speaker should be able to perceive at a glance what comes next. Copy should be clear, large enough to be easily read, and arranged in proper order. For a manuscript speech, typewritten copy double- or triple-spaced on one side of each sheet is preferable to a longhand draft. If speaking extemporaneously, the speaker should type or write the outline or notes on small cards that are unobtrusive, easy to handle, and enable the speaker to gesture while holding them.

Use of the Speaker's Stand

A speaker's stand or lectern often can be more of a handicap than a help to beginning speakers. While a lectern is useful for holding a manuscript, visual aids, or reference works, too many speech students use it as a crutch to lean upon or a place to hide. It seems to invite lounging and poor posture. Some speakers grasp it so tightly that they fail to gesture once during an entire speech. Others employ gestures that are hidden from the view of the audience by the lectern. Speakers who might normally move about on the platform stand rooted behind it and, if absolutely forced to move away to use a blackboard or visual aid, promptly scurry back as if it were home base. Short speakers remain almost completely hidden behind it, and lanky speakers stoop over it, straining to see their notes. Speakers fondle it, cradle it, embrace it, play with it, lean on it, entwine their legs around it, and do almost everything but leave it alone. Some speakers become so dependent upon it that if confronted with a speaking situation in which a lectern is not available, they are unable to speak.

If a lectern is actually *needed*—for example, to hold a manuscript or other materials a speaker may need—it should by all means be used. If there is no real need for a speaker's stand, a speaker should learn to do without one.

Eye Contact

"Look me in the eye and say that" is a familiar expression used in determining whether another person is telling the truth; it implies that dishonest speakers are "shifty-eyed." While many speakers who are unable to look the other person in the eye are undoubtedly honest and sincere, most listeners place greater confidence in someone who looks at them directly and steadily. Direct eye contact is also important because it enables a speaker to observe the listeners, gauge their reaction, and adapt to their response.

To achieve and maintain good eye contact, a speaker should look directly

A prominent educator's gestures, facial expression, and eye contact reinforce his message. (Menschel, *Christian Science Monitor*)

at the audience—not over the tops of their heads, not out the window, not at the ceiling or the floor. A speaker who stares out a window or at a corner of the room is likely to so arouse the curiosity of the listeners that they may turn around to discover what has caught the speaker's interest. Obviously such behavior interferes with effective communication. The speaker should also avoid directing eye contact to a single segment of the audience throughout the speech. The speaker's goal, although physically impossible, should be to look at all of the audience all the time.

Facial Expression

The speaker's facial expression is important. To be effective, the speaker's countenance should be consistent with and reinforce those ideas and emotions they seek to convey. Speakers who smile while relating the grim details of a fatal automobile accident, remain calm when describing the winning play in a thrilling football game, or frown while describing an enjoyable vacation trip are almost certain to diminish listener interest; inappropriate facial expression will support insincerity or deception.

A fault of many beginning speakers is their almost complete impassivity in delivering a speech. From beginning to end, their facial expression betrays not the tiniest glimmer of feeling: the speaker never smiles, frowns, appears

No phrase can convey the idea of surprise so vividly as opening the eyes and raising the eyebrows. A shrug of the shoulders would lose much by translation into words.

HERBERT SPENCER

excited, or shows concern. The entire speech is delivered as if the assignment were the most boring type of drudgery. Such behavior may result from nervousness, a poor choice of topic, or lack of interest on the part of the speaker. Whatever the explanation, speeches delivered in this manner are never successful. To overcome a monotonous presentation, a speaker must control nervousness, develop a desire to communicate, select a subject of deep interest, and become personally involved in the speech.

This speaker's facial expression clearly indicates that he is interested in the response of his young listener. (Wide World)

VISUAL AIDS

Another aspect of delivery the speaker should consider is the use of visual aids. A wide variety of visual materials—including charts, graphs, maps, drawings, paintings, blackboard sketches, models, photographs, slides, and motion pictures—is available to a speaker in preparing and presenting his or her message.

Visual aids are not only often helpful in communicating an idea to the audience but at times may be almost essential to an effective presentation. For example, a speaker who relies on words alone may experience difficulty in describing the operation of a machine, the geography of an unfamiliar place, or a statistical trend; yet, in each instance, the information could be presented clearly by using a model, map, or graph.

Visual aids can be particularly helpful in presenting statistical information. Take, for example, the challenge of trying to explain a complicated state budget to almost any audience, no matter how well-informed. How many dollars are allocated to education, highways, social services, welfare, law enforcement, salaries, and other functions? A long list of statistics indicating how much is to be spent in each area will only confuse most listeners. However, a simple pie chart can easily clarify the division of funds by showing the size of the cut for each service.

Bar graphs are particularly useful in presenting statistical comparisons—between different years, countries, states, companies, groups, and other units. A line graph can clarify trends, fluctuations, increases, and declines in areas such as crime, unemployment, population, and cost of living in a way that words alone cannot.

Anyone who has ever had to ask for directions in a strange place knows how helpful a map—a visual guide—can be in learning how to reach one's destination. Newspapers and television newscasts regularly utilize maps to show the location of unfamiliar sites where newsworthy events are occurring. For example, the media rightly realize that the average person may have little knowledge of the locations of major news events—hurricanes, plane crashes, earthquakes—and rely on maps to convey this information.

Visual aids are almost essential in discussing subjects that are largely visual, such as art, design, photography, and architecture. It is difficult to imagine how a speaker could meaningfully discuss Picasso's paintings, Stonehenge, Cecil Beaton's photographs, and Rodin's sculptures without visual materials.

While visual aids often make it easier for an audience to grasp an idea, they are not always helpful. In deciding whether to employ visual aids, a speaker should ask: Do I need a visual aid? Can I effectively display it? Will it develop my subject without detracting from the speech? Each question is important. In determining whether to use a visual aid, the speaker should recognize that visual aids contribute very little to the development of some topics. If a speaker does not truly need a visual aid to clarify an idea, one

FIGURE 10.1   Various kinds of graphs.

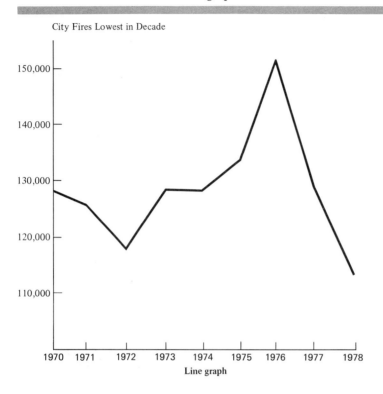

City Fires Lowest in Decade

Line graph

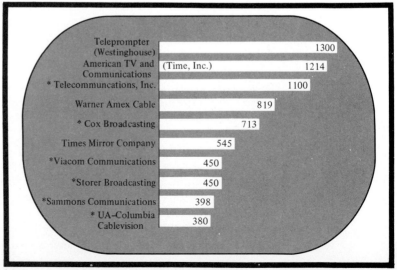

Top Ten Cable TV System Operators
Number of subscribers, in thousands, as of October 10, 1980; parent company,
if any, in parentheses

* Indicates potential merger candidate

Source (subscriber data only): Paul Kagan Associates

Bar graph

Various kinds of graphs.

Ethnicity

Where the Immigrants Have Come From
(1957 to 1977)

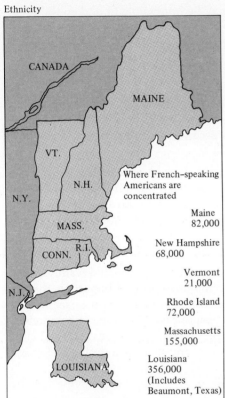

Where French–speaking
Americans are
concentrated

Maine
82,000

New Hampshire
68,000

Vermont
21,000

Rhode Island
72,000

Massachusetts
155,000

Louisiana
356,000
(Includes
Beaumont, Texas)

Visual aid map

Graph with shading

Federal power distribution

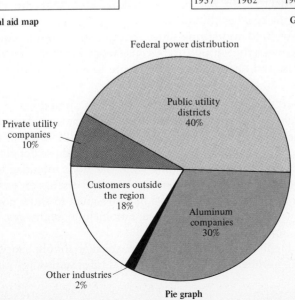

Pie graph

should not be employed. Second, the speaker must consider whether the circumstances will permit the effective use of visual aids. For example, the audience may be too large to see the visual aid; electric outlets for a slide projector may not be available; or it may be impossible to darken the room. Finally, a speaker must make certain that the visual aid will not prove so fascinating that the audience will be more interested in it than in the speech.

Preparation of Visual Aids

Assuming a visual aid is needed, that it can be effectively displayed, and that it will not detract from the speech, the speaker is now ready to begin its preparation. An effective visual aid is accurate, legible, clear, and simple.

ACCURACY.   An inaccurate visual aid serves no useful purpose, for it merely misleads. The careful speaker will make certain that the data are current; that the chart, map, or diagram contains no errors; that the model operates properly; that parts are properly identified; and that names and labels are spelled correctly.

LEGIBILITY.   A visual aid that cannot be easily seen and readily understood contributes little to effective communication. It is important that the visual aid be *easily* seen and read; if the listeners must strain to see the aid, they will quickly tire of the effort. To ensure easy viewing and comprehension by the audience, the speaker should make certain that the visual aid is large enough, that all labels are of good size, and that the lettering is clear and can be read easily.

CLARITY.   In addition to making sure that the visual aid is large enough, the speaker should strive for clarity. Clarity can be achieved through the use of bold and strong lines, shading, and contrasting colors. Adequate space between the various parts, consistency in the size and type of print used for labels, and neatness also contribute to a clear and effective visual aid.

SIMPLICITY.   Inexperienced speakers sometimes mistakenly assume that visual aids must be completely self-explanatory, forgetting that they will have the opportunity—indeed, the obligation—to explain the visual materials. A good visual aid is simple. It includes only those details that are pertinent and necessary for understanding what the aid is intended to show. Inclusion of information the speaker does not intend to discuss only clutters the aid and may confuse the listener. Thus a map designed to show population distribution in the United States should not include highways, rivers, mountain ranges, and similar irrelevant details.

To facilitate comprehension, the speaker should simplify visual aids by rounding numbers, relegating incidental information to "miscellaneous" categories, and omitting unimportant details. The aim, of course, is not to distort the facts through omission of information but to direct the audience's attention to the important aspects of the subject.

Speakers should also avoid complicating their visual aids with too many labels. Since the speaker has the opportunity to explain the visual aid, it may not be necessary to label all its parts.

Use of Visual Aids

Fully as important as the preparation of a visual aid is the use of it during the speech. In planning the speech, the speaker should decide when to introduce a visual aid, where to place it, how to use it, and how to handle notes or manuscript while referring to the aid.

If presented at the wrong time, a visual aid can interfere with the development of a topic. If a speaker displays a visual aid before beginning the speech, the audience may be more interested in it than the speech. If the speaker distributes visual aids in advance, the audience is likely to spend several minutes studying the visual aid before they begin paying attention to the speaker. If a single visual aid is circulated, the speaker's difficulties are even greater, for at any moment some member of the audience is examining the visual aid rather than listening to the speaker.

To prevent such interference, the speaker should determine exactly when the audience should see the visual aid and keep it out of sight until then. If materials are to be passed out, the speaker should determine exactly when to place them in the listeners' hands and arrange efficient distribution at the proper moment.

The speaker must also determine where to place a visual aid. Well in advance of the speech, the speaker should investigate the availability of easels, flannel boards, blackboards, screens, projectors, and any other equipment necessary for the display of visual material.

Assured that the necessary equipment is available, the speaker still must determine such things as whether to hold the visual aid or place it on an easel, where to place the easel or screen so that the audience can see it, who will operate the projector, when and how the room will be darkened, and similar related items.

After deciding when and where to display the visual aid, the speaker should next plan how to use it. The speaker should not forgetfully block the audience's view by standing in front of it, lose contact with the audience by turning away in order to see the material, or repeatedly obstruct the audience's view while pointing to various parts of it.

Finally, the speaker should anticipate any problems that may arise because of the visual aid. For example, if colored slides are to be shown, the room will have to be darkened, which will deprive the speaker of the light needed to see notes or manuscript. If a model or object is employed, the speaker may have to move away from the lectern or use both hands, which will also preclude the use of notes. If the visual aid must be held, it will be difficult to handle simultaneously a set of note cards or a manuscript. For a speaker who plans to hold a visual aid, one solution may be to write the notes on the reverse side of the aid.

SUMMARY

Speech delivery refers to *how* the speech is presented as opposed to *what* is presented (content). Delivery consists of the speaker's vocal and physical activity.

Four methods of speech presentation are manuscript, memory, extemporaneous, and impromptu. Each has advantages and disadvantages. The method the speaker chooses for a particular speech will depend on the nature of the speech, the audience, and the occasion. Probably the most widely used is the extemporaneous method, in which the speaker carefully prepares a talk and then delivers it from a few notes or a brief outline.

What the audience sees, as well as what it hears, is important in determining its response to a speech. Among the physical factors of delivery that may influence the listeners' reception of a speech are the speaker's appearance, manner of approaching and departing from the podium, posture, movement, gestures, handling of notes, use of the lectern, eye contact, and facial expression.

The speaker's physical characteristics should never distract the listener. Good nonverbal communication reinforces the speaker's ideas, appears natural and spontaneous, and is appropriate to the audience and the occasion.

Speakers who use visual aids such as charts, maps, diagrams, models, and slides should give careful attention to their preparation and display. Visual aids should always be accurate, legible, clear, and simple. They should not dominate the speech or detract from any portion of it but should supplement the speaker's oral presentation at the appropriate time in the speech.

STUDY QUESTIONS

1. How does the content of a speech differ from its delivery? Which is more important to effective communication?
2. Cite a speech that *you* might be required to give where you would want to use a manuscript; a memorized speech; the extemporaneous method.
3. How do the physical attributes of delivery differ from the vocal attributes? Which, in your opinion, are more important?
4. How much movement should speakers permit themselves when giving a speech? Under what circumstances could movement detract from a speech? Cite a speaker whose movement impaired effectiveness.
5. Of what value are gestures while speaking? Can a speech have too many gestures? Can a speech without gestures be effective? As effective as with gestures?
6. Why do you think television announcers always look straight at the screen? What relevance does this practice have to effective public speaking?

7. When should a speaker employ visual aids? How might a visual aid detract from a speech?

EXERCISES

1. Attend in person (not via radio or television) a speech, sermon, lecture, or debate and note the physical aspects of the speaker's delivery. Prepare a 3- to 4-minute oral report analyzing the strong and weak points of his or her nonverbal communication. Present the report in class.
2. Observe the actions of someone you might describe as a character type. Present a 2-minute pantomime of the behavior of this person, working out as much specific action or "business" as possible. In your pantomime give careful attention to the subject's age, size, physical characteristics, personality, and mannerisms.
3. Prepare a 3- to 4-minute informative speech in which you demonstrate some physical activity (for example, artificial respiration, driving signals, bowling, a golf stroke, fly casting, archery, a dance step).
4. Prepare a 4-minute speech in which you employ at least two different kinds of visual aids. Give careful attention to their preparation and presentation.
5. In a 2-minute oral report, demonstrate two or three physical characteristics of delivery you find particularly distracting or annoying when used by speakers.

FURTHER READINGS

Ehninger, Douglas, Bruce E. Gronbeck, Ray E. McKerrow, and Alan Monroe, *Principles and Types of Speech Communication,* 10th ed. (Glenview, IL: Scott, Foresman, 1986), chap. 13, "Using Visual Aids in a Speech," and chap. 14, "Using Your Voice and Body to Communicate."

Lucas, Stephen E., *The Art of Public Speaking* (New York: Random House, 1986), chap. 11, "Delivery," and chap. 12, "Using Visual Aids."

Minnick, Wayne C., *Public Speaking* (Boston: Houghton Mifflin, 1979), 127–133.

Mudd, Charles S., and Malcolm O. Sillars, *Speech: Content and Communication* (New York: Crowell, 1975), chap. 13, "Delivery."

Taylor, Anita, *Speaking in Public* (Englewood Cliffs, NJ: Prentice-Hall, 1979), 159–168.

Verderber, Rudolph F., *The Challenge of Effective Speaking,* 6th ed. (Belmont, CA: Wadsworth, 1985), chap. 8, "Using Visual Aids."

Zannes, Estelle, and Gerald Goldhaber, *Stand Up, Speak Out,* 2d ed. (Reading, MA: Addison-Wesley, 1983), chap. 8, "Delivering the Message."

CHAPTER 11

DELIVERY: VOICE USAGE

The way speakers use their voices may make the difference between a lack-luster performance and an effective address. During one presidential campaign, Franklin D. Roosevelt evoked a roar of approval from the crowd simply because of the enthusiastic way he announced, "I've had a wonderful day in New England." His opponent, Wendell Wilkie, strained his voice so badly that he was barely able to speak for much of the campaign. A problem John F. Kennedy had to overcome was that he spoke so rapidly listeners often had difficulty following him. Other speakers—including Jimmy Carter and Lyndon B. Johnson—found their regional accents a handicap in speaking to some audiences. The vocal characteristics of William F. Buckley and Howard Cosell prove distracting to many. These are a few examples of speakers whose vocal attributes, at least at times, have greatly influenced their effectiveness. Almost everyone probably can recall similar examples among less well known speakers.

The vocal or audible elements of delivery are what the auditor hears. The voice quality, pitch, rate, volume, articulation, and pronunciation of the speaker affect the auditor's reaction to the message. If the speaker's delivery is marred by too rapid a rate, inadequate volume, distracting voice quality, confusing pitch inflection, sloppy articulation, mispronunciation, or other faults, the listener may find it difficult to grasp the message. To prevent this, speakers should give careful attention to the vocal attributes of delivery.

Vocal delivery is effective if it aids in the realization of six main goals:

1. *The speaker's vocal attributes should help the audience understand what the speaker is saying.* The volume should be loud enough and the rate slow enough to enable the listeners to hear without difficulty. Words should be clearly articulated and properly pronounced so that they are readily recognizable.

2. *The vocal characteristics should create interest in the speaker's message.* A monotonous pitch, lack of emphasis, or a too slow rate will prove to be boring with most audiences. A good speaker will use variety to create a high level of interest.

3. *The speaker's vocal usage should reinforce the ideas.* The manner of speaking should contribute to the mood the speaker seeks to create—serious, light-hearted, exciting, or inspiring.

4. *The speaker should sound natural and spontaneous,* not artificial, stilted, or rehearsed.

5. *The speaker's voice usage should be suited to the audience, medium, and the occasion.* An address by radio or television, for example, differs significantly from a speech to a live audience. Although the auditors for a broadcast talk could number in the millions, the speaker is really talking to many small groups of three or four persons seated in their homes and not to a multitude. Conscious of this difference, the speaker will modify volume, rate, emphasis, and voice quality accordingly.

6. *The speaker's vocal presentation should not distract the listener.* It should be free of anything that calls attention to itself, such as errors in pronunciation, too many vocalized pauses, voice breaks, articulation errors, and a too rapid or too slow rate of speaking.

In a telephone conversation, a speaker must rely solely on the vocal attributes of delivery to convey ideas. (Beth Shore, LSU Publications)

With these goals in mind, let us examine several specific aspects of voice usage.

VOLUME

Volume is the loudness or softness of the speaker's voice. Speech begins with exhalation of air from the lungs. The speaker's volume is determined by the amount of air supporting the sound production. The greater the quantity of

> Words were given us to communicate our ideas by; and there must be something inconceivably absurd in uttering them in such a manner as that either people cannot understand them or will not desire to understand them.
>
> LORD CHESTERFIELD

air supporting a sound, the louder it will be; the less the amount of air support, the fainter it will be.

Among beginning speakers, the most common difficulties are insufficient volume and lack of flexibility. The speaker who cannot be heard is simply wasting the listeners' time. Communication is a two-way process; if the other party cannot hear what the speaker says, no communication can take place.

A speaker who talks with little variation in loudness, in addition to being monotonous, gives the impression that everything is of equal importance. The monotony and lack of emphasis may confuse the listener.

Other problems of volume include speaking too loudly, improper emphasis, and patterns (such as beginning each sentence strongly and fading away at the end).

To achieve effective volume control, the speaker should:

1. *Maintain an adequate supply of air.* To do this, one must learn to breathe deeply and to control exhalation. Adequate breath support can be maintained through either abdominal or thoracic breathing. However, speakers whose breathing is shallow will find that they are almost constantly short of breath.

2. *Adapt volume to the size of the room and the number of listeners.* No communication will take place if the listener cannot hear or tires of trying to hear and stops listening. But speakers should also take care not to speak too loudly. Few things are more irritating than a speaker who shouts at a small group as if addressing a multitude at Madison Square Garden.

3. *Speak loudly enough to overcome distracting noises.* The hum of an air conditioner, the noise of outside traffic, or simply the shuffling of feet in the audience can make it difficult to hear, either momentarily or for a prolonged period of time. A speaker needs to be alert to competing sounds and compensate for them.

4. *Vary volume to maintain interest.* The speaker can stress important words, phrases, and sentences by varying volume. At times, something may be emphasized by saying it with additional volume. Other times, contrast can be achieved by speaking more softly. Some speakers habitually begin each sentence with considerable volume and then "run down," fading away at the end, which is distracting.

5. *Discover and eliminate the causes of persistent problems with loudness.* Failure to achieve proper volume and emphasis at times may be because the speaker has

a hearing problem or may be speaking in a pitch range that strains the voice and precludes greater volume. In other instances, the speaker's problem may not be related at all to sound production but simply be a problem of shyness or insecurity. Whatever the reason, if problems of loudness persist, the speaker should ask the instructor for advice in an effort to discover the causes of the difficulty.

PITCH

Pitch refers to the highness or lowness of the speaker's voice and inflections. Pitch originates with the vibration of the vocal folds. As a speaker exhales air, it passes through the throat (pharynx) to the vocal folds. The vocal folds, located in the larynx, just behind the cricoid cartilage (commonly known as the Adam's apple), can best be described as two "blobs" of muscle. *Blobs* is used here because the appearance of the vocal folds almost defies description; and it is important to realize that, contrary to the implication of the term vocal "cords," the vocal folds are not taut bands.

As the air from the lungs reaches the vocal folds, the speaker must tense them to produce a sound. As the air passes over the tensed folds of muscle, they vibrate and sound is formed. The degree of tension of the vocal folds as they vibrate determines the speaker's pitch: the greater the tension, the higher the pitch; the more relaxed the vocal folds, the lower the pitch.

The most common pitch problems among beginning speakers are use of a pitch range that strains the voice, use of a pitch level inconsistent with the audience's expectations of the speaker, and lack of variation in inflection. To achieve effective pitch usage, the speaker should:

1. *Discover and speak in the pitch range best suited to his or her voice.* Everyone has an optimum pitch level, or a range of tones best suited to that individual's voice. People who habitually speak in a range above or below their optimum pitch level are likely to strain their voices, have difficulty being heard, and develop a hoarse or raspy voice quality.

A speaker may speak at an unsuitable pitch level for physical or psychological reasons. A protracted illness—bronchitis, laryngitis, or some other disability—that interferes when most youth's voices change may interfere with normal change.

A more common cause for the use of an unsuitable pitch is a conscious or subconscious imitation of some admired person. Children and adolescents model their speech after those they most respect—parents, a teacher, an athlete, or a prominent public figure. If the model's pitch level is unsuitable to the individual's vocal mechanism, the speaker's pitch level can severely strain the voice.

Feelings of insecurity may lead to improper pitch usage. The speaker who fears the responsibilities of adulthood may be reluctant to "cut the apron strings." To maintain the parent-child relationship, the individual speaks with a high-pitched "little girl" or "little boy" voice.

To determine one's optimum pitch level, a speaker should sing from the lowest pitch possible to the highest pitch reachable with a falsetto voice, count the number of full-step tones in the entire range of voice, divide by three, and then count up from the lowest pitch one-third of the total range. This is the optimum pitch. Speakers, of course, should not use only that tone, but most normal speaking should center on pitches in the general vicinity of this note.

2. *Speak in a pitch range that does not distract the listeners.* Occasionally a speaker will find that his or her optimum pitch level, while comfortable and natural, disturbs the auditors. The big, rugged-looking man whose optimum pitch level happens to be high may sound effeminate to listeners who expect a deeper, more masculine voice; the small, demure woman whose optimum pitch is much lower than that of most women may also be distracting. In such instances, the speaker may wish to try to adjust to the audience's expectations.

3. *Avoid monotony in pitch.* Few speakers are more boring than the one who speaks at the same pitch throughout a speech. Monotonous speakers are often the victim of their own lack of interest. They simply do not care enough about the subject to make it interesting. At other times, monotony in pitch is caused by overdependence on a manuscript by a speaker who cannot read well or on memorization by a speaker who cannot recite effectively. At times, monotony may result from tone deafness or a hearing impairment.

To overcome these handicaps, speakers should choose topics which they are interested in and eager to discuss. To determine whether one is speaking with enough variation in pitch, it is helpful from time to time to record a speech and listen to it. If the speech is monotonous, the speaker should experiment with different methods of attaining variety of pitch—perhaps saying the same sentence in as many different ways as possible, imitating the pitch patterns of celebrities, or copying TV commercials to "loosen" voice usage. Speakers may also achieve greater flexibility by repeating a single sentence aloud with varying patterns of rising and falling inflections. For example, they might speak the following sentence in several different ways by following the arrows indicating rising and falling inflections:

The broad, ⟋ flat meadow was covered with daisies.

The broad, flat ⟍⟶ meadow was covered with daisies.

The broad, flat meadow ⟶ was covered with daisies.

The broad, flat meadow was covered ⟶ with daisies.

The broad, flat meadow was covered with daisies. ⟋

The broad ⟍⟶ , flat meadow was covered with daisies.

The broad, flat ⟶ meadow was covered with daisies.

The broad, flat meadow ⟍⟶ was covered with daisies.

The broad, flat meadow was covered⟍   with daisies.

The broad, flat meadow was covered with daisies.⟍⟶

The broad ⟋, flat meadow was covered ⟍with daisies.

The broad⟍, flat meadow ⟋ was covered ⟍with daisies.

Any simple sentence and any combination of variations in pitch can be used in the above exercise. The important factor is the speaker's ability to achieve variety in pitch by saying the sentence in different ways.

4. *Avoid distracting pitch patterns.* The speaker who varies pitch but does so in the same way throughout the speech is almost as boring as the speaker who never alters pitch. Repetitious inflections, or pitch patterns, are detrimental to effective communication. English is a complex language, capable of conveying an almost infinite number of ideas, depending on how it is used. An unvarying pitch pattern eliminates one of the principal means of indicating precisely what one wishes to say, for without meaningful inflection a whole range of nuances, shadings, and interpretations is lost.

VOICE QUALITY

Voice quality—or timbre—refers to the distinctive characteristics of one voice that distinguish it from all other voices. For example, when people answer the telephone, in spite of the low fidelity of that instrument, they often immediately recognize the voice they hear. What is familiar to the listener is not the speaker's pitch, volume, rate, articulation, or pronunciation, for thousands of other people say "hello" in almost the same way. The distinguishing feature is the speaker's voice quality. Each person's voice quality is unique, so much so that "voiceprints" are increasingly being accepted in courts as a means of identifying individuals.

A speaker's voice quality is the result of the resonance of the sound formed in the vocal folds. The sound produced by vibration of the vocal cords is not the same sound the listener hears, for following its production it travels through the upper larynx, mouth, and nose. As it passes through these cavities, it is resonated—altered and modified. The size, shape, and texture of the resonating cavities determine the sound the listener eventually hears.

Understanding voice quality and how it is determined may be helped by comparing it to the quality or timbre in musical instruments. If one were to ask a clarinetist, a trumpeter, and a violinist to play a note at the same volume for the same period of time for auditors who could not see the performer, most of the listeners could without difficulty identify the various instruments. The distinguishing characteristic would not be the pitch, duration, or loudness but the quality or timbre of the instrument. To carry the analogy a step further, the principal reason for the difference in the sound of the three instruments is the size, shape, and texture of the resonating cavities: in the clarinet it is a long wooden tube; in the trumpet, a circular brass tube; and

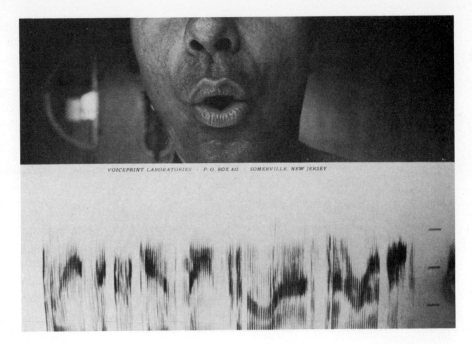

VOICEPRINT LABORATORIES · P. O. BOX 835 · SOMERVILLE, NEW JERSEY

A voiceprint. (Arms, Jeroboam)

in the violin, an unusually shaped wooden box. A modification of the size and shape of the resonating cavity (for example, the substitution of a viola for a violin or a French horn for a trumpet) would result in a change in the quality of the sound.

In much the same manner that the size, shape, and texture of the resonating cavities determine the timbre of a musical instrument, the size, shape, and texture of the mouth, nose, and larynx alter and modify the quality of the sound produced by the vocal cords. At this point, however, it should be pointed out that not all the sounds used in speech are produced by vocalization and resonation. All vowels require vocalization. Many speech sounds, however, are made without the use of the vocal folds. These include *t, p, k, f, s, sh, th, w,* and *wh.* The *t, p,* and *k* sounds are formed by building up a slight pressure of air and then "exploding" it. The *f, s, sh, th, w,* and *wh* sounds are produced by blowing breath over the tongue, teeth, and lips in various ways. If the vocal cords are vibrated while producing these sounds, with only slight modifications in the set of the mouth, tongue, teeth, and lips, *t* becomes *d, p* becomes *b, k* becomes *g, f* becomes *v, s* becomes *z, sh* becomes *z* (as in *azure*), and the silent *th* (as in *think*) becomes the voiced *th* (as in *those*). Voice quality is not influenced by the voiceless sounds. Only those sounds produced by vibration of the vocal folds contribute to the speaker's voice quality.

Although good vocal quality can be defined as a voice that is pleasant and easy to listen to, this definition is too vague to be very helpful. Good voice quality can best be defined by telling what it is *not:* it is a voice whose quality is *not* harsh, husky, hoarse, breathy, shrill, strident, or nasal.

The causes of poor voice quality are many. A permanent huskiness or hoarseness may be the result of a prolonged cold or laryngitis. Inadequate breath support may lead to a whispering or breathy quality. Enlarged adenoids may contribute to nasality. Prolonged use of an unsuitable pitch level may lead to harshness.

But the most common cause of poor voice quality is imitation, either conscious or subconscious. Some young people deliberately try to develop speaking voices similar to those of admired adults. At times the effort may strain the young person's voice and result in an unpleasant voice quality. Others, totally unaware of it, model their speech on persons whose voices are unpleasant. Thus a son may develop a strident voice similar to that of his father, or a daughter may speak with the nasal quality of her mother's voice.

The process of improving voice quality requires time and effort. One must hear, recognize, and try to get rid of an undesirable voice quality used for many years and then adopt and practice a new voice quality until it becomes natural and habitual.

To improve one's voice quality:

1. The speaker should learn to hear his or her voice as others hear it. An almost universal reaction of people hearing a recording of their voices for the first time is "That's not me. There must be something wrong with the recorder." But of course nothing is wrong with the recording, as friends will verify; the sound is a faithful reproduction of the individual's speech. Speakers often don't hear themselves as others do. They are so accustomed to hearing their own voices that they really do not carefully listen to themselves.

   The first step in learning to hear one's voice as others hear it is to record and listen to your speech and develop an awareness of how you sound.
2. To avoid strain, one should speak at a comfortable pitch level. For a discussion of how to determine optimum pitch level, see page 193.
3. The speaker should maintain adequate breath support.
4. The speaker should remain relaxed while speaking.
5. If strain or hoarseness occurs regularly, the speaker should consult a speech therapist.

RATE

Rate is the speed at which the speaker talks. It consists of the duration of individual sounds and syllables, pauses, fluency, and rhythm. A speaker's rate is determined primarily by the speed with which the tongue, teeth, and lips are manipulated to formulate sounds, syllables, and words. It is more, however, than mere physical rapidity, for a speaker's rate also depends on verbal facility and thought processes. If speakers lose their train of thought or cannot find the word they want, they will be forced to pause before continuing.

A desirable rate of speaking is one that is neither too fast to permit the hearer to grasp what the speaker says nor too slow to hold listeners' interest; it is varied, flexible, and free from awkward hesitancies, pauses, and nonfluencies.

Common problems of rate are speaking too rapidly and lack of variety and vocalized pauses. To achieve a good rate of speaking, you should:

1. *Know what you are talking about.* Speakers who are uncertain of their material are going to have difficulty presenting their ideas fluently, remembering what they want to say, and locating the right word.

2. *Practice aloud and often.* Only by actually saying a speech aloud in practice can the speaker locate sentences that are difficult to say, tongue-twisting phrases, and awkward constructions, nonfluencies, and vocalized pauses. Extensive oral practice helps speakers develop familiarity with their material so they can speak smoothly and meaningfully.

3. *Make sure that your rate is neither too fast nor too slow.* A good way for speakers to check on their rate is to record and listen to themselves during preparation or ask a friend to listen to them. Speakers who normally speak too rapidly because of nervousness should commence at a deliberately slow pace, because many speakers have a tendency to accelerate their rate as they progress. A slow start may discourage too rapid a rate.

4. *Vary the rate.* Speaking at the same speed throughout a speech detracts from the effectiveness of the speaker. In addition to being boring, speakers whose rate is monotonous convey the impression that everything is of equal importance—that no idea or statement is more important than another. Variations in rate add force, emphasis, and meaning to what one is saying.

5. *Avoid excessive vocalized pauses.* Some speakers are uncomfortable if every moment is not filled with a sound of some kind. So instead of pausing naturally, they fill each pause with "uh," "and uh," "er," "uhm," "okay," "you know," or some similar vocalization. An occasional vocalized pause is not distracting, but a speaker who fills almost every pause with a vocalization can distract the auditor.

ARTICULATION

Articulation is the process of forming sounds, syllables, and words. Articulation differs from pronunciation in that articulation is primarily a matter of skill or habit, whereas pronunciation is a matter of knowledge. For example, people who say *stastistics* instead of *statistics, jist* instead of *just,* or *git* instead of *get* are guilty of poor articulation, since they undoubtedly know that these words are not pronounced *stastistics, jist,* and *git,* but through carelessness or habit they nevertheless continue to say them incorrectly. On the other hand, people who pronounce the *s* in *Illinois* or say *revelant* for *relevant* probably do so because of lack of knowledge. They cculd say *Illinois* or *relevant,* but they do not know that they should. These mistakes are classed as pronunciation errors.

Good articulation is clear and correct without being overly precise or pedantic. It is clear in the sense that each sound is distinct and each word is easily recognized. It is correct in that words are free from addition, omission, substitution, and transposition of sounds. In improving articulation, a speaker needs to be familiar with four common errors:

1. *Addition of sounds.* This mistake occurs when a speaker adds to a word a sound that should not be included. An example would be *ath-a-lete* for *ath-lete.*
2. *Omission of sounds.* This error consists of omitting from a word a sound that should be included (e.g., *doin* for *doing, goverment* for *government*).
3. *Substitution of sounds.* This results from the speaker's substituting an incorrect sound for the correct one (e.g., *git* for *get, jist* for *just,* and *undoubtebly* for *undoubtedly*).
4. *Transposition of sounds.* This mistake occurs when the speaker inverts the order in which two sounds are uttered, saying the second sound first (e.g., *hunderd* for *hundred* and *modren* for *modern*).

The above examples are articulation errors rather than mistakes in pronunciation because in each instance, if given a choice between the two ways of saying the word (*jist* or *just, goverment* or *government,* etc.), the speaker would be able to identify the proper pronunciation. Nevertheless, through carelessness or habit, one might continue to say the word incorrectly.

Additional examples of common errors in articulation are found on page 199.

The causes of poor articulation are many. It may result from such physiological factors as a cleft palate, a malocclusion of the teeth, the spacing of the teeth, or other physical impairments. However, most articulation problems, rather than being caused by some physiological factor, are learned. If a child's speech model speaks carelessly and indistinctly or omits, distorts, or slurs certain sounds, the child is likely to develop the same articulation problems.

The speaker who is unable to make a particular sound needs the assistance of a speech correctionist, as does the speaker whose articulation is poor because of some physiological defect. However, others whose articulation is characterized by additions, omissions, and substitutions of sounds or by imprecision can improve their speech by following these suggestions:

1. *Develop a perceptive ear.* Many speakers whose articulation is unclear simply are poor listeners. They don't listen carefully to their own speech or

the speech of others. They not only are unaware of what sounds a word should contain but may fail to recognize their own faulty articulation of it. The first step in improving articulation is to become aware of the sounds each word contains.

2. *Isolate articulation errors.* Having become conscious of their own and others' articulation, speakers next must seek to detect the specific problems that mar their speech. They must look for words and sounds that cause them trouble and for evidence of general carelessness and indistinctness.

3. *Seek to break bad habits of articulation.* Having determined the nature of one's articulation difficulty, the speaker must learn to monitor his or her own speech in everyday conversation in order to detect and eliminate the articulation errors.

Common Articulation Errors

	Word	Misarticulation
Additions	idea	idea*r*
	athlete, athletic	ath-*a*-lete, ath-*a*-letic
	statistics	sta*s*tistics
Omissions	film	fim
	help	hep
	self	sef
	government	goverment, govement
	doing, coming	doin, comin
	going, nothing	goin, nothin
	seeing, morning	seein, mornin
	Europe	Eurpe
Substitutions	any, many	*i*nny, m*i*nny
	undoubtedly	undoubte*b*ly
	just	j*i*st
	want	w*o*nt
	get	g*i*t
	gone	go*a*n
	can't	ca*i*n't
	Massachusetts	Massa*t*usetts
	Baptist	Ba*bd*ist
	escape	e*x*cape
	ask, asked	a*x*, a*x*ed
Transposition	hundred	hund*er*d
	children	child*er*n
	modern	mod*re*n
	nuclear	nu*cu*lar

4. *Substitute new habits of good articulation.* In addition to being conscious of personal mistakes, the speaker should make a deliberate effort to incorporate new, correct articulation into daily speech.

PRONUNCIATION

Pronunciation is knowing how a word should be said. Unlike an articulation error, which occurs because of carelessness or inability to say the word properly, a mistake in pronunciation is the result of a lack of knowledge of the accepted way of saying the word.

Speakers who mispronounce words usually do so because the word is new and unfamiliar, because it resembles another word with which they are familiar, or because they have frequently heard it mispronounced. For example, someone who has come across the word *predaceous* many times in reading might be well acquainted with its meaning yet, never having heard it spoken, may pronounce the word incorrectly. Another speaker may mispronounce the word *relevant* as *revelant* because it resembles *revelry* or *reverent.* Or a speaker who has regularly heard *Italian* pronounced *Eye-talian* may adopt this incorrect pronunciation.

In seeking the accepted pronunciation of a word, a speaker's first recourse should be an up-to-date standard dictionary. The dictionary will provide a guide to which sounds are silent, how the vowels should be pronounced, and what syllables should be stressed. The dictionary, however, usually will not reveal accepted regional variations. Most dictionaries indicate only acceptable general American pronunciation. Even dictionaries that include regional variations may be of little help, for speakers in different regions of the country often pronounce the same sound in different ways. For example, many southern speakers tend to prolong or diphthongize several vowel sounds. Thus a southern speaker consulting the dictionary to determine the correct pronunciation of a word such as *fate* would see that it is pronounced *fāt* with a long *a* as in *ape.* But because the speaker normally prolongs the *a* in *ape* as if it were *ayup,* he or she will probably pronounce *fate* in the same manner: *fayut.* A midwesterner, on the other hand, would pronounce it *fāt.* So, unless the speaker is well acquainted with the symbols used to indicate the correct pronunciation of the words, the dictionary is not an entirely satisfactory guide to pronunciation.

A better source of information is a pronouncing dictionary such as John S. Kenyon and Thomas A. Knott's *A Pronouncing Dictionary of American English.* This volume, which includes no definitions, provides a comprehensive guide to acceptable regional variations in pronunciation. However, for this dictionary to be of help one must know the phonetic alphabet, because all pronunciations are noted phonetically.

In view of the shortcomings of both standard dictionaries and Kenyon and Knott's pronouncing dictionary, how can a speaker decide how a word should be pronounced? The authors suggest two criteria. These are:

1. For most words, speakers should adopt the pronunciation of the educated people of the region in which they live.
2. The names of people and places should be pronounced as they are pronounced by the possessors of the name or the inhabitants of the place.

The United States, unlike some nations, has no official dialect or pronunciation. Instead the country has three major dialects that are spoken in different regions and several variations within each of these dialects. The most common dialect is the General American or Midwestern, which is spoken by the majority of Americans. The Southern dialect is generally spoken in the states that constituted the Confederacy, with the exception of west Texas. The New England dialect is spoken by people in the six New England states

Common Errors in Pronunciation

Word	Mispronunciation	Accepted Pronunciation
often	*off*-ten	*off*-en
genuine	*gen*-you-wine	*gen*-you-win
gesture	*guest*-ure	*jest*-ure
direct	*dye*-rect	dir-*rect*
event	*ee*-vent	ee-*vent*
police	*po*-lice	po-*lice*
insurance	*in*-sur-ance	in-*sur*-ance
theatre	thee-*ate*-r	th*ee*-a-ter
err	air	er
relevant	*rev*-e-lant	*rel*-e-vant
illegal	ee-*le*-gal	ill-*le*-gal
iron	arn	eye-urn
homage	*hom*-mage, *hom*-age	*omm*-age
subtle	*sub*-tul	*sut*-tl
aria	*air*-i-a	*are*-i-a
program	*pro*-grum	*pro*-gram
clique	click	cleek
cooperation	cor-po-*ra*-tion	co-oper-*a*-tion
mayonnaise	*my*-on-aise	*may*-on-aise
ambulance	ambu-*lance*	*am*-bu-lance
legislator	leg-is-la-*tor*	*leg*-is-la-ter
suite	suit	sweet
route	rout	root

Common Errors in the Pronunciation of Names of People and Places

Name	Mispronunciation	Accepted Pronunciation
Illinois	Ill-i-*noise*	Ill-i-*noy*
Detroit	*Dee*-troit	De-*troit*
United States	*U*-ni-ted States	U-*ni*-ted States
Des Moines	De *Moins,* Des *Moins*	De *Moin*
Pierre (South Dakota)	Pi-*air*	Peer
Iowa	*I*-o-way	*I*-o-wuh
Italian	Eye-*tal*-ian	It-*tal*-ian
New Orleans	New Or-*leens*	New *Or*-lee-uns
Syracuse	*Sa*-rah-cuse	*Seer*-a-cuse
Biloxi	Bi-*lock*-si	Bi-*luck*-si
Louisiana	Lou-*ee-sy*-an-na, Lou-zee-an-na	*Lou*-is-ee-an-na
Richard Wagner	*Wag*-ner	*Vahg*-ner
Mozart	*Mose*-art	*Moats*-art

and northeastern New York. The speech of people living along the boundaries of the major dialect regions, as might be expected, usually displays characteristics of the dialects of both regions. Within each region, variations in dialect are found also. For example, while both are regarded as Southern, the speech of Virginia differs considerably from that of Mississippi. Differences also occur in large cities, where the influence of immigrant groups has altered the dialect. Ethnic groups speaking a language other than English have also modified the dialect of some areas. For instance, the French in southern Louisiana, the Germans in Wisconsin, and Spanish-speaking Americans in the Southwest have contributed to variations in those areas. Black Americans in many parts of the country also have a distinctive speech dialect.

Since the United States has no officially approved standard of pronunciation, it seems sensible to recommend that one adopt the pronunciation of the educated people in the region where one lives.

An exception is the pronunciation of names of people and places, where the speaker should accept the pronunciation of those who possess the name or inhabit the place. Thus the town of Monroe in Louisiana is pronounced *Mon*-roe, whereas Monroe, Michigan, is Mon-*roe*—these are the pronunciations used by residents of the two communities. For the same reason, Arkansas is pronounced *Arkansaw* rather than *Arkansas;* the capital of South Dakota, Pierre, is pronounced *Peer* rather than Pi-*air,* and Detroit is correctly pronounced with the accent on the second rather than the first syllable.

An exception to the above rule is in determining the pronunciation of foreign places, where not only the pronunciation but the actual name may differ markedly from American usage. For example, the names that inhabitants of the following places use are quite different from what Americans call them:

Name of Place	Anglicization
Norge	Norway
Sverige	Sweden
München	Munich
Helvetia	Switzerland
Österreich	Austria
Wien	Vienna
Suomi	Finland
Firenze	Florence
Deutschland	Germany
Köln	Cologne
Maroc	Morocco
Kobnhavn	Copenhagen

Commentator Eric Sevareid has said that one of a broadcaster's problems concerns the pronunciation of the listener's hometown:

> For example, it's plainly Versailles in France, but just as plainly Versayles in Kentucky. That Illinois town is Willamette but that Oregon river is Willam'ette.
>
> Prague rhymes with frog in Europe, but it rhymes with plague in Oklahoma. Vienna is good enough for Europeans, but Vyenna suits Georgia. Madrid is in Spain, but Mad'rid is in Iowa; Peru is in South America, but Peeroo is in Illinois. How the French town of Calais' got to be the town of Ca'lace in Maine, we'll never understand, nor why Rheims, in France, rhymes with Screams in New York. Every third Frenchman is named Pi-erre, but the one and only capital of South Dakota is named Peer. There are more than a dozen Berlins in America, but most of them are called Ber'lin. Newark couldn't be anything else in New Jersey, but it can be in Delaware, where it's New'Ark. Around New Smyrna, Florida, they are insulted unless you call it New Summerna. Montevide'o is in Uruguay, but Montevid'eo is in Minnesota; Bogo'ta is New Jersey, but they call it Bogota' in Colombia. And the g in Elgin is soft in Illinois and hard in Texas.
>
> You see what we go through in this business.
>
> This is Eric Sevareid—or Sevareed—in Washington. (Eric Sevareid, *In One Ear,* New York: Knopf, 1952, pp. 257–258.)

SUMMARY

The audible or vocal elements of delivery include the speaker's volume, pitch, voice quality, rate, articulation, and pronunciation. The speaker's volume should be flexible, adapted to the speech situation, and neither too loud nor too soft. Pitch should be pleasant, varied, and suited to the speaker's vocal mechanism. The speaker should strive to develop a voice quality that is easy to listen to and free from distracting characteristics. Good speakers vary their rate, speaking neither too rapidly nor too slowly.

Articulation is the speaker's skill or facility in saying a word correctly, while pronunciation is a matter of knowing how the word should be said. Good articulation is clear, distinct, and free from omissions, additions, distortions, or transpositions of sounds. The speaker's guide in pronunciation for most words should be the pronunciation of educated people in the region in which he or she lives. However, proper names of people and places are correctly pronounced as the possessors of the name or inhabitants of the place pronounce them.

STUDY QUESTIONS

1. What is meant by the audible or vocal elements of delivery?
2. What are some possible causes of persistent volume problems?
3. What is pitch? What is a speaker's optimum pitch level?
4. What is an inflection? What are pitch patterns?
5. How does voice quality differ from pitch? How may they be related?
6. What is the difference between an articulation error and a pronunciation error?
7. What standard of pronunciation should a speaker adopt for most words?
8. What should guide the speaker in the pronunciation of the names of persons and places?

EXERCISES

1. Prepare a 3- to 4-minute oral report in which you evaluate the vocal attributes of some speaker you have heard in person in the last two weeks. Possible subjects might be a classroom lecturer, a clergyman, a guest speaker, a political candidate, or a student speaker (other than a member of your speech class). Evaluate the speaker's voice quality, pitch, rate, loudness, articulation, and pronunciation, pointing out both good and bad qualities. You need not identify the speaker by name. Present a report in class.
2. Listen to several radio or television commercials delivered by announcers of your sex. Try to ignore what the announcer is saying and concentrate on the pitch usage. Attempt to imitate the speaker's use of pitch. Then compare his or her range and variation with your own voice.
3. Select a short passage from a speech, editorial, article, or column in which the speaker or author is attempting to persuade. Read the passage aloud first as if you believed deeply in what you were saying; second, as if you were bored by the passage; and, third, in a manner suggesting that you are skeptical of what you are reading.
4. From a speech you have already delivered or from one on which you are working, select a short passage of eight or ten sentences. Speak these extemporaneously and record your speaking. Play back the recording and listen carefully to your pitch variation, rate, and emphasis. Then:
   a. Speak and record the passage again, attempting to achieve greater variety of pitch. Don't worry about using exactly the same words. Then play back and

compare the two versions. Repeat this several times and attempt to achieve a different pitch usage in each recording. Finally, play back each version and try to decide which sounds best.

b. Perform the same exercise listed above only vary the rate of speaking for different sentences and phrases. Experiment with pauses, with speaking faster at times, and with slowing down at other times. Again, replay the several versions and select the best.

c. Perform the same exercise a third time, now varying emphasis and volume. Again seek to determine which version you think sounds best.

5. To train yourself to be more acutely aware of articulation and pronunciation, during the next week jot down every articulation or pronunciation error (or doubtful usage) that you hear in classroom lectures, student speeches, class discussions, and conversations. At the end of the week, check to see how many—if any—of these mistakes you are likely to make.

6. Determine your optimum pitch. Then record your voice, speaking impromptu for about one minute on some subject with which you are familiar. As you play the recording, hum your optimum pitch tone and attempt to determine whether you normally speak at this level.

FURTHER READINGS

Ehninger, Douglas, Bruce E. Gronbeck, Ray E. McKerrow, and Alan Monroe, *Principles and Types of Speech Communication,* 10th ed. (Glenview, IL: Scott, Foresman, 1986), "Using Your Voice to Communicate," 267–274.

Gibson, James W., and Clifton Cornwell, *Creative Speech Communication* (New York: Macmillan, 1979), chap. 13, "Saying Things."

Lucas, Stephen E., *The Art of Public Speaking* (New York: Random House, 1986), "The Speaker's Voice," 229–236.

Minnick, Wayne C., *Public Speaking* (Boston: Houghton Mifflin, 1979), 127–133.

Mudd, Charles S., and Malcolm O. Sillars, *Speech: Content and Communication* (New York: Crowell, 1975), "Vocal Elements," 293–300.

Taylor, Anita, *Speaking in Public* (Englewood Cliffs, NJ: Prentice-Hall, 1979), 159–168.

Zannes, Estelle, and Gerald Goldhaber, *Stand Up, Speak Out,* 2d ed. (Reading, MA: Addison-Wesley, 1983), "What the Audience Hears," 205–212.

CHAPTER 12

PRESENTING INFORMATION

In the classroom, the shop, the business firm, the laboratory, the office, the consulting room, and elsewhere, the communication of information is a daily activity. Even in specialized fields such as medicine and law, communicating information in simple, understandable language is an important part of the practitioner's job. For example, a study conducted not long ago showed that a main reason why patients often fail to follow their doctor's advice is because they simply don't understand it. In the field of law, according to Charles Bunn, most of a lawyer's work consists of obtaining and conveying information. "I do not mean information about the law," Professor Bunn emphasizes, "I mean information about the client's problems and the facts connected with them. A lawyer's work is seldom *about* law."

Regardless of vocation or level of education, almost every person needs to be able to present simple, everyday information clearly and understandably. Journalist James Reston explains the importance of this ability, saying:

> I think that I could convince any group of children that there are two things that are absolutely fundamental when they leave school—no matter what work they're going into—whether they're going into a garage to fix a car or going into medicine, or law, or to higher education—and that is simply to learn the arts of accurate observation and accurate speech . . . because he ought to be able to explain himself so that a man can understand. The higher up the ladder he goes, and the educational scale, of course, the more important that is. (*Representative American Speeches, 1983–1984*, New York: H. W. Wilson Co., 1984, p. 113.)

While our main use of speech probably always has been to communicate information to others, in recent years "the information explosion" has made this function even more important. With the scientific-technological breakthrough in this century, the expansion of knowledge has been so rapid that experts find it difficult to keep abreast of their own fields. Louis Martin, of the Association of Research Libraries, says that the amount of new information each year is "staggering." So many scholarly journals are being published that no one has been able to count them, although authoritative estimates range from 200,000 to 600,000 titles per year! Physics journals published by the American Institute of Physics alone form a stack 20 feet high, and the world output in the field is estimated at 60 feet, with production doubling every 8 years; the National Library of Medicine receives more than 18,000 different journals. A recent survey showed that the number of scientific and technical publications in the world had reached 59,000, with 9,000 published in this country alone. In other areas the increase has been comparable.

One result of this explosion has been that scholars, scientists, doctors, and researchers find it almost impossible to keep up-to-date with the latest discoveries in their fields. It is alarming that much of what has been learned is of great import to the whole of society but fails to reach the majority of people. Muriel Beadle stresses that:

> The experts can't (or at least *shouldn't*) make decisions for all of us on the control of radioactive fallout or the right of people with inherited diseases to reproduce as freely as people without such diseases. Whether one race has inherited superiority to another race is no longer an academic question. (*Saturday Review,* April 3, 1965, pp. 53–54.)

She believes that the formation of intelligent opinion is possible only when ordinary citizens understand new discoveries better than they do now.

Inadequate information concerning scientific advances evokes widespread confusion and fear among the general public, as was evidenced when congressional hearings on the safety of birth control pills produced an epidemic of anxiety. Doctors were deluged by inquiries from frightened women who had not understood the findings presented to the committee.

The ability to present information clearly is as important to the ordinary individual as to the expert. Whatever one's status or occupation, skill in providing others with information is essential to effective communication.

When presenting information, a speaker's choice of supporting materials is vital in determining success or failure. Supporting materials may be divided into two classes according to their use. Materials used for informing the listeners are called expository. Materials selected to alter the listeners' opin-

Most teaching consists of informing students.
(Matheny, *Christian Science Monitor*)

ions, to reinforce beliefs, or to influence actions are known as evidence. Speeches to inform and to entertain consist almost entirely of expository material. Argumentative speeches—discourse designed to convince or to persuade—rely mainly on evidence, although they may also include expository material. Inspirational talks usually contain both expository and argumentative supporting material.

Selecting the materials to be used in developing the topic begins after the speaker has chosen a subject, determined the purpose, studied the topic, and decided how to approach the subject. In informative speaking, the supporting material is used to explain or clarify. At other times, a speaker may use expository materials to amplify or develop an idea more fully. Still another use of expository supporting materials may be to make the information more vivid, interesting, and easily remembered.

The principal supporting materials used in exposition are details, examples, description, narration, definition, comparison, contrast, and statistics.

TYPES OF INFORMATIVE SUPPORTING MATERIALS

Details

Details are specific characteristics or features of an object, event, or concept. Speakers present details in order to clarify the listeners' understanding with specific information.

The statement "Automobile for sale," for example, is very general. However, if specific details are added, giving the brand, make, model, color, design, size, interior, optional equipment, special features, and price of the automobile, the reader or listener has a much better understanding of what is being offered for sale.

A speaker usually employs details in order to clarify an idea, to make it more concrete or specific in the mind of the listener. Just as a map without labels, a recipe omitting the amount of each ingredient, or a newspaper with only headlines would be unclear, specific details are essential to the understanding of many concepts speakers discuss. Details, however, may serve another function. They may also amplify, embellish, or develop a concept, making the idea more vivid and easier to recall.

Former CBS News President William A. Leonard used details to support his ideas in the following excerpt from a speech to a convention of journalists:

> As a nation, we are widely, even wildly, informed. Some people call it "electronification," others call it the information age. Whatever the terms, . . . we are surrounded by information, we are bombarded by news, we are engulfed in entertainment. Stores and elevators have cam-

> eras, cars have cassettes, homes have video tape recorders. And as you have noticed on city streets these days, it appears that most people under 25 are walking around with wires coming out of their ears. (*Representative American Speeches, 1981–1982,* New York: H. W. Wilson Co., 1982, p. 137.)

In a speech discussing a Supreme Court ruling that a citizen's bank records are not his private property, Senator Charles M. Mathias, Jr., employed details as follows:

> A bank record is not just a collection of miscellaneous, anonymous scraps of paper. It is a raw material for a collage that, if pieced together, will reveal not only your income and net worth, but your politics, what you read, what you owe, what you buy, the charities you support, the causes you oppose, where you take your vacations, what and how much you eat and drink, and even what your allergies are. (*Representative American Speeches, 1978–1979,* New York: H. W. Wilson Co., 1979, p. 74.)

Examples

Examples consist of instances and illustrations—real or hypothetical. An example is a citation of one instance out of many. To explain what a *fad* is one might cite as examples the Hula Hoop, streaking, the twist, Pac-Man, Rubik's Cube, and Cabbage Patch dolls.

Note the extended use of examples, in a speech by historian Ray A. Billington:

> I am sure that most of you will agree when I say that the "Wild, Wild West" is alive and well in much of the world today, nearly a century after the last cowboy blazed a path of virtue across the Great Plains with his six-shooters. . . . For the myth of the American frontier as a land of romance, violence, and personal justice has persisted and grown.
>
> The persuasive influence of the frontier image is nowhere better exhibited than by the cultists of other nations who try to recapture life in that never-never land of the past. In Paris, western addicts buy "outfits" at a store near the Arc de Triomphe called the Western House, spend weekends at Camp Indian clad in Comanche headdresses and moccasins, or don cowboy sombreros and spurred boots to gallop through the Bois de Boulogne on Vespas. Frontier buffs have brought affluence to the late George Fronval, a novelist who has written nearly 600 westerns, 54 of them about "Buffalo Bill" Cody, under such improbable titles as *The Cavern of the Mammoths* and *The Prisoner of the Ku Klux Klan.*
>
> In Austria children play Cowboys and Indians, or walk Indian file through the cobbled streets, their makeshift costumes contrasting strangely with half-timbered houses. In West Germany enthusiasts buy

Rodeo After Shave and a deodorant called Lasso, purchase western clothes from two thriving chain stores (some buffs refuse to watch westerns on television unless properly garbed), and belong to one of the 63 societies in the Western Clubs Federation whose members spend weekends in log houses, dress as Sioux Indians or cowboys, and carry realism to the uncomfortable extreme of using saddles for pillows and barring Indian impersonators from the club saloon. In Norway a "western" author, Morgan Kane, is a national hero among the young; in Japan "Frontier" restaurants vie for customers, and a *Frontier* magazine has recently appeared. (*Representative American Speeches, 1975–1976,* New York: H. W. Wilson Co., 1976, p. 177.)

At times a speaker may use only one or two examples to illustrate a point, as President Ronald Reagan did in the following passage:

We don't have to turn to our history books for heroes. They're all around us. . . . Just 2 weeks ago, in the midst of a terrible tragedy on the Potomac, we saw again the spirit of American heroism at its finest—the heroism of dedicated rescue workers saving crash victims from icy waters. And we saw the heroism of one of our young government employees, Lenny Skutnik, who, when he saw a woman lose her grip on the helicopter line, dived into the water and dragged her to safety. (*Representative American Speeches, 1981–1982,* New York: H. W. Wilson Co., 1982, p. 24.)

Description

Another way that a speaker might develop a subject is through description. Description is the process of depicting the appearance or atmosphere of a scene, place, or object, based on one's visual observations and impressions. A speaker's impressions of the appearance of the Grand Canyon, the explosion of a volcano, Stonehenge, the Great Wall of China, or a Rio Mardi Gras parade are examples of description. A news story detailing the wreckage following a hurricane would be largely descriptive. Society-page reports of weddings often describe the bride's costume in considerable detail. Accounts of the feelings and reactions of a passenger on a hijacked airplane or of a witness to a fire or flood are other examples of description.

The main value of descriptive materials in developing a subject is that they assist the auditor in visualizing clearly and vividly a situation, scene, or event.

In the following passage, a high school principal at a school in a poverty-stricken area of a large city describes conditions before that school began a character-education program:

The building resembled a school in a riot area. Many, many windows had been broken, and the glass had been replaced with masonite. . . . Most of the pupils were rude, discourteous, and insolent to members of the faculty. . . . The children had no school pride, very poor self-image, and were most disgruntled because they had to attend "that old school."

A vivid example of description is found in Mark Twain's lecture, "The Sandwich Islands," first delivered in 1866:

Each island is a mountain—or two or three mountains. They begin at the seashore—in a torrid climate where the cocoa palm grows, and the coffee tree, the mango, orange, banana, and the delicious chirimoya; they begin down there in a sweltering atmosphere, rise with a grand and gradual sweep till they hide their beautiful regalia of living green in the folds of the drooping clouds, and higher and higher yet they rise among the mists till their emerald forests change to dull and stunted shrubbery, then to scattering constellations of the brilliant silver sword, then higher yet to dreary, barren desolation—no trees, no shrubs, nothing but tern and scorched and blackened piles of lava; higher yet and then, towering toward heaven, above the dim and distant land, above the waveless sea, and high above the rolling plains of clouds themselves, stands the awful summit, wrapped in a mantle of everlasting ice and snow and burnished with a tropical sunshine that fires it with dazzling splendor! Here one may stand and shiver in the midst of eternal winter and look down upon a land reposing in the loveliest hues of a summer that hath no end. Such is Mauna Loa—16,000 feet by recent and accurate measurement, and such is Mauna Kea, 14,000 feet high. (Mark Twain, *Life as I Find It*, Garden City, NY: Hanover House, 1961, pp. 183–188.)

Narration

Narration is similar to description except that it depicts an event or act. A narrative relates what happened, usually in chronological order. Most accounts of personal experience are narratives. Reports of trips, sporting events, programs, and meetings are often given in narrative form.

Congressman Morris Udall of Arizona used narration to relate a personal experience in the following passage:

Some years ago, when I was practicing law here, a troubled businessman of modest means came to me as an old friend. His closest friend during a terminal illness had asked him to help the sick man's son, who was just starting in business. He readily agreed; in other words, he made a solemn commitment. Subsequently he loaned the boy $5,000 after his friend's death. It soon became apparent the boy didn't have any business sense, but the agreement was a solemn one. Soon he had $25,000 of his own money and half his working hours invested in a clearly losing venture, and he was neglecting his own business affairs. When he came to see me, he had just talked with his banker about mortgaging his home. It was apparent to me he was on a course that would eventually lead to bankruptcy. . . . I told my Tucson friend that he had kept the spirit and word of any commitment he had made to his dead friend and that now he should tell the boy frankly that he could go no further. (*Representative American Speeches, 1967–1968,* New York: H. W. Wilson Co., 1968, p. 21.)

Definitions

In developing a topic, a speaker often finds it necessary to employ a definition to explain what an unfamiliar word or concept means. A definition may be brief, such as: *gauche* means awkward, tactless, or lacking grace, especially social graces; or a *French leave* is a secret, hasty, unnoticed, or unceremonious departure. At other times, a speaker may go into greater detail in defining a concept.

Two examples of short definitions by speakers are (1) Dean Acheson's definition of *ethical* in which he said, "We are told what is ethical is characterized by what is excellent in conduct and that excellence may be judged by what is right and proper, as against what is wrong, by existing standards," and (2) George Bernard Shaw's succinct definition of an agnostic as "only an atheist without the courage of his opinions." Examples of more detailed definitions are:

> Nike-Zeus was subject, as I believe all the later systems are, to something called *blackout;* that is, if a nuclear explosion were set off to destroy an incoming missile, it also upset the gas in the air, "ionized" it—electrons strip off from the molecules and for a while the gas acts like a metal rather than a gas so that radar waves cannot go through it and you cannot see what is behind it. (Jerome B. Wiesner, "An Argument Against the ABM," *Representative American Speeches, 1968–1969,* New York: H. W. Wilson Co., 1969, p. 19.)

In a speech in which he contended that violence in this country had reached epidemic proportions, Surgeon General C. Everett Koop defined *epidemic* in the following manner:

> Violence in American public and private life has . . . assumed the proportions of an epidemic. Assaults, child and spouse abuse, homicides and suicides among young adults, these indicators of violence in our population are still climbing. They are occurring at a rate "beyond what is normally expected," to use the phrase used by epidemiologists to define the term *epidemic.* The occurrence of a case of an illness *beyond what we might expect, based upon past experience,* is an epidemic. ("An Epidemic of Violence," *Representative American Speeches, 1983–1984,* New York: H. W. Wilson Co., 1984, p. 165.)

In a sermon, Reverend F. Forrester Church defined *companion* as follows:

> Regardless of faith or creed, . . . we are all companions. You know what the word *companion* means. It goes back to the Latin roots, *con* meaning with, and *pan,* meaning bread. A companion is one with whom we break bread. In a spiritual, rather than material sense, the ultimate bread we mortals break together is the bread of life and death. This bread is precious. It is salty and bitter and good. ("Love and Death," *Representative American Speeches, 1983–1984,* New York: H. W. Wilson Co., 1984, p. 159.)

For a detailed discussion of how to define terms, the reader should consult Chapter 15.

Comparison

Comparison is a process by which the speaker seeks to clarify a concept by showing how it is similar to another. Comparisons or analogies may be literal or figurative. A literal comparison develops actual existing similarities. Comparisons between American agriculture and Australian agriculture, between economic conditions in 1967 and 1987 or between Fords and Chevrolets would be literal analogies. In a figurative comparison, the two items being compared possess no real or physical resemblances. Thus, comparisons of poverty to cancer, or raising a child to writing a book, or of education to a game of chess would be figurative.

In exposition the main function of a literal comparison is to clarify an idea, while a figurative comparison serves more to dramatize or vivify what the speaker wishes to convey.

Comparison can be particularly useful in explaining an unfamiliar concept by showing its resemblance to something better known. In the following example, William J. McGill, past president of Columbia University, uses a literal comparison to clarify a point. He says:

> A department or faculty is in many ways a family, living in intimate contact with one another. They have the capacity to protect one another, or to irritate one another unbearably. (*Representative American Speeches, 1971–1972,* New York: H. W. Wilson Co., 1972, p. 189.)

The following passage by speech critic Lester Thonssen contains a figurative comparison that seems to have been more to enliven the speaker's thought than to inform:

> Several years ago, an uncommonly snide trick was played on some unsuspecting members of the animal kingdom. A day-long festival was held commemorating the one hundredth anniversary of the development

of the Rhode Island Red chicken. There were speeches memorializing the hen; a plaque to the hapless creature was dedicated; and the Rhode Island Red was singled out for its contribution to the multibillion dollar poultry industry.

After the kind words were spoken, do you know what the audience did? You are quite right. It ate one hundred Rhode Island Reds at a festive barbecue. A cynical attitude, it would seem, with a bit of reverse English.

Yet it is not unlike the practice of some anthologists and critics who, with academic fanfare, select so-called great speeches or other creative expressions for special remembrance, and then promptly tear them to pieces with such cavalier delight as to make the readers wonder why they were chosen to begin with. (*Representative American Speeches, 1967–1968,* New York: H. W. Wilson Co., 1969, p. 3.)

Contrast

Contrast is similar to comparison except that it stresses differences rather than likenesses. For example, one might clarify a description of the British educational system by showing how it differs from American schooling; one speaker might use contrast to show how the invention of the computer has changed our lives.

Robert S. Browne employed contrast as follows:

A black child in a predominantly black school may realize that she doesn't look like the pictures in the books, magazines, and TV advertisements, but at least she looks like her schoolmates and neighbors. The black child in a predominantly white school and neighborhood lacks even this basis for identification. (*Representative American Speeches, 1968–1969,* New York: H. W. Wilson Co., 1969, p. 144.)

In an address to the California Bar Association, reporter Daniel Schorr employed contrast to describe changed attitudes toward the press, saying:

Once, a reporter was perceived as a relentless and usually impecunious pursuer of the truth. Today, the reporter is, often as not, perceived as the well-heeled and arrogant offspring of a giant amusement industry. The journalist appears on the tube as lost in the wasteland blur among the prime-time programmers, the docudrama titillators, the happy-news chucklers and the Saturday morning sugar-plugging hucksters. It seems a long way from John Peter Zenger of colonial times, or even from Hildy Johnson of "The Front Page."

The press, once typically antiestablishment, is perceived now as itself a huge establishment. (*Representative American Speeches, 1978–1979,* New York: H. W. Wilson Co., 1979, p. 208–209.)

Statistics

Statistics are simply numbers. They may be totals, fractions, percentages, proportions, or ratios. *Two million, doubled, three to one, 65 percent, one-third, 11,* and *643,981* are all statistics. The following are some examples of the use of statistics by speakers to amplify or clarify their ideas.

> During the next 60 seconds, 200 human beings will be born on this earth. About 160 of them will be black, brown, yellow, or red. Of these 200 youngsters now being born, about half will be dead before they are a year old. Of those that survive, another half will be dead before they are 16. The 50 of the 200 who live past their sixteenth birthday, multiplied by thousands and millions, represent the people of this earth. (*Representative American Speeches, 1976–1977,* New York: H. W. Wilson Co., 1977, p. 152.)

A similar example is found in the following passage:

> If the world were a single town with a population of 100, one of those 100 people would have a college education, 30 would be able to read and write, 15 would live in adequate housing (the rest would live in huts), and 50 would be hungry most of the time. Six of the 100 would control half of the wealth of the town, and of these six, three would be Americans. (*New Era,* Parker S.D., November 10, 1983, p. 1.)

TESTING INFORMATIVE SUPPORTING MATERIALS

In expository speaking, speakers should ask the following five questions about the supporting materials they are thinking of using to amplify or clarify their ideas.

Is the Supporting Material Correct?

Speakers have three reasons for investigating the accuracy of supporting materials. First, they have an ethical responsibility not to mislead their listeners by presenting inaccurate information. The audience expects speakers to know their material, not to misinform them. Second, since exposition is primarily informative, a speaker cannot expect listeners to understand a subject if the supporting material is incorrect. Third, inaccurate information, if detected, can destroy a speaker's credibility. A single incorrect detail, example, or statistic may be enough to disillusion an audience. For example, a student speaking on improving one's tennis game instantly lost credibility with an inaccurate visual aid illustrating how a tennis court is laid out.

Similarly, another student speaker lost credibility in a speech on the Battle of New Orleans when it became clear that she did not know that the battle was fought after, not before, the end of the War of 1812. Even though the error in each of these instances was minor, it was enough to make the audience question the speaker's knowledge of the topic and the reliability of other supporting material.

Is the Supporting Material Relevant?

Supporting materials should be necessary and pertinent and should contribute to the achievement of the speaker's goal. Common mistakes in selecting supporting materials include the introduction of interesting but unnecessary or irrelevant information and the overdevelopment of a point the audience has already grasped.

Common mistakes speakers sometimes make include straying from the topic as they remember a humorous anecdote, becoming so enthusiastic that they go into unnecessary detail, and at times developing material that is totally unnecessary to the audience's understanding of the subject. A speaker should carefully examine each piece of supporting material. Only materials that contribute to the achievement of the speaker's purpose should then be used.

Is the Supporting Material Specific?

All expository supporting material has the function of making a speech more meaningful by making it less abstract or general. In expository speaking, supporting materials primarily serve to elaborate or amplify the speaker's ideas so the listener can more easily understand them.

If the supporting materials are vague, unclear, or difficult to follow, they contribute little to comprehension. Furthermore, specific supporting data is more interesting than abstract concepts. For these reasons, the speaker should keep the supporting materials specific and concrete.

Saul Alinsky stresses the difference in the way a listener will react to generalizations and to specific, personal information:

> People understand only in terms of their own experience. . . . A classic example of the failure to communicate . . . is the attempt . . . to indicate to the poor the bankruptcy of their prevailing values. "Take my word for it—if you get a good job and a split-level ranch house out in the suburbs, a color TV, two cars, and money in the bank, that just won't bring you happiness." The response without exception is always, "Yeah. Let me be the judge of that one—I'll let you know after I get it."
>
> Communication on a general basis . . . carries a very limited meaning. It is the difference between being informed of the death of a quarter of a million people—which becomes a statistic—or the death of one or two

close friends or loved ones or members of one's family. . . . In trying to explain what the personal relationship means, I have told various audiences, "If the chairman of this meeting had opened up by saying, 'I am shocked and sorry to have to report to you that we have just been notified that Mr. Alinsky has just been killed in a plane crash and therefore this lecture is canceled,' the only reaction you would have would be, 'Well, gee, that's too bad. I wonder what he was like, but oh, well, let's see, what are we going to do this evening.'

"Now suppose after finishing this lecture, let us assume that all of you have disagreed with everything I have said, you don't like my face, the sound of my voice, my manner, my clothes, you just don't like me, period. Let us further assume that I am to lecture you again next week, and at that time you are informed of my sudden death. Your reaction will be very different, regardless of your dislike. You will react with shock: you will say, 'Why, just yesterday he was alive, breathing, talking, and laughing. It just seems incredible to believe that suddenly like that he's gone.'

"What is of particular importance here, however, is the fact that you were dealing with one specific person and not a general mass. . . ." It should be obvious by now that communication occurs concretely, by means of one's specific experiences. (*Rules for Radicals,* New York: Random House, 1971, p. 95.)

Is the Supporting Material Clear?

At times, supporting material can be correct, relevant, and specific without being clear. Some audiences lack the educational background needed to comprehend highly technical or specialized concepts. Yet the speaker may find it virtually mandatory to include such material. For example, the average person probably has only the most elementary understanding of such concepts as gross national product, balance of payments, and deficit spending; but if the speaker's purpose is to explain the government's fiscal policy, it will be almost impossible to exclude materials related to these concepts. In such a situation, the speaker must be sure to recognize and explain unfamiliar technical materials.

A speaker should also be careful to present statistics in a way that will not confuse the listeners. Unless a precise number is required, statistics often should be simplified by rounding off, thereby enabling the auditor to grasp them more easily. For example, instead of *9,883,412,* a speaker might say *approximately ten million; 26.2 percent* could be stated as *a little more than a fourth; 51.6 percent* becomes *about one half;* and a *98.73 percent increase* is *nearly double.*

In the passage below, quoted from a speech by Robert C. Weaver, note how the speaker has simplified his statistics:

Median family income among nonwhites was slightly less than 55 percent of that for whites; for individual incomes, the figure was *50 percent.*

> *Only a third* of the black families earned sufficient income to sustain an acceptable American standard of living. Yet this involved *well over a million* black families, of whom 6,000 earned $25,000 or more. . . . Blacks have made striking gains in historical terms; yet their current rate of unemployment is *well over double* that among whites. *Over two-thirds* of our black workers are still concentrated in five major unskilled and semiskilled occupations, as contrasted to slightly *over a third* of the white labor force. [Emphasis added] (*Representative American Speeches, 1963–1964*, New York: H. W. Wilson Co., 1964, p. 88.)

Visual presentations in the form of charts, diagrams, and graphs are also helpful in presenting statistics.

Because a speaker can communicate only within the areas of experience of the auditors, materials difficult to comprehend often should be clarified by relating the unfamiliar to the known. Thus, in explaining communism to an audience in a capitalistic country or socialized medicine to a group familiar only with the private practice of medicine, rather than discussing these concepts in the abstract, the speaker might describe a day in the life of a Communist farmer or tell how a patient goes about seeing a doctor, entering a hospital, and obtaining treatment under a program of socialized medicine.

Listeners sometimes have difficulty grasping the extent of huge numbers. To make such statistics more meaningful, a speaker might compare them to something more readily understood, as Notre Dame University President Theodore Hesburgh did in a speech on foreign aid:

> "But we are spending billions on foreign aid." Yes, about 4 billion annually to be exact. But again, about half of this is military aid, and the 2 billion that are left seem hardly sacrificial when you compare it to the 6 billion we spend annually for tobacco, the 12 billion for alcohol, the 20 billion for that ancient pastime called gambling. I shall spare you the bill for entertainment. (*Representative American Speeches, 1970–1971*, New York: H. W. Wilson Co., 1971, p. 85.)

Another example of clarifying statistics by relating them to something more easily understood is found in a television commercial, "Automotive travel in the United States totals more than one trillion miles a year, the equivalent of two thousand round trips to the moon."

Is the Supporting Material Interesting?

In choosing materials, the speaker should select those most likely to interest listeners. If the material is interesting, the auditor will not only grasp it more quickly but will also be more likely to remember it.

Specific material usually is more interesting than abstract support. Materials related to the listeners' experiences generally are more likely to be of interest. If the material is up-to-date, it seems more immediate and relevant and therefore more interesting.

Interest can be enhanced by vivid language. Descriptive adjectives, forceful verbs, alliteration, parallelism, rhetorical questions, and other stylistic devices can make an idea more striking and memorable.

Wit or humor also adds interest to a speaker's supporting material. For example, President Malcolm Moos, of the University of Minnesota, in relating how he somewhat reluctantly concluded that he must play a more active role in the future of his institution, illustrated how he reached this decision, saying, "You will recall the bullock who, being pursued by a ferocious tiger in India, shouted to a monkey: 'Do you think I can climb this tree?' 'Brother, it's no longer a matter of opinion. You've got to climb this tree.' "

SUMMARY

Supporting materials are of two kinds: those used for exposition and those used for argumentation.

Expository supporting materials are employed mainly to clarify, amplify, elaborate, and embellish. Common types of expository supporting materials are details, examples, description, narration, definition, comparison, contrast, and statistics.

Details are the specific characteristics or features of an object, event, or concept.

Examples consist of instances and illustrations, actual or hypothetical. An example is a citation of one instance out of many.

Description is the process of depicting the appearance, nature, or atmosphere of a scene, place, object, or experience. Description is the result of one's personal observations and impressions.

Narration resembles description except that it recreates an event or act. Narration is concerned with what happened and usually is presented chronologically.

Definitions are explanations of what a word or concept means. The purpose of a definition is to make sure that the listener understands what a word means or how the speaker is using a particular word.

Comparison is the process by which a speaker seeks to clarify his subject, showing how it is similar to another situation, event, process, or development. Comparisons may be literal or figurative.

Contrast resembles comparison except that it stresses differences rather than similarities.

Statistics are numbers: totals, fractions, percentages, proportions, or ratios.

In the selection and use of supporting materials for the purpose of exposition, a speaker should apply five tests:

1. Is the material correct?
2. Is the material relevant, pertinent, and necessary?

3. Is the material specific?
4. Is the material clear? If not, the speaker should take pains to simplify or clarify the supporting materials.
5. Is the material interesting?

If the supporting material meets these five tests, a speaker will probably be successful in holding the interest of the listener, in presenting a message in such a way that the hearer will have no difficulty understanding the ideas, and in accomplishing the purpose of the speech.

MODEL INFORMATIVE SPEECH

Toward the end of 1985, the media became interested in the return of Halley's comet after 76 years. The publicity surrounding this anticipated event aroused the curiosity of a student, Jerald L. Boykin, and led him to embark on an investigation of the comet and its earlier appearances. What he found out prompted him to prepare an informative talk on the subject for his speech class.

In reading and analyzing Boykin's speech, identify the kinds of informative supporting materials used by the speaker to develop his subject, his organizational techniques, and the sources of his material.

Halley's Comet: Since the Last Time

Jerald L. Boykin, Jr.

Throughout history, the eyes of man have gazed toward the heavens and the appearance of a comet has always been regarded with bewilderment and fear. No comet is more historic than Halley's comet. I would like to discuss with you tonight the impressions of the comet, when it was last seen, what is being done to prepare for the comet's return in 1986, and the changes that have taken place over these past 76 years.

Halley's comet is named after Edmund Halley, an English astronomer who saw the comet in 1682 and was the first to recognize that it had appeared many times before. He predicted the comet would return in 1758. However, he died in 1742; but because his calculations proved correct, the comet was named after him.

The comet returns to its perihelion, the point at which it is closest to the sun, approximately every 76 years and is expected to reach perihelion on February 9, 1986.

What did Americans think about Halley's comet in 1910? Among some Americans, anticipation of the comet was mixed with fear. In 1910, as before, some saw Halley's comet as an omen. Many people believed that the comet would collide with the earth, while superstition led others to believe that the dangers lay in the comet's poisoned tail.

America's popular writer Mark Twain died on April 21, 1910, just after the comet reached perihelion. Newspapers noted Twain had been born only two weeks before the comet reached perihelion on its 1835 visit, and just before the comet's tail touched the earth King Edward VII died.

"Chicago is terrified. Women are stopping up their doors and windows to keep out the cyanogen." This was the first line to an article in the *New York Times* dated May 17, 1910.

Cyanogen had been detected by scientists in the comet's tail. Professor S. A. Mitchell of Columbia University described cyanogen to a *New York Times* reporter in 1910. "Cyanogen is found in prussic acid and is a poison so powerful that a single drop on the tongue would cause instant death."

But while some Americans feared the return of Halley's comet, others looked forward to its reappearance. They looked forward to seeing one of nature's greatest and most famous spectacles.

In New York City, major hotels were the sites of roof parties and similar gatherings of people who were anxious to witness the comet's return.

Eighty-seven-year-old Tommy Hotchkiss told Peter Jones of *American History Illustrated Magazine* that he was only 12 years old on May 13, 1910, when he climbed into the bell tower of his Taylortown, New Jersey school so that he could get a better look at the comet.

How have things changed since 1910 as far as Halley's comet is concerned? Research and technology over the past eight and one-half decades have shown that Halley's comet is a hunk of rocks, dust, and frozen gases that follows a seven and one-half billion mile elliptical orbit around the sun at speeds varying between 2,000 and 122,000 miles per hour. In the 30 reported returns of the comet, it is obvious that it has not destroyed the earth by colliding with it, nor has its poisoned tail wiped out all of mankind. According to John E. Bortle, astronomer and consultant to *Astronomy* magazine, this is not likely to happen in the next 2,000 years.

In 1910 Americans could simply step out into their own backyards and view Halley's comet at its best for free. However, in 1986 the best views of the comet will not be in the United States, and faithful stargazers will have to pay for some of the best views.

Tour packagers are planning week-long or longer comet-watching ocean cruises and overland expeditions into the Southern Hemisphere where the comet will be best seen. These prices range from $1,100 to over $10,000 per person.

Entrepreneurs and marketers are supplying faithful stargazers with every comet gimmick the imagination can think of.

William C. Banks of *Money* magazine says that some of these offerings include official comet T-shirts for $8.00, jackets for $50.00, comet pills for $4.00, and for only $9.95 General Comet Industries of New York City will sell you 100 shares of comet stock.

The sellers of telescopes and binoculars are expecting their best business ever, with prices ranging from $150 to over $700.

The most impressive change since 1910 has to be the fact that in 1986

Americans will be able to view color close-ups of Halley's comet in their living room on television.

Powerful earthbound telescopes will be focused on the comet and five spacecrafts, launched by the Soviet Union, Japan, and the European Space Agency, will inspect the comet up close.

In 1910 the lack of technology and the superstitions of people led many to fear Halley's comet, while others were fascinated by it. In 1986, because the comet will be best seen in the Southern Hemisphere, those of you who decide not to view it on television and would like to see it firsthand may have to pay as much as $10,000 for a tour excursion below the equator.

Halley's comet was last seen when Model T Fords chugged over dirt roads, and when the airplane was just a little more than a motorized kite. It returns in the age of space shuttles, yuppies, and cola wars. What will the world be like in 2061 when the comet returns again? That speech has yet to be written.

STUDY QUESTIONS

1. What is the difference between exposition and argumentation?
2. How does development by comparison differ from development by contrast?
3. What are five tests of good expository supporting material?
4. Why do speakers sometimes introduce irrelevant or unimportant expository materials? Is this practice desirable?
5. Why should the speaker seek to employ materials that are specific?
6. What are some ways of clarifying or simplifying statistics? When should this practice be avoided?
7. What are some methods that the speaker can use to make the supporting material interesting?
8. Indicate why the ability to present information clearly would be important to each of the following:
   a. the foreman of a construction crew
   b. a nurse
   c. a police officer
   d. a librarian
   e. a football coach
   f. an air-conditioner salesman
   g. a travel agent

EXERCISES

1. In a newspaper or magazine, find an example of each of the eight types of expository materials discussed in this chapter.
2. List three topics that would lend themselves to expository development by details, by examples, by description, by narration, or by definition.
3. Select one of the topics below and write three 75- to 100-word paragraphs, each developing the subject with a different kind of expository material: (a) basketball, (b) Sunday afternoon, (c) the library, (d) procrastination, (e) roommates, (f) the Fourth of July, (g) a pep rally, (h) blind dates.

4. Prepare and deliver a 4-minute expository speech in which you utilize one kind of supporting material throughout.
5. Read a speech in *Vital Speeches* or *Representative American Speeches* that is primarily expository or informative and identify the kinds of supporting materials used by the speaker. Applying the tests of good expository supporting material, evaluate the use of supporting materials.
6. Listen to a newscast on radio or television and list the different types of expository materials used by the speaker. What kind was used most frequently? Was the newscast strictly informative? Write a paper summarizing your findings.
7. Analyze a lecture by one of your teachers in order to determine what kinds of supporting materials were employed. Evaluate the use of supporting material. Were there places where you felt additional supporting material was needed to aid your understanding of the lecture? Did the supporting materials clarify and add interest to the speech?

FURTHER READINGS

Ehninger, Douglas, Bruce E. Gronbeck, Ray E. McKerrow, and Alan Monroe, *Principles and Types of Speech Communication,* 10th ed. (Glenview, IL: Scott, Foresman, 1986), chap. 15, "Speeches to Inform."

Lucas, Stephen E., *The Art of Public Speaking* (New York: Random House, 1986), chap. 13, "Speaking to Inform."

Mudd, Charles S., and Malcolm O. Sillars, *Speech: Content and Communication* (New York: Crowell, 1975), chap. 16, "Speaking to Inform."

Osborn, Michael, *Speaking in Public* (Boston: Houghton Mifflin, 1982), chap. 9, "The Design and Development of Informative Speeches."

Ross, Raymond S., *Speech Communication: Fundamentals and Practice,* 7th ed. (Englewood Cliffs, NJ: Prentice-Hall, 1986), chap. 9, "Presenting Information."

Taylor, Anita, *Speaking in Public* (Englewood Cliffs, NJ: Prentice-Hall, 1979), chap. 9, "Giving Information: A Technique and an End."

Vasile, Albert J., and Harold K. Mintz, *Speak With Confidence: A Practical Guide,* 4th ed. (Boston: Little, Brown, 1986), chap. 11, "Inform Them."

Verderber, Rudolph F., *The Challenge of Effective Speaking,* 6th ed. (Belmont, CA: Wadsworth, 1985), chap. 7, "Principles of Informative Speaking," chap. 9, "Explaining Processes," and chap. 12, "Expository Speeches: Using Resource Materials."

CHAPTER 13

PERSUASION

Since Aristotle's proclamation that rhetoric is "the faculty of discovering in the particular case what are the available means of persuasion," scholars have been interested in speech as a major form of social influence and control. As citizens in a free society and in a competitive economy, we are constantly designing communication strategies to garner others' support, favor, and aid. These persuasive ploys begin as early as the child's attempts to gain an extra hour before going to bed or to coax an extra serving of dessert. Early persuasive attempts involve relatively simple strategies—a smile, a kiss, a promise to be good. As the individual matures, the strategies become more complex and the planning of them often consumes a great deal of time. The arguments that a teenager develops to prove the need for the use of the family car or later hours on weekends are often elaborate conundrums. The salesperson who attempts to persuade a business manager to use a particular brand of paper or electronic duplicator in an office constructs even more sophisticated strategies of persuasion.

The fact that individuals and groups design persuasive strategies strongly suggests that there is someone to be persuaded. We are, perhaps, better defined as consumers than as designers of persuasion. For example, from the time we wake up in the morning until the time we retire at night we are constantly bombarded by radio and television with commercials for automobiles, soft drinks, detergents, insurance, sporting goods, laxatives, energy-giving compounds, and headache-relief pills. While driving along the highway, we see billboards displaying persuasive messages such as "Be a Pepper," "Keep fit," and "Shop at Macy's—A Family Store." Americans are mass consumers of persuasive campaigns.

As both architects and consumers of persuasive messages, we should recognize that the roles are complementary rather than antithetical. For example, persons who are persuaded to play golf on Saturday must, in turn, persuade their spouses that the garden doesn't really need care this weekend. The executive who agrees to adopt an advertising campaign proposal must, in turn, present it to a superior or to the board of directors to win their support.

Several aspects of persuasion are evident from these examples. First, every person is at once a persuader and one persuaded. Second, persuasion takes place incessantly and in various settings—at home, at work, while driving, while eating. Third, persuasion is transmitted via numerous media—radio, television, billboards—and in face-to-face contact with colleagues, friends, and members of the family. Fourth, persuasion can be aimed at different types of audiences—mass (radio, television), small group (committee or board), or individual (student-to-teacher or teacher-to-supervisor).

PERSUASION DEFINED

Generally, persuasion may be defined as an attempt by one person to influence the behavior of another. More specifically, persuasion is a strategy consciously designed to shape perceptions, modify attitudes, or influence responses of one or more persons to concur with those of an initiating agent.

Since all communication in a very real sense influences our behavior, the consciousness of our effort to persuade takes on significance. To design a strategy of persuasion in order to win the support of another, the persuader must make a deliberate effort to discover the goals of the communicative act and the means by which those goals can be accomplished.

An example of the importance of using persuasion to influence behavior is found in the experience of the manager of a small business. The manager realized that some of his decisions had produced an unspoken hostility between him and the workers. It became apparent that his authoritarian control was the source of these hostilities, and he decided to investigate alternatives. After discussing the matter with other managers, he altered his approach. Instead of dictatorially announcing plans by memo, he discussed matters with the employees, seeking their advice and opinions. By involving the employees in decisions and infusing his own recommendations into their discussions of the problem, he not only obtained his goal but also won the respect and cooperation of his staff. To persuade the employees, the manager cited historical evidence, listing the companies that successfully utilized the new procedures he advocated; he used the prestige, but not the authoritativeness, of his own position, a factor sometimes called ethical appeal; and he used logic, showing the reasons his proposed innovations probably would succeed. The manager learned to influence responses by consciously designing a communication strategy.

CONSTITUENTS OF PERSUASIVE COMMUNICATION

The four major constituents of persuasive communication are (1) a persuader, (2) a purpose, (3) a persuasive message, and (4) an audience to be persuaded. Each of these constituents influences the persuasive act.

The Persuader

The persuader, or sender of the message, has several rhetorical tools with which to execute a persuasive act. The persuader may use the power of office and the appeal of ethos (speaker credibility), employ rational or logical appeals, and employ appeals that aim at emotional responses from those to be persuaded. The principal appeal used by the speaker is variously referred to in communication literature as ethos, ethical appeal, personal appeal, or source credibility. We shall use the term *speaker credibility.*

Speaker Credibility

It is impossible to separate the speaker's effect on the audience from the content of the message. If listeners regard a speaker highly, they will adopt a more favorable attitude toward the proposition than if they had a negative impression. Consequently it is important that the speaker bring to the platform a strong, positive, personal appeal. The importance of source credibility cannot be minimized and can be reinforced in seven principal ways.

POSITION.   Why do millions of people listen with respect to the words of the president of the United States on a matter of policy? Not necessarily because the president represents the political views of the listeners or is more brilliant than they are but because the nature of the position commands deference. The president of the United States brings to the speaking situation a respect derived from the prestige and powers of the office. In a similar manner, employees will listen with great interest when the president of the company speaks, even though their contact may be minimal or purely formal. The very fact that someone is the president of the company and represents the firm to the outside world creates respect that he or she might not otherwise enjoy. Similarly, most students are attentive and deferential to their teacher because of the teacher's position or status.

REPUTATION.   The persuader's reputation accounts for a second source of credibility. A good reputation based on past performances, accomplishments, publicity, and honors will contribute to the audience's acceptance of the speaker as a credible source. In addition, the chairperson of a meeting can, in an introduction, enhance the speaker's reputation and prestige by listing the speaker's qualifications as an expert on the topic. Favorable publicity preceding the speech also adds to the speaker's credibility. Most important, however, are those methods employed in the speech to reinforce the speaker's reputation.

GOODWILL.   Speakers may create goodwill by reminding the listeners of their association with persons, institutions, and goals respected by the audience. Not infrequently, politicians invoke the family, God, and country as a means of improving their image with voters. Although this triumvirate is a bit obvious, it clarifies the point.

> When the conduct of men is designed to be influenced, *persuasion,* kind, unassuming persuasion should ever be adopted. It is an old and true maxim, that a "drop of honey catches more flies than a gallon of gall." So with men. If you would win a man over to your cause, first convince him that you are his sincere friend. Therein is a drop of honey that catches his heart, which, say what he will, is the great high road to his reason.
>
> ABRAHAM LINCOLN

Speakers who can identify with the heroes, ideals, and causes admired by the audience will improve their chances for acceptance. Speakers may create goodwill by praising the audience, its leaders, or its accomplishments. Simply by demonstrating familiarity with the group or community, speakers may earn a favorable reaction. By displaying modesty, a sense of humor, and pleasure at being permitted to talk to the audience, speakers may enhance the listeners' goodwill.

INTELLECTUAL INTEGRITY.   Intellectual integrity, a fourth source of credibility, is imperative for the persuader. A person who is both self-assertive and self-effacing, honest and yet obviously wary of bravado, exaggeration, and deception, will elicit the approval of the audience. On the other hand, the public is not easily fooled, at least not for long. When we begin to doubt the honesty of a speaker, that speaker loses credibility. Honesty is essential to trust, and trust is essential to acceptance. When persons in positions of leadership provide the public with false information, the listener begins to question their integrity. Listeners also believe that the words and ideas expressed by speakers should reflect their own ideas and be of their own creation. Although it may be necessary at times for some persons to employ ghostwriters, knowledge that a speaker has personally prepared the speech increases ethical appeal. Such was the case with Adlai Stevenson, who was admired almost as much for the fact that he wrote his own material as for the ideas that material conveyed. Listeners value honesty; they respect rhetorical effort.

KNOWLEDGE.   A fifth ingredient of source credibility is knowledge, learning, or wisdom. The pretender to wisdom, the pseudointellectual, will soon be discovered, while the caretaker of legitimate knowledge will earn respect. A speaker must know his or her subject. The accumulation of evidence to support a position or proposition is an important aspect of persuasion. Supportive evidence not only enables the speaker to present logical reasons for accepting a position, it also creates a favorable impression with the audience.

If speakers present ideas and supporting materials with thoroughness and confidence, the audience will be impressed. However, if speakers belabor the obvious or talk at a level beyond their comprehension, an audience is less likely to accept them. As still another method of advancing reputation as knowledgeable persons, speakers may tactfully and unobtrusively indicate their qualifications as experts.

SINCERITY.   Sincerity is a sixth ingredient of credibility. There is probably no greater example of the power of sincerity than that represented by the election of President Harry Truman in 1948. While all the polls predicted overwhelming defeat, President Truman embarked on a whistle-stop campaign, talking to thousands of voters from the back of a train. A frequent comment by those who heard Truman was, "He sounds so sincere." Truman's sincerity proved a significant factor in his winning the election. Some more recent persons who seem to enhance their images because they appear to be sincere might include Bill Moyers, Jesse Jackson, Gloria Steinem, and Lee Iacocca.

After gathering facts, statistics, and other supporting materials, the speaker should digest them thoroughly and present them with conviction. Beware, however, of the "persuasive fallacy," the pretense of unparalleled intelligence and unquestionable knowledge. A speaker should never make the audience appear ignorant or stupid or belittle or embarrass them. As a persuader, the speaker must approach the listener in a spirit of goodwill. The speaker must make it clear that the argument is in the interests of the listeners. The speaker who identifies with the listeners as a member of their group or supporter of a common cause may dispel any predisposition on the part of the audience to question his or her motives. An audience is likely to reject the arguments of one who appears to be soliciting support for a selfish cause or for self-aggrandizement.

DELIVERY.   The speaker's delivery is a seventh source of credibility. One who exhibits timidity, nervousness, indirectness, or lethargy may well be immediately rejected by the audience. On the other hand, the speaker who approaches the audience with confidence, firmness, and self-assurance will probably earn the respect of listeners. For this reason, the speaker should, from the outset, establish direct eye contact with the audience and adopt a sure and enthusiastic manner of delivery—attributes attained by vigorous vocal and physical presentation. The speech should be lively, for most audiences are unimpressed by sobriety, no matter how erudite.

The Purpose of Persuasion

We defined persuasion as discourse consciously designed to influence others, to make them agree with us. Thus the second constituent of a persuasive speech is the speaker's purpose or the specific response desired from the audience. The persuasive speaker's purpose may be to actuate, to obtain some definite observable performance from the audience, such as asking the listeners to vote for a particular person or issue in a referendum. In the case of an evangelist, the desired observable performance may be in the form of raised hands or verbal testimonies expressing belief in the message proposed by the evangelist.

A second possible response desired by the speaker may be to change the attitudes or beliefs of the members of the audience. In the case of a court trial, the ultimate goal for a defense attorney is to persuade the jury to hand down a verdict of "not guilty," but in the process of the trial, the attorney will attempt to shape the jury's attitude favorably toward the defendant.

A third purpose of the speaker may be to inspire members of the audience, to arouse their enthusiasm, or to strengthen their existing feelings of respect or devotion. The function of the president of a labor union at its annual convention, for example, is to heighten the members' loyalty to the union. The football coach at a pregame rally usually seeks to stimulate the loyalty and enthusiasm of the student body.

The specific purpose of the speech to persuade may be to influence beliefs, to arouse emotions, or to actuate audiences.

The Message

The third constituent of a persuasive speech, the message, may take many forms. Aristotle defined three types of messages: deliberative, forensic, and epideictic or demonstrative. He further clarified these types by describing the deliberative speech as appropriate to matters of probability and future action, the forensic speech to events, and demonstrative speeches to concerns of praise or blame. Contemporary rhetoricians define these three types of speeches as those that affirm propositions of policy (deliberative), those that affirm propositions of fact (forensic), and those that affirm propositions of value (demonstrative).

Deliberative speeches, or those affirming propositions of policy, concern themselves with the wisdom or expediency of courses of action affecting the future welfare of the audience. Members of Congress, when devising and debating laws to guide the country, utilize the deliberative form. For instance, when a bill is debated for final passage, supporters of the legislation usually argue that the new legislation will improve society. Opponents often argue that passage of the bill will create more problems than already exist. Whether the issue is tax reform, conservation, or population control, debates in Congress are usually concerned with legislation affecting future events.

The forensic form of speeches to persuade is best illustrated by courtroom speaking. The questions answered in the courtroom involve the determination of the facts surrounding past events and are all forms of the basic question "Is the defendant guilty?" The propositions presented are basically propositions of fact. Who actually pulled the trigger during the armed robbery? Was the defendant's gun the murder weapon? But speeches that affirm propositions of fact extend beyond the courtroom and include such questions as "What is the major cause of air pollution?" "Are grades a reliable index of how much a student knows?" "Is the 'energy crisis' real or contrived?" "Who is responsible for terroristic acts?"

The demonstrative speech was defined by Aristotle as a speech to praise or blame. Eulogies delivered at memorial services are good examples of this type of speaking. Fourth of July orations and Labor Day speeches also fall into this category. We might think of this type of speech, however, as being more inclusive than just praising or blaming, and also include speeches that affirm propositions of value. A speech of this nature attempts to determine the value of an object or policy by comparing it with values of similar acts or policies. Examples of propositions of value would include the value of requiring study of a foreign language, the value of owning a subcompact car, or the values of jogging, health foods, ethics commissions, or yoga.

Appeals

Whatever the form of the message, it must contain information that appeals to the intellect and the emotions of the audience and creates for them a belief in the speaker. When developing the message, the speaker should consider three types of appeals to make the speech attractive and compelling to the audience. To make an argument intellectually acceptable, the speaker should employ logical appeals. To compel the audience to believe, the speaker should employ ethical appeals. And to motivate the listeners to act as desired, the speaker should employ emotional appeals. Each of these types of appeals or proofs is discussed separately below, although often a single statement may contain all three types of appeal.

LOGICAL APPEALS.   People like to think of themselves as rational beings. Consequently, if a persuasive message is to be effective, reasons for accepting the ideas and actions called for by the speaker must be provided. The reasoning process and the supporting materials used to give credence to the proposition are the elements of logical proof. An academic adviser, for instance, might recommend that a student majoring in English take a course in logic. The student might well ask "Why?" The adviser is then required to furnish support for the recommendation. That support might consist of the testimony of other English majors who said that logic had assisted them in understanding the subject matter of English or the testimony of a well-known and respected educator, or some examples of benefits to be gained from taking the course. The forms of evidence available to the persuader and the tests of that evidence are discussed later in this chapter.

ETHICAL APPEALS.   Ethical proof concerns the attitude of the audience toward the speaker. The concept of ethical proof is based quite simply on the assumption that listeners are more likely to agree with people they

In order to persuade a man of sense, you must first convince him, which is only done by satisfying his understanding of the reasonableness of what you propose to him.

HUGH BLAIR

like, trust, and admire than with people they dislike, distrust, or do not respect. Thus they are likely to place more confidence in the statements of a friend than in those of an enemy or rival, more credence in the information of a reliable acquaintance than that of the neighborhood gossip, and more respect for the opinions of an experienced courtroom judge than those of a first-year law student. We discussed earlier in this chapter the elements of speaker credibility that constitute ethical appeal. Speakers who are known to an audience bring with them a built-in credibility based on their prior reputation and deeds. However, the able speaker will seek to enhance that credibility by including in the speech specific information demonstrating the speaker's qualifications as an authority on the topic, the speaker's good character, and the speaker's modesty and appreciation and respect for the audience. The speaker may, at times, seek to remove any negative impressions that an audience may have. For a discussion of this aspect of speaker credibility, see pages 112–113.

EMOTIONAL APPEALS.   The use of emotional appeals by a speaker is thought by some scholars to be antithetical to the use of rational or logical appeals, because emotional excitement often impairs rational judgment. However, philosopher Lionel Ruby contends that logic has its proper place and so has emotion. He says, "A purely intellectual approach to life is as insufficient as a purely emotional one." When, then, is logical, rational support required in a speech, and when should one employ emotional appeals? According to Ruby, "When we assert beliefs which may be questioned, then we have an obligation to be rational . . . [and] we ought to support our beliefs with adequate evidence. When we say we know something is true, we ought to be able to justify our belief by adequate evidence.

In other words, speakers have an obligation to be logical when logic is relevant. Ruby continues, arguing:

> And when we act on emotion without concerning ourselves with the facts, we are likely to rush into disaster. Usually, when a politician . . . substitutes emotional appeals for proof, propaganda for rational persuasion, when he inflames rather than informs, we shall find that he does so for one of two reasons. Either he has a contempt for the people, treating them as if they were children, incapable of understanding the issues, or he doesn't want them to know the truth.
>
> We are not saying that emotional appeals are never appropriate. On the contrary. When the facts are not in question, and action is desired, then an emotional appeal is appropriate, even indispensable. In the critical days of 1940 Prime Minister Winston Churchill made his great "blood, sweat, and tears" speech to the British people. He inspired his people and spurred them to heroic efforts. Emotion is the best fuel for this kind of energy, and this kind of stimulus is needed even in the best of causes.

> Let us pause for a moment to get our bearings. . . . We have not condemned emotional appeals under all circumstances but only when we substitute emotion for proof when proof is required. The latter form of behavior is the essence of what is meant by "How Not to Argue." (Lionel Ruby, *The Art of Making Sense,* Philadelphia: J. B. Lippincott Co., 1954, pp. 78–80.)

The speaker who appeals only to the emotions abrogates responsibilities to the audience. But emotional appeals can be used to reinforce logical arguments and, if used well, can be a major factor in exciting human motives. Emotional excitement tends to express itself in action. It is not surprising that in the heat of competition an athlete occasionally will attack an opponent, or that teams sometimes "clear the benches" in a general melee. Because emotion provokes action, persuasive speakers often seek to arouse the feelings of their listeners.

For centuries, philosophers, scholars, and observers of human behavior have attempted to understand the forces that impel people to act. Various concepts of "emotion," "drive," "need," "desire," and "motive" have been set forth. It is not surprising, then, that today no two rhetoricians, philosophers, or psychologists are likely to agree completely on what emotional needs motivate an individual to action. Generally, however, they make a distinction between basic physiological drives and secondary, socially derived, or learned motives. The basic physiological needs include such drives as self-preservation, hunger, thirst, shelter, security from bodily harm, and sex. Secondary drives might include a wide range of emotions related to the desire for freedom from restraints, acceptance, physical well-being, and pleasure. Other such secondary motivating factors might be labeled as a desire for power, for financial gain, for ownership, for respect, for adventure, for friendship, and for relief from distress. They would also include curiosity, loyalty, love, fear, hate, jealousy, security, justice, sense of fair play, sympathy, and anger.

Because people hold on with varying intensity to different goals and attitudes, the effective persuader will analyze an audience to determine the goals and attitudes to which the listeners are most intensely committed.

A proper blending of logical, ethical, and emotional appeals is needed to produce a desired response from an audience. This blending requires a thorough knowledge of the topic and of the audience.

The passions are the only orators who always convince. They have a kind of natural art with infallible rules; and the most untutored man with passion is more persuasive than the most eloquent without.

LA ROCHEFOUCAULD

SUPPORTING MATERIALS FOR PERSUASION

Effective supporting material is particularly important when a speaker seeks to convince or persuade. Audiences tend to listen to informing, entertaining, and inspiring speeches with an open mind or even a favorable attitude, so the speaker, in these cases, need be concerned only with maintaining interest while clarifying the topic. However, in argumentative speeches, speakers face the difficulty of dealing with audiences that are, at least in part, apathetic, skeptical, or opposed to the speakers' ideas. The critical or questioning attitude of listeners toward persuasive messages demands that the speaker apply rigorous standards in the choice of supporting material.

Effective argumentation is based on sound supporting material, or evidence, and valid reasoning. Although a speaker's message may be made more attractive by appeals to the feelings of the listeners (emotional proof) or enhanced by a good reputation (ethical proof), it is rare that an antagonistic audience can be won over by these factors alone. Essential to any argument that will withstand critical scrutiny, both at the time of delivery and upon later reflection, is a solid foundation of factual evidence (logical proof).

The responsible speaker's main appeal will be to the minds of the listeners, with emotional and ethical appeals used sparingly and appropriately.

Facts

WHAT ARE FACTS?   Although everyone talks a great deal about facts, most people probably could not explain what a fact is. To the scientist, a fact is empirically verifiable data. More generally defined, facts are the materials from which we attempt to draw conclusions or between which we seek to establish relationships. Facts—in contrast to theories or opinions, which are merely speculative—have to do with the existence and nature of things.

Facts are regarded as true only because those best fitted to judge proclaim them so. Most of what is considered fact can be determined by the judgment of the general population and is based on simple observation. For example, the reader undoubtedly feels competent to decide whether this is a book, whether the sun rises in the east, and whether it is raining at any given moment. Most people, however, probably do not feel qualified to determine

> Our judgments when we are pleased and friendly are not the same as when we are pained and hostile.
>
> ARISTOTLE

many other matters, such as the genetic effects of atomic radiation, the acoustical properties of an auditorium, or how leukemia affects the blood. In these instances, the layperson defers to the judgment of accepted authorities in the field. The practical test of facts, then, is whether they are sanctioned by common knowledge and by the judgment of experts. But we must remember that both the rank and file of people and the experts continually demonstrate that they are not infallible in assessing facts.

ARE FACTS PROVABLE?   It is not uncommon to hear references to "proven facts" and statements such as, "I know that is true. It has been proved to be a fact." Such comments raise the question: Can facts always be proved? The answer is no. And, because facts cannot always be proved, it follows that some things that are regarded as fact have never been proved.

While much of the body of knowledge considered to be fact can be demonstrated through some kind of systematic "proof," if proof is regarded as a scientific, mathematical, or experimental testing, then a great many facts can be said to be unproven or unprovable. Much of what is fact is the result of observation rather than methodological testing. For example, "John was absent from class Wednesday," "That is a desk," "The Declaration of Independence was written in 1776," "The Mississippi River flows through Louisiana," and "I have a pear tree growing in my backyard" are statements that, if correct, are factual. They are facts, however, not because they have been scientifically proved to be so but because persons qualified to judge such matters agree that each statement is a fact. Their status as facts rests not on their being proved, but on personal observation. Even facts that are derived through scientific research and carefully controlled experimentation are based, in the final analysis, on the observations of the scientists or researchers who must interpret what they have discovered or proved.

ARE FACTS ALWAYS TRUE?   Surprisingly, facts are not always true. To the best of our knowledge, everything we accept as fact is true; we regard it as truth and, accordingly, base our reasoning and decisions on it. However, at any moment, materials accepted as factual may be demonstrated to be false or untrue. For example, experts at one time regarded it as a fact that the earth was not round. All charting, mapmaking, and scientific thought rested on the fact that the earth was flat. It would have been unthinkable then to suggest that the earth was round, just as today it is unthinkable to suggest that the earth is not spheroid. Later, when it was demonstrated that the earth was not flat, it was necessary to correct and readjust all calculations and thought based on the formerly accepted fact. With our advanced technology, it seems inconceivable that what we *know* to be facts today could be in error, but time and progress will probably demonstrate that many presently accepted facts are untrue. So while one may say that all facts are true today, or at least presently

> Let our discourses be founded upon reason, and let us establish everything we advance with solid and convincing arguments.
>
> THOMAS GIBBONS

regarded as being true, it cannot be said that all that is now considered as factual will always be true.

If facts deal with what is certain or true, what is the opposite of a fact? A falsehood or untruth could hardly be regarded as its opposite, for if something is accepted as being false or untrue, it has much the same status of certainty as a fact. Thus if certainty and acceptability are criteria for calling something a fact, words indicating uncertainty would be appropriate opposites. So one might say that the opposite of a fact is an *uncertainty*, a *theory*, an *opinion*, a *controversy*, a *belief*, or a *hypothesis*.

If a division of opinion is the mark of a nonfact, how widely must something be accepted before it may be regarded as fact? If the majority of those capable of deciding believe something to be true, is it then a fact? Certainly not, for if that were the case, it would be necessary to classify as fact a great many things that clearly are opinions. Popularity does not guarantee that one political candidate is better qualified than another, that a particular product is best, or that one philosophy is correct, whether the judges be lay or experts.

As long as a difference of opinion exists among competent observers, the matter remains in the realm of belief, opinion, or theory. Unanimity of opinion is necessary before the label *fact* can correctly be applied to a condition, circumstance, or relationship. By this formula, anything universally acclaimed as fact becomes theory, opinion, or belief when qualified judges begin to doubt its accuracy. This is not meant to suggest that a fact becomes an opinion whenever human error or misunderstanding temporarily leads an otherwise competent judge to dissent. Everyone misjudges from time to time. Therefore, it is quite possible that well-qualified judges might momentarily question the validity of an otherwise accepted fact. If after further investigation they perceive their error and unanimity of opinion is restored, the fact remains a fact. If, on the other hand, the critics continue to question the accuracy of an alleged fact, then clearly the matter has fallen into the realm of controversy or conjecture and can no longer be regarded as fact.

That a concept is not a fact should not lead one to dismiss it as having no worth. A large part of every person's life is based on theories, opinions, and attitudes. Most religious, political, philosophical, and moral beliefs and codes rest largely on theory rather than fact.

In speech, both theoretical and factual materials are useful in influencing others. However, it is important that the speaker recognize the difference between the two, between what is accepted as fact, and therefore needs no proof, and what is not factual and requires supporting documentation before it will be accepted by some listeners.

To test your knowledge of the difference between facts and theories or opinions, read the 15 statements listed below and classify each as either factual or theoretical.

1. Democracy is the best form of government.
2. A good personality is important to success.
3. A college education is beneficial.
4. George Washington was a great president.
5. The United States is a peace-loving country.
6. Training in speech is valuable.
7. The Chicago Symphony is one of the world's great orchestras.
8. Colleges and universities should grant students a greater voice in their education.
9. Intercollegiate athletics make a worthwhile contribution to education.
10. American medicine is the best in the world.
11. The U.S. Congress consists of two houses: the Senate and the House of Representatives.
12. The Minnesota Twins won the World Series in 1987.
13. Glacier National Park is in Montana and is 1538 square miles in size.
14. Bismarck is the capital of North Dakota.
15. The United States was the first nation to explode an atomic bomb.

The first 10 of these statements are opinions or theories. In other words, any one of these 10 statements might evoke both agreement and disagreement among competent, intelligent people. The last 5 statements are factual. No informed persons would be likely to disagree with any of the final 5 statements, unless they were temporarily misinformed. If any of the first 10 statements were to be used in a speech, the speaker would have to present supporting material to prove the point. Note, however, a difference between the first 5 statements and the second 5. The first 5 are so widely accepted by most Americans that with many audiences little evidence would be required to support these points. Numbers 6 through 10, being more controversial, would demand substantial support to make them convincing to the audience.

Testing Sources of Evidence

The sources of supporting material for an argumentative speech may include books, magazines, encyclopedias, government documents, newspapers, specialized reference works, professional journals, pamphlets, broadcasts, bulletins, surveys, speeches, and personal interviews.

In studying a topic, the speaker should critically evaluate all sources, for if the source is unreliable, the speaker has little reason to place any faith in what it says. Among the questions that should be asked about the source are: (1) Is it clearly identified? (2) Is it reliable? (3) Is it unbiased? (4) Is it honest? (5) Is it recent? (6) Is it corroborated by other sources?

IS THE SOURCE CLEARLY IDENTIFIED?   In identifying sources, the speaker should ask: Who is responsible for this publication or broadcast? If the author, publisher, or sponsor is not indicated, the speaker should waste no time on it. Until one knows who prepared or authorized the work, one has no way of judging whether it is trustworthy. Furthermore, even when authors, publishers, and sponsors are indicated, the speaker should investigate these individuals or groups. Pressure groups and others with special interests often create "foundations," "research institutes," and other front organizations with respectable names in order to issue publications designed to influence public opinion. The less responsible an organization, the greater need it has to conceal its true identity.

Failure to investigate sources can lead to public embarrassment, as a former administrator of the Environmental Protection Agency (EPA) learned when he mentioned in a speech the findings of a "federally aided experiment" in California. Following the speech, when the EPA was flooded with requests for more information about the study, the agency belatedly discovered that the administrator had misunderstood a conversation with a colleague and that no such study existed.

IS THE SOURCE RELIABLE?   Having established who is responsible for the work, the speaker should next ask whether the source is reliable. Does it have a reputation for integrity? Does it aim at accuracy rather than sensationalism? Is it more interested in education than in propaganda? Does it have a staff adequate in size and experience to undertake the type of study or investigation it purports to present? If it is a magazine or journal, are the articles signed? Do you know exactly who is responsible for the different parts of the publication? With the most reliable sources, the answers to all of the foregoing questions will be yes.

While it would be impossible to compile a list of all the sources considered reliable and futile to try to prepare one with which everyone would agree, some sources generally regarded as dependable can be suggested. Recognized encyclopedias such as the *Encyclopedia Americana,* the *Encyclopaedia Britannica,* and the *World Book Encyclopedia* have a reputation for reliability, as do other standard reference works such as *World Almanac* and various yearbooks. Publications by government agencies such as the United States Census Bureau, the Library of Congress, the Department of Agriculture, the Department of Commerce, and others are usually dependable if the work consists of a presentation of purely factual information. On the other hand, one should be suspicious of publications whose purpose seems to be to prove the success of some political program, to justify a committee's existence, or to demonstrate the competence of a bureau or agency. Reports of internal security committees, state sovereignty commissions, and other investigatory groups often fall into one of these categories.

In the field of newspapers, the *New York Times,* the *Washington Post,* the *Los Angeles Times,* the *Louisville Courier-Journal,* the *St. Louis Post-Dispatch,* the *Wall Street Journal,* and the *Christian Science Monitor* have reputations for honesty and dependability. In surveys of publishers, these newspapers consistently rate among the most reputable.

In evaluating sources, the speaker should be careful not to misjudge the reliability of one part or one article because of the publication in which it appears. The *Congressional Record,* for example, may seem to be a highly reputable source because it publishes the speeches and debates of Congress. However, since members of Congress are allowed to insert anything they wish into the *Record,* a great deal of inaccurate material appears within its pages. Even the speeches may not be authentic, because members are permitted to revise them before publication. In 1972 the *Record* published a speech allegedly given by a congressman who, tragically, had been killed in a plane crash a few days before the date on which he supposedly delivered the address. Perhaps the sublime in the realm of unreliability was the publication in 1978 of an eight-volume, 4500-page report on the "hearings" of a congressional committee on the budget. In fact, the committee *never* met! On the other hand, *Playboy* and *Esquire* magazines, which are better known for other diversions, often publish works of significance by reputable writers.

IS THE SOURCE UNBIASED?   A source may be said to be biased when it has a vested interest in the outcome of an issue. The source may sincerely believe it is objective, but because it stands to gain or lose depending on the way the issue is resolved, it cannot be trusted to observe impartially. Thus, for example, a newspaper published by a labor union may strive for objectivity in discussing a proposed wage increase, but it is unlikely that it will be wholly unbiased. Furthermore, even if it were objective, the general public would probably question its impartiality.

As this example suggests, publications by groups with special interests are likely to be biased. Such sources would include many publications issued by political parties, business firms, religious organizations, pressure groups, minorities, and others. In addition, some publications designed to serve special segments of the community are not likely to publish anything offensive to them. *Fortune,* for example, is a magazine for and about big business and depends heavily on industry for advertising. For this reason, one might question the impartiality of *Fortune* on issues affecting business. On the other hand, some of the most reliable, objective evidence available concerning business trends might well be found within the pages of *Fortune.*

Among the biases a reader might expect to find in a few other publications are: the *Journal of the American Medical Association,* opposed to national health insurance and federal interference in medical matters; *Broadcasting,* against stringent regulation of radio and television by the federal government; *Democratic Digest,* a publication of the Democratic party; *Chicago Tribune,* politically conservative; *American Legion Magazine,* politically conservative, especially regarding defense and foreign affairs; *Monthly Review,* Marxist oriented; *The Worker,* pro-Communist; and *Independent American,* prosegregation.

IS THE SOURCE HONEST?   Although the publishers of biased sources may give a slanted analysis of a problem, many do so in the sincere belief that they are telling the truth. Others, however, sometimes set out deliberately to mislead the public. Such sources can be said to be intellectually dishonest. A popular national magazine once placed on its cover what appeared to be a secret photograph of a famous wealthy recluse who had not been seen in public for many years. The magazine made no mention of the fact that the photograph was a fake. While trivial, this is an example of intellectual dishonesty.

A more serious example occurred when a television station was found repeatedly to have shown films supposedly depicting current events that actually were old films taken from the files and relabeled. A film of a crowd in Bucharest, Romania, for example, was said to show Prague during the Soviet occupation of Czechoslovakia.

Authors sometimes deliberately falsify in order to promote a cause or to create a better public image for an organization or individual. Campaign biographies written to advance the prospects of a candidate often omit unpleasant details, gloss over some facts, and emphasize others. Political tracts written to win support for or against some piece of legislation frequently quote out of context, select materials favorable only to their point of view, and in other ways distort the facts. A notorious example of intellectual dishonesty was the publication in 1978 of a book purportedly written by a black urging other blacks to purchase weapons and instructing them on how to organize an attack on the white population of the United States. Later, it was discovered that the book actually had been written and published by a leader of the all-white Ku Klux Klan.

Disclosures of deliberate deception by prominent government and military officials in the 1960s and 1970s regarding the war in Vietnam, the bombing of Cambodia, and the Watergate break-in did much to undermine the confidence of the American public in the honesty and integrity of its leadership. Clearly, if there is any evidence of dishonesty on the part of the author or publisher, the speaker should place no confidence in the work.

IS THE SOURCE RECENT?   The speaker should check the publication dates of sources to determine whether they contain the latest available information. Conditions change rapidly, and out-of-date information may be highly unreliable in analyzing a current situation. If the publication is a second, third, or fourth printing or edition, also check to see whether material in the latest issue has been brought up-to-date.

IS THE SOURCE CORROBORATED BY OTHER SOURCES?   If information available in one source is not corroborated by other sources, the speaker has good reason to regard it with suspicion. The fact that other sources fail to corroborate it does not actually disprove the reliability of the evidence, but if the material is at all significant, its unavailability in other sources where one might reasonably expect to find it certainly raises doubts about its validity.

Anything that has been reprinted from another source should be verified by checking the data in the original source to make sure that it has been fully and accurately reported.

Testing the Evidence

Having determined the reliability of sources, the speaker is now ready to test the evidence. While a speaker may employ any of the types of supporting material used in exposition, in argumentative speaking the principal forms of evidence are specific instances, statistics, comparisons, the testimony of authorities, and causal relationships.

The speaker should support arguments with the best available evidence for two reasons: (1) to make sure that the speaker's own analysis and understanding of the subject are correct, and (2) to provide listeners with the most conclusive case possible.

TESTING SPECIFIC INSTANCES.   In arguing from specific instances, the speaker attempts to support contentions inductively by citing specific examples, illustrations, or instances to prove a more general conclusion. The following excerpt from a speech by history professor Larry R. Gerlack is an example of the use of specific instances. In attempting to prove that sport is an important part of our society, he said:

> The enormous capacity of television to reach people has sold sport. If TV moguls devote so much programming time to sport, then sport must be important. If television devotes virtually an entire day to covering the Super Bowl, then that contest must be important. And by extension, sport itself must be very important. I would suggest that sport is regarded as being much more influential in our society than it really is because of the attention that television pays to it. (*Representative American Speeches, 1983–1984,* New York: H. W. Wilson Co., 1984, p. 84.)

In developing an argument by employing specific instances, the speaker should apply the following tests:

1. *Are enough instances presented?* To present an argument that is to be convincing, the speaker must cite enough specific instances to justify the conclusion drawn. For example, an audience will not accept the conclusion that college students are rude if the speaker mentions only two or three examples of student discourtesy. Likewise, citing four or five faculty members who are poorly prepared for their classes is not enough to warrant any broad generalization about the competence of the entire faculty. Whereas no fixed number of instances necessary to prove a contention can be prescribed, because the number will depend on what argument the speaker hopes to prove, enough should be presented to convince the audience.

Even when a large number of instances are cited, however, the speaker should be careful not to overstate the argument, not to be too sweeping in the use of generalization. Arguments claiming to prove contentions covering *all, every,* or even *most* parts of the whole are difficult to support with specific instances. The speaker is probably wise to qualify the conclusion with terms such as *generally, usually, frequently,* and *commonly;* or the speaker might contend that the specific instances demonstrate a *serious* problem, a *major* failure, or a *pattern* of error.

2. *Are the instances fairly chosen?* If the speaker wishes to generalize about a group or class, it is necessary for specific instances to be representative and typical of the whole, rather than exceptions or the unusual. Anyone who reads a daily newspaper has come across examples of clergy who have been involved in scandals, government employees who have given secret information to foreign agents, respected business executives who have been guilty of bigamy, college presidents with phony degrees, and judges who have committed criminal acts. However, these instances are so unrepresentative that it is difficult to see how they could be used as a basis for any kind of generalization about the clergy, the government, business, educators, or the judiciary. Arguments based on specific instances are valid only when the instances are representative.

3. *Are there significant exceptions to the instances?* At times, a speaker may be able to compose an argument based on specific instances that are both frequent and representative but that fail to prove the generalization because of significant exceptions. For example, the contention that a big-time intercollegiate athletic program lends prestige to a college or university might be supported by examples of outstanding schools that are well-known for their athletic teams. Among such instances, the speaker could cite Notre Dame, Southern California, Ohio State, Texas, Michigan, Penn State, U.C.L.A., and many others. In spite of the adequacy of these instances, the speaker could not logically conclude that emphasis on athletics was *essential* to the prestige of an institution, because too many ex-

ceptions exist. One need only look to Harvard, Yale, Columbia, the other Ivy League schools, Johns Hopkins, M.I.T., and the University of Chicago, where athletics are not stressed, to see the fallacy in the speaker's argument. Whenever a speaker argues from specific instances, he or she must investigate carefully to determine whether exceptions exist that invalidate the conclusions.

4. *Are the instances true?* Are the examples what they appear to be? In verifying the accuracy of specific instances, the speaker should first determine that each instance actually exists or occurred. After being satisfied that the instance is true, the speaker should investigate whether it actually is an example of what it seems to be. For example, whether a newspaper photograph of a police officer striking someone being arrested is evidence of police brutality would depend on the circumstance that led up to the act. If a business has more men than women in executive positions, is this an example of discrimination against women? Often a condition or action that appears to illustrate one thing will, upon closer scrutiny, turn out to illustrate something quite different.

5. *Are the instances recent?* Since out-of-date instances are of little value in proving anything about current conditions, the speaker should make certain that specific instances are recent enough to be applicable to the problem being discussed.

Just how recent the instances should be will depend on the speaker's subject. In some fields, data become outdated very quickly. A discovery, a new law, a change in management or ownership, a court decision, adoption of new policies, or the election of different officials may drastically alter a situation almost overnight. For example, not long ago, poliomyelitis was a serious national health problem. But the discovery and use of polio vaccines virtually eliminated the disease within a few years. Many questionable practices of manufacturers and lenders were curbed as soon as "fairness in packaging" and "fairness in lending" legislation went into effect. Recent decisions of OPEC (the Organization of Petroleum Exporting Countries) on the price of oil have affected almost every American. In each of these instances, the nature of the problem changed completely within a short period of time. In other areas, change may be more gradual. But in either case, the speaker should take care that instances are sufficiently recent to represent conditions accurately.

TESTING STATISTICS.   When used properly, statistics often are the most conclusive kind of evidence for proving one's contention. A statistical total showing exactly how many armed robberies occurred over a fixed period of time, for example, is a far more accurate index of the incidence of this crime than a series of specific instances of armed robberies. However, although statistics may be highly accurate and definitive, they often are difficult to interpret.

Statistics may be employed in various ways to support an argument or contention. Examples are cited below:

One out of every three blacks in this country is officially listed below the poverty line.

One out of every three blacks lives in substandard housing.

One out of five black adults is unemployed.

One out of two black youths can't find work.

Black infant mortality is twice as high as that of whites.

Despite the progress we have made in the area of voter participation, less than one percent of the more than 500,000 elected officials are black.

In the House of Representatives there are a total of 21 black congresspersons, including the nonvoting delegate from the District of Columbia, out of 435.

In the United States Senate, since the defeat of Senator Edward Brooke, there are no blacks in the U.S. Senate out of 100 senators.

Of the top Fortune 500 corporations, less than 125 have blacks on their boards of directors.

Black enrollment in medical schools is less than 5 percent, in dental schools less than 3 percent, in law schools less than 4 percent of the totals.

In the area of business, according to the most recent survey, there are a total of 321,203 black firms, but they have a combined gross receipt of only $8.6 billion. This, in a nation with over a trillion dollars gross national product. The life expectancy for a black American is 6.1 years fewer than that of whites. The black median family income is 56 percent of that of white families. (Benjamin L. Hooks, *Representative American Speeches, 1983–1984,* New York: H. W. Wilson Co., 1984, pp. 84–85.)

The number of reported cases of child abuse has more than doubled over the past half dozen years, from 416,000 cases in 1976 to 851,000 cases in 1981. The National Center for Child Abuse and Neglect, however, estimates there may be another million cases of child abuse and neglect not reported and not seen, known only to the family members involved and maybe a friend or neighbor. If the center is right, that would mean close to 2 million instances of child abuse and neglect occurring each year in our society. That is certainly beyond anything we might "reasonably expect." Some of these statistics are open to question because our systems of reporting violent episodes are not what they should be. (C. Everett Koop, *Representative American Speeches, 1983–1984,* New York: H. W. Wilson Co., 1984, p. 167.)

The 28 hours a week that the majority of American adults sit inertly in front of their TV sets amounts to 1456 hours a year, or about a quarter of their waking hours. This means that if our addiction to television continues unabated . . . a one-year-old child, whose life expectancy will exceed 75 years, will spend at least 110,000 hours of his or her life in front of the tube. And if my arithmetic is correct, that amounts to 12 total years of your precious child's life. (I mean 24 hours times 365 days of a year.) (David Manning White, *Representative American Speeches, 1982–1983,* New York: H. W. Wilson Co., 1983, p. 90.)

To make certain statistics are being used properly, the speaker should ask several questions:

1. *Are enough statistics presented?* As with specific instances, speakers should determine whether they have enough statistical data to warrant the conclusion drawn from them. Statistics measuring only a part of the whole may not be a fair index to the complete picture. For example, statistics showing a rise in the cost of clothing or of dairy products reveal little about the overall cost of living. Likewise, figures on the incidence of asthma in one part of the country are virtually useless as an index to the incidence of this disorder nationally. The speaker should employ statistics that are comprehensive— that cover the entire population with which one is concerned.

2. *Are the statistics representative?* Surveys that are restricted to one segment of the whole, that pertain to one class or group, or that are obtained under unusual or artificial circumstances may not be typical and representative. Surveys requiring the respondent to complete a questionnaire may be misleading because they exclude the illiterates in the population. A survey conducted by telephone is likely to be biased because it does not include the lowest-income group—people who do not have telephones. Statistics obtained by interviewing people in one part of a city or one section of a state may not be representative of the whole city or state population. A survey of student opinion might be greatly affected by whether the surveyor conducted interviews at the library or at the student center, by the ratio of upperclassmen to freshmen, and by whether the sample has a fair proportion of students from the various colleges, divisions, or departments. Realizing that such factors affect statistical tabulations, the speaker should try to discover how the compiler obtained the statistics in order to verify that they are representative.

Many people place little confidence in surveys based on a sample of the whole, such as the Nielsen television ratings and the Gallup and Harris polls. Statisticians, however, agree that such surveys can be highly reliable indices of the entire population if they are based on a representative sample and if the sample is large enough. The most representative sample is one in which the interviewees are chosen entirely at random or, in other words, in which every person has an equal chance of being selected to be counted or interviewed. A completely random sample, however, is difficult to obtain in many instances, and so several of the polls that purport to survey a representative sample—that is, a sample containing allegedly correct ratios of persons of different religions, politics, income, age, sex, marital status, occupation, and other characteristics—do not, in fact, do so. So when using surveys, the speaker should seek to discover the polling methods employed in collecting the statistics.

3. *Are there significant exceptions to the statistics?* Some statistics can be highly misleading. Averages often give a false impression. For example, the statement that the homes in the block where I live have an average value of $250,000 gives the impression of an affluent neighborhood, when, in truth, one family may live in a million-dollar mansion and the remaining three families consist of paupers residing in cardboard shacks. Averages often conceal exceptions, thereby tending to hide serious problems and gross inequities. Thus the average income of retired persons, the average salary of teachers, or the average number of years of education completed by a group may hide the fact that substantial numbers of retired persons live on pittances, that many teachers are underpaid, or that widespread illiteracy exists.

4. *Are the statistics recent?* It is obvious that statistics that measure changing conditions such as the crime rate, gross national product, cost of living, wages and salaries, incidence of disease, production costs, defense spending, and similar factors must be recent if they are to reflect accurately the situation as it exists at the time. How recent should the speaker's statistics be? The only answer to that question is that they should be the most recent possible. Sometimes the passage of only a few weeks or months can greatly alter the accuracy of a speaker's statistics. For example, on the basis of public opinion surveys, it was freely predicted that Thomas Dewey would be elected president in 1948. However, the last survey was taken nearly two months before the election and, as the results indicated, did not reflect changing public attitudes which led to Harry Truman's victory. A single event—a scientific discovery, an invention, a political announcement, the outbreak of war, the enactment of a law, an assassination—may sometimes have great repercussions almost overnight on public opinion, the economy, and political conditions. An example would be the almost immediate increase in support of President Ronald Reagan following the release of Americans held hostage by Palestinian terrorists in 1985. The speaker must recognize that the most recent statistic available is the most reliable and that even that statistic may no longer be accurate.

5. *Are the units properly defined?* Since statistics are based on counting, it is important that the speaker know exactly what the compiler has counted. The speaker should determine how the compiler defined the units counted. For example, if the statistics concern the student body at Metropolitan University, the speaker should know what the compiler means by *students*. Does *students* include graduate students as well as undergraduates? Does it embrace part-time students, students enrolled in short-term workshops, seminars, and institutes? Are extension and correspondence students included? Students in branches or departments of the university located in other places? Unless

How recent are the statistics? (UPI)

these questions are answered, the speaker does not really know what the statistics reveal.

6. *Are the statistics an index to what they claim to measure?* At times, it is difficult to determine exactly what a set of statistics measures. For example, is a capacity audience at a campus lecture an indicator of student interest in the speech? Or were most of the students required to attend? Or was the audience composed mainly of faculty and townspeople?

Is a poll of coaches or sportswriters ranking college athletic teams a reliable indicator of which school has the best team? If so, why are highly ranked teams often defeated by lower-ranked or unranked teams?

Does a large increase in a city's population show that it is a prosperous, growing community? The 1980 census might show one city's population as having increased from 475,000 to 745,000 and another as jumping from 200,000 to 528,000 in 10 years. In both instances, the increase may have been accomplished simply by incorporating large areas of land outside the cities' limits.

Does a decline in the number of arrests for speeding show that the public is driving more carefully? Or is it a sign of less stringent law enforcement?

Is an increase in attendance at football games throughout the country an indicator of increased popularity of that game? Or does it merely reflect the increase in population? Could it indicate that more people can afford to attend sports events? Could it be related to the expansion of professional football to several new cities?

If a country has a high suicide rate, is the statistic an indicator of the tension of daily life in that nation, of the mental instability of the people, or of stricter and more accurate reporting of suicides than in other places? Could the suicide rate be related to the predominant religious belief of the country?

If a significant number of people refuse to participate in a survey, how reliable are the findings? For example, even the highly regarded United States Census is considered suspect by some authorities who believe that millions of illegal aliens in this country were not counted in 1980 because they refused to return the forms for fear of being deported.

As the above questions suggest, interpreting statistics can be a tricky task. So before speakers assert that statistics prove something, they should make sure that they know exactly what they measure.

7. *Were the statistics collected at the proper time or over a sufficient period of time?* Often the time of year, the particular day, or even the hour when a statistic is obtained can affect the accuracy of the tabulation. For example, a count of the number of vehicles passing a particular intersection to determine whether a traffic signal is needed can be misleading if the survey is taken on Sunday, on a holiday, early in the morning, or late in the evening.

In determining trends, the speaker should be certain that the statistics cover a sufficiently long period of time to permit an accurate judgment. For example, surveys of economic factors such as the unemployment rate, gross national product, cost of living, and inflation, or surveys of social trends such as crime, birth, and divorce rates are meaningless if they cover only a limited span of time, because temporary fluctuations or aberrations may have severely distorted the general direction or nature of the trend.

The success of many experiments, laws, and programs often cannot be accurately measured until a considerable period of time has passed. For example, the introduction of a new method of teaching in a school system probably can be evaluated only after large numbers of children have been taught under the plan for several years. The effectiveness of the "No Pass-No Play" rule adopted in Texas in 1985 cannot be measured until a substantial amount of time has elapsed. Legislation to curb inflation, laws to discourage drunken driving, public education campaigns, and similar measures may have little immediate effect, but in the long run they may prove effective. Or in other instances the measure may seem highly successful at the outset only to diminish in effectiveness with the passage of time. Statistics purporting to measure the consequence of such programs, laws, and experiments cannot be regarded as valid if the period of time covered is brief.

8. *Have the statistics been accurately collected and classified?* Even in national elections, where great care is taken to ensure accuracy, the original unofficial announcement of the vote always differs from the final official tabulation, indicating that some errors were made in the initial count. In elections where a recount of the votes is ordered, additional mistakes are usually discovered. If inaccuracies of this type can occur in a carefully supervised election, it is not difficult to imagine the likelihood of error in collecting and classifying data in less well organized polls.

The speaker who plans to use statistics should try to determine how the statistics were collected and tabulated. If questionnaires were used, learn to whom they were sent, of what they consisted, how they were worded, and what percentage of them were returned. If interviews were conducted, discover whether the interviewers were qualified and trained to conduct the interviews impartially. If the statistics are based on reports of several different bodies, groups, agencies, or collectors, ask whether each participating unit collected and tabulated its data in the same way.

The speaker should also be aware that some subjects do not lend themselves to accurate statistical tabulation. For example, no one really knows how many heroin addicts there are in the United States, because heroin is unlawful in this country and addicts simply are not going to confess to using it. On many topics, all we have is estimates. For example, how many alcoholics, narcotics pushers, income tax evaders, AIDS carriers, and dishonest medical doctors are there in the United States?

Until the speaker knows how the statistics were collected and is assured that they were reliably tabulated, little confidence can be placed in their accuracy.

TESTING COMPARISONS.   Perhaps the least conclusive form of evidence is an argument based on comparison or analogy. In constructing an argument by analogy that will be both logical and convincing, the speaker's principal problem is in finding two entities, conditions, or sets of circumstances enough alike that he or she can argue that what is true of one will also be true of the other.

Although argument by comparison is difficult to establish, at times the speaker has virtually no other means of support. For example, if the speaker proposes to demonstrate the effects that allegedly will result from the adoption of some untried policy, no statistics, instances, or testimony are available on how the proposed policy has functioned in the past. The best that one can do is to show how the policy has worked elsewhere and, by comparison, attempt to predict how it will operate in the specific circumstances with which one is concerned. For example, a speaker who wished to argue for the creation of ombudsmen in the United States would have to look to various European countries for evidence of the utility of these officials. The basic premise of the argument would be: If ombudsmen serve a useful function in Europe, an ombudsman would be useful in the United States. However, unless the speaker can demonstrate that the United States and those European countries with ombudsmen are much alike, the argument falls apart.

Educator Clark Kerr resorted to argument by comparison in advocating creation of 67 urban-grant universities. Kerr began by contending that throughout their existence the 67 land-grant colleges had contributed enormously to American agriculture and technology. The speaker then introduced his proposal and proceeded to support it by analogy, saying:

> Tonight, I should like to suggest that we need a new model to add to our . . . universities in the United States, . . . the urban-grant university. . . . I use the term *urban-grant* . . . to indicate a type of university which would have an aggressive approach to the problems of the city, where the city itself and its problems would become the animating focus, as agriculture once was and to some extent still is of the land-grant universities. . . .
>
> The suggestion that the federal government should help with the land and with the money to build these new campuses or to change existing campuses is altogether reasonable. When the land-grant movement began, over 50 percent of the people in the United States lived on the land; today, only 10 percent do. The reasons for an urban-grant university now are at least as compelling as were those for the land-grant university in 1862. . . .
>
> Today, great national problems have to do with the cities, with equality of opportunity, with the ending of poverty, with the quality of life, and I think that the federal government might logically respond to these problems by again aiding the proper activities of higher education. The urban-grant university might parallel the land-grant institution not only via city-oriented curricula and on-campus research studies but also by setting up experiment stations to work on the problems of the city as they once worked on the problems of the land, and by setting up intensified urban extension services like agricultural extension. As a counterpart to the county agent, I can visualize a school agent, for example—one who through the research at his university is informed about the best new techniques for language teaching and who can take this knowledge directly into the public schools in his particular city area. It is true that many urban problems are more complex than those of the land, but this very complexity makes the prospect of confronting them more important and more challenging. (*Representative American Speeches, 1967–1968*, New York: H. W. Wilson Co., 1968, p. 90.)

Kerr's use of comparison effectively illustrates how the speaker at times has no other alternate means for developing an argument. Since the United States had not tried a system of federally supported urban-grant universities, Kerr could not point to statistics, specific instances, or testimony of authorities to prove their worth. Instead he was required to locate a similar program and to argue on the basis of its operation that a system of urban-grant institutions would be comparably successful.

In arguing from analogy, the speaker should apply the following tests:

1. *Do the two entities being compared actually have many similarities?* In argument by comparison, the speaker must have two entities that possess a large number of actual, not figurative, similarities. Because both football and warfare are characterized by two opposing forces engaged in a contest that each seeks to win, one might conclude that the two constitute a suitable comparison. However, the resemblances between the two are largely figurative, for the grim realities of death and destruction, the seriousness of the conflict, and the international repercussions dependent on the outcome of a war are totally absent in a football game.

A comparison between the operation of a business firm and the administration of government also would be invalid because the two really have little in common; one is concerned primarily with making a profit, whereas the other seeks to govern the people.

Comparisons between two different eras or two different types of activity usually are ineffective because of the lack of similarities. Space exploration, for example, has almost nothing in common with earlier types of exploration. Conditions today are so unlike those of a hundred years ago that in most fields a meaningful analogy cannot be drawn.

In argument by comparison, the speaker should make certain that the two entities being compared possess enough actual similarities so that the speaker can convincingly contend that what is true of one is likely also to be true of the other.

Former Chief Justice of the United States Supreme Court, Warren E. Burger, compared advertising by lawyers to selling commodities:

> We see some lawyers using the same modes of advertising as other commodities, from mustard, cosmetics, and laxatives to used cars. A hypothetical case will make my point.
>
> Imagine a day when thousands of eyes are focused on a football game. An ad comes on the TV, perhaps during the halftime. The scene is much like the contest the viewers have just been observing—a spectacular 90-yard touchdown run in which the star eludes all tacklers. The scene then changes. A fine-looking fellow comes on the screen in business clothes, and it turns out he is a popular football star. He says something like this: "If you have a legal problem or case—and if you want to score—go to my friends, Quirk, Gammon & Snapp." At this

point, one by one, three well-dressed fellows come on stage, perhaps against the background of the *United States Code Annotated* or the *United States Reports.* The speaker goes on:

"If you really want to make a touchdown against your opponents, go to Quirk, Gammon & Snapp. For an appointment call (800) 777–1111. They are the best! There will be no charge for the first conference on your problems. They have a special rate on uncontested divorces during the holidays. Don't wait." (*Representative American Speeches, 1983–1984,* New York: H. W. Wilson Co., 1984, pp. 193–194.)

2. *Are the similarities significant?* The speaker also needs to ask whether the observable similarities are significant ones. Two entities may possess many likenesses, but the resemblances may be unimportant. For example, both a kindergarten class and a college seminar are concerned with education. In each the students attend for the purpose of learning. Both involve a teacher, students, assignments, study, and class discussion. Both meet regularly in classrooms with basically similar equipment and facilities. However, except perhaps for the basic goal, most of the resemblances are not significant and, in spite of their number, do not constitute the basis for a convincing argument by analogy. One certainly could not expect an audience to accept the argument that because the sandbox proved popular in the kindergarten, the seminar too should have one, or that term papers should be required of the kindergarteners because they were valuable in the seminar.

In argument by comparison, then, a large number of similarities is not enough for the development of a satisfactory analogy. In addition, the likenesses must be significant ones.

3. *Do important differences occur?* Having constructed an argument by comparison between two entities possessing significant similarities, the speaker should look for any important differences that may invalidate the argument.

For example, two colleges may have a great deal in common, but because one is state supported and the other private, a comparison may not be possible. An analogy involving the urban problems of two similar cities could be invalidated by a difference in the laws of the states in which they are located. A comparison between two periods of time could be invalidated because of the enactment or repeal of a law. For example, repeal of all laws forbidding the sale and use of marijuana would greatly alter the number of arrests for the illegal use of narcotics, thereby making it difficult to compare drug addiction before and after the laws were repealed.

Even though two entities may appear much alike in significant ways, the speaker must be alert to the possibility that a single important difference may prevent a persuasive analogy between the two from being drawn.

TESTING AUTHORITIES.   In argument by authority, the strength of the argument rests upon the reputation of the expert or witness cited by the speaker. The authority may be a convincing source because of learning and intelligence, because of a reputation for honesty and integrity, or because of specialized knowledge derived from personal observation or investigation. In arguing from authority, if the authority is not acceptable to the audience, the audience will attach no significance to what the speaker says.

An example of argument by authority is found in Franklyn S. Haiman's speech at Louisiana State University:

> My problem with *legal* requirements of truth, fairness, rationality, good taste or civilized discourse in the political arena is that they place in the hands of some state commission, judge or jury the power to decide what is true, what is rational, what is fair, what is civilized, what is in good taste. But it is my understanding of democracy that these are questions which only the public may decide—not a government agency or the courts.
>
> Justice Louis Brandeis summed up what I believe to be the proper understanding of the First Amendment when he wrote, in *Whitney v. California* in 1928: "If there be time to expose through discussion the falsehood and fallacies, to avert the evil by the processes of education, the remedy to be applied is more speech, not enforced silence."
>
> Or, as Thomas Jefferson put the same thought, in words now engraved on that beautiful memorial to him in our nation's capital, when referring to political rebels: ". . . let them stand undisturbed as monuments of the safety with which error of opinion may be tolerated where reason is left free to combat it." (*Representative American Speeches, 1983–1984*, New York: H. W. Wilson Co., 1985, p. 57.)

In determining the effectiveness of an authority, speakers should employ the following tests:

1. *Is the authority known to the audience?* If the listeners are not familiar with the experts cited, they are not going to attach much weight to what they say. Identifying the source as "a leading doctor," "a high government official," "the author of one of the best books on the subject," or "a prominent physicist" leaves the audience in doubt as to just who the expert is and how much confidence they should place in his or her testimony. For this reason, the speaker should always give the authority's name.

If, after the expert has been named, it is likely that the listeners still do not know who he or she is, the speaker should briefly indicate the person's qualifications as an authority with a short phrase such as "who is at present an undersecretary in the State Department, was formerly the United States ambassador to Pakistan, and has written three books on American foreign policy in Asia," or "who is editor of the *St. Louis News-Courier* and won the Pulitzer Prize for his exposé of the influence of organized crime in Missouri," or "who is head of the speech department at Midland State University and a former president of the Speech Communication Association." Well-known public figures, of course, need not be identified in this manner.

2. *Is the authority recognized as an expert in the field?* Almost everyone has an opinion on something observed firsthand. Students have opinions on education; veterans regard themselves as knowledgeable about the armed forces and military matters; tourists consider themselves experts on places they have visited, and Monday-morning quarterbacks authoritatively replay the game they saw on Saturday. But none of these qualify as authorities simply on the basis of their observations or personal involvement.

Whenever possible, the speaker should select authorities whose knowledge of the subject is not restricted to limited observation, partial understanding, or fleeting involvement. The best authorities are those who speak from a broad background of study, experience, and observation. Thus a speaker would probably rely on a well-qualified educator for information about teaching; on an experienced statesman for an analysis of international affairs; on a trained historian for knowledge of the past; and on a recognized theologian for an interpretation of religious concepts.

In discussing specific events or incidents, however, the eyewitness is a highly respectable authority regardless of lack of expertise. The person who observed a traffic accident, for example, is much better able to discuss it than a traffic safety engineer who was not present, just as a witness to a crime is more of an expert on this particular act than a criminologist, judge, or law enforcement officer.

3. *Is the authority qualified to discuss the subject?* Many experts in one field take an interest in and frequently speak out on other matters. For example, Benjamin Spock, who is regarded as an expert on child care, often discusses political affairs as well; evangelist Billy Graham frequently expresses opinions on political subjects; and Marianne Moore, the poet, occasionally discussed baseball, in which she was keenly interested. Actors, entertainers, and athletes such as Marlon Brando, Bob Hope, Carroll O'Connor, Jane Fonda, Vanessa Redgrave, Robert Redford, Hank Snow, Linda Ronstadt, Lauren Bacall, Muhammad Ali, Carol Burnett, Shirley MacLaine, Anita Bryant, and Billie Jean King have in recent years been active spokespersons for or against a variety of political and social causes.

While it is commendable for these individuals to take an interest in subjects other than their own areas of competence, it would be a mistake to assume that because they are well-informed in one field, they automatically qualify as experts on other, unrelated matters. When developing an argument by authority, the speaker will construct a more persuasive case if the quoted experts are known for their knowledge of the speaker's subject rather than for expertise in another subject.

4. *Has the authority had opportunity to observe?* No matter how eminent experts may be, they can be regarded as authorities only on those conditions or events they have had ample opportunity to observe and study. Statements based on

limited observation, secondhand information, or hearsay reports cannot be regarded as authoritative. For example, a speaker who wants evidence concerning socialized medicine in Britain should seek the views of the minister of health or prominent British physicians or health officials who have been closely associated with the program, rather than the opinion of an American physician whose knowledge comes largely from reading and limited observation.

Even an expert who has had an opportunity to observe conditions personally does not qualify as an authority unless the period of study or observation was an extended one. For example, government officials, politicians, reporters, and tourists who spend a few days in a foreign country or a few hours at the scene of a natural disaster, riot, or battle probably depart with only a superficial understanding of what they have observed. Likewise, hastily written biographies, books, and reports that seek to capitalize on public curiosity following the sudden death of a prominent figure, a disaster, or a major news event often are of questionable reliability because of the speed with which they have been prepared. An example of the hastily written study is a book on the victory of the United States hockey team in the 1980 Olympics that was written and published in a single week.

5. *Is the authority unbiased?* As pointed out in the discussion of prejudiced sources, bias is the inability of one to judge objectively because of self-interest or some preconceived attitude. The opinions of biased authorities are of little value either in understanding a problem or in persuading an audience, so the speaker should rely on the testimony of impartial experts.

6. *Is the authority acceptable to the audience?* Some people who truly are authorities on the subjects they discuss may be unacceptable to some audiences because of allegedly unethical, illegal, or scandalous conduct. Such people often will not be regarded as authorities even if their misconduct is in no way related to the subjects on which they have expert knowledge.

Even people who have committed no crime or breach of conduct may at times be unacceptable to an audience because of their associations with controversial causes or organizations such as the Ku Klux Klan, the Communist party, the American Nazi party, the National Organization for Women, the Moral Majority, Synanon, the Unification Church, gay liberation, or right-to-work, right-to-life, or other groups or movements regarded as radical, reactionary, or subversive.

The views of controversial figures of the types just described are not necessarily wrong, but so long as an audience is unwilling to trust them, the speaker will find their testimony of little value in influencing listeners.

7. *Is the authority correctly quoted?* In a famous libel suit brought against the publisher of a book critical of the House of Commons, British barrister Thomas Erskine convincingly demonstrated that by quoting out of context one may construe another person's statements to prove almost anything. Inaccurate quotations are not always deliberate or malicious. Paraphrasing, the need to condense to meet space limits of newspapers and magazines,

and honest errors in understanding what a speaker said are some reasons statements of authorities are sometimes inaccurately reported. In other instances, a person's remarks may be deliberately distorted for political or other reasons.

Whatever the explanation, it is important that speakers verify the statements of the authorities they plan to cite. To check on the accuracy of a quotation, one should go to the original source. If this cannot be done, a statement may sometimes be verified by comparing two or more independent reports of it.

TESTING CAUSAL ARGUMENTS. Argument from causation, or cause-to-effect argument, is not so much another kind of supporting material as a different way of using evidence to construct one's arguments. In cause-and-effect reasoning, the speaker may employ specific instances, statistics, comparisons, and testimony but use them to establish a relationship between an action and its consequences or between a condition and its causes. In causal argument, the speaker seeks to explain why or how something happened or will happen. In a speech about air pollution, for example, the speaker might attempt to clarify the problem by explaining its causes or discussing its effects. Or in a speech on foreign trade, the speaker might try to predict the consequences of lowering our tariffs.

In a speech to the United States Senate, Senator Frank R. Lautenberg employed a cause-to-effect argument in an effort to show the effect of breaking up AT&T. He said:

> The American Telephone & Telegraph Company, our national phone system, is being broken up. Local telephone companies will be spun off and will provide basic telephone service.
>
> For years, profits from long-distance and equipment charges have held down the cost of local telephone rates. But that day is ending. We are fast approaching a time when local telephone users will have to pay the full cost of local service. Local rates may double or triple. In my state, regulatory officials predict that basic telephone rates could rise as much as 150 percent by early 1984.
>
> The effect could be devastating. For every 10 percent rise in price, we can expect that 1 percent of telephone users will drop service. Projected price increases would lead to a fall off of telephone service to more than 10 percent of the population. Further increases will cut millions more from the most basic of our information networks—the telephone system.
>
> Cut off will be the poor, the sick, and the elderly, in need of telephone service for emergencies, for contact with the outside world.
>
> Cut off will be the unemployed, who will become further isolated from job opportunities.

> Cut off will be whole areas of our poorest cities, adding another impediment to the revival. (*Representative American Speeches, 1983–1984,* New York: H. W. Wilson Co., 1984, p. 31.)

In a causal argument, the speaker should test the causal relationship with the following four questions:

1. *Can a causal relationship be established?* Just because two events occur one after the other does not prove that the two are in any way related to each other. The rooster, for example, crows every morning, and the sun rises shortly thereafter, but no one will contend that the sun would not rise if the rooster failed to crow. So, clearly, there is no causal relationship between the two.

On the other hand, take the example of John, who failed the final examination in his speech course. In trying to explain his failure, John relates that a severe storm occurred during the test and that the thunder and lightning so badly distracted him that he could not concentrate on the exam. Is it possible that a relationship could exist between a storm and poor performance? Although this is conceivable and one may conclude that a causal relationship *could* exist, it still has not been established that a causal relationship *did* exist.

2. *Is the suggested cause adequate to produce the effect?* Whereas a possible relationship between two phenomena can sometimes be established, one must look further to determine whether the alleged cause actually was important enough to produce the result attributed to it.

Continuing with the example of John's failure on his final examination, if the duration of the storm was only five minutes of the two hours he had to complete the test, it seems unlikely that the proposed cause (the storm) was adequate to produce the consequence (distraction leading to failure). On the other hand, if the storm raged violently for most of the two hours, then perhaps the cause was sufficient to account for the effect.

3. *Does the effect result from one or many causes?* In attempting to establish a cause-to-effect link between two phenomena, after demonstrating that the alleged cause could have produced the effect, one should not overlook the possibility that other causes may also have contributed to the consequence.

Thus, while admitting that the prolonged storm could have caused John to fail his examination, one might also discover that John had gone to a party the night before, that he had slept only a few hours, that he had not reviewed for the examination, that he had not read the daily assignments, that he had not attended classes regularly, and that his fiancée had broken their engagement just before the examination. Any or all of these are possible explanations for why he failed the test, and all are probably just as plausible as the explanation that the storm distracted him.

When speakers are aware of the existence of other plausible causes, they cannot logically claim that the alleged cause singly produced the effect. One might still argue, however, that it was one of the causes or perhaps even the most important cause.

4. *Is there evidence that the alleged cause did not or could not have produced the effect?* When attempting to determine which of several causes might have produced an effect, the speaker should investigate each alleged cause to see if evidence exists that would discredit one or more of the causes.

Continuing with the illustration of John's failure on his final examination, one might ask whether other students were distracted by the storm. Did any students complain of the distraction? Did the class do as well as usual on the examination? Was John in a position in which the storm may have distracted him more than the other students? If no one else complained about the storm, the class performance was generally good, and John was in no way more exposed to the thunder and lightning than the others writing the examination, it seems unlikely that the storm was the cause of his failure. Still, it is possible that John is unusually nervous and finds thunderstorms particularly unnerving, so one might try to determine how John reacted to the storm. Should this lead to the discovery that John dozed off and slept through part of the storm, it would seem unlikely that the storm could be considered a possible cause of his failure.

The example used above to illustrate the four tests of causal argument demonstrates how difficult it may be to establish a causal relationship even when dealing with a relatively simple question. One can imagine, then, the difficulty of trying to determine causes and effects when analyzing such complex problems as crime, civil rights, poverty, national security, inflation, unemployment, birth control, taxation, urban decay, pollution, the energy crisis, and foreign aid. Yet many speakers propound simplistic explanations of these highly intricate issues. Unemployment, they say, is caused by laziness; just kick the shirkers off the welfare rolls and the problem will be solved. Riots and demonstrations are caused by lack of respect for law and order; just call the cops to bash the participants' skulls and the problem will go away. Some speakers attribute the country's economic problems to an international conspiracy. For others, behind almost every problem is a Communist plot to overthrow America. Such easy resolutions of difficult issues are detrimental to the democratic process, which depends on an informed and compassionate electorate in dealing with the problems that confront the country. The speaker has an ethical responsibility to scrutinize critically and exhaustively all possible causes and effects of every problem before recommending an analysis to the public.

Stephen Birmingham, in his novel *The LeBaron Secret,* gives an example to illustrate the difficulty one sometimes encounters in trying to establish causal relationships. He writes:

Every day, right before our very eyes, under our very noses, accidents happen, mistakes are made. The newspapers are full of these stories.

They fill the files of the psychologists. Years ago, in an obscure mill town in northern Ohio, a worker in a steel mill is laid off his job because of hard times. To fill his days, he whittles a crude slingshot, fastens to it a stout strip of rubber sliced from an old inner tube, and presents this plaything to his two young sons, showing them how they can use it to dispatch empty beer cans lined up on a fence rail in the backyard, much the way their father taught them to swim in the Cuyahoga River and taught them to skip flat pebbles across the surface of a pond. The two brothers are close, but they are young and excitable, and three days later the older boy aims the slingshot, playfully, at his younger brother. No harm was meant, but the younger boy's eye is lost, and the sight of that single, bloodied eyeball, dangling by the thinnest filament of muscle tissue from his brother's head, and the brother's look of, at first, sheer surprise, will not go away and reappears forever in the older brother's dreams and nightmares. The half-blinded brother becomes a priest, administering to the sick and elderly. And is it guilt over his brother's disfigurement, that vision of the dangling eyeball that will not erase itself, that causes the older brother to become a motorcycle racer, experimenting with one daredevil feat after another, until, inevitably, he is thrown from his bike into a concrete retaining wall beside a levee in California, and his own face is left brutally scarred, with most of his lower jaw torn away? The sight of him after the accident turns his wife permanently from him. Is this why, one night sitting alone in a drive-in theatre in Texas in 1972, during a showing of *Deliverance*—during the famous sodomy scene, in fact—he quietly reaches for the automatic rifle on the passenger seat beside him and begins shooting at the moviegoers in their cars? Before he has finished, five lie dead—two women, a man, and two teenagers on their first date—and four others are injured. Is this why the older brother is now waiting on Death Row, while the younger, half-blinded brother has been placed in charge of an important parish in Detroit? Where, in this chain reaction, does the blame lie? Who must account for this physical and emotional carnage—the wife who would not let her husband touch her, the father who whittled the slingshot for his handsome and beloved sons, the owner of the mill that laid the father off, the producers of films like *Deliverance* that fill our screens with so much unnatural sex and violence, our loose gun-control laws, or our increasingly depersonalized society? You tell me. (Stephen Birmingham, *The LeBaron Secret,* Boston: Little, Brown & Co., Inc., 1987, pp. 338–339.)

SUMMARY

The persuasive speaker consciously designs communication strategies that will shape perceptions, modify attitudes, or influence actions of other people. It is important, therefore, to employ all the means available to make the message compelling to the audience. An element that plays a vital role in the audience's acceptance is source credibility, derived from a variety of influences, including the position of the speaker and the speaker's reputation, goodwill, intellectual integrity, knowledge, sincerity, and delivery.

The message of persuasive speech can be deliberative (affirming propositions of policy), forensic (affirming propositions of fact), or demonstrative (affirming propositions of value). Whatever the form of the persuasive message, it should include logical, ethical, and emotional appeals—all phrased in compelling language characterized by energy and vividness.

Because of the more critical attitude of the listeners, in argumentative speaking the speaker must be particularly careful in the selection of supporting material and should understand the difference between factual evidence and theories, opinions, and beliefs. The speaker's supporting documentation should be drawn from reputable, recent, and reliable sources.

The speaker who argues from specific instances should make sure that enough instances are presented; that they are representative, recent, and true; and that they are not invalidated by significant exceptions. If developing an argument with statistics, the speaker should use statistics that are adequate in number, representative, recent, properly defined, accurately collected, and not contradicted by important exceptions, statistics that truly measure the phenomenon they purport to investigate.

If comparisons are employed to prove a contention, the two entities being compared should have many important similarities and should not differ in any significant feature. Authorities, witnesses, and experts who are cited in support of an idea should be recognized experts familiar and acceptable to the audience; they should be regarded as unbiased and trustworthy by the listeners. Authorities' testimony should be confined to those areas of their field of competence that they have had an opportunity to study or observe carefully. In arguments based on causal reasoning, the speaker should determine whether a causal relationship is possible, whether it is probable, whether more than one cause acted to produce the effect, and whether evidence exists to contradict the alleged relationship.

MODEL PERSUASIVE SPEECH

Drug Testing in the Marketplace

Earl Omer

The speech reproduced below was given to a beginning Fundamentals of Speech class. The assignment was to prepare and present a 5-minute persuasive speech well suited to the audience of fellow students. Before preparing the speech, the class had studied and discussed most of the principles discussed in this chapter.

In reading and analyzing the speech, keep in mind that the listeners consisted of about twenty other students, mostly college freshmen and sophomores. Specific questions to consider include: does the speaker (1) create interest in his topic and involve his listeners? (2) adapt his speech to the class members? (3) provide adequate materials to support his contentions? (4) cite the sources of his information? (5) indicate his own concern? (6) attempt to refute counterarguments? (7) organize the speech so that it is easy to follow?

How many of us plan to seek a job with a major corporation in the next few years? As we all know, when you go job hunting, you have to go on a job interview. During this interview, you're going to be asked questions about yourself and your aspirations with the company, but there's something you might not be prepared for. Your interviewer hands you a small plastic bottle and asks you to follow him or her to the rest room. There you are requested to give them a small sample of your urine for drug testing while the interviewer watches you to maintain the integrity of your sample. A little embarrassing or disgusting, you say? Well unfortunately this type of job interview is becoming more and more commonplace in the market today. A recent survey by the *Wall Street Journal* found that 35 to 40 percent of the Fortune 500 companies in the United States today use drug testing as part of the initial interview process. Now admittedly, drug testing is necessary for people who are seeking jobs as airline pilots, law enforcement officials, and high-ranking government offices. But there are problems associated with drug testing in the workplace. Two of these problems are the poor quality of the drug testing industry itself and the lack of legal liability for false test results. These two problems, which represent only the tip of the controversial iceberg in drug testing, are reason enough to suspend drug testing until solutions can be found.

First, the problem of the poor quality of the drug testing industry. This one should be of concern to all of us as potential job applicants. Currently this quarter of a billion dollar industry is not regulated or supervised by any government agency. The only thing you or I need in order to set up our own drug testing lab is a machine to do the analysis and a technician to keep the machine running.

I'd like to tell you how the testing procedure works, according to a 1986 United States Department of Health and Human Services study.

Once you give your interviewer your small sample of urine, he'll place a label over the cap with your signature and social security number on it. From there it is transported to the lab to be maintained in a temperature- and humidity-controlled room. Now it's not uncommon, and it has been proven, that in this dry humidity and cool temperature your adhesive label can come unfixed from your bottle and fall to the floor. What happens is that the technician comes in, picks up the label, looks on the table for what bottle is missing a label, and sticks your label on it. That sample now becomes your sample. When a technician is ready to make the test, he'll take a small portion of that sample, place it in a tray configuration which may hold 35 to 40 other urine samples. All these are tested simultaneously, and the technician is supposed to keep track of where your urine sample is in the tray.

However, in a United States Center for Disease Control survey done in October of 1986, 13 labs were chosen at random around the United States. Of these 13, all of them were found to have an average error rate of 66 percent, and none were found to be performing the test correctly. Now a 66 percent error rate is inexcusable by anybody's standards, and this brings me to my second point, the lack of legal responsibility for false test results. Currently if a drug company calls your employer back and says you test positive for drug use, your employer has every right to refuse to hire you or fire you if you've already been employed. Your only legal recourse is to go to court and challenge the accuracy of the test.

But let's say your employer thinks you're a worthy effort; maybe he thinks you might be innocent. He can do one of two things; he can either have you retake the same test, or he can have you take a different test. But as we've seen, the average error rate of 66 percent gives you less than a 50/50 chance of passing even if you're innocent. Some of you might say, I'll refuse to take the test again; but your employer has every right to refuse to hire you or fire you if you refuse to take a urine test. There's been no legal precedent set in the court as of now and the issues of constitutionality and privacy are still being debated.

Some of us might say, well, the military has been using urinalysis for quite a few years, with a lot of success. Well, the military is very different from the business community. The military's opinion is that until a better system comes along, they're going to continue to use what they have. In other words, you've got to sacrifice a few innocent people to get the quality, and so be it.

Unfortunately, we here in the civilian world believe you are innocent until proven guilty beyond a reasonable doubt. And I think there's plenty of reasonable doubt in this system with a 66 percent error rate.

When I was in the military, I used to laugh at the guys who came up positive on the drug test and would swear they never used drugs. Of course, nobody believed them. Well, knowing what I know now makes me think maybe some of those guys really were innocent.

Until we demand a regulation and supervision of the drug testing industry and until the courts set a precedent for a legal liability of false test results, we need to suspend drug testing in the workplace.

Each time you or I take a drug test, it's like playing Russian roulette with our careers and our lives.

STUDY QUESTIONS

1. Why is effective supporting material particularly important in a speech to convince or to persuade?
2. What is a fact?
3. Are facts always true? Can facts always be proved?
4. How are facts determined? By whom?
5. Why is it important that a speaker be able to differentiate between facts and theories or opinions?
6. What six tests should a speaker apply to the sources of evidence?

7. What is the difference between a biased source and a dishonest one?
8. What are the tests of argument by specific instances? Why is it important that the instances be representative?
9. What is the principal difficulty in constructing a valid argument using comparison? Why, in spite of this problem, is the speaker sometimes required to argue from comparison?
10. What is argument by authority? What is an authority?
11. What is a causal argument?
12. What tests should the speaker apply to test an argument based on statistics?

EXERCISES

1. From a newspaper, find five statements (complete sentences) that are facts. Also find five statements that clearly are opinions.
2. In a newspaper or magazine article, find an example of statistics being used to prove a point. Apply the tests of statistics and decide whether the statistics constitute conclusive proof.
3. Name someone who would be regarded as an authority by most students in your class in each of the following fields: newspaper publishing, medicine, professional football, college education, crime.
4. List three speech subjects where the speaker probably would employ causal argument to prove the central thought.
5. Test the following as authorities to support an argument in a persuasive speech. Be prepared to indicate why each one would or would not be satisfactory.
   a. A quotation by the British prime minister on American education.
   b. Testimony of a Big Ten football coach on qualities of leadership in college youth.
   c. Actor Bob Hope's opinion on pollution.
   d. The conclusions of a missionary who has just returned from two years' work in Ecuador on needed political reform in Ecuador; on poverty in South America.
   e. The recommendations of an FBI agent for handling student disciplinary problems in a high school.
6. Test the following as evidence to support one's arguments in a speech to persuade. Be prepared to state why each would or would not be satisfactory.
   a. A comparison between German treatment of the Jews in the 1930s and the American treatment of blacks today to prove the need for a solution to United States racial problems.
   b. Statistics showing that the major television networks devoted more time in their newscasts during the 1980 presidential campaign to Jimmy Carter than to Ronald Reagan as evidence of biased reporting and distortion of the news.
   c. An eyewitness account of how eight different passersby failed to come to the assistance of a man being beaten by three assailants in a parking lot as evidence of the apathy and indifference of the American people to crime.
   d. Statistics showing that American blacks enjoy a standard of living higher than that of blacks in any other country in the world as evidence that blacks are not discriminated against economically in this country.
   e. Several examples of violent crimes committed by juveniles resembling criminal acts depicted on television programs they had watched as evidence of the harmful effect of television upon youth.

7. Prepare a 1- to 2-minute talk in which you prove a single point. Members of the class will be asked to evaluate how conclusive you were in your proof.

8. Prepare a 4- to 5-minute speech to convince or persuade the class of an unpopular view. At least half of the class should be either opposed or neutral toward your proposition when you begin. Select a topic in which you believe strongly.

9. Prepare a 4- to 5-minute speech to persuade your listeners to do something within the next week that they otherwise would not do. At the end of the week, check to find out how many carried out the action urged. Report to the class the results of your survey, and explain the reasons for your relative success or failure.

10. Write a 500 to 750 word evaluation of Earl Omer's persuasive speech, "Drug Testing in the Marketplace," pp. 261–263. Give special attention to the seven questions listed before the speech.

FURTHER READINGS

Ehninger, Douglas, Bruce E. Gronbeck, Ray E. McKerrow, and Alan Monroe, *Principles and Types of Speech Communication,* 10th ed. (Glenview, IL: Scott, Foresman, 1986), chap. 16, "Public Reasoning and Argumentation," and chap. 17, "Speeches to Persuade and Actuate."

Lucas, Stephen E., *The Art of Public Speaking* (New York: Random House, 1986), chap. 14, "Speaking to Persuade."

Mudd, Charles S., and Malcolm O. Sillars, *Speech: Content and Communication* (New York: Crowell, 1975), chap. 17, "Speaking to Persuade."

Osborn, Michael, *Speaking in Public* (Boston: Houghton Mifflin, 1982), chap. 12, "The Challenge and Design of Persuasion," and chap. 13, "Developing, Outlining, and Wording the Persuasive Speech."

Ross, Raymond S., *Speech Communication: Fundamentals and Practice,* 7th ed. (Englewood Cliffs, NJ: Prentice-Hall, 1986), chap. 10, "Persuasive Speaking," and chap. 11, "Reasoned Supports of Persuasion."

Vasile, Albert J., and Harold K. Mintz, *Speak with Confidence: A Practical Guide,* 4th ed. (Boston: Little, Brown, 1986), chap. 12, "Persuade Them."

Verderber, Rudolph F., *The Challenge of Effective Speaking,* 6th ed. (Belmont, CA: Wadsworth, 1985), chap. 13, "Principles of Persuasive Speaking," and chap. 14, "Reasoning with Audiences: Speeches of Conviction."

CHAPTER 14

LANGUAGE IN COMMUNICATION

"Communication by means of language is man's distinctive activity," states Stuart Chase. Language is the most important element in any culture, not only for day-to-day communication but also for preserving the community from generation to generation, he continues; for, although individuals die, the culture that flows through them and that they help to create is all but immortal. Without words the flow would cease and the culture wither away.

Without language, speech could not exist. Although we might still communicate through the use of signs and gestures, lacking a system of words recognizable to others, we would be incapable of speech. It is therefore obvious that effective use of language is essential to good oral communication.

WORDS AS SYMBOLS

Words are symbols. Language is a system of symbols intended to convey ideas. When language is used by persons who know what the symbols stand for, communication occurs.

The symbols employed in the act of communicating are both audible and visible. The most common audible symbols are the sounds of human speech, which, when put together in a certain manner, convey messages to hearers acquainted with the language being spoken. The most common visible symbols of communication are written or printed words, which consist of marks

A referee uses a visible symbol to indicate a score.
(Focus on Sports)

of various kinds and shapes (letters) arranged to convey a message to some-one familiar with the language.

People have many forms of symbolic communication. One is gesture. By the way they signal, hitchhikers clearly ask passing motorists, "Will you give me a lift?" The referee at a football game, the officer directing traffic, the conductor of a symphony, and the bicycler signaling a turn all relay specific information through a system of visible gestures. Other physical movements that convey meaning are the raised arms of surrender, military salutes, nodding the head in agreement or disagreement, removal of the hat as a sign of respect, turning one's thumbs down, the sign of the cross, and waving goodbye.

Abstract marks are another means of symbolic communication. Many of these identify groups, as do the Christian cross, the swastika, the hammer and sickle, the Star of David, the Republican elephant, the Democratic donkey, the interlocked rings of the Olympic games, the maple leaf of Canada, the lone star of Texas, the twin arches of McDonald's restaurants, and the distinctive marquees of Holiday Inns. Some convey messages, such as the arrow indicating a turn in the highway or the skull and crossbones warning of poison.

Even colors may be used as symbols to communicate messages. The red, green, and amber of traffic signals, the yellow line down the middle of a highway, the black armband of mourning, the red flag of communism, the green of the Irish, and a school's colors are examples.

One more type of symbolic communication would include the torch of liberty, the scales of justice, the dove of peace, the olive branch, the motion picture industry's Oscar, and Uncle Sam.

Words are but another set of symbols for conveying ideas. As symbols, words have no connection or relationship to anything—except in the mind. Words are not things, but they make people think of things. James McCrimmon explains:

> The letters *b-o-o-k* make you think of this thing you are reading or of a similar thing. But any other combination of letters could perform the same function, provided people had agreed on that combination. Because of this general agreement, the same object is known by different names in different languages. Thus what we call a book in English is also referred to as *buch* (German), *bock* (Dutch), *bok* (Swedish), *bog* (Danish), *livre* (French), *libro* (Spanish), and so on. No one of these names is the "real" name for book. No one is better than the others. In so far as they point to the thing which we choose to call a book, they are all satisfactory names. (James McCrimmon, *Writing with a Purpose,* Boston: Houghton Mifflin, 1950, pp. 197–198.)

McCrimmon might have gone on to point out that we could even devise an entirely new set of letters or sounds—*pxkwobby* or *zuzu*—to refer to a book and,

Flying the flag at half-mast: a symbol of respect.
(Main, *Christian Science Monitor*)

> Perhaps of all the creations of man language is the most astonishing.
>
> LYTTON STRACHEY

so long as they were understood by others to designate a book, they would be entirely satisfactory.

MISCONCEPTIONS ABOUT LANGUAGE

Effective use of language in communication is sometimes impaired because of misconceptions about the nature of words. Six common misunderstandings about language are the misconceptions of (1) singularity, (2) permanency, (3) authority, (4) mystical power, (5) morality, and (6) superiority.

The Singularity Misconception

A widespread misunderstanding about language is the belief that every word has only one meaning. This may be called the misconception of singularity, because it implies that a single, correct definition exists for every word. In fact, however, many words have more than one meaning. For example, the 2,000 words most frequently used by educated people have 14,000 dictionary definitions. Besides the words with more than one dictionary meaning, many others with only one definition in the dictionary are capable of expressing different ideas and shades of meaning depending on how they are used.

The statement "All men are created equal" illustrates how words may possess more than one meaning. In this sentence, the word *equal* may be used to mean that all persons are born with identical traits and abilities; or, more likely, *equal* may mean that no person is inherently superior or inferior to another by reason of race, religion, class, or nationality and that all persons, therefore, are entitled to just and equitable treatment. Obviously, failure to understand how the word *equal* is used could lead to misunderstanding. In the same sentence, the word *men* could have more than one interpretation. It could mean all members of the human race or it might refer only to the male of the species.

Other examples of how meaning is altered depending on the definition of a particular word include the following:

He was a *poor* student. (Academically weak? Financially hard up?)
Mr. Jones was a *religious* worker. (Diligent? Church worker?)
The man was *unemployed* at the time. (Idle? Out of a job?)
Mary bought some new *glasses*. (Spectacles? Tumblers?)

Father had *retired.* (Gone to bed? No longer working?)
He was witty and *gay.* (Happy and debonair? Homosexual?)

Sometimes the meaning of a word is clear when written but unclear when spoken. Look at these two examples.

It was a *democratic* meeting. (Democratic? democratic?)
The graduating class sat in *tiers.* (tiers? tears?)

The italicized words in the above illustrations are ambiguous. Each word has at least two different definitions, and if listeners are unaware of which meaning the speaker intends, they probably will have difficulty in understanding the sentence.

In addition to the problems caused by ambiguous words, communication can be impaired by vague language. Vague words have no clear-cut meaning, and even though the hearers think they understand how the speaker is using the word, the speaker and the listeners may have two very different concepts of what the word means. Some words of this type are *moral, free press, free speech, obscene, right-to-life, human rights, justice, cult,* and *fanatic.* For example, two people may both use the word *obscene* to mean pornography without being able to agree on whether a particular book or movie is obscene.

Liberal and *conservative* are words with no clear-cut meaning. For example, a politician might be liberal in his views on social security and civil rights and conservative in his views on education and defense spending.

Advertisements frequently contain words that, if one stops to think about them, actually have no specific meaning. For example, what is meant by the word *quality* in the claim "All aspirins are not alike. . . . For *quality,* Bayer is superior"? Or what is meant by *living color* (the opposite of *dead* color?), the *ketchupy* ketchup, *uncola,* "It's the *real* thing," or "Sparko cleans your oven 33 percent *better"* (better than what?)?

The meaning of a word may also differ from group to group and from area to area. For example, some people call the midday meal *lunch* or *luncheon* and the evening meal *dinner,* while others refer to the noon meal as *dinner* and

"When I use a word," Humpty Dumpty said, in a rather scornful tone, "it means just what I choose it to mean—neither more nor less."
"The question is," said Alice, "whether you can make words mean so many different things."
"The question is," said Humpty Dumpty, "which is to be master—that's all."

LEWIS CARROLL,
Through the Looking Glass

the evening meal as *supper.* Thus, when invited to dinner, one should make certain which meal is intended.

Many southerners use the word *evening* to refer to any time after noon, while in the rest of the country it generally means after 6 PM. Also, in the South, *camp* may be used to describe what others would call a *cabin* or *lodge.*

The meanings of words also differ from one country to another. For example, a comparison of unemployment statistics in the United States and Britain, even if based on reliable records, could be highly misleading because of the different ways the two governments define *unemployment.* To be regarded as unemployed in Britain, one must fit a set of criteria quite different from those the United States government uses in determining whether a person is unemployed.

Other British terms that could be confusing to an American include the following:

British Word	*American Equivalent*
public schools	private schools
ground floor	first floor
first floor	second floor
lift	elevator
the underground	the subway
lorry	truck
flyover	overpass
chemist	pharmacist
turf accountant	bookmaker, bookie
dual carriageway	two-lane road
gaol	jail
flat	apartment
coach	bus
one stone	14½ pounds
water closet	toilet, bathroom
to queue	to stand in line

Differences in customs, institutions, laws, and social mores between nations can cause words to have different meanings in different societies. Thus a *high school diploma* or a *college degree* may not reflect the same educational attainment in two different countries; *petit larceny* in one country might be classified as *grand larceny* in another; and an act considered criminal by one nation might be perfectly legal in another.

Some words in one language have no equivalent or counterpart in another. For example, Greek has no word for *blue.* English words for color distinguish color spectrally by the hue. The Greek words have to do almost entirely with depth and brightness, with the result that no single Greek word means *blue,* although it is possible to find a word that sometimes refers to the color we call *blue.* Because many words mean different things in other cultures, one must take care to understand exactly how a word is being used and what it means to the user.

Even within a culture, persons from different groups often find it difficult to communicate because of their experiential backgrounds. A civilian in un-bombed America can never understand war in the same way that it is known to a returned serviceman who has seen combat duty or to the survivors of a bombing raid. In a like manner, employer and employee, male and female, black and white, farmer and banker all may be at a loss to understand how the other is using words. Anthropologist Margaret Mead believed that the "generation gap" between youths and adults results from the fact that the young will never experience what their parents have experienced and that adults can never experience what the younger generation has experienced. She observed:

> In most discussions of the generation gap, the alienation of the young is emphasized, while the alienation of their elders may be wholly over-looked. What the commentators forget is that true communication is a dialogue and that both parties to the dialogue lack a vocabulary. . . . Once the fact of a deep, new, unprecedented worldwide generation gap is firmly established, in the minds of both the young and the old, commu-nication can be established again. But as long as any adult thinks that he, like his parents and teachers of old, can become introspective, invoke his own youth to understand the youth before him, then it is lost. But this is what most elders are still doing.

To regard words as having a single, correct meaning is a misconception. Words may have more than one meaning, no clear-cut meaning, or somewhat different meanings depending on who is using the word and how it is being used.

The Permanency Misconception

Related to the misconception that words have only one meaning is the belief that, once defined, the meaning of a word remains forever the same. The idea that the meanings of words do not change is the misconception of perma-nency.

In spite of the objections of purists, language is constantly changing: Some words drop out of use; other words acquire different meanings or uses; and new words are regularly introduced into our vocabularies.

Etymology, the study of the origins and derivations of words, reveals how greatly language has changed over the years. The word *surgeon,* for example, once meant anyone who worked with his or her hands and was properly applied to craftsmen and laborers. Today, however, it is used to denote a medical practitioner who performs operations. *Doctor* at one time referred to any learned person. But today, even though people holding doctoral degrees in academic fields are addressed as *Doctor,* when one hears "I have an appointment with my doctor tomorrow," one almost invariably concludes that the person is going to see a medical doctor.

Through usage, many words acquire meanings other than their original ones. When the United States was founded, it was regarded as a *republic,* not a *democracy.* In fact, the founding fathers probably would have objected to having the government described as a democracy. However, repeated use of the terms *democracy* and *democratic* in reference to the kind of government in this country has led to the acceptability of these words as accurate descriptions of the American system of government. In a similar manner, the word *flammable* has come to mean *inflammable* and *gas* to mean *gasoline.*

Other words drop out of the language because they are seldom used. *Canst, hast, shan't, 'tis,* and *whilst,* for example, fall strangely upon our ears because we rarely hear them. Still other words fall into disuse because they are no longer needed: *talkies, rumble seat, roadster, running board, icebox, antimacassar, washboard, speakeasies, moonshiner, boogie-woogie, victory garden, marcel, bloomers, flappers,* and *spats.* Some words are heard less often because they have been replaced by others. *Spectacles* today are generally called *glasses;* the *parlor* has become the *living room; dungarees* are called *jeans; saloons* have been replaced by *bars, taverns,* and *cocktail lounges;* the *veranda* has become the *porch;* and *hillbilly music* has become *country and western,* or *folk music.*

Words are also constantly being replaced by others because they have fallen into disrepute. For example, some people feel that there is an odium attached to the term *insane asylum* and prefer to call such institutions *mental hospitals. Old people* or the *aged* similarly are called instead *elderly* or *senior citizens. Retarded* or *mentally retarded* are the words substituted for *feebleminded; janitors* are *custodians;* and *garbage collectors* become *sanitation workers.*

To replace words that are dying out or no longer used, language is constantly being replenished and enlarged by the introduction of new words. Many of these new words are needed to describe new discoveries, processes, or conditions. In the following list, most of the words were nonexistent or, at best, little known no more than 25 years ago: *microchip, Teflon, junk food, laser, quasar, space shuttle, silicon chips, slam dunk, high five, stonewall, smog, transistor, WASPs, quadraphonic, Third World, tape cassette, panty hose, Super Bowl, frisbee, cablevision, Ms., Sun Belt, subcompact, gays, thalidomide, Polaroid, Watergate, jogging, the Pill, microwave ovens, light beer, punk rock,* and *snowmobile.* The above list could be extended by the inclusion of the myriad of slang words and jargon terms such as *nerds, wimps, preppy,* and *Yuppies* that come and go.

The speed at which language changes is illustrated by the glossary of new words and expressions prepared by the United States Air Force for returning prisoners of war following the cease-fire in Vietnam. The brochure listed 85 new words or phrases that had come into popular usage in only about 10 years time, including *acid, Afro hairstyle, blow your cool, bread* (money), *cop out, dude, ego trip, happening, rap, rip off, split, uptight, vibes,* and *zap.*

Political changes also affect language. The following countries, for example, either did not exist or had different names not very long ago: Sri Lanka, Zaire, Bangladesh, Zimbabwe, Zambia, Botswana, Malawi, and Mozambique.

Clearly, language is constantly changing as words fall into disuse or acquire different meanings and as new words and phrases are added. To insist that the meaning of words never changes is unrealistic. Indeed, if language is to serve us in our communication efforts, it must constantly evolve to meet the changing circumstances of the times.

The Authoritative Misconception

Do you prefer the *super-giant* box to the *large* size, the *new, improved* product to its *regular* predecessor, and the *bargain economy* item to its standard-priced counterpart? Would you rather live in *Leafy Glen Estates* than in *Briar Patch Hollow,* or on *Magnolia Plantation* than on the *Jones farm?* Would you rather have a *gown* from a *haute couture house* than a *frock* from *Molly's Bargain Dress Shop?* Does *continental cuisine* seem more inviting than *eats?* Does *Windsor Preparatory Academy* sound like a better school than *Public High School Number 34?* Are you interested in *antiques,* but not *used* furniture? Do you find *Aunt Beulah's pipin' hot fluffy wheat cakes with rich creamy dairy-fresh butter and honest-to-goodness homemade Vermont maple syrup* more appetizing than *flapjacks with butter and syrup?* Are you tempted by *discount* and *bargain* sales in contrast to *retail* prices? If so, you may be suffering from the delusion that words guarantee quality, value, or worth.

Unaware that words are simply arbitrary symbols, some people tend to accept them at face value. If a product is described as *new* or *improved,* they unthinkingly believe that it must be better. The labels *discount* and *wholesale* are no guarantee of lower prices, but some people assume they are. *First-class* accommodations may not differ in any way from those described as *tourist* or *economy class*—in fact, exactly the same seat may be designated *first class* on some flights and *tourist* or *executive* on other flights.

Nevertheless, many people believe that because a word says something is so, it must be so. One shrewd college football coach exploited this tendency by renaming his first, second, and third platoons the *Go team, White team,* and the *Chinese Bandits.* The stratagem was highly successful, particularly with the third team. No longer regarded as bench warmers and inspired by the fearless, marauding implications of their name, the Chinese Bandits became a highly effective platoon and the darlings of the fans. (How much this tactic contributed to the squad's success is debatable; however, it might be noted that the team was undefeated that season.)

Another illustration of this phenomenon is found in the ranking of various college sports teams by panels of "experts" for the Associated Press and United Press International. Great prestige is attached by most fans to the title of *national champion,* which these groups award to the top-ranking team at the end of the season. Coaches of the second- and third-place teams complain loudly, and local sportswriters berate the panels for their failure to recognize that Popcorn College was really better than Notre Dame. One

DELTA   UNITED AIRLINES   EASTERN

Corporate symbols give businesses a visual image.

politician, irate that his state university's football team was ranked only second in the final polls, went so far as to introduce in the state legislature a bill to declare the local team *national champion.*

What coaches, scribes, and fans alike forgot is that the terms *number one* and *national champion* are no guarantee that the team in fact is the best in the country. If, indeed, the *national champions* were better than all others, how could one account for the defeats these squads frequently suffer in postseason bowl games and tournaments? One *national championship* basketball team lost a postseason tournament game by 30 points! In other words, as in the examples cited earlier, simply calling a team *national champion* is no guarantee of the caliber of the players.

Other examples of the authoritative misconception are provided by those persons who believe in graphoanalysis, biorhythms, astrology, flying saucers, and various new medical cures simply because they have been told or read that these are *based on fact* or have been *clinically tested* or *scientifically proven.*

The same type of thinking is also sometimes found in politics. Aware of the public's susceptibility to high-sounding titles, special-interest groups often seek names that inspire confidence. Thus groups may decide to call themselves the League of Christian Mothers, the Patriotic Sons of Democracy, the Better Government Party, or the Guardians of Decency (GOD). These must be good groups, as their names imply, for who is opposed to Christian mothers, patriotism, democracy, better government, or decency? But of course, the name provides no assurance that the organization represents a worthy cause. In reality, the goals of such groups might be highly questionable or even subversive.

The authoritative misconception can easily lead to a type of fallacious reasoning that is known as *begging the question.* Examples of this are: "He should know, he has a Ph.D. in the field"; "Of course he's impartial, he's the judge, isn't he?"; "How can you say it's no good, when it says on the bottle that it has been scientifically tested?"; "It should be a good place to eat; they adver-

tise 'home cooking' ''; "It must be effective—after all, they named it 'Rely' '';
and "For the first time there's a soap pure and mild enough to be called 'Pure
and Natural.' ''

A want ad appearing in a London newspaper effectively illustrated the
dangers of the misconception of authority regarding language. It stated forth-
rightly: "We buy junk—We sell antiques."

The Mystical Power Misconception

"Open Sesame," says the genie, and the door magically swings open. "Abra-
cadabra," mutters the witch, and the spell takes effect. While these examples
are obviously the ingredients of a child's fairy tale, some adults suffer from
the delusion that words possess a similar kind of mystical power that can alter
their fortunes for good or ill.

This misconception is basically a form of superstition. The individual
who makes a statement about good luck such as, "Fortunately, I have never
had an automobile accident" or "No one in our family has ever had cancer"
and then quickly adds, "I'd better knock on wood" illustrates the superstitious nature of this misconception. Obviously the words can have no effect
on a person's driving habits or on family health—nor can the knocking on
wood—but the speaker irrationally fears that they might.

Baseball players and sports announcers have long observed the taboo
against any mention of the fact when a pitcher is throwing a no-hit game for
fear that the words *no-hitter* will spoil the pitcher's success. Thus it is sometimes possible to listen to a broadcast of a baseball game without ever being
told that it is a no-hitter until someone gets a hit or the game ends.

The constant chatter of players rolling dice—"shooting craps"—as they
implore the dice to bring them good luck is another example of this misconception.

To ward off bad luck, some people say *bread and butter* or *salt and pepper* if
they happen to pass on opposite sides of a tree, pole, or post when walking
with someone else.

An additional manifestation of this misconception is the refusal of most
hotels to number their thirteenth floor *13* for fear that guests would object
to staying on this floor.

While these superstitious beliefs about the power of words are probably
harmless, they represent another misunderstanding about the nature of language.

The Morality Misconception

Probably the most widely accepted misconception about language is the
belief that words possess moral qualities—that there are "good" and "bad"
words, "nice" and "dirty" words, and "acceptable" and "objectionable"
words. If one keeps in mind the fact that words are nothing more than

symbols, how can the marks on a sheet of paper that make letters and words or the vocal sounds we use in speech be either "good" or "bad"? Is the letter *E* or *A* or *T* good or bad? If individually they are neither good nor bad, do they acquire desirable or undesirable qualities when used in combination? Is EAT good or bad? Are TEA, ATE, and ETA acceptable or improper? When spoken aloud, do these symbols become good or bad? Obviously not. They are simply sounds.

Yet many people, ignoring the fact that words are only symbols, do regard some words as inherently bad, or improper, whereas others are considered acceptable. Certain words are taboo in polite society, banned in public broadcasts, and likely to shock the reader or hearer. Because of this misconception, a speaker who wishes to achieve a goal will avoid their use in most situations. Nevertheless, speakers and hearers should recognize that words are simply symbols that inherently are neither good nor bad. Words that may prove offensive can be divided into two classes: (1) disreputable language, words that are considered obscene or profane, and (2) derogatory language, words having an unpleasant or degrading connotation.

DISREPUTABLE LANGUAGE.   In spite of the furor and indignation their use arouses, the number of English words regarded as disreputable is small and probably diminishing. Disreputable language consists of words that are considered obscene or profane.

Obscene words refer to bodily functions or organs generally regarded as intimate. They are, almost without exception, short, which has led to their being called "four-letter" words. Profanity is language considered blasphemous or irreverent.

The concepts of obscenity and profanity are products of one's culture. What is vulgar or blasphemous in one culture may be considered harmless in another. Thus *bloody* used as an adjective is objectionable to the British but not to Americans. Although most American families would consider it blasphemous to name a son *Jesus,* the Spanish do it constantly.

As a culture changes, so do its concepts of obscenity and blasphemy. Victorian society, for example, regarded any reference to a woman's legs as vulgar. People of that era moved about on *limbs,* which were expected to be fully covered. The show of an ankle by a lady was considered indiscreet. In their propriety, Victorians even went so far as to cover the legs of tables, pianos, and benches with frilly lace skirts. In those august times, no one became *pregnant,* although of course ladies occasionally found themselves *in a family way.* At that time the terms *white* and *dark meat* came into use because the proper Victorians could not bring themselves to refer to a chicken's *thigh, breast,* or *legs.* While these evasions sound ridiculous now, it should be remembered that not too long ago use of the words *sex* and *condoms* was forbidden among respectable people. Unquestionably, some words considered obscene or profane today will become acceptable to future generations.

More people probably object to obscenity than to profanity. Although the English language probably would not suffer if no one used "four-letter" words, the outrage which they often trigger seems excessive. The use of words considered by some to be obscene has resulted in the banning of books and movies, the arrest of speakers, federal, state, and local prosecutions, and innumerable lawsuits. While the number of words considered obscene is very small, they provoke controversy far out of proportion to their possible effect.

Understanding obscene language requires that a distinction be made between ideas and the words used to represent the ideas. Many subjects that are unpleasant to consider are not regarded as obscene: for example, murder, cancer, and drug addiction. Any revulsion experienced when such topics are discussed is the result of the nature of the subject itself rather than the language used. Even sex, venereal disease, and perversion can be discussed without offending most people if the speaker's language is discreet. However, if the speaker employs certain words generally regarded as vulgar in discussing these subjects, many people will be distressed.

For example, the following statements all convey the same information in different ways: "They spent the night together"; "They slept together"; "They made love"; "They had an affair." These statements contain enough information to enable every reader to understand what is being described. Whereas some may regard the act as immoral, probably no one would be offended by the language. If one were to become more specific, the following descriptions might be added: "They had intercourse"; "They engaged in sexual intercourse"; or "They had sex." None of the last three statements should offend the reader any more than the earlier ones, because they all convey essentially the same information. If the example were to be carried one step further, however, and a common "four-letter" word used, some readers probably would be upset. Why, it may be asked, since the same idea is conveyed? Clearly it is the language, not the information, that produces such a response.

Why are people offended by the use of certain symbols when they find the same information inoffensive when conveyed by other symbols? The answer is that many people have been so thoroughly conditioned from childhood to regard some words as dirty that they automatically react to them with disgust. The belief that some words are inherently immoral is dangerous, because it is likely to confuse one's moral judgments and values. Armed with the misconception that certain words are inherently evil, well-intentioned would-be censors and guardians too often focus their attention almost solely on "four-letter" words and neglect the possibly damaging effects of speeches, books, magazines, movies, and television programs glorifying violence, greed, prejudice, and corruption.

A second form of disreputable language, profanity, consists of words and phrases that are offensive on religious grounds. Oaths and curses that invoke the name of God are usually regarded as blasphemous, regardless of whether the speaker gives thought to the meaning of the words or simply uses them out of habit. The objection to profanity stems from the Biblical injunction

"Thou shall not take the name of the Lord thy God in vain." It is understandable that people of deep religious conviction should find language that violates this commandment repugnant. Even many nonreligious persons regard such language as improper.

The words *God, Jesus Christ, hell,* and *damn* are not objectionable in most contexts; it is only when they are used to express certain ideas that they are deemed profane. So clearly, profanity is a matter of intent.

What about circumlocutions used to avoid outright profanity? For example, are *G-d d--n, J---s Ch---t, g- to h--l* profane? All that has been done here is to substitute different symbols (dashes) for more readily recognizable symbols (letters). Since the reader clearly comprehends the messages conveyed by the symbols, it is difficult to see how this circumvention is in any way less profane than the same words without the substitution of dashes for letters.

Conversely, some people regard Xmas as sacrilegious, forgetting that letters and words are simply symbols. So long as readers recognize that Xmas means the same thing as *Christmas*—and not *Exmass* or *Thanksgiving*—there is nothing objectionable about using a different symbol to convey the same idea. Indeed, in other languages totally different sets of symbols are used to represent *Christmas.*

UNDESIRABLE LANGUAGE.   "What's in a name?" asked Shakespeare. "That which we call a rose, by any other name would smell as sweet." But to some people, a rose by another name would not smell as sweet. The National Marine Fisheries Service, for example, recently reported that several species of fish do not sell well apparently solely because of their names. They include ratfish, dogfish, gag, snook, pigfish, pout, and pollock. However, when called such names as *Boston bluefish* and *ocean perch,* they sell much better and seem to improve in taste among consumers. Other words are considered derogatory, demeaning, or indelicate. In discussing this phenomenon, we are not talking about words that are used with the intention of degrading or demeaning, such as *nigger, kike, coward, queer, bigot, stupid, slob,* and *liar.* Instead we are concerned about words that the ordinary person uses with no thought of being offensive or insulting but that others may regard as derogatory. For example, some people frown on the use of the word *slum,* preferring to call such neighborhoods *depressed areas.* Similarly, some people consider *sanitation worker* more acceptable than *garbage collector.* Additional examples include the following:

Undesirable Term	*Preferred Term*
ignorant, uneducated	culturally deprived
insane, crazy, lunatic	mentally disturbed
janitor	custodian, maintenance engineer
politician	legislator, statesman
funeral parlor	mortuary

used car	preowned car
corpse	dearly departed, loved one
insane asylum	mental hospital, rest home
crippled	physically handicapped
false teeth	dentures
wigs, toupées	hairpieces
hairdresser	beautician, cosmetologist
charity	welfare
mentally disturbed children	exceptional children
fat	stout, overweight
sweat	perspiration
old maid, spinster	unmarried, single
constipation	irregularity

At times, attempts to substitute more delicate language for other terms verge on the ridiculous. Consider the following excerpt from the report of a junior high school committee of teachers appointed by the principal to find ways of saying things more tactfully on students' report cards:

Somewhat Harsh Expressions	*Euphemisms*
Could stand more baths; dirty; has bad odor	Needs guidance in development of good habits of hygiene
Lies	Shows difficulty in distinguishing between imaginary and factual material
Steals	Needs help in learning to respect the property rights of others
Lazy	Needs ample supervision in order to work well
Noisy	Needs to develop quieter habits of communication
Has disgusting eating habits	Needs help in improving table manners
Is a bully	Has qualities of leadership but needs help in learning to use them democratically
Disliked by other children	Needs help in learning to form lasting friendships

Both derogatory words and their preferred substitutes are merely symbols. It is a mistake to assume that one set of words is inherently bad or degrading and the other is good or uplifting. Regardless of whether a person is called a *garbage collector* or a *sanitation worker,* the person still picks up the trash. There is a danger that the substitution of more complimentary terms for commonly used words may tend to disguise the true nature of a situation. For example, slum neighborhoods constitute a serious national problem. Calling these sections *depressed areas* in no way changes conditions in the slums and may actually disguise the seriousness of the problem.

The Superiority Misconception

Most children in the United States are taught to read and speak in what is known as *standard* dialect, with standard pronunciations and standard grammatical and syntactical constructions. Some people believe persons who speak something other than the accepted dialect are substandard in their language development. For instance, the child who says, "I have 10 cent" or "They gone" or "They be gone" or "Don't nobody care" is considered deficient in language development and intellectually inferior. This attitude reflects the superiority misconception.

Most research on dialect differences supports the conclusion that persons whose dialect and grammar differ from the speech of the majority are not inferior. The studies generally conclude that rather than being substandard they are nonstandard or different. Nonstandard means that although the children do not use the standard dialect, they may very well have a systematic language pattern that enables them to communicate effectively in their environment (for example, among blacks, Hispanics, and Asian and other recent immigrants).

The assumption that nonstandard speech is in some way substandard may impair the educational development of persons who do not speak a standard dialect. The myth can be harmful if a teacher's or adult's expectation becomes a self-fulfilling prophecy. One who labors under the superiority misconception runs the risk of classifying persons who speak a nonstandard dialect as inferior and then, in turn, convincing them that they actually are inferior by criticizing their language development and thought processes. Convinced of their inferiority, they give up hope of acceptance and development of an acceptable dialect and grammar.

TYPES OF LANGUAGE

Language can be classified in several ways. Three categories are (1) concrete and abstract language, (2) emotive and neutral words, and (3) informative, directive, and expressive language.

Concrete-Abstract Language

One way of understanding language is classifying it according to how specific it is. Words that are very specific are referred to as *concrete.* They include tangible objects—persons, places, and things. The following words are specific and so would be considered concrete: *aspirin, Time magazine, eighty-nine,*

Golden Gate Bridge, a lemon, Rembrandt's Night Watch, and *my wristwatch.* Less specific terms—intangible or theoretical ideas, conditions, and relationships—are called *abstract.* More abstract words than those above are *medicine, communications, many, transportation, food, art,* and *time.*

Actually it is more accurate to say that some are more concrete than others than it is to classify language as being *either* concrete *or* abstract. There are degrees of concreteness and abstraction. One might illustrate this by placing several words on a continuum ranging from the highly abstract to the very concrete, as shown in Figure 14.1. At no place on the continuum can one draw a line and say all the words on one side are abstract and all the words on the other side are concrete. Instead it is a matter of some words being more or less concrete than others.

In the following passage, italics indicate the highly abstract language used in a speech by Henry Kissinger:

> Today the *forces of democracy* are called upon to show *renewed creativity* and *vision.* In *a world of complexity*—in *a world of equilibrium and coexistence,* of *competition and interdependence*—it is our *democratic values* that *give meaning to our sacrifice and purpose to our exertions.* Thus the *cohesion of the industrial democracies has a moral* as well as a political and economic significance. (*Representative American Speeches, 1975–1976,* New York: H. W. Wilson Co., 1976, p. 52.)

Most listeners would find it extremely difficult to grasp the meaning of such a highly abstract statement.

Emotive-Neutral Language

Another way of classifying language is according to how much emotion or feeling it arouses in the listener. Words that stimulate emotional responses are called *emotive* or *connotative;* words that evoke little or no emotional reaction are referred to as *neutral* or *denotative.*

Emotive or connotative language may affect the listener either favorably or unfavorably. It can arouse warm, pleasant feelings, such as love, friend-

FIGURE 14.1

A B S T R A C T	Mankind	A woman	An American woman	A woman from Ohio	A woman from Akron, Ohio	A police-woman from Akron, Ohio	Sgt. Elaine Q. Smith of Akron, Ohio	C O N C R E T E

ship, goodwill, forgiveness, nostalgia, gratification, pride, and generosity. Or it can create unpleasant, irritating emotions, such as hatred, fear, selfishness, anger, shame, and insecurity.

A speaker's choice of words for conveying an idea can greatly influence the hearer's emotional response. Note the differences in the following passages, each embodying essentially the same thought:

He delivered a strongly worded attack.
He delivered a vicious tirade.

It was an unpleasant scene.
It was a disgusting spectacle.

She proposed major reforms.
She demanded radical changes.

Jones, president of the women's rights organization . . .
Jones, who claims to be the leader of the so-called equal rights group . . .

Smith, who is regarded as a successful business executive . . .
Smith, known to be a shrewd dealer (or slick operator) . . .

The troops made a strategic withdrawal . . .
The troops were driven back . . .

His resolute, determined opposition to . . .
His pigheaded, stubborn attitude toward . . .

The following excerpt from a speech by then FBI Director Clarence M. Kelley provides an excellent example of the use of emotive language. The emotive language is in italics.

> The *terrorist* neither listens to reason nor engages in reasoning with others. His aim is *to generate fear—to frighten people into submission.* He measures success by the *magnitude of the fear he generates* through *brutal, savage acts of violence.* How proud those responsible must have been of the *bombing* at Fraunces Tavern . . . last year—a *bombing* in which four persons were *killed* and *scores were injured.* Members of the Armed Forces of Puerto Rican Liberation *crowed* that they *committed* that *vicious act* and others. *Terrorists* like these are *prepared to kill* . . . to further whatever cause they claim to be pursuing. And the *heinousness of these murders* is accented by the fact that they *murder without passion.* They *murder* with *cool deliberation and careful planning.* . . . A *perverted* sort of courage and profound dedication sustains them. . . . They are *utterly amoral.* (*Representative American Speeches, 1975–1976,* New York: H. W. Wilson Co., 1976, p. 119.)

Because human beings differ, not everyone will respond with the same reaction or intensity of feeling to a particular word or phrase. Differences in culture and experience shape each person's emotional responses to words. The individual who has never experienced poverty will not react to the word *hunger* in the same way as someone who has gone to bed on an empty stomach night after night. The word *torture* has unpleasant connotations for almost everybody, but for the person who actually has been tortured the word will have a different meaning from the meaning it will have for the individual who has never undergone this experience. *Charity* is a word that suggests generosity to the giver, but to someone who must rely on it for existence it may have a less favorable connotation.

Recognizing that cultural and experiential factors determine the way people respond to a message, radical organizer Saul Alinsky urges speakers to gain an understanding of the background, values, and aspirations of their listeners. He says:

> Communication with others takes place when they understand what you're trying to get across to them. If they don't understand, then you are not communicating, regardless of words, pictures, or anything else. People only understand things in terms of their experience, which means that you must get within their experience. (Saul Alinsky, *Rules for Radicals,* New York: Random House, 1972, p. 81.)

The emotive content of a word depends, of course, on how it is used and what meaning it has in its particular context. Describing a balloon as *yellow* produces no emotional response; calling a man *yellow* would undoubtedly evoke emotion. In the same way, when *plot* is used in reference to a story, it is neutral, but a *plot* to kidnap someone would be regarded as sinister.

Some words that have no emotional overtones for most people may produce a profound reaction in others. A traumatic experience resulting from the injury or death of a loved one might lead to a permanent emotional reaction, which most people would not share, to words associated with the tragedy.

Informative, Expressive, and Directive Language

Language can also be classified according to its use. Depending on the speaker's purpose, language may be described as informative, expressive, or directive.

Informative language contributes to the listener's knowledge or understanding. Its purpose is to enlighten rather than to influence the reader. Some examples of informative language are

I saw Mike at the supermarket this morning.
We had 6 inches of snow yesterday.
Enrollment last semester was 11,642.
The concert begins at 7:30.

Expressive language consists of statements made by speakers to indicate their feelings. It seeks neither to inform nor to persuade. Examples of expressive language are:

Ouch!
What a beautiful day.
I'm worn out.
I wish I were taller.

Directive language, unlike informative or expressive language, seeks to influence beliefs or behavior. Some directive statements are:

Will you please pass the salt?
Save money by shopping at O'Neils.
Vote for me.
Aw c'mon, Jane, please.

DIFFERENCES BETWEEN ORAL AND WRITTEN LANGUAGE

Charles James Fox, the great British debater, once said that "if a speech reads well it is not a good speech." While this probably is not entirely true, it does suggest that speech and writing are not the same. Differences between oral and written communication require speakers to give special attention to the language they use.

One of the principal differences between communicating orally and in writing is that when deciphering the written message, the reader has many visual aids to help comprehend the message. For example, if you look at a few pages of this book you will see that reading is made easier by the use of headings, different sizes and kinds of type, dividing the material into paragraphs, periods, question marks, exclamation points, commas, colons, semicolons, parentheses, and dashes within sentences to show relationships, subordination, and qualification. None of these visual cues is available to understand a speech. The listener must rely entirely on the speaker's inflections, pauses, emphases, and changes of rate in order to grasp meaning.

Another important difference between the two kinds of communication is that readers control the pace at which they receive the message. They can pause, reread, stop to look up unfamiliar terms, and review earlier passages. Because readers set their own pace, writers can develop their material stylistically in a way that is considerably more complex and abstract than can the speaker. In a speaking situation the listener has no control over the rate at which the message is presented but must grasp the meaning instantly. Because of this, the speaker must use language the listeners can comprehend immediately.

A third difference between oral and written communication is in the

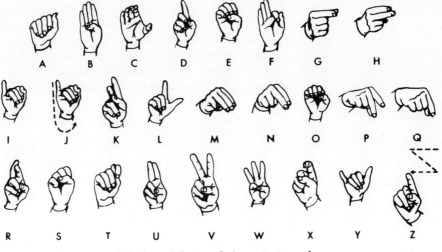

The sign language alphabet. (National Association of the Deaf)

vocabularies the speaker and writer can employ. Most people have a considerably larger reading than listening vocabulary; they recognize in print many words that they would not recognize when spoken. Because of this, good oral style is usually characterized by the use of more familiar words and shorter and simpler sentences than are found in written messages.

Because speakers confront listeners in a face-to-face situation, they also tend to be more direct, making extensive use of the personal pronouns *you, we, our, your,* and *us.* The printed word, however, because it is not aimed at any single, visible audience, tends to be somewhat more formal, making less frequent use of the personal pronouns cited above.

The speaker also tends to be more colloquial and conversational than the writer and will usually use the contractions *won't, don't, can't, couldn't, shouldn't, wouldn't, we'll, I'll,* and others rather than the more formal *will not, do not, cannot, could not, should not, would not, we will,* and *I will.*

A final difference is in the syntax of oral and written communication. Writers, because their work must withstand careful scrutiny and study, usu-

It should be observed that each kind of rhetoric has its own appropriate style. That of written prose is not the same as that of spoken oratory.

ARISTOTLE

ally are more exacting in their sentence structure, grammar, and syntax. A speaker, however, often violates the rules of good composition, leaving some sentences unfinished, starting other sentences anew, and inserting parenthetical digressions. Yet frequently these errors in no way detract from the clarity of the message because of the speaker's use of inflection, pause, emphasis, rate, and gestures to supplement the verbal presentation.

SUMMARY

Language is the basis of our communication with others. Although also employing visible symbols, a speaker uses primarily audible symbols or spoken sounds. Understanding the nature of language is essential to its effective usage in oral communication. Six common misconceptions about language interfere with effective communication. The singularity misconception, or the belief that words have only one meaning, may lead to misunderstanding between the speaker and listener. The belief that the meanings of words never change can also cause a breakdown in communication. A third misconception is that words carry authority or in some way guarantee the worth or value of something. Some people even regard words as having mystical powers. Another misconception is that words can be inherently good or bad. A final misconception is the belief that the standard-dialect speaker communicates more effectively and thinks more logically than the nonstandard speaker. The effective communicator is cognizant of these misconceptions and chooses language accordingly, defining and clarifying where necessary, avoiding taboos, and making certain at all times that the speaker and listeners are using words in the same way.

Language may be studied in several ways. Words may be classified according to their degree of specificity or tangibility into concrete and abstract language. They may also be analyzed according to the emotional responses they arouse in listeners. Still a third approach is to analyze language according to its use, whether the words are informative, directive, or expressive.

Although both oral and written communication rely on words to convey their messages, language is used somewhat differently in speaking than in writing. The writer is assisted by many visual clues not available to the speaker in getting ideas across to an audience. On the other hand, the speaker has the advantage of various vocal techniques to help clarify meaning. The two methods of communication also differ significantly in the vocabularies and syntax they use and in the degree of control the receiver has over the reception of the message. Because of these differences, the speaker's approach to style will differ from the writer's.

STUDY QUESTIONS

1. What is the singularity misconception of language?
2. How does ambiguous language differ from vague language? Give an example of each.

3. What is meant by the permanency misconception of language? Why does it cause confusion?
4. What is the authority misconception? Give some examples of this misconception that you have observed.
5. How widely held is the morality misconception of language? Can a speaker afford to violate this misconception in a speech?
6. What are the differences between disreputable and derogatory language?
7. Are some words inherently bad, evil, or obscene? Defend your answer.
8. How does abstract language differ from concrete language?
9. What is the key to classifying words as either neutral or emotive? Can a word be both neutral and emotive?

EXERCISES

1. Define and give an example of each of the following kinds of language: (a) informative, (b) expressive, and (c) directive. Which kind do you think is used most frequently?
2. From a newspaper or magazine editorial, syndicated column, or speech, find a passage (at least 10 sentences long) containing an unusually large number of emotionally colored words. After copying the passage, underline all the emotive words and then rewrite the passage, replacing the emotive words with neutral ones.
3. List 10 abstract words and for each word find a more concrete counterpart (for example: *fruit* and *a candied apple; journalism* and *The New York Times*).
4. From a book, magazine article, or speech, find a passage containing several abstract words. Rewrite the passage, substituting more concrete words for the abstract terms.
5. Locate several advertisements that illustrate the authoritative misconception.
6. Locate a passage of approximately 150 words in a book or magazine. Rewrite the passage using an oral style. Read both versions aloud before the class.

FURTHER READINGS

Brown, Charles T., and Paul W. Keller, *Monologue to Dialogue* (Englewood Cliffs, NJ: Prentice-Hall, 1979), chap. 5, "Meaning: What Language Does to Us and for Us."

Chase, Stuart, *Power of Words* (New York: Harcourt, Brace, Jovanovich, 1954).

Civikly, Jean M. (ed.), *Messages: A Reader in Human Communication* (New York: Random House, 1974), 52–77, 81–86, 321–331, 338–345.

Jacobovits, Leon A., and Murray S. Miron (eds.), *Readings in the Psychology of Language* (Englewood Cliffs, NJ: Prentice-Hall, 1967).

Myers, Gail E., and Michele Tolela Myers, *Communicating When We Speak* (New York: McGraw-Hill, 1978), chap. 3, "Symbols and Messages."

Ross, Raymond S., *Speech Communication: Fundamentals and Practice,* 7th ed. (Englewood Cliffs, NJ: Prentice-Hall, 1986), chap. 2, "Language Habits."

Ruby, Lionel, and Robert E. Yarber, *The Art of Making Sense* (Philadelphia: Lippincott, 1974), chap. 2, "Words and Ambiguity," chap. 3, "Define Your Terms," and chap. 4, "What Kind of Language Are You Using?"

Vetter, Harold, *Language Behavior and Communication: An Introduction* (Itasca, IL: Peacock, 1969).

CHAPTER 15

USING LANGUAGE EFFECTIVELY

During the Crimean War, in the late 1850s, John Bright made one of the most magnificent speeches in British parliamentary history. He spoke in opposition to the war. "The Angel of Death has been abroad throughout the land," he said to a hushed House of Commons, "you may almost hear the beating of his wings." Afterward, when being congratulated, he said, "Ah, yes, but if I had said 'the flapping of his wings' they would have laughed." Bright's comment emphasizes the importance of selecting the right words to express one's ideas.

The speaker's use of language is known as oral style. Good oral style is clear, correct, concrete, vivid, and appropriate. The speaker's language should be clear so that the listener understands without difficulty. Words and sentence structure should be correct so that they accurately express the speaker's ideas. The speaker should strive to employ concrete language because it contributes to a precise communication and increases the audience's interest in the message. Through the use of vivid language, the speaker can make ideas more colorful, more forceful, and more easily remembered. And the speaker should use appropriate language that neither offends nor interferes with the communication of ideas.

ACHIEVING CLARITY

In any speech situation, if the speaker is to gain the desired response, it is essential that the hearer understand what the speaker is saying. The basic test of a speaker's choice of words, according to Quintilian, is "not that language may be understood, but that it cannot be misunderstood."

Lack of Clarity

A speaker's language may not be clear for various reasons, but three of the most common are that (1) the words may be totally unfamiliar to the listener; (2) they may have no clear-cut meaning; and (3) they may have more than one meaning. In each of these instances, the speaker must either define terms or specify the precise meaning of the word as it is being used. Speakers who employ technical jargon, abstract language, or unfamiliar terminology must clarify the meaning of these words if they expect to get their message across to the listeners. Furthermore, communication sometimes is unclear because the speaker is guilty of what has been called the COIK fallacy—Clear Only If Known.

> Style is the dress of thoughts.
>
> PHILIP DORMER STANHOPE

Speakers commit the COIK fallacy for three reasons:

1. *Speakers often do not appreciate the complexity of what they are communicating.*
Edgar Dale gives an example of this:

> For years I have puzzled over the poor communication of simple directions, especially those given me when traveling by car. I ask such seemingly easy questions as: Where do I turn off Route 30 for the bypass around the business district? How do I get to the planetarium? Is this the way to the university? The individual whom I hail for directions either replies, "I'm a stranger here myself," or gives me in kindly fashion the directions I request. He finishes by saying pleasantly, "You can't miss it."
>
> But about half the time you do miss it. You turn at High Street instead of Ohio Street. It was six blocks, not seven. Many persons tell you to turn right when they mean left. You carefully count the indicated five stoplights before the turn and discover that your guide meant that blinkers should be counted as stoplights. Some of the directions turn out to be inaccurate. Your guide himself didn't know how to get there. (*The News Letter,* Columbus: Ohio State University, School of Education, April 1966, p. 1.)

2. *Speakers fail to consider how much or how little the other person knows about the subject.* Imagine that you are a third party to this conversation: A. "Have you tried the MX10A?" B. "It dumps sidebands all over the spectrum." A. "What about the Verion?" B. "The midrange is hooded. I hear the new Koetsu is quite something." A. "Without correct lateral tracking, forget it." The conversation is about sound, but unless you are an audiophile familiar with tweeters, subwoofers, oscilloscopes, and other technical items, the discussion will make little sense.

3. *Speakers are more technical and detailed than necessary.* For example:

> A plumber once wrote to a research bureau pointing out that he had used hydrochloric acid to clean out sewer pipes and inquired whether there was any possible harm. The first written reply was as follows: "The efficacy of hydrochloric acid is indisputable, but the corrosive residue is incompatible with metallic permanence." The plumber thanked them for this information approving his procedure. The dismayed research bureau wrote again, saying, "We cannot assume responsibility for the production of toxic and noxious residue with hydrochloric acid and suggest you use an alternative procedure." Once more the plumber thanked them for their approval. Finally, the bureau, worried about the New York sewers, called in a third scientist, who wrote: "Don't use hydrochloric acid. It eats hell out of the pipes." (*The News Letter,* Columbus: Ohio State University, School of Education, April 1966, p. 3.)

A speaker should be particularly careful to define vague, technical, and ambiguous words. In defining terms, a speaker has many methods of definition from which to choose.

Methods of Definition

DEFINITION BY SYNONYM.   A synonym is a word having the same or nearly the same meaning as another. Defining by synonym consists of citing other words that mean the same or approximately the same thing as the word being defined. In defining by synonym, the speaker should be sure that the synonym actually increases the listener's understanding. A vague or unfamiliar synonym will not increase the listener's knowledge. For example, to define a *god* as a *deity; virtuous* as *morally good;* or *legerdemain* as *prestidigitation* contributes little to understanding what the speaker is talking about. If one uses a synonym to define, the synonym must have a clear and specific meaning for the listener.

Trying to define by synonym also may not be practical because there may be no other word with precisely the same meaning. For example, it is difficult to find another word with the same meaning as *house. Home* has an emotional connotation and implies that someone is living in the structure. *Cottage, bungalow, villa, chalet,* and *mansion* all suggest specific types of houses and so are not satisfactory. So a speaker may find it difficult to define a word by using synonyms.

DEFINITION BY EXAMPLE.   Defining by example consists of giving an illustration—actual or hypothetical—of a word. A definition by example might prove helpful in explaining a word that is difficult to explain and for which there is no exact synonym. For example, defining *empathy* as "projection of one's own feelings into the feelings of another" contributes little to understanding the concept. However, if the speaker could provide examples of *empathy* that the listeners had experienced, the meaning of the term might be clearer. For example, one could ask: "When you see someone bite into a lemon, do you pucker your lips and almost taste it?" "When someone scrapes

"You should say what you mean," the March Hare went on.
"I do," Alice hastily replied, "at least—at least I mean what I say—that's the same thing, you know."
"Not the same thing a bit!" said the Hatter. "Why you might just as well say that 'I see what I eat' is the same as 'I eat what I see'!"

LEWIS CARROLL
Alice's Adventures in Wonderland

a fingernail across a blackboard, do you feel chills up and down your spine?''
''When you see someone do a belly flop into the swimming pool, do you gasp
as the diver hits the water?'' Each of these is an example of *empathy*, and
listeners who have experienced them will probably understand what the term
means.

Remember: for the definition to be meaningful, the speaker's examples
must be familiar.

DEFINITION BY DETAILS.   A common method of definition is for the
speaker to provide enough details about a word for the listener to understand
its meaning.

In a speech on the environment, William D. Ruckelshaus used details to
define *usufruct.* He said:

> Note the term *usufruct.* Under an agreement of usufruct, a tenant may use
> the fruit of the orchard and the land, but he is bound to preserve the basic
> resources as they were received. He has the use of the land in his own
> time, but he must pass it on without damage. (*Representative American
> Speeches, 1971–1972,* New York: H. W. Wilson Co., 1972, p. 127.)

Each of the following also illustrates how a term may be defined by
details.

Jodhpurs are riding breeches made loose and full above the knees and close
fitting below them.
A *kiosk* is a small structure resembling a summerhouse or pavilion, which is
open at one or more sides and often is used as a newsstand, bandstand,
or covering for the entrance to a subway.
A *jingo* is a person who boasts of his or her patriotism and favors an aggressive, threatening, warlike foreign policy for his or her country.
A *trifle* is a popular English dessert consisting of sponge cake soaked in wine
and covered with fruit, macaroons, almonds, and custard or whipped
cream.
Aphasia is the total or partial loss of the power to use or understand words,
usually caused by brain disease or injury.

DEFINITION BY COMPARISON AND CONTRAST.   Sometimes a
word can be most effectively defined by comparing or contrasting it with
something else. This method is useful in explaining concepts with which the
audience has little familiarity.

Nobel laureate George W. Beadle's skillful use of comparisons to clarify
the principles of genetics to lay audiences illustrates the value of this method
of definition. By comparing a concept in genetics to something familiar, Dr.
Beadle was able to discuss highly technical, scientific ideas with listeners

having little knowledge of the subject. For example, to illustrate evolution by natural selection, he told of a housewife who made such good angel food cake that many people asked for her recipe.

> On one occasion when she wrote it out, however, she listed thirteen egg whites instead of the twelve egg whites she should have specified. The cook who followed that copy of the recipe got a cake so light and delicate that her recipe for angel food cake became the one that all members of the Ladies Guild requested. The twelve-egg cake thus became extinct and the thirteen-egg cake survived. The original cook's mistake when copying the recipe . . . was a mutation; and the subsequent replacement of the twelve-egg cake by the thirteen-egg cake was a perfect example of evolution by natural selection. (*Saturday Review,* April 3, 1965, pp. 52–54.)

Historian Daniel Boorstin used contrast as a method of definition to describe a *pseudoevent* as follows:

> A politician's visit to a dairy farm is an example of a pseudoevent; a fire is an example of a real event. If the television cameras don't show up, the fire will burn anyway, but the politician is not likely to make the visit. (For additional examples of different methods of defining pseudo-event, see Daniel Boorstin, *The Image: A Guide to Pseudoevents in America,* New York: Harper & Row, 1961, pp. 9–12.)

At times, comparison and contrast can be used to pinpoint the precise meaning of a word by showing how it both resembles and differs from a closely related idea. In this method, the speaker points out the similarities between the two concepts but also emphasizes the distinguishing differences. An example of this method is provided by Ken Follett:

> There is no such thing as a safe level of radiation. Such talk makes you think of radiation like water in a pool: if it's 4 feet high you're safe, if it's 8 feet high you drown. But in fact radiation levels are much more like speed limits on the highway—30 miles per hour is safer than 80, but not as safe as 20, and the only way to be completely safe is not to get in the car. (Ken Follett, *Triple,* New York: Arbor House, 1980, p. 79.)

Concepts such as *libel* and *slander; agnostic* and *atheist;* and *legal, ethical,* and *moral* can be better understood if compared and contrasted.

The following are examples of definition by comparison and contrast:

Libel and *slander. Libel* is a written or printed statement, sign, or picture, not made in the public interest, tending to expose a person to ridicule or contempt or to injure the person's reputation. *Slander* is the utterance or spreading of a false statement or statements harmful to another's character or reputation. Legally, *slander* is spoken, as distinguished from *libel*, which is written.

Agnostic and *atheist.* An *agnostic* is a person who thinks it is impossible to know whether there is a God or future life. An *atheist,* on the other hand, is convinced that there definitely is no God or future life. An *atheist* rejects all religious belief and the existence of God, while an *agnostic* simply questions the existence of God because of the absence of proof of His existence and an unwillingness to accept supernatural revelation. The *atheist* would say "There is no God," while the *agnostic* would say, "I don't know whether there is a God."

Legal, ethical, and *moral.* The term *legal* implies conformity with written, statute law. *Ethical,* on the other hand, means conforming to the standards or codes of conduct of a group or profession, while *moral* refers to conformity with accepted standards of rightness or goodness. For example, it is unethical for doctors and lawyers to advertise, but it is not illegal or immoral. Running a red light would be illegal but not unethical or immoral. Telling a lie is neither unethical nor illegal; however, it is generally considered immoral.

Other concepts that might lend themselves to definition by comparison and contrast include *nationalism* and *patriotism; sympathy* and *empathy; apartheid* and *segregation; liberal, radical, conservative,* and *reactionary; illiteracy* and *ignorance; intelligence* and *knowledge; romanticism* and *classicism; character* and *personality;* and *inflation* and *deflation.*

DEFINITION BY CLASSIFICATION AND DIFFERENTIATION. Definition by classification and differentiation consists of placing a word within a class and then differentiating it from other concepts within that classification by pointing out its dissimilar characteristics. For example, if one were to define *automobile* by this method, one would first place it in the general class of *vehicles* and then show how it differs from other vehicles by listing such details as the following: it is four-wheeled, operated on land, runs on gasoline, is usually used for private transportation, and so on. It is thereby distinguished from vehicles such as trains, bicycles, motorcycles, trucks, boats, and airplanes.

DEFINITION BY HISTORICAL BACKGROUND.   Some concepts can be understood only by placing them in historical context and showing how they came into being. For example, the *romantic movement* or *romanticism* in music, art, and literature probably is understandable only if one knows something about the times and conditions that gave rise to it.

Other words that require historical background in order to be fully understood are *populism, muckrakers, protestant, popular sovereignty, cold war, witch hunt, feudalism, lend-lease, McCarthyism, spoils system, bluestocking, blitzkrieg, Watergate, women's liberation, Reaganomics, Irangate,* and *glasnost.*

DEFINITION BY ETYMOLOGY.   Etymology is the study of the origins and derivations of words. Occasionally, a term may be better understood if its origin—what it initially meant—and how its meaning has changed are known.

Some words that might be more easily recognized and remembered through definition by etymology are listed below.

Pyrotechnics is derived from the Greek *pyr* or *pyros,* meaning "a fire," and the Greek *technic,* meaning "art." Combined, these words mean "the art of making or using fireworks or a display of fireworks." From this, it has also come to mean a dazzling display of eloquence or wit.

The word *heterogeneous* is based on the Greek words *hetero,* meaning "other or different," and *genes,* meaning "race or kind." Thus, *heterogeneous* means "composed of unrelated or unlike elements or parts; varied; miscellaneous; dissimilar; or differing in structure or quality."

The concept of *jurisprudence* is based on the Latin *jus* and *juris,* which mean "right of law," and *prudentia,* which means "a foreseeing, knowledge, or skill." When combined, they refer to the science or philosophy of law, a system of laws, or a part or division of law.

The word *orthodox* comes from the Greek *orthos,* which means "correct," and *doxa,* which means "opinion." Thus *orthodox* means "conforming to the usual beliefs or established doctrines; proper; correct; or conventional."

Daniel J. Boorstin, head of the Library of Congress, defined *encyclopedia* etymologically in a speech when he said, "Encyclopedia originally meant the circle of knowledge of the arts and sciences essential to a liberal education."

While an etymological definition is helpful in understanding some words, this method is of little value and may even be misleading in explaining others. Because the meanings of words change, the original meaning of a term sometimes bears little relationship to its present meaning. For example, *surgeon* is derived from the Greek words *cheir* and *cheires,* meaning "the hand," and *ergein,* which means "to work," and originally referred, as discussed earlier, to people who worked with their hands, such as artisans and craftspeople. Obviously the meaning of the word has changed greatly since then, today referring to a doctor who treats disease or injury in a particular way. With a concept such as this, citing the origins of the word will add little to the audience's knowledge.

DEFINITION BY OPERATION, USE, OR FUNCTION.   Some concepts can be understood only if the listener understands their operation or purpose. To define such concepts, it is necessary to explain how they work, what they are intended to accomplish, and their uses. For example, it is almost impossible to understand *inflation* without knowing how it operates and what are its effects. Similar terms that necessitate explanation of their operation, action, or purpose in order for listeners to comprehend their meaning include:

polarization	balance of payments
natural selection	fluorescence
survival of the fittest	milk homogenization
fermentation	schizophrenia
food processor	balance of power
X-ray	eggbeater
crop rotation	hydroplane
pogo stick	corkscrew
napalm	metronome synthesizer

DEFINITION BY NEGATION.   At times, the meaning of a word can be clarified by telling what it is *not.* Speakers may decide to use this method because (1) the word has more than one meaning, and they wish to make certain that the listener understands which meaning they attach to the term; (2) the word is misunderstood, and they wish to eliminate false conceptions; or (3) they wish to define the term in a new and different manner.

For example, in discussing *freedom of speech,* a speaker might point out that free speech does not include the right to say anything regardless of its consequences: that it does not give the speaker the right to slander others, to incite a riot, or to demand free radio or television time.

An example of definition by negation is the following excerpt from a speech by Barbara H. Franklin to a consumer conference:

> The challenge to all of us—and, I believe, the opportunity—is to make America work better again.
>
> When I say "better" I do not mean a bigger government which crowds out the private sector or the individual.
>
> I do not mean a more meddlesome government, burrowing deeper into the affairs of business "to fix things that ain't broke."
>
> But I also do not believe that we can turn back the clock, championing only those solutions which fit other times in our national life 50, 30, or even 20 years ago.
>
> We must learn from our mistakes of the past—so that we can do better in the future. Our country was not built by complacency or excessive caution, but by boldness, innovation, and competition. (*Representative American Speeches, 1978–79,* New York: H. W. Wilson Co., 1979, p. 140.)

Another example of a speaker using negation to help clarify his meaning was Professor Glenn A. Crosby's definition of the *purpose of a university:*

> A primary purpose of a university is not to prepare students for a good job, not to obtain grants from the federal government, not to be an

instrument of social justice, not to compete with community colleges and state colleges for the "student pool," not to screen candidates for professional schools, not to provide a hostel for prolonging adolescence, not to conform to the whims of a fickle public, not to field athletic teams, not to provide a haven for the unprepared, the indolent, and the irresponsible. This list goes on. Many of you gasp. Why, one of these purposes is exactly the reason I am here. . . . (*Representative American Speeches, 1976–1977,* New York: H. W. Wilson Co., 1977, p. 159.)

VISUAL DEFINITION.   Visual concepts often are difficult to define using only words. For example, imagine a speaker trying to explain what the color *chrome yellow* looks like using nothing but words. However, the concept is immediately clear if the speaker shows the audience something that is chrome yellow. Colors that most listeners probably could not visualize without actually seeing them include *burnt umber, cobalt blue, cadmium orange, yellow ocher,* and *French ultramarine blue.* The same is often true of definitions involving shapes, spatial relationships, textures, and concepts in the visual arts. For example, it is easier to draw a parallelogram on the blackboard by way of definition than it is to try to explain what a parallelogram looks like. Likewise, a map of Thailand showing the location of Bangkok is more explicit and meaningful than verbal directions locating the city. Other concepts best explained by a visual representation include: *iridescent, montage, hieroglyphics, impressionism, surrealism, pentimento,* and *optical illusion.* (See Figure 15.1.)

AUDIBLE DEFINITION.   Just as some concepts are most easily explained by presenting them visually, others are best understood if the listener can hear them. Many musical terms, concepts, and instruments are difficult to comprehend unless the speaker's explanation is accompanied by an audible illustration. For instance, imagine the problems a speaker would encounter in trying to explain the sound of an unfamiliar musical instrument such as the *flügelhorn, oboe, harmonium, lute, melodeon, harpsichord,* or *clavichord* without playing either a recording of its sound or a few notes on the instrument itself. Other musical concepts that require audible demonstrations if they are to be understood include *fanfare, syncopation, jazz, pizzicato,* and *leitmotiv.* Other concepts more easily understood if they are accompanied by audible illustration include *nasality, resonance, timbre, alliteration, yodeling,* and *speech dialects.*

COMBINATION OF METHODS.   The most effective definitions usually combine more than one of the methods just discussed. For example, a speaker might first list *synonym* and then follow with an example; or one might trace the origins of the word and then present details; or, after discussing the history of the concept, compare or contrast it with related concepts. The advantage to combining two or more methods of definition is that if one method does not completely clarify its meaning, perhaps another type of definition will clear up any uncertainty in the listener's mind.

FIGURE 15.1 Visual explanations can sometimes clarify better than words.

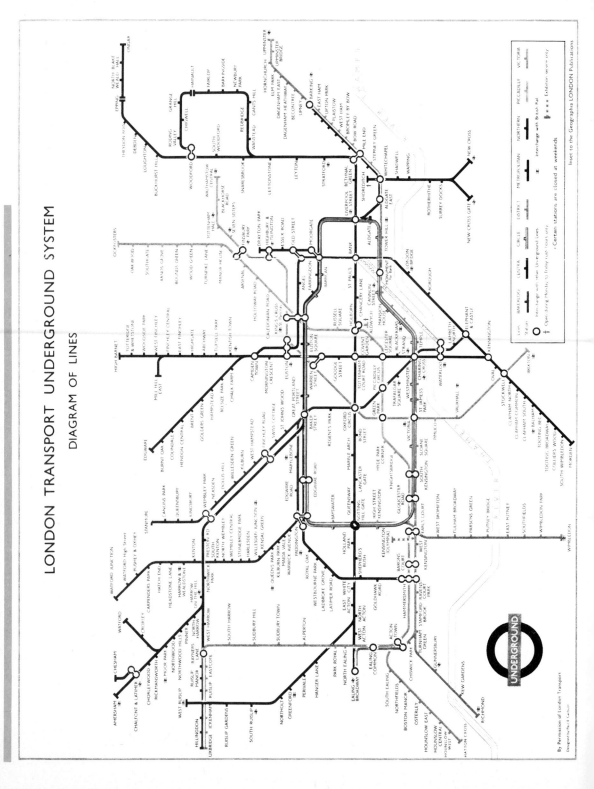

LONDON TRANSPORT UNDERGROUND SYSTEM

DIAGRAM OF LINES

ACHIEVING CORRECTNESS

A second characteristic of good oral style is correct use of language. Correctness implies not only correct grammatical use, but the right choice of words for expressing the speaker's ideas.

Correct language is important for three reasons. The first and foremost is that an incorrect choice of words may mislead or misinform. For example, the speaker who does not know the difference in meaning between *persecute* and *prosecute,* or *rational* and *rationalization* and mistakenly uses one for the other may convey a false or misleading meaning.

Second, language that is incorrect may simply confuse the hearer. Rather than being misinformed, listeners will simply not know what the speaker means.

Third, incorrect language often distracts the listener. Language errors call attention to themselves. Listeners, instead of thinking about what the speaker is saying, notice the incorrect language. A question that sometimes bothers speakers is whether to use slang words. The answer should not be based on whether the word has been included in a standard dictionary, because inclusion in a dictionary simply indicates that the word is in common usage. Actually, whether one should use slang is more a question of appropriateness than of correctness. Slang is neither correct nor incorrect. It may be unfamiliar to some audiences, and it may be inappropriate for some topics or occasions. But on the other hand, it may be highly effective in communicating the speaker's message.

Television commercials, lyrics of popular songs, and slogans of special-interest groups that employ incorrect language are frequently repeated so often that the correct usages sound strange. Most people have heard "Tell it like it is," "Winston tastes good like a cigarette should," "the real thing," and "very unique" so often that they no longer notice the incorrectness of the language. If few people notice these mistakes, should a speaker feel free to employ similar language? Probably not. The main reason is that such usages convey no useful information.

Incorrect language usage usually is the result of an inadequate education, both at home and at school. There probably is no solution to such errors other than to study grammar and to develop an ear for the language.

A speaker's language may also suffer from an inadequate vocabulary: the

The difference between the right word and the almost right word is the difference between lightning and the lightning bug.

MARK TWAIN

inability to find the right word to convey an idea or the exact shade of meaning. A speaker who repeatedly uses the same word (for example, "It was a *very* enjoyable play. It was *very* well directed. The acting was *very* good. The last act was *very, very* funny" instead of "It was a *very* enjoyable play. It was *well* directed. The acting was *exceptionally* good. The last act was *hilarious*") is handicapped by an inadequate vocabulary. Speakers who frequently resort to imprecise words, such as "you know," "stuff like that," "et cetera," "and so forth," should embark on a program of vocabulary development to achieve more precise expression. In addition, every educated speaker should own a standard dictionary and a thesaurus for consultation in determining the precise meanings of words, synonyms, and antonyms.

Probably the most common reason persons use words incorrectly is that they don't fully understand what they are talking about. A well-informed speaker will have no trouble finding the right words to convey his or her ideas.

Among commonly heard mistakes in language usage are the following:

1. *like* and *as*
   INCORRECT: Do like your mother says.
   CORRECT: Do as your mother says.
   CORRECT: She looks like her mother.
2. *only*
   INCORRECT: I only have a quarter.
   CORRECT: I have only a quarter.
3. *even*
   INCORRECT: He criticizes everyone; he even criticizes his mother.
   CORRECT: He criticizes everyone; he criticizes even his mother.
4. *lay* and *lie*
   INCORRECT: I think I will lay down for a while.
   CORRECT: I think I will lie down for a while.
5. *is* and *are*
   INCORRECT: None of them are going.
   CORRECT: None of them is going.
6. *enthused* and *enthusiastic*
   INCORRECT: All of the critics were enthused about the performance.
   CORRECT: All of the critics were enthusiastic about the performance.
7. *regardless, irrespective,* and *irregardless*
   INCORRECT: We decided to enter irregardless of our chances of winning. (There is no such word as *irregardless.*)
   CORRECT: We decided to enter regardless of our chances of winning.
   CORRECT: We decided to enter irrespective of our chances of winning.
8. *further* and *farther*
   INCORRECT: The church is further down the street.
   CORRECT: The church is farther down the street.

9. *less* and *fewer*

   INCORRECT: Some schools play less basketball games than others.

   CORRECT: Some schools play fewer basketball games than others.

10. *most* and *best*

    INCORRECT: You are the most educated person in the organization.

    CORRECT: You are the best-educated person in the organization.

11. *between* and *among*

    INCORRECT: Let's keep this secret strictly between the three of us.

    CORRECT: Let's keep this secret strictly among the three of us.

    CORRECT: Let's keep this secret strictly between the two of us.

12. *than* and *from*

    INCORRECT: Conditions are no different now than when you were young.

    CORRECT: Conditions are no different now from when you were young.

13. *unique* and *unusual*

    INCORRECT: It is a very unique school.

    CORRECT: It is a unique school.

    CORRECT: It is a very unusual school.

14. *real* and *very*

    INCORRECT: It was a real entertaining show.

    CORRECT: It was a very entertaining show.

15. *so* and *very*

    INCORRECT: It was so well planned.

    CORRECT: It was very well planned.

    CORRECT: It was so well planned that everyone found it easy to follow.

16. *hard* and *difficult*

    INCORRECT: He gave a hard examination.

    CORRECT: He gave a difficult examination.

    CORRECT: The seat was hard.

17. *orient*

    INCORRECT: The meeting was to orientate the new students.

    CORRECT: The meeting was to orient the new students.

18. *crown*

    INCORRECT: She was coronated queen of homecoming.

    CORRECT: She was crowned queen of homecoming.

19. *comment*

    INCORRECT: Her job was to commentate the style show.

    CORRECT: Her job was to comment on the style show. (Or probably better: Her job was to serve as commentator for the style show.)

20. *infer* and *imply*

    INCORRECT: Your answers are insulting and infer that I am lying.

    CORRECT: Your answers are insulting and imply that I am lying.

CORRECT: Your answers are insulting, and I infer from them that you think I am lying.
21. double negatives
INCORRECT: They don't know nothing about it.
CORRECT: They don't know anything about it.

These are examples of words often used incorrectly. To avoid misusing language, a speaker should study grammar, rely on a dictionary to learn the precise meanings of words, and develop an awareness of the way in which reputable speakers use language to convey their ideas.

ACHIEVING CONCRETENESS

Words that refer to specific and usually tangible persons, places, and things are called concrete words, in contrast to abstract language, which refers to general, often intangible concepts. From ancient times to the present, rhetoricians have urged speakers to employ concrete language because it reduces the likelihood of misunderstanding, is more quickly grasped, and usually is more interesting than abstract language. Abstract words tend to evoke a different image or meaning in the mind of each listener. For example, when a speaker uses the abstract word *charity,* some members of the audience will think of large, philanthropic foundations; others will visualize a campaign such as the March of Dimes drive; a few will think of the charitable work carried on by churches and religious orders; still others will be reminded of small gifts to beggars, tramps, and the destitute.

Speakers should use concrete language because it is more readily grasped and understood than abstract language. For example, even though this country has only one *national anthem,* the words *The Star-Spangled Banner* are more immediately meaningful than *the national anthem* to most people. Some examples of fairly concrete terms that could be replaced by even more specific words are:

Fairly Concrete	*More Concrete*
the chief executive	Presidents Carter or Reagan
the state university	Ohio State University
the nation's largest city	New York
in the spring	May
the largest automobile manufacturer	General Motors
the state capital	Madison, Wisconsin
the chief justice	Chief Justice William Rehnquist

Another reason for preferring concrete terms to abstract words is that listeners usually find concrete language more vivid and interesting. *Rolls-Royce,*

> It is a good thing to use few words and the best words, which are those which are simple and forcible.
>
> JOHN BRIGHT

for example, tells us more and is more interesting than *a big car. A six-year-old girl* is more interesting than *a child. Bad weather* is not as specific or vivid as *a blizzard, a hailstorm,* or *a tornado.*

Still another reason for using concrete language is that some common expressions are so extremely general that they can mean almost anything and so should be avoided, especially in the speaking situation. As mentioned on page 302, these include words and phrases such as *you know, things like that, too much, lots of, stuff like that,* and *et cetera.*

ACHIEVING VIVIDNESS

Whether talking to one person or addressing a large audience, a speaker may use language that is clear, correct, and concrete and still fail to attain a vivid, interesting oral style. To achieve vividness, the speaker should employ fresh and colorful words to stimulate the imagination and feelings of the listener. Two kinds of language help achieve vividness: emotive words and figurative language. Emotive language, as discussed in Chapter 14, consists of words and phrases that arouse the feelings of the listeners. Thus *home, mother, brother, hero, America, slaughtered,* and *war* are more emotive than *house, parent, sibling, soldier, this country, killed,* and *conflict.* Because emotive words stimulate the hearer's feelings, they usually are more useful than neutral terms in arousing, inspiring, or persuading others.

Figurative language consists of words used in such a way that they are pleasing, stimulating, and easily retained by the listener. Figurative language includes parallelism, repetition, alliteration, metaphor, simile, antithesis, quotations, and rhetorical questions. To illustrate the value of figurative language in enhancing an idea, consider the following paraphrases of famous statements by prominent speakers:

"Instead of trying to find out what you can get from the government, you should try to figure out some things that you can do to help it" clearly is less memorable than John F. Kennedy's "Ask not what your country can do for you; ask what you can do for your country."

"This is a fateful time" is less striking than Franklin D. Roosevelt's "This generation has a rendezvous with destiny."

Had Adlai Stevenson in his acceptance of the Democratic party presidential nomination in 1952 said, "When the convention is over, we have to face up to a lot of problems," his audience probably would not have been impressed. What he actually said, however, struck many listeners as eloquent: "When the tumult and the shouting die, when the bands are gone and the lights are dimmed, there is the stark reality of responsibility in an hour of history haunted with those gaunt, grim specters of strife, dissension, and materialism."

At times a speaker can add color and interest through the choice of a single word that is particularly striking or vivid. Notice how the italicized word in each of following enhances the entire sentence or phrase:

Few things *rankle* in the human breast like a sense of injustice.
the great *travail* of race
an *agony* of the spirit
zestfully they informed us
mortared together by common sentiment
Our economic system is a *cornucopia* of goods and services piled high.
Shattered lies the myth of American omnipotence.
the Greek colonels who *strangled* freedom in democracy's home

Lack of Vividness

To achieve a more vivid oral style, the speaker should keep in mind the following suggestions.

AVOID TRITENESS, CLICHÉS, AND HACKNEYED LANGUAGE. Triteness, clichés, and hackneyed language are phrases and expressions that have become commonplace by overuse and have lost any freshness, originality, or novelty. Such expressions may at one time have been unusual, but they have been worn out by constant usage. A few examples of trite language would include *but that is another story, who hails from, a legend in his/her time, have a nice day, it is a known fact, the good old days, the real thing, to coin a phrase, light at the end of the tunnel, at that point in time, without further ado, in conclusion let me say, the tip of the iceberg, build a better mousetrap, the bottom line, opening a new can of worms, bite the bullet, the bitter end,* and *if it's the last thing I do.*

The speaker who hopes to achieve an interesting style will shun overworked language and find more original ways of expressing ideas.

SEEK VARIETY IN LANGUAGE AND SENTENCE STRUCTURE. Although repetition at times can be an effective means for achieving emphasis, some speakers make the mistake of repeating the same word too frequently and of using the same type of sentences throughout their speeches. To overcome the monotony resulting from overuse of the same word, the speaker should use synonyms to achieve greater variety. For example, instead of repeating "he *said,*" "then he *said,*" and "next he *said,*" the speaker might use words such as *pointed out, commented, remarked, noted, mentioned, discussed, claimed, argued, explained, contended, asserted, charged, stated,* and *told.*

Speakers should also seek to achieve variety in sentence structure and length. Instead of all simple sentences, they should vary them with compound, complex, and complex-compound sentences as well. They should not speak entirely in declarative sentences but should also employ imperative and interrogative statements. If the sentences are all approximately the same length, they will be boring; instead try to heighten interest by varying sentence length.

Useful Techniques

USE REPETITION.   While too much repetition can become monotonous, at times the speaker can effectively emphasize and stress important ideas through a graceful or forceful reiteration of key words, phrases, and even complete sentences. For example, Edward Brooke used the word *alike* three times in one sentence to emphasize his point in a speech to the United States Senate when he said, "We do not want a world where all people look *alike,* talk *alike,* and, even worse, think *alike.*"

In a speech to the United Nations, President Jimmy Carter used repetition in the following manner:

So, true peace—peace embodied in binding treaties—is essential. It will be *in the interest of* the Israelis and the Arabs. It is *in the interest of* the American people. It is *in the interest of* the entire world.

Senator Edward Kennedy, in a rousing speech to the 1980 Democratic national convention, repeated the word "new" as follows:

We are the party of the *new* freedom, the *new* deal and the *new* frontier. We have always been the party of hope.

So this year, let us offer *new* hope—*new* hope to an America uncertain about the present, but unsurpassed in its potential for the future.

Former Secretary of Agriculture Earl L. Butz effectively employed repetition, saying:

World food conferences *don't produce food;* state farm bureaus *don't produce food;* politicians *don't produce food.* Only a farmer and his family on the land *produce food.*

A famous illustration of the repetition of a complete sentence was Charles James Fox's challenge to the British House of Commons in his Westminster Scrutiny speech. Knowing that the House was aware of the government's unjust attempt to deprive him of his seat as the elected member for

Westminster, Fox repeatedly defied the Speaker and the House by asserting at five different times early in the speech: "I have no reason to expect indulgence, nor do I know that I shall meet with bare justice in this House."

USE PARALLELISM.   Parallelism or balanced construction is the arrangement of words, phrases, or sentences in a similar manner or in a pattern. Parallel construction often involves repetition. Note the repetition of words in several of the following examples of parallelism:

> The choice was clear. We would stay the course. We shall stay the course. (Lyndon B. Johnson)

> The task is heavy, the toil is long, and the trials will be severe. (Winston Churchill)

> We have been told of success and seen defeat. We have been told of life and seen death. We have been told of tunnels of light and seen graves of darkness. We have been told of freedom and seen repression. (John V. Lindsay)

USE ANTITHESIS.   Antithesis is a type of parallel or balanced construction in which the parts contain opposing or contrasting ideas. Following are several examples of antithesis:

> Let us never negotiate out of fear. But let us never fear to negotiate. (John F. Kennedy)

> We believe it is better to discuss a question even without settling it than to settle a question without discussing it. (Adlai E. Stevenson)

> It's the duty of a newspaper to comfort the afflicted and afflict the comfortable. (Daniel J. Boorstin)

> Now this is not the end. It is not even the beginning of the end. But it is, perhaps, the end of the beginning. (Winston Churchill)

USE SIMILE AND METAPHOR.   Similes and metaphors are figures of speech that compare two essentially different or dissimilar things. In a simile, the comparison is actually stated through the use of words such as *like* or *as.* The metaphor, on the other hand, omits *like* or *as* and merely implies the comparison.

The following are examples of the use of similes to make an idea more vivid:

> We move students around like pawns on a chessboard through bits and pieces of academic time and campus space—from two-year college to

four-year college, from college to graduate school, from technical center to liberal arts center. (William T. Birenbaum)

Unfortunately, people are individuals, and institutions deal in multitudes. There is never time to inspect each person, to grade him like a cut of beef, and stamp him prime, choice, or good. (Harold Howe II)

The world at our mid-century is, as someone has said, like a drum—strike it anywhere and it resounds everywhere. (Adlai Stevenson)

The overthrow, for a while, of British and United States sea-power in the Pacific was like the breaking of some mighty dam; the long-gathered, pent-up waters rushed down the peaceful valleys, carrying ruin and devastation forward on their foam, and spreading their inundations far and wide. (Winston Churchill)

The following are examples of metaphors used by speakers to add color to their ideas:

If youth tells me that the Church is a religious chain store, run by the Establishment, doling out packaged worship, packaged doctrine, packaged comfort, then I want to listen before I reply. (David H. C. Reid)

We are using a slingshot for a job that calls for nuclear weapons. We are applying Band-aids in the curious expectation of stopping the growth of an advanced cancer. (Whitney Young, Jr.)

The roller coaster of inflation followed by recession is out of control. (Edmund C. Brown, Jr.)

USE COMPARISON. In addition to using the figurative metaphor and simile, a literal analogy or comparison at times will help the speaker to make an idea more clear or vivid. Following are examples of the use of comparison:

In this continuing furor over the credibility gap, the reader associates the untrue statement of a public figure with the paper that publishes it. This is like getting mad at the local editor because the weatherman goofed. But it undoubtedly has a lot to do with public disbelief of journalism. (Wes Gallagher)

This reporter has spent the last week trying to fish and think simultaneously and is obliged to report with some reluctance that both the fish and the ideas hauled up from the depths were pretty small, barely inside the legal limit, unsuitable for framing. So, after some contemplation, the contents of both catches were tossed back where they came from in the hope that they would survive and grow to more impressive proportions. (Eric Sevareid)

USE PERSONIFICATION.   Another figure of speech the speaker may use to achieve vividness is personification, or the endowment of ideas and objects with human traits, qualities, or attributes. Examples of personification are:

American higher education is currently suffering from an acute case of dyspepsia brought on by our inability to acknowledge our own digestive problems. (Edward D. Eddy)

There is a cancer here and the country is ready for surgery. (Robert S. McNamara)

The Cherokee nation was never dead; only asleep. Today it stirs and begins to waken. (W. W. Keeler)

Economic injustice has shown its ugly head in millions of American homes where five years ago it was unknown. (Shirley Chisholm)

It does not take overt censorship to cripple the free flow of ideas. (Frank Stanton)

The spirit of dissent stalks our land. (Daniel J. Boorstin)

USE ALLITERATION.   Alliteration is a stylistic device in which the initial sounds in words or in stressed syllables within the words are repeated in a pleasing or memorable manner. Some illustrations of alliteration selected from recent speeches by prominent speakers follow:

reality not rhetoric
the professed purpose of protecting the peace
a day of dissent and divisiveness
masculine mystique
headless and hostile men
take a few facts and flail away
deluged daily
design of democracy
unnoticed and unused
virtue over vice
lower level of life
trifle with truth
our differences and our diversity
adversaries and allies
tragedy and travail

hallowed halls
a center of stillness surrounded by silence
without peer or precedent
maddening magnitude
political platitudes and promises
a sham and a shuck
mythology of murder
monopoly on madness
demented decade
barbarous bombing

USE RHETORICAL QUESTIONS.   Speakers can also create interest by introducing an idea in the form of a question. Rather than employing a direct statement, speakers phrase their thoughts as questions that they do not expect the audience to answer. Some examples of rhetorical questions are:

What is to come? Is this the year when women's political power will come of age? Or are we just going to make noise but no real progress? (Bella Abzug)

How many millions of immigrants have come to these American shores to avoid European conscription, from the days of Napoleon I to the 1930s? (Dudley T. Cornish)

Have we achieved the best medicine if we "cure" our patient only to find that he wishes we hadn't? (Seymour M. Farber)

What does that mean? What does it take to be a certified teacher? (Harold Howe II)

USE QUOTATIONS.   Another way speakers may enhance their oral style is by the use of a quotation that is particularly apt, graceful, or memorable. The quoted statement may be familiar or unfamiliar, folksy or lofty, direct or paraphrased. Unlike the quotation by an expert or authority to support a contention, the speaker's purpose here is not to *prove* a point but rather to embellish an idea in a pleasing, vivid, or forceful manner. Some examples of quotations used by recent speakers include the following:

The needs of blacks and whites are too strongly entwined to separate. As Whitney Young used to say, "We may have come here on different ships, but we're in the same boat now." (Vernon E. Jordan, Jr.)

As Thomas Jefferson, one of the moving forces of American independence, observed 150 years ago, "If a nation expects to be ignorant and free, it expects what never was and never will be!" (Robert F. Kennedy)

The public is like Mrs. Einstein, when she was asked if she could make sense of her husband's theories.

"I understand the words," she said, "but I don't always understand the sentences." (John W. Hanley)

The speaker who wishes to locate a quotation for use in a speech will find that most libraries own several collections of quotations. The best known probably is Bartlett's *Dictionary of Familiar Quotations.* Collections of quotations are also available in inexpensive paperback editions. Most of these works are arranged both by subject and author.

ACHIEVING APPROPRIATENESS

A fifth characteristic of good oral style is that it is appropriate to the speaker, the subject, the listener, and the occasion.

We expect others to use language that is consistent with their education, status, and profession. Most people expect members of the clergy to use language that is not vulgar or profane. University professors are expected to be correct in their choice of words. On the other hand, sportscasters, entertainers, and after-dinner speakers may use much more informal language without offending the listener. So the first step in developing an appropriate oral style is to use the language appropriate to the speaker's education and position.

Second, a speaker's language should be appropriate to his or her purpose and message. To inform, the language should be clear and objective. To convince or persuade, one should use words that are more emotive, directive, and vivid. The speaker who wishes to inspire will need words that stimulate the feelings of the auditors and arouse respect and admiration. On the other hand, in social conversation or in situations where the speaker only wants to entertain, one can use a highly informal style, employing slang, colloquialisms, and even grammatically incorrect expressions.

The speaker's language should also be appropriate to the auditors. The speaker should be aware of the educational background, occupations, and interests of listeners in order to gauge their knowledge of the subject and what vocabulary they will understand. With poorly educated listeners, the speaker will need to use less technical language than would be employed in talking to better-educated persons. Psychologists, sports fans, housewives, musicians, automobile mechanics, and other groups all have specialized vocabularies of which a speaker should be cognizant. Terms such as *deuce, birdie, baste, carburetor,* and *contrapuntal* will be immediately recognized by those people who are familiar with the fields in which these terms are used, but for others the words are meaningless. Children, obviously, have to be addressed in simpler language than adults. In avoiding the use of language hearers will not understand, a speaker should take care not to give the impression of "talking down" to the listener.

Speakers should also know something about a listener's attitudes and beliefs. If they are trying to win over an antagonistic or skeptical listener, speakers must be much more careful in their choice of language than they would be if the hearer already agreed with them. The language a speaker uses in talking to a highly religious individual or group probably will differ from what would be employed before less pious auditors. Whether the listeners are male or female, young or old, conservative or liberal, of similar or different background, race, or nationality all might affect a speaker's choice of words.

Regardless of who the listeners are, the speaker's language should be in good taste. Words that refer to ethnic groups in a contemptuous or disparaging manner should be avoided. Such words not only irritate many members of these groups, they may also alienate others who will regard such language as bigoted or intolerant. Thus the speaker will refrain from the use of terms such as *kike, kraut, frog, spic, limey, wop, dago, Chink, Jap, Polack, yid, nigger, coon, spook, jigaboo, redneck, honky, whitey,* and *white trash.* Words disparaging groups, such as *frat boys, jocks, fuzz, pigs, head shrinkers, pill pushers, ambulance chasers,* and *holy rollers* may also give offense. Since it is possible to get a message across without resorting to name-calling, a speaker should also avoid such words as *fink, S.O.B., slob, commie, queer, pervert, pansy, fruit, slut, hick, nut, kook, lush, wino, goon, nigger lover,* and *quack.* Making fun of personal handicaps such as stuttering, palsy, crossed eyes, deafness, blindness, a limp, or a foreign or regional accent will generally be considered to be in bad taste.

The speaker's language should be adapted to the occasion. The number of listeners or participants, their reason for assembling, and the site may be important factors in determining the speaker's language. If the auditors have assembled for a special reason, such as a business meeting, to present an award, to honor an outstanding individual, to commemorate an event, or to pay their respects to the deceased, a somewhat formal choice of language is dictated. If, on the other hand, the occasion is purely social, greater informality of language would be permissible. In like manner, one's choice of language would probably differ for a large outdoor rally as opposed to a small gathering in someone's home. The language the speaker uses in a church or synagogue should be more decorous and formal than that used in other places.

In choosing the words in which one's ideas will be clothed, one should strive to develop an oral style that is appropriate to oneself, to the message, to the listeners, and to the occasion.

INVOLVING THE LISTENER

Throughout this book, attention has been given to the differences between oral and written style. Most speakers are much more direct than writers in addressing the receiver of the message, making extensive use of first- and second-person pronouns, such as *you, we, our, your,* and *us,* to involve the auditor.

In the following excerpt from a commencement address at Barnard College, note how author and playwright Lillian Hellman uses *you, your,* and *we* to achieve directness and establish rapport. Note also the bluntness of her style in this address.

> It is my deep belief that if *you* live in a country, *you* owe it something, as it, of course, owes *you. You* who are graduating today . . . [have] very possibly lived through the most shocking period of American history. *You* have seen a White House disgraced. *You* have heard a President of *your* country lie over and over again to *you. You* have seen a pious-talking Vice President thrown out because he was a crook.
>
> Perhaps more important . . . *you* know that government agencies— the CIA, the FBI, the Department of Justice, and God knows what yet hasn't come to light—have spied on innocent people who did nothing more than express their democratic right to say what they thought. *You* have read that the CIA has not alone had a hand in upsetting foreign governments they did not like, but have very possibly been involved in murder, or plots to murder. Murder. *We* didn't think of ourselves that way once upon a time.
>
> I came here today—I don't like to make speeches—to say that I think it is *your* duty to put an end to all that. *Your* absolute duty. I wish *you* well.

IMPROVING ONE'S ORAL STYLE

Clear, correct, appropriate, and impressive language usage cannot be achieved overnight. One must develop standards of judgment and taste, a sensitivity to the meanings of words and their nuances, and skill in the selection and use of the right words at the proper time and occasion. To improve oral style, the student of speech needs to follow a systematic program of study and observation.

Six steps toward improving one's use of language in the speech situation are:

1. *Acquire a library of language reference works.* With the availability of inexpensive paperback editions of standard reference works, there is no excuse for not having a reputable, up-to-date dictionary, a thesaurus, and at least one collection of quotations in your own personal library. In addition, you may wish from time to time to acquire additional works dealing with semantics, style, rhetoric, and speech preparation.

2. *Enlarge your vocabulary.* Look up the meanings of unfamiliar words in a dictionary; consult a thesaurus to find synonyms and related words; and try to incorporate these words into your vocabulary by using them in writing, speaking, and everyday conversation.

3. *Become language conscious.* Listen critically and analytically to the language used by effective speakers and study the word choice and composition of reputable speakers and writers. Try to note differences in oral style among speakers of different personalities, on different occasions, and in treating different kinds of subjects.

4. *Keep a notebook of effective language usage.* Record and file for future use words, phrases, quotations, figures of speech, slogans, puns, bits of humor, and other expressions that seem to be unusual, interesting, or particularly effective. In time, this collection should prove helpful in suggesting language you may wish to incorporate in your conversation and public speaking.

5. *Revise your style.* Certainly a speaker who plans to give a manuscript or memorized speech should rewrite and revise the speech as often as is necessary to achieve the most felicitous choice of words. However, even in preparing an extemporaneous speech, you may at times find it helpful to write out the speech in its entirety and work on improving your style. Although you probably will not recall the precise language of the written version when you deliver the talk from your notes or outline, you may find that you remember some of the terminology and phraseology on which you have worked.

6. *Differentiate between oral and written style.* Speak or read aloud your speech manuscripts. Often you will discover that what reads well on paper does not sound well when spoken aloud. You will then want to rewrite those passages in a more conversational, colloquial vein.

SUMMARY

Oral style refers to the language the speaker selects to express ideas. Good oral style is clear, correct, concrete, vivid, and appropriate.

Clarity of language is achieved by using words that the listener understands and by defining unfamiliar terms. The speaker has a variety of methods of definition available, including definition by synonym; example; details; comparison and contrast; classification and differentiation; historical background; etymology; operation, action, or purpose; negation; and audible and visible examples. The best definitions often combine two or more of these methods.

Correctness of style refers to the use of language that is grammatically acceptable and properly chosen to express accurately the speaker's ideas. The speaker should also use words that are concrete wherever possible because such language is more readily grasped by listeners and is usually more interesting than abstract language. To achieve vividness, the speaker should employ emotive and figurative language to stimulate the imagination and feelings of the hearer. He or she should avoid clichés and trite, hackneyed expressions. Variation in sentence structure and the use of such stylistic devices as repetition, parallelism, antithesis, simile, metaphor, comparison, contrast, personification, alliteration, and rhetorical questions are all helpful in achieving a vivid oral style. Language is appropriate when the words are suitable to the speaker, the purpose, the subject, the listener, and the occasion.

Improving oral style is a long-range process requiring the speaker to become language conscious through a constant and systematic program of vocabulary and stylistic development.

STUDY QUESTIONS

1. What kinds of language make it difficult for listeners to understand a speaker's ideas?
2. What are some of the problems that are encountered in defining with synonyms?
3. Explain definition by classification and differentiation.
4. How does definition by historical background differ from definition by etymology?
5. What is definition by negation? When is this method useful?
6. Cite three or four words where visual or audible definitions would be almost essential to the listeners' understanding.
7. Which method of definition do the authors recommend?
8. Why is correct language usage desirable in a speech?
9. Why should speakers strive whenever possible to use concrete rather than abstract language?
10. What is meant by triteness? What are clichés?
11. What steps should speakers follow to improve their oral style?

EXERCISES

1. Explain the meaning of a definition by details. List five words other than those discussed in the text that would lend themselves to effective definition by details.
2. Define and give an example (other than one in the text) of each of the following: (a) parallelism, (b) repetition, (c) antithesis, (d) simile, (e) metaphor, (f) personification, (g) alliteration, and (h) rhetorical question.
3. In 100 words or less, write your own definition of one of the following: (a) a well-rounded education, (b) a successful person, (c) the average person. Be as concrete as possible in your definition.
4. Prepare a 3- to 4-minute informative speech in which you define one of the terms listed below. Use at least two of the methods of definition discussed in this chapter:

a. aristocracy	m. gross national product
b. justice	n. existentialism
c. gauche	o. agnosticism
d. jazz	p. rationalization
e. intuition	q. empathy
f. heresy	r. romanticism
g. loyalty	s. humane
h. impressionism	t. bel canto
i. integrity	u. socialism
j. serendipity	v. automation
k. cubism	w. nationalism
l. ethnocentrism	x. intelligence

After you have delivered the speech, your instructor may call on some member of the class to explain what your concept means in order to test the effectiveness of your definition.

5. Locate five quotations you might use to achieve a more vivid style in discussing one of the following concepts:
   a. trust
   b. ignorance
   c. China
   d. gardens
   e. puzzles
6. Consult a thesaurus and list six synonyms for each of the following words:
   a. ostentation
   b. fluidity
   c. sedate
   d. perforator
   e. consanguinity
7. For your next speech, write out the speech in its entirety. Then revise the entire speech, seeking to improve your oral style. At the time of delivery, submit both your original and final drafts to your instructor.

FURTHER READINGS

Ehninger, Douglas, Bruce E. Gronbeck, Ray E. McKerrow, and Alan Monroe, *Principles and Types of Speech Communication,* 10th ed. (Glenview, IL: Scott, Foresman, 1986), chap. 12, "Using Language to Communicate."

Lucas, Stephen E., *The Art of Public Speaking* (New York: Random House, 1986), chap. 10, "Using Language."

Verderber, Rudolph F., *The Challenge of Effective Speaking,* 6th ed. (Belmont, CA: Wadsworth, 1985), chap. 5, "Speech Wording."

Zannes, Estelle, and Gerald Goldhaber, *Stand Up, Speak Out,* 2d ed. (Reading, MA: Addison-Wesley, 1983), chap. 7, "Wording the Speech."

CHAPTER 16

SPEAKING ON SPECIAL OCCASIONS

What do all the following speech occasions have in common: the inauguration of a president, presentation of an award, a pep rally, dedication of a new building, a funeral service, and commemoration of an important event? The answer, of course, indicated by the title of this chapter, is that each constitutes a special occasion demanding a particular kind of speech and dictating to a considerable extent the speaker's choice of subject and materials. Addresses of this type are known as ceremonial speeches, occasional speeches, and speeches for special occasions. They can be divided into three types: (1) speeches of courtesy, (2) speeches of inspiration, and (3) speeches of goodwill. This chapter examines the nature of these special occasions, analyzes the expectations of the audiences in each situation, and offers suggestions to the speaker for meeting the demands of the audience and occasion.

SPEECHES OF COURTESY

Speeches of courtesy are of six kinds: introductions, welcomes, responses, farewells, presentations, and acceptances. The audience for a speech of courtesy usually is favorably predisposed to the speaker and his subject and expects to hear a talk that is positive, favorable, tactful, sincere, and in good taste. To understand courtesy speeches better, each of the six main types is discussed below.

Introductions

Speeches of introduction are required when one must acquaint an audience with the qualifications, background, or accomplishments of someone who is going to deliver a lecture, participate in a workshop, symposium, or debate, or perform in some other capacity.

WHAT TO SAY.   What the speaker giving a speech of introduction will say depends on the audience's knowledge of the person being introduced. If the auditors are familiar with the person's background and qualifications, very little need be said by way of introduction. For example, "Ladies and gentlemen, the president of the United States" is all that is usually said in introducing the president of this country. If the person is not well known, the introducer probably will wish to cite some of the speaker's accomplishments, background, and qualifications, such as offices held, honors, awards, appointments, publications, areas of special knowledge, and unusual experiences.

HOW TO SAY IT.   The speaker's remarks in a speech of introduction should be accurate, relevant, positive, moderate, and brief.

In preparing an introductory speech, the speaker should make sure that all information is correct. Inaccurate details may mislead and confuse the audience, causing them to expect a speech or performance quite different from what the person being introduced has planned. Furthermore, a speaker whose accomplishments and qualifications are inaccurately announced may

319

feel compelled to correct a misleading introduction—a situation embarrassing for both the introducer and the person being introduced. To obtain accurate information, the speaker may wish to consult sources such as *Who's Who in America, Current Biography,* the *Dictionary of American Scholars,* or various "who's who" volumes for specific professions and regions of the country. Information can also be obtained by letters or telephone calls to the party to be introduced. Finally, if unable to obtain information by any of these means, the speaker can ask the individual for such data just before making the introduction.

In addition to being accurate, speakers making introductions should limit their remarks to information that is relevant. Reminiscences about having known the subject years before, humorous anecdotes from the subject's past, and trivia about the subject's hobbies, idiosyncrasies, and personal life usually add little to the introduction and actually may make it more difficult for the person being introduced to achieve his or her goal.

In an introduction, the speaker should stress the positive. No useful purpose is served in reminding an audience about controversial, questionable, or unpleasant incidents in the subject's past. A good introduction assists, not hinders, the subject in performing effectively.

While avoiding negative comments and emphasizing positive elements, speakers delivering introductory speeches should take care not to overstate the qualifications of the person being introduced. Introductions of this type are a disservice to both the audience and the person being presented. The audience is disappointed when the individual does not live up to the introduction, and the person being introduced is intimidated because it is now impossible to meet the audience's expectations. Imagine having to follow an introduction such as this: "I have heard Winston Churchill and Franklin D. Roosevelt speak. I have been in the audience when John F. Kennedy and Martin Luther King, Jr. delivered stirring speeches. I have listened to Pope John Paul I and Billy Graham, but I have never been so moved by a speaker as I was when I first heard Tommy Atkins, who is a freshman enrolled in Fundamentals of Speech at . . ."

Finally, be brief. In most situations requiring a speech of introduction, the audience is more interested in the person being introduced than in the individual delivering the introduction. A long introduction can irritate and alienate both the auditors and the subject of the introductory remarks. The audience wants the program to get going, and the subject resents the time that is lost to him or her because of the long introduction.

Welcomes

A speech of welcome is required on any occasion when a group, organization, or official wishes to extend hospitality and cooperation to visitors or newcomers. Such a speech might be given by a civic leader to welcome to the community a prominent person, visiting delegation, or touring study group. For example, one might give such a speech to welcome the governor of another state, the president of France, a group of Japanese educators studying American education, or representatives of Monsanto considering building a plant in the city or state. Often a "key to the city" is presented to the visitors. Prominent officials often also welcome groups holding meetings, conferences, and conventions in their cities or on their campuses. A speech of welcome also is in order when greeting new members of an organization or community. For example, on the campus of one of the authors of this book there is a "Newcomers Club" to acquaint new faculty with the university and the community. In addition, the city annually sponsors a breakfast, to which all new residents within the past year are invited. In both situations, an essential element of the occasion is a speech to welcome the newcomers. Such speeches are also given at meetings of fraternal, charitable, professional, and civic groups—such as Alpha Tau Omega, United Givers, Sigma Delta Chi, Kiwanis, the Rotary Club, and other organizations—to welcome visiting groups.

In a speech of welcome, the speaker must determine what to say and how to say it.

WHAT TO SAY.   In a speech of welcome, the speaker should provide the individual or group with good and meaningful reasons why their visit, interest, or membership is appreciated. The speaker may also wish to provide information to those being welcomed regarding the background of the group or unit extending the welcome, to heighten the visitors' appreciation. The speaker might, for example, cite the purpose, goals, achievements, membership, and special concerns of the welcoming group.

HOW TO SAY IT.   Obviously a speech of welcome must be sincere and warm. It must also be honest and accurate. To be effective in impressing the individual or group being welcomed, a fine line must be drawn between depicting the welcomers in a favorable light and outright bragging. A good speech of welcome also should be concise.

Responses

In a speech responding to a welcome, introduction, or presentation—by a public official or representative of some organization—the speaker will wish to speak in such a way that the group will be favorably impressed. To realize this goal, it is necessary to give attention to what the welcoming or inducting group expects before considering what to say and how to say it.

WHAT TO SAY.   In a speech of response, the speaker should express appreciation for any courtesies, kindnesses, or praise extended to him or her. The respondent also should display a knowledge of the nature, interests, goals, and accomplishments of the group or organization that has extended the welcome.

HOW TO SAY IT.   The speaker's response should be presented sincerely, concisely, and in a manner that demonstrates appreciation.

Farewells

A speech of farewell is required in situations when a group has assembled to mark a pending departure and to pay tribute to an admired, respected, or loved associate, leader, employee, or group. The departure may be occasioned by the person being transferred to another office, retirement, or simply a decision to leave for personal reasons. The settings for such speeches range from a regular meeting of an organization to a special luncheon or dinner marking the occasion, to a formal ceremony in honor of the departing individual or group.

WHAT TO SAY.   The farewell speech basically is a speech of commendation (discussed later in this chapter) and consists of expressions of affection, appreciation, and admiration. The most common components of such talks are examples of the contributions of the individual or group to the organization, department, institution, or community, and descriptions of the subject's personal qualities that have earned the respect and affection of those assembled. References to any past difficulties or disagreements with the person leaving probably should be avoided.

The farewell speech should not be a maudlin, sad, or depressing message. In situations when a friend or associate is leaving, many persons feel a sense of loss, but most also probably harbor a hope that the departing member will prosper and will not regret the change. Whatever the reason for the subject's departure, a speaker delivering a farewell speech should "accentuate the positive" and "eliminate the negative."

HOW TO SAY IT.   The farewell speech should be delivered in a warm, sincere manner, with a sense of camaraderie. The occasion should be approached in a serious manner, and there should be nothing insincere in the speaker's expression of appreciation. But the tenor of the speech should be positive, upbeat, and optimistic.

Presentations

Of all the different kinds of speeches for special occasions, the speech of presentation is probably the most familiar to Americans. We know of the Oscars, Tonys, Emmys, Grammys, and a variety of others in the field of entertainment. Nobel Prizes, Pulitzer Prizes, National Book Awards, and other awards honor scholars, authors, scientists, and humanitarians. In athletic competition, we have the World Cup, the Davis Cup, the Cy Young Award, the Heisman Trophy, the MacArthur Trophy, and many other designations of distinction. Almost all business and professional, educational, and religious organizations—to name only a few—bestow annual awards on individuals who have made outstanding contributions to their fields.

At the local level, community and professional groups honor outstanding individuals with presentations of the "Golden Deeds" award for community service, with designations of a teacher, secretary, or nurse of the year, and with awards for accomplishments in other fields.

College and university organizations often honor outstanding individuals at end-of-the-year meetings.

Speeches of presentation are often given to express thanks, appreciation, or respect on occasions other than award ceremonies. These may be given upon the retirement of an associate or completion of a term of office, a project, or a drive. For example, the Speech Communication Association presents its outgoing president with a gavel in appreciation of his services, the director of the annual United Way drive in one community is presented with a plaque, and coaches of successful athletic teams frequently are given awards ranging from jewelry to automobiles.

WHAT TO SAY.   In a speech of presentation, the speaker should make certain that the audience understands the nature of the award. Is it for a specific accomplishment or for a cumulative series of contributions? Does it recognize excellence, service, personal qualities, or all of these? Often the audience will already know the nature of the award—as is generally true of the Academy Awards and the Pulitzer Prizes—in which case the speaker, of course, need not explain the nature of the honor.

Make sure that the auditors are familiar with the criteria used in determining the recipient of the award. For example, what qualities, qualifications, and achievements did the selection committee consider in determining the annual civic "Golden Deeds" award, the secretary of the year, or the department leadership award?

Finally, the speaker should relate those qualities and accomplishments that led to the recipient being chosen for recognition.

HOW TO SAY IT.   As in speeches of introduction, welcome, and farewell, the speaker's remarks should be accurate, relevant, positive, and brief, and the speaker's manner should be warm, respectful, and enthusiastic. It is important that the speaker avoid any appearance of uncertainty about the nature of the award and the qualities of the person being recognized. To enhance the appreciation of the listeners for the accomplishments of the recipient, many presenters of awards prepare their speeches with great care. To make sure that the speech is appropriately worded, they may write it out, revise and polish, and deliver it from manuscript or memory.

Acceptances

The speech of acceptance is given in response to a speech of presentation, described above, when one is being recognized for a distinguished accomplishment, achievement, contribution, or service. Most television viewers have had an opportunity to hear a great many acceptance speeches given on awards ceremonies for the motion picture industry, Broadway stage shows, television, recording performers, country-western music stars, and an assortment of other groups. A few of the speeches of acceptance on these occasions are moving, most are banal, and many are downright bad. In discussing the speech of acceptance, one should keep in mind that such televised ceremonies constitute only a small percentage of the speech occasions in which outstanding individuals are recognized and which call for an acceptance speech.

WHAT TO SAY.   In a speech of acceptance, the speaker's first responsibility is to express appreciation for the recognition. When it is appropriate, the speaker may wish to compliment the group making the award on its activities and achievements. When the recipient of an award has been substantially aided by others in the accomplishments that led to the recognition, it is appropriate to acknowledge this assistance. For example, the "coach of the year" probably should give credit to team members and assistants, while the recipient of a citation from a charitable or civic organization might wish to include mention of the cooperation of others. Although care should be taken not to overlook anyone whose aid was vital, the speaker should not feel compelled to list—and to bore the audience with—the names of everyone from the cradle to that moment who has made some contribution, however minor, leading to the award.

HOW TO SAY IT.   Since most people who are going to be recognized or given an award will have been notified in advance, they are provided with the opportunity to work out carefully exactly what they wish to say in acceptance. Even though a person knows only that he or she has been nominated, that person should prepare an appropriate acceptance speech in advance. A speaker also should not take advantage of being chosen for recognition to harangue a captive audience on an irrelevant political theme, social cause, or personal bias. The occasion for audiences gathering to hear speeches of presentation and acceptance usually is ceremonial, and speakers should recognize that the audience has assembled to honor or express appreciation to an individual or group and not for a rally or debate. When all the nominees for an award, but not the winner, are known in advance, all potential recipients have an opportunity to prepare in advance. This they should do, because a speech that is thought out, carefully worded, and well organized usually is more effective than an impromptu response. In presenting the acceptance speech, the speaker will seek to appear to be appreciative, sincere, and modest.

SPEECHES OF INSPIRATION

The speech to inspire seeks to strengthen or intensify attitudes, opinions, or beliefs already held by the listeners. Unlike a speech to convince or persuade, in which the speaker realizes that some members of the audience disagree with his or her ideas, a speech to inspire begins with the speaker knowing that the listeners are in basic agreement. The audience may be very enthusiastic or passive and only mildly interested, but in each instance the speaker is not required to deal with hostility and disagreement. Instead, the speaker's goal is to stir greater fervor and enthusiasm.

Inspirational speeches are of three types: the eulogy is a speech that commends the character and actions of a deceased person or group; the speech of commendation shows admiration or respect for a living person; and the speech of a commemoration celebrates the anniversary of an important event.

Inspirational speeches are built around a single theme, key sentence, or proposition. Examples of central thoughts for each of the three types of inspirational speeches are:

Eulogy
John F. Kennedy was a great American whose spirit lives on.
This country should never forget the character and athletic ability demonstrated by Jesse Owens in the 1936 Olympic games.

Commencement exercises call for a special kind of speech. (Louisiana State University)

Helen Keller was one of the most remarkable, courageous, and inspiring women in American history.

Commendation

We owe a debt of gratitude to Charles Schulz and his "Peanuts" characters for the pleasure and insights they provide.

Luciano Pavarotti is a great singer, teacher, and humanitarian.

Julia Child should be given a special culinary medal for bringing haute cuisine into millions of American homes.

Commemoration

Today marks the anniversary of the adoption of one of the most important documents in history: the United States Constitution.

The discovery of penicillin by Alexander Fleming in 1929 was one of the most important medical advances in the twentieth century.

Today we celebrate the founding of our great university.

This anniversary of the first person to walk on the moon marks one of the most important events in history.

Speech for a special occasion: British Prince Charles addresses a Harvard University convocation observing the 350th anniversary of the school. (Main, *Christian Science Monitor*)

SPEECHES OF GOODWILL

Speeches of goodwill may appear to be informative but really are aimed at maintaining or improving the image of an institution, organization, company, or group. Speeches of goodwill are given to groups who either already admire the subject of the address or who, if not already favorably predisposed, are open-minded. For example, a speech praising one of the following groups probably would be favorably received by most people: the YMCA, the YWCA, the Boy and Girl Scouts, the Red Cross, the Salvation Army, the Volunteers of America, the United Givers, the American Cancer Society, the symphony auxiliary, and "friends of the library." Addresses commending the following organizations would be classified as a speech of goodwill if the audience attitude was favorable or neutral at the outset: the American Legion, the American Civil Liberties Union, the National Education Association, the Moral Majority, the Teamsters Union, the National Organization of Women, the American Medical Association, and various charities. While the above groups have many supporters, they also have their critics. If the audience already is favorably predisposed, the speaker can draw upon their reservoir of goodwill in preparing and presenting the speech. For example, if the audience consists of teachers who belong to the National Education Association or doctors affiliated with the American Medical Association, the speaker will not need to "prove" that the organization is deserving of support. However, if the audience includes persons opposed to or skeptical about the group, the speaker faces a different task. Instead of heightening goodwill, he or she will need to try to convince or persuade those who are critical of the worthiness of the group.

In preparing a goodwill speech, the speaker should stress the group's accomplishments, goals, contributions, and ideals. In addition, the speaker may appeal for sympathy, understanding, and support.

PREPARATION OF OCCASIONAL SPEECHES

Preparing a speech for a special occasion does not differ markedly from putting together other kinds of addresses. However, in preparing such talks, the speaker should pay particular attention to the following suggestions. In choosing a subject, remember that the audience and reason for assembling for occasional speeches virtually dictate the speaker's choice of topic. In addition, the topic should be limited. Audiences for occasional speeches usually are favorably disposed, have a knowledge of and appreciation for the individual, group, or institution, and can be easily bored by a lengthy recitation of information they already know. The audience has assembled for a specific purpose and expects a particular kind of speech. Since the listeners usually already know quite a bit about the subject, the speaker faces the challenge of finding new and interesting material. This may entail limiting the topic to a little-known aspect of the subject or concentrating on a personal response or experience. For example, in a short tribute to John F. Kennedy on the anniversary of his assassination, Thomas J. Scanlon focused on how Kennedy, whom he had never met, influenced his life (see this speech at the end of the chapter).

In organizing a speech for a special occasion, the speaker should have a limited number of subpoints or ideas. These may consist of traits, accomplishments, goals, or crucial decisions made by the individual or group.

The speaker's choice of language in achieving the desired response probably is more important in speeches for special occasions than in other spoken communication. Eulogies, commendations, and commemorative addresses re-

The inaugural address: a speech for a special occasion.
(Brack, Black Star)

quire more moving language than is needed in most other speaking situations. The language needs to be vivid, impressive, and appropriate. Chapter 15 discusses ways to achieve a colorful and memorable oral style. Since speeches of goodwill generally are short and to be effective must be carefully worded, speakers may wish to write out the speech in its entirety so they can give special attention to word choice. In addition to writing out the speech for a special occasion, at times a speaker, to make certain that the carefully chosen wording is not lost, may memorize the talk or use a manuscript.

In delivery of the speech of courtesy, inspiration, and goodwill, the speaker should seek to convey the impression of sincerity, respect, and conviction.

SUMMARY

In preparing a speech for a special occasion, a speaker should recognize that the audience has preconceived expectations that must be met. The auditors for the presentation of an award, a eulogy, a commendation, a commemoration, or a speech of goodwill, for example, expect a particular kind of address. Failure to meet their expectations will disappoint them. Audiences for most occasional speeches are favorably disposed to the group, event, or organization that is the subject of the speech. The speaker's task is not to convert or convince them but to heighten their affection, respect, and goodwill. Occasional speeches can be divided into three categories: (1) speeches of courtesy, which include introductions, welcomes, responses, farewells, presentations, and acceptances; (2) speeches of inspiration, which include eulogies, commendations, and commemorations; and (3) speeches of goodwill.

MODEL INSPIRATIONAL SPEECHES

Below are three models of inspirational speeches. The first was given by Albert Keller, Jr., then national commander of the American Legion, at the dedication of a memorial to American Vietnam veterans in Washington, DC, on November 13, 1982. Keller was one of several speakers participating in the dedication ceremonies. In reading the speech, note the speaker's brevity and pay special attention to his use of emotional appeals and language.

A Memorial to American Vietnam War Veterans

Albert Keller, Jr.

Thank you, Jan. Today we dedicate a memorial to a generation of Americans who fought a lonely battle. We dedicate the Vietnam Veterans Memorial to those who died in that war, yes. But, more than that, we dedicate it to those countless thousands who survived that war, only to face a battle that honor bound them to.

In the jungles and the dusty deltas of Vietnam, our young soldiers stood together and cared for their wounded and dead. If no other characteristic distinguished the Vietnam veteran, it was his unfaltering devotion to his comrades. They let no wound go untended. They left no dead behind. And they came home expecting the nation to care about their comrades as they did.

But instead, they encountered indifference and a deep desire to have Vietnam, and those who fought there, left behind.

But this generation of veterans would not have it so. For years the wounded spirit festered. And for years the Vietnam veteran tended to himself and did what he would alone. And for years the wounded memory of his comrades cried out to be healed, waiting, hoping, crying out in a hundred tortured ways.

The Vietnam veterans yearned for a way to tend to this last wound of the war. And, finally, they decided, as they had learned in the war itself, that they would have to tend to one another alone.

But today, we know they were wrong. The American people, inspired by the undaunted determination of those men and women, responded in a historic conversion of compassion, caring and generosity. Standing at last before them was the opportunity to express the gratitude and the honor that they longed to give, but knew not how to grant.

There are those who say that the war in Vietnam brought shame on America. There are those who say this memorial would bring shame on those who fought the war. But there are those, like the men and women that I represent, who say, "Not so." There is no shame in answering the nation's call. There is no shame in serving with honor and courage in difficult times. And there is no shame in enshrining the names of fallen comrades in immutable stone for generations to recall.

There is a legacy left for us from the Vietnam experience, and it was left to the young who fought there to show it to us. And that is the rediscovery of our capacity to care, to give, and to honor. That is no small legacy for a nation to receive.

This memorial symbolizes, not only the supreme gift of nearly 58,000 young Americans, but also the priceless gift of renewed awareness in our capacity as a people.

With this dedication, we come not to the end of America's commitment to Vietnam veterans, but the beginning of a new awareness of their unparalleled contribution to the nation.

Generations to come will walk before these gleaming walls and, like them, will reflect. They will consider the memories of those who died. They will consider the legacy of the living veterans left. And they will take from this Memorial a promise to be ever true to their American heritage.

My fellow veterans, families and friends, we are here today to honor, to remember, and to consecrate forever this piece of America, to insure that coming generations understand how dearly we hold those who served our nation in Vietnam. How painfully we recognize that the debt we owe those listed here can never be paid. And how hopefully we stand together as a nation of peace.

There are some very special people here with us today. They symbolize America's future. They are the children of our nation's Vietnam veterans.

Let us salute this nation's Vietnam [veterans] this afternoon by joining hands in a silent pledge that together we will care for their children, as we pray that Vietnam was America's war to end all wars.

Source: Albert Keller, Jr., *Representative American Speeches, 1982–1983,* New York: H. W. Wilson Co., 1983, pp. 171–174.

The second speech was a eulogy to President John F. Kennedy given at a concert at the Kennedy Center for the Performing Arts in Washington, DC, commemorating the twentieth anniversary of Kennedy's assassination. Throughout the week preceding the speech, which was delivered on November 22, 1983, the mass media had carried many articles and television programs reminding the country of the former president's accomplishments. In view of this, Thomas J. Scanlon wisely decided not to review all of Kennedy's career and contributions but to focus on just one, the Peace Corps. Since he himself had been a member of the Peace Corps, the choice of topic was particularly appropriate for the speaker. As you read the speech, note Scanlon's choice of examples to reinforce his ideas.

Tribute to John F. Kennedy

Thomas J. Scanlon

I have been asked to pay tribute to President John F. Kennedy tonight, and I feel honored. I held no position in his administration. I did not know him personally. I am here only as one of the thousands whose lives were profoundly influenced by him.

When John Kennedy took the oath of office, I was a graduate student in philosophy. Six months later, I entered the Peace Corps. Today, I am still involved with the problems I worked on then. The Peace Corps experience led me to a new life work.

I hope that I speak not only for myself here but for all of us whose lives and careers were inspired by John F. Kennedy.

In the past few weeks, television has enabled all of us to remember President Kennedy again in life—how alive he made us feel and how proud to be Americans. In fact, the greatest sacrifice for me in being in the Peace Corps was to be outside our country during much of that magical period.

Yet we volunteers were never really very far from events in the United States. I was stationed in Chile in a small village 6000 miles south of here. One day I drove my jeep as far as I could toward the coast, walked a few miles to a local mission, and continued on horseback for three hours to a remote Indian neighborhood. I was feeling very proud of myself. Certainly no other American had ever been there. Perhaps they had never even heard of the United States. After a customary cup of tea with my Indian host, he said to me, "Did you know that yesterday was President Kennedy's birthday?"

There are many achievements that will secure John Kennedy's place in history. But the Peace Corps is the one that I choose as my text because it tells us so much about him.

The Peace Corps reflects John Kennedy's vision of America. He brought out a sense of idealism and participation that runs like a deep stream in all of us. Through the Peace Corps he challenged us to go to the remotest parts of the world, to live without privileges of any sort, to learn a new language, and to put our skills and energies to work as a symbol of our country's concern for others.

Ten thousands of us responded to that challenge in the first three months. Today there are over 89,000 Americans who have returned to the United States after serving two years as Peace Corps volunteers in 88 countries.

The impact of these volunteers—and the 5200 who are serving today—is incalculable. Perhaps it was summed up best by a little girl in Africa who wrote adoringly to her volunteer teacher—in not so perfect English, "You are a blot on my life which I will never erase."

The Peace Corps exemplifies the quality President Kennedy admired most—courage, in this case the willingness to take a risk. There was considerable opposition to the Peace Corps when President Kennedy first announced it. Some called it a children's crusade and a publicity stunt.

The Kennedy administration pressed forward. But one of Sargent Shriver's aides did ask him, fairly early, "Aren't we really going out on a limb with the Peace Corps? We still don't know whether the idea will work or whether the volunteers will be accepted."

"Out on a limb, nothing!" Shriver replied, "We're out there walking on the leaves."

The Peace Corps symbolizes John Kennedy's commitment to world peace. The Peace Corps itself was a peace initiative. In teaching hundreds of languages to volunteers, the Peace Corps learned that in many languages the word for "stranger" is the same as the word for "enemy." The Peace Corps has shown that the more we know about each other, the less likely it is that we will consider one another as enemies. As John Kennedy said to the Irish Parliament in the summer of 1963, "Across the gulfs and barriers which divide us, we must remember that there are no permanent enemies."

Today the question of peace involves no less than our survival as a planet. In the tragic operas or dramas which we witness here at the Kennedy Center, simple misunderstandings lead the action unavoidably toward its tragic end. This is the essence of tragic art. In the real world of international politics, one such misunderstanding could bring the ultimate tragedy which would end all music and all art.

John Kennedy was possessed by this realization. His eloquence and conviction were prophetic. Popular consciousness of the dangers of nuclear war is only now beginning to catch up with him.

Finally, the Peace Corps highlights John Kennedy's compassion for the billions around the world who live in an abject poverty and misery. People ask why John Kennedy is so beloved in the developing world? The answer to that question is clear. John Kennedy truly cared about that half of humanity which lacks the basic necessities. He made promises to them and he delivered. He convinced the Congress to approve levels of development assistance and Food for Peace which have never been equaled since.

Then, of course, there was the Peace Corps itself. The people in developing countries saw us as the direct expression of John Kennedy's interest in them. "Children of Kennedy" we were called in many parts of Latin America; "wakima Kennedy" or "followers of Kennedy" in Africa.

Twenty years ago this evening, there were 5937 volunteers serving in 46 countries. Each of them remembers vividly the outpouring of grief which his death occasioned. In Nepal, some villagers walked for 5 days to where the volunteers were to bring them the sad news. In Iran, a local coworker told a volunteer, "Our president is dead." In Bangkok, people dressed in mourning garb. Schools everywhere searched for flags to fly at half-mast. A volunteer wrote from Brazil:

If then this awful thing could reach out to the farthest corner of the world and have the effect on all people that I believe it did—then there is a real brotherhood among men—only one family of man.

History must judge John Kennedy not only by what he was able to accomplish in a thousand days but also by what he inspired all of us to volunteer—in the broadest sense—to do for our country.

So might I suggest that there is a most fitting tribute which all of us can pay to John Kennedy here this evening. We can pay him this tribute in our own lives; in our concern for a just and compassionate society here at home; in our willingness to assist the masses of poor throughout the world; and, most important, in assuring our nation's commitment to take the first steps toward peace. We can be prepared, in his memory and in his honor, to go out and "walk on the leaves."

Source: Thomas J. Scanlon, Representative American Speeches, 1983–1984, New York: H. W. Wilson Co., 1984, pp. 153–157.

The third model inspirational speech differs from the two preceding ones in that it was given in honor of a famous person who the speaker knew not as a statesman and president, but as a father. The occasion was a joint meeting of the United States House of Representatives and Senate on the one hundredth anniversary of the birthday of President Harry S Truman, and the speaker was his daughter, Margaret Truman Daniel. Preceding Mrs. Daniel's speech, several prominent former associates of President Truman had paid tribute to Truman's accomplishments as a senator and president. Mrs. Daniel's speech is an excellent example of the speech of eulogy or commendation that heightens the audience's appreciation and respect by focusing on personal and little-known aspects of the honoree.

The Remarkable Man from Missouri

Margaret Truman Daniel

Mr. Speaker, Mr. President, ladies and gentlemen, first I would like to say that dad would have loved all of the music, as I am sure we all did.

You cannot imagine what a delight and honor it is for me to find myself once again in this place. It is both exhilarating and humbling to be standing in the same spot where my father stood when he delivered his annual State of the Union message.

This monumental building and its majestic site, towering over the capital of our republic, was once my playground. I skipped through its long corridors with my schoolbooks, I became familiar with the great men and great events memorialized here, I wandered casually into the family gallery of the Senate and listened to the nation's business being transacted.

It was a simpler, easier time, with no passes required for a daughter of the Senate, the guards all knew me and no electronic surveillance of visitors.

Most delightful of all, I rode the subway back and forth between the Senate Office Building and the Capitol to my heart's content.

And while my father labored in room 240 of the Old Senate Office Building, I did my homework until it was time for him to drive me home in his spiffy Chrysler.

When as a child you walk beside a good man, a warmhearted man, and find comfort, love and protection in his embrace, you never think of him as a great man. He is just your dad and you love him. It is only when you grow up and step back from him or leave him for your own career and your own home, it is only then that you can measure his greatness and fully appreciate it. Pride reenforces love.

My father was a great man and his greatness grows with time. I am given evidence of that in some way every day. Wherever I go, even in the hinterlands of China, where I was last fall, people came up to me and said, "I just want to tell you how much I admired your father." That is all, but they had a compulsion to say it.

Now on his 100th birthday the attention of the whole nation and much of the world beyond is focused on his accomplishments and his character. Without the character there would have been no accomplishments.

What was his character as it was revealed to his daughter, his only child? First of all, there was never a man more devoted to his family. You can see that in the letters he wrote to his wife, his mother, his sister, and to me. Even though with youthful carelessness I rarely replied, his letters kept coming.

It is extraordinary in this electronic age, an age of instant contact and communications, to recall that he wrote every word laboriously by hand. And even when he was President, he licked a three-cent stamp and pasted it on my personal letter. Actually, for those of you who are so young here, there really was once a three-cent stamp.

How in the midst of one of the most difficult and dangerous periods of American history did he as President and Commander in Chief, find time to write those letters every day? They were expressed in the homely idiom of Missouri and with the affection and longing of a man often separated from his family by his compelling sense of duty. They reflected his simplicity, directness, wisdom, and resolve, qualities that he had demonstrated in his public behavior, as well as his private life.

There was at the core of the man a gentleness that was often obscured by the brusqueness he sometimes displayed as a partisan politician and the firmness he showed as a statesman. Giving them hell was a rhetoric device, permissible in a politician context, but he really loved people. He was supremely confident of the people's ability to govern themselves, if properly led.

Above all, he loved the United States of America next to his family and he served it devotedly in war and peace.

His forthrightness was not an expression of irritation, but a sign of strong will and high purpose. And he was a great teaser. He liked to get your goat and then grin about it. His grin was as wide as his hat brim and as quick as his temper. Of course, he was capable of occasional expressions of anger. That is to say he could get fighting mad. But if you were the beloved beneficiary of his anger, as I was, and not its target, you kind of enjoyed it.

Every girl has a white knight in her dreams and he was mine. Now I have five white knights. My husband, Clifton Daniel, my sons, Clifton Truman Daniel, William Wallace Daniel, Harrison Gates Daniel, and Thomas Washington Daniel. At least I hope they are my white knights.

So it is with great pride that I have sat here today and seen dad honored, revered and eulogized. This august convocation would have delighted him. He would have felt right at home in the midst of it. He jokingly called the presidential mansion the Great White Jail, but he felt a sense of liberation, a certain expansiveness in the halls of Congress.

He loved the work and reveled in the comradeship he found here. Being one of the boys was his greatest pleasure. And he took pride in belonging to the world's most exclusive club, the U.S. Senate.

He was prouder still to be a member of that even more restricted group, Uncle Sam Rayburn's board of education, the bourbon and branch water college of congressional knowledge.

He loved politicians, even Republicans. True.

I hope that somewhere, somehow, he is watching these impressive proceedings and listening in. If he is, he probably thinks we are making too much of the occasion, but he is nevertheless enjoying it.

He was a modest man, but not fanatically so.

On his behalf, I conclude with heartfelt thanks to all those who have made possible this great celebration and are contributing to all the other events marking the Truman centennial. You have worked long, hard, and successfully. My father would be grateful. My family, every branch of it, is honored. And we thank all of you.

Source: Margaret Truman Daniel, *Representative American Speeches, 1984–1985,* New York: H. W. Wilson Co., 1985, pp. 151–154.

STUDY QUESTIONS

1. What are the three main types of speeches for special occasions?
2. How does the audience for a speech for a special occasion differ from the audience for a persuasive or convincing speech?
3. Describe the purpose of the speaker in each of the following types of courtesy speeches: (a) introductions, (b) welcomes, (c) responses, (d) farewells, (e) presentations, and (f) acceptances.
4. What is a eulogy? What should a speaker delivering a eulogy seek?
5. What is a speech of commendation? What is the speaker's goal in a speech of commendation? What usually is the audience's attitude toward the subject?
6. What is a speech of commemoration? What does the speaker hope to accomplish in a speech of commemoration?
7. How important is the speaker's language in an occasional speech? Is it more or less important than in a speech to inform, to convince, to persuade, or to entertain? Why?

EXERCISES

1. Prepare a 3-minute speech of introduction to introduce a visiting speaker at a convocation at your college or university. Choose an actual person as your hypothetical speaker, but not someone so well-known as to need little in the way of introduction. For example, you might choose to introduce a prominent legislator, business leader, journalist, scientist, educator, clergyman, or athlete. Deliver the speech in class as if it were the convocation.
2. Prepare a 3-minute speech welcoming one of the following groups who are visiting your campus to learn more about your college or university: (a) the senior class of a high school within the state; (b) a small group of British educators touring the country visiting American schools; (c) a group of high school guidance counselors attending a short workshop; (d) the officers of a social sorority, fraternity, or club from other schools in the state who are holding a meeting on your campus; (e) a delegation of leading officials from the Ministry of Education of a Latin American country; (f) the representatives of a student religious group (any denomination) who are holding an annual conference; (g) high school students on campus to participate in a music festival; or (h) some similar group. Deliver the speech in class, pretending that your fellow classmates constitute the visiting delegation.
3. Prepare a 3-minute speech in which you present an award for achievement of an outstanding accomplishment to an individual. Select an actual person from any of the fields discussed on page 322. Be sure to explain the significance of the award, the criteria upon which it is based, and the qualifications of the recipient. Deliver the speech in class as if it were an assembly of persons who have come together for this purpose.

4. Prepare a 4-minute eulogy of an outstanding individual who is no longer alive, to be presented at a special observance of his or her birth or death. You should use a manuscript and give careful attention to your choice of language. For suggestions on preparing and delivering a manuscript speech, see pp. 167–169. Deliver the speech in class.

5. Prepare a 3- to 4-minute speech of commemoration to be given at a meeting arranged specifically to mark the anniversary of the event. You may choose to commemorate a discovery, invention, victory, founding, publication, disaster, movement, or enactment. Remember that you are commemorating an event, not a person. Deliver the speech from manuscript. In preparation, be sure to give careful attention to your choice of language. For suggestions on preparing and delivering a manuscript speech, see pp. 167–169. Deliver the speech in class.

6. Prepare a 3- to 4-minute speech of goodwill to be given at the annual banquet of the group you choose to honor. See p. 327 for suggestions of some of the types of groups you might honor. Deliver the speech from manuscript in class.

7. Analyze one of the three model inspirational speeches by Albert Keller, Jr., Thomas J. Scanlon, or Margaret Truman Daniels, giving special attention to the speaker's supporting materials, emotional appeals, and language. Write a 300–400 word evaluation based on your analysis.

FURTHER READINGS

Lucas, Stephen E., *The Art of Public Speaking* (New York: Random House, 1986), chap. 15, "Speaking on Special Occasions."

Monroe, Alan H., and Douglas Ehninger, *Principles of Speech Communication,* 7th brief ed. (Glenview, IL: Scott, Foresman, 1975), chap. 12, "Speeches for Special Occasions."

Ross, Raymond S., *Speech Communication: Fundamentals and Practice,* 7th ed. (Englewood Cliffs, NJ: Prentice-Hall, 1986), chap. 12, "Forums and Special Occasions."

Vasile, Albert J., and Harold K. Mintz, *Speak With Confidence: A Practical Guide,* 4th ed. (Boston, MA: Little, Brown and Co., 1986), chap. 13, "Saying a Few Words."

Verderber, Rudolph F., *The Challenge of Effective Speaking,* 6th ed. (Belmont, CA: Wadsworth Publishing Co., 1985), chap. 18, "Adapting to Special Occasions."

White, Eugene E., *Practical Public Speaking,* 3d ed. (New York: Macmillan, 1978), chap. 14, "Speeches of Special Types."

CHAPTER 17

ETHICAL AND LEGAL RESPONSIBILITIES OF THE SPEAKER

SPEECH IN A DEMOCRATIC SOCIETY

Speech achieves its greatest importance in the conduct of human affairs in those societies placing the fewest restraints on what the speaker may say. Politically, states encouraging the widest expression of opinion on all issues and relying on the judgment of an informed electorate for their policies produce the most effective public discussion. Where freedom of expression is restricted, speech tends to become little more than the mouthing of government-approved doctrine and dogma. In the totalitarian state, speech deteriorates into mere propaganda. Under a one-party system, no real exchange of ideas occurs and the lack of competition among conflicting ideologies often prevents the people from inventing and instituting needed reforms.

Even in a democratic state, fear and intolerance of certain beliefs can restrict the exchange of ideas. The United States experienced this during and after World War I, when more than 2000 prosecutions were brought against people under the Espionage Act of 1917 and the Sedition Act of 1918. These laws permitted people to be prosecuted for urging taxes rather than bond issues for financing the war, for defending the legality of the sinking of merchant vessels, for advocating a referendum on participation in the war, and for calling the war un-Christian. Again, during the McCarthy era of the 1950s, a wave of hysteria resulting from fear of communism silenced many speakers who feared investigation by congressional committees and possible loss of jobs if they spoke out. The politics of confrontation of the 1960s illustrates the importance of freedom of speech in a democratic society. The attempts of minorities to force their views on the majority by demonstrations and the seizure of buildings almost invariably led to rioting, bloodshed, and public reaction against what may have been legitimate grievances.

In areas other than politics, freedom of expression is equally important. Whether communication occurs in the form of a speech, debate, discussion, or conversation, whether it takes place in the classroom, church, business conference, committee session, organization meeting, or social intercourse, the most stimulating and productive discourse results when the participants express themselves freely. Through the open exchange of ideas and information, better understanding and acceptable solutions to group problems are more likely to occur. Worthwhile communication seldom takes place when the participants are inhibited or restrained by fear of retribution or reprisal and whenever speakers believe that their ideas will have no influence on the actions of others.

> The most important tenet of our democratic elective process is the obligation of each candidate to speak out on basic issues in order to present the electorate with a suitable basis for judgment.
>
> JAMES MADISON

> My view is, without deviation, without exception, without any ifs, buts, or whereases, that freedom of speech means that you shall not do something to people either for the views they have or the views they express or the words they speak or write.
>
> HUGO LAFAYETTE BLACK

> If the press is not free, if speech is not independent and untrammeled, if the mind is shackled or made impotent through fear, it makes no difference under what form of government you live, you are a subject and not a citizen.
>
> U.S. SENATOR WILLIAM E. BORAH

While it is desirable to have the widest possible scope in the discussion and debate of ideas, some restrictions are necessary even in the most open and democratic society. When freedom of expression begins to conflict with other rights guaranteed to citizens, some resolution must occur. This resolution may require legal restraints on the exercise of free speech for such reasons as to protect the democratic process, to guarantee the rights of others, to maintain order, and to provide equal opportunity of expression to all.

These safeguards alone, however, cannot ensure either responsible communication or an enlightened exchange of ideas on the issues. Basic to the understanding and decisions required in a democratic society is the acceptance by the speaker of certain ethical responsibilities. The word *ethical* comes from the Greek *ethos* and refers to the adherence to acceptable standards of conduct and moral judgment. Unless speakers—and audiences—accept responsibility for abiding by accepted standards of conduct, the kind of free exchange of ideas essential to discovering the best means of resolving conflicts and reaching decisions cannot occur.

This chapter examines the ethical and legal responsibilities of speakers and auditors in a democratic society.

ETHICAL RESPONSIBILITIES OF THE SPEAKER

The first and most important of the speaker's ethical responsibilities is to be well-informed about the subject. While the right of free speech is guaranteed to anyone, no matter how ignorant or ill-informed, there is no excuse for a speaker to mislead the public simply because of laziness or carelessness. If democracy is to work and the people are to make intelligent decisions, it is imperative that their choices be based on the best information and analysis available. To mislead the public through ignorance is no less reprehensible

Some very young Americans learning about freedom and democracy. (Matheny, *Christian Science Monitor*)

than to operate an automobile without knowing how to drive or to perform surgery without the necessary medical training.

To be well-informed, a speaker must examine all sides of a question as honestly and impartially as possible, utilize all the available information, weigh the reliability of the sources, and test the validity of his or her own reasoning. A speaker must attempt to foresee the consequences of any proposed action.

Second, the speaker has an ethical obligation to present facts supporting his or her ideas. If public confidence is to be maintained, audiences must believe that the speaker is telling the truth, is not distorting the facts, and is not suppressing vital information. Confusion and distrust result when people believe they are being misled. The term *credibility gap* came into being to describe the feeling on the part of many Americans that they were not being told the truth by their leaders. Disclosures of lying and deception by government and military leaders regarding the war in Vietnam and Kampuchea, undercover activities of the CIA and FBI, the Watergate cover-up, and similar attempts to suppress or distort the truth contributed to a dangerous lack of confidence in the government.

Unquestionably, information essential to national security cannot be widely circulated. However, except for items of this kind, the public has the right to know the facts. The example of Winston Churchill during World War II suggests that when people are being told the truth, however unpleasant, they can be trusted to act in the best interests of the country. Never mincing words about the hardship of the war, Britain's setbacks and defeats, and the grimness of the struggle ahead, Churchill nevertheless so inspired the British with his words that the beleaguered island stood alone against the Nazis for more than a year before the United States entered the war.

Third, the speaker has an ethical obligation to accept full responsibility for all that is said. This applies equally to prominent public figures and to student speakers. At a time when busy politicians, executives, educators, and others rely more and more on ghostwriters in the preparation of speeches, the speaker has an ethical obligation to take an active part in the formulation of the speech. Ideally speakers should prepare speeches themselves, without any extensive assistance from others. This enables the listeners to understand the speaker better than any statement prepared by professional speech writers or public relations agencies whose aim is to sell the person—as a product— rather than to enlighten and inform.

Seldom or never will a man be eloquent, but when he is in earnest and uttering his own sentiments.

HUGH BLAIR

At the student level, speakers are expected to prepare their own speeches. The whole purpose of presenting a classroom speech is to gain knowledge and skill in preparing and delivering speeches. Anyone who has not done this cannot possibly have learned anything about speech making. Although students should consult outside sources to obtain ideas and information, the final speech should be the result of their own thought. If material from other sources is used, the speaker should always give proper credit to the author or publication. To simply lift an entire speech or article from a file, book, or magazine and to pass it off as one's own is not only unethical but also constitutes plagiarism—an offense that at most schools is subject to severe penalties.

A fourth ethical responsibility of the speaker is to present the message in a way that listeners are able to respond intelligently. We are not governed by intellect alone; instinct and emotion are important factors in our decisions. But few people would claim that decisions resulting mainly from one's feelings are better than those based on knowledge and facts. Indeed, this is the assumption underlying all education. Thus, if people are to make wise choices, communicators must supply them with the necessary information to judge intelligently.

Having said this, it is important to acknowledge that facts alone often are not enough to motivate a person to take action. For example, in spite of all the statistics showing a high correlation between smoking and cancer, millions of Americans continue to smoke cigarettes; in spite of almost incontrovertible evidence that operating an automobile while intoxicated is dangerous, people continue to drive while drunk; and in spite of conclusive evidence that exceeding speed limits leads to more automobile accidents, many drivers either resent or refuse to obey speed limits. As these examples indicate, factual evidence is not always enough to influence others. For this reason, speakers often must resort to emotional appeals to motivate listeners.

However, the fact that a speaker may find it necessary to appeal to the emotions of the audience to secure the desired response does not constitute a license to substitute sentiment for intelligent thought or to try to influence listeners primarily through appeals to their feelings, no matter how important or virtuous the cause. In a free society, the end never justifies the means. If people do not base their decisions on information and understanding, the democratic process fails. The substitution of slogans for rational thought, oversimplifications, appeals to hysteria and intolerance, and other tricks of propagandists seek to confuse and, even though they may succeed at times, are ethically irresponsible.

A fifth ethical responsibility is to let the other side be heard. Instead of promoting a free exchange of ideas on controversial topics, some individuals and groups seek to silence their critics. Their techniques include shouting speakers down, disrupting meetings, and physical attacks, threats, and intimidation. They try to deny access to public halls, parks,

Where free speech flourishes: the members of Congress assembled in the
House of Representatives for a president's State of the Union address. (Wide
World)

and other facilities. Many organizations refuse to invite speakers whose
ideas they oppose. Although such groups have no legal obligation to hear
both sides of a question, if they really wanted to make intelligent choices,
it would seem that they would avail themselves of the opportunity to
hear many diverse views. Persons who are unwilling even to hear contra-
dictory ideas have no real faith in democracy, free speech, or their own
cause.

No individual or group has an ethical responsibility to solicit a contradic-
tory point of view for every idea expressed in a speech, but any attempt to
suppress opposing viewpoints is not in the best interest of freedom of inquiry
and democratic government.

> Slogans are both exciting and comforting, but they are also powerful opiates for the conscience. . . . Some of mankind's most terrible misdeeds have been committed under the spell of certain magic words or phrases.
>
> JAMES B. CONANT

LEGAL RESPONSIBILITIES OF THE SPEAKER

In addition to ethical responsibilities, a speaker must be aware of his legal rights and restrictions. In the United States, the principal restrictions concern advocacy of the forcible overthrow of the government; speech that provokes a breach of the peace; obscenity; the regulation of time, location, and manner of speaking; defamation of character; and the use of radio and television.

Advocacy of Forcible Overthrow of the Government

Because the government of the United States provides for peaceful change through democratic elections and amendment of the Constitution, laws prohibiting the overthrow of the government by force have consistently been upheld by the courts. The constitutionality of acts banning the *advocacy* of forcible overthrow of the government, however, is not so clear. At one time, the Supreme Court stated that:

> One may not counsel or advise others to violate the law as it stands. Words are not only the keys of persuasion, but the triggers of action, and those which have no purport but to counsel the violation of law cannot by any latitude of interpretation be a part of that public opinion which is the final source of government in a democratic state.

However, the Court later modified its position, applying a criterion known as the "clear and present danger" test. The test does not prohibit abstract discussion of violent overthrow of the government but only speech that actually urges the listeners to take overt action to overthrow the government. In 1969 the Court ruled that advocating violent overthrow of the government was punishable only if the speaker intended to produce imminent lawless action and that violence was likely to occur as a result of the speech. The speaker must have both the intention and capacity to accomplish the violent overthrow of the government.

Furthermore, the Court has specified that the danger must be both clear and present—in other words, neither a vague statement that might be construed by some as urging violence nor a statement that proposes action at some unspecified future date could be considered illegal. Mere membership in a political party dedicated to changing the form of government of the United States (the Communist party, American Nazi party, or some other group) cannot be deemed an attempt to overthrow the government, and members of such parties are allowed the same freedom of speech as members of other political organizations. Participation in a *conspiracy* to overthrow the government can be prosecuted only if the conspirators actually take steps to implement their plan. They must act; merely plotting such action is not unconstitutional.

Breach of the Peace

Restrictions are also placed on speech that provokes a breach of the peace or breaking the law. Cases involving a breach of the peace usually result from some speaker arousing an audience to the point where they destroy public property, attack others, or assault the speaker. Since the Constitution does not deprive a speaker of the right to be intolerant, offensive, ignorant, or bigoted, some speakers evoke intense hostility. The problem facing public officials is to protect the right of free speech of such speakers while preventing them from inciting their listeners to commit violence or break the law.

Decisions of the courts have repeatedly held that the police cannot be

---

The ultimate good desired is better reached by free trade in ideas. The best test of truth is the power of the thought to get itself accepted in the competition of the market. . . . We should be eternally vigilant against attempts to check the expression of opinions that we loathe and believe to be fraught with death, unless they so immediately threaten immediate interference with the lawful and pressing purposes of the law that an immediate check is required to save the country.

OLIVER WENDELL HOLMES

A believer in democratic rights who denies a hearing to speakers whom he regards as opposed to democratic rights is acting on their alleged principles, not on his.

EDITORIAL COMMENT
The Observer (London)

used to suppress unpopular views, yet they have also recognized that when the speaker passes the bounds of peaceful argument and undertakes incitement to riot, the police should not be powerless to act.

In the case of a speaker with a hostile audience that threatens his or her safety, the courts have ruled that the police must make all reasonable efforts to protect the speaker.

Although the courts have never set forth a clear formula for determining when a speaker can be restrained, the factors that have been important in their decisions in such cases have been the place where the speech is given, the character and temper of the audience, and the exact nature of the danger at the critical moment when breaking the law is likely to occur. Even when the entire situation presents an immediate danger of violence, the police face the question of whether to try to restrain the audience or to stop the speaker. Obviously every effort must be made to permit the speaker to continue, for to do otherwise would be an invitation to opponents to silence the speaker simply by threatening disorder. Examples of the necessity for restraining the audience rather than stopping the speaker are found in political campaigns, public meetings, and protest demonstrations that attract protestors hoping to disrupt the speaker. Failure to restrain the demonstrators would effectively silence the speaker, thereby depriving him or her of the right of free speech.

Obscenity

Another area in which freedom of the speaker is restricted is that of obscenity. Obscenity is not governed by the "clear and present danger" test. Instead the courts have held that obscenity simply is not constitutionally protected under the First Amendment and that both the state and federal governments have the right to enact legislation to suppress obscenity. During the 1960s, the courts became increasingly reluctant to ban anything as obscene. Arguing that "any material having any social importance" is permissible—regardless of how crude or offensive it may be to some members of the community—the courts frequently reversed state and local laws governing obscenity on stage presentations, in motion pictures, and in night club performances. As the courts relaxed their attitude toward obscenity, so did several voluntary regulatory agencies such as the Motion Picture Association, with the result that nudity, sexual acts, and language not permitted a short time before were allowed on the stage and screen.

However, in 1973 the Supreme Court handed down a new set of guidelines on obscenity, giving states and communities greater scope in banning books, magazines, plays, and movies offensive to local standards. Among the important guidelines set forth in its decision, the Court ruled that in judging whether a work appeals to prurient interests, a jury should apply the views of "the average person, applying contemporary community standards," rather than any hypothetical national definition. The Court further ruled that showing that the work had some "redeeming social value" would no longer be a defense against prosecution for obscenity. The 1973 ruling raised difficult questions that the courts will have to resolve. For example, how does a jury determine who is an "average person" and what are "contemporary community standards"? The courts will also have to justify imposing standards of the "average person" on everyone else in the community. Finally, they will have to deal with the challenge to the doctrine of equal protection under law raised by empowering authorities in one locality to prohibit and prosecute as obscene works which in other communities would be judged permissible.

Time, Place, and Manner of Speaking

Because the right of free speech often conflicts with other rights and may interfere with the orderly functioning of a community, the courts have held that certain regulations on the time, place, and manner of speaking may be justified. However, the courts have clearly ruled that the government, under the guise of preserving law and order, has absolutely no power to prevent a speaker from presenting a message to a particular audience; at the same time, they have also made it clear that the speaker's constitutional right does not mean that the message can be conveyed at any time or any place under any circumstances.

Among the situations in which public officials may intervene to regulate the use of speaking facilities are the following: when the speech obstructs traffic or the passage of pedestrians; when more than one speaker seeks to use a particular podium, park, or public hall at the same time; when the presentation of a speech interferes with another speaker; when extensive police protection is required to preserve order; and when the speaker disturbs the tranquility or the health of individuals through excessive noise (for example, a public meeting outside a hospital, extreme amplification, or the use of sound trucks at particular times and locations).

In regulating situations of the kind just described, the courts have repeatedly emphasized that none of the restrictions may have anything to do with the content of the speech and that all groups must be treated equally. Although the government may insist that speakers secure a permit or register on a sign-up sheet, it cannot show any preference in the granting of permits. At times, government bodies may even charge fees to cover expenses for

---

If all mankind, minus one, were of one opinion, and only one person were of the contrary opinion, mankind would be no more justified in silencing that one person, than he, if he had the power, would be justified in silencing mankind.

JOHN STUART MILL

Workers demonstrate to support their message.
(© 1982, Johnson, The Picture Cube)

services such as providing police protection or cleaning up after the meeting, or simply for processing the applications for rallies or meetings; but when fees are charged, they cannot be so large that they discourage small groups or unpopular speakers, and they must be equal for all seeking permits.

Furthermore, although the courts have ruled that state and local governments are under no obligation to make public facilities available to any speaker whatsoever, if they do permit the hall to be used for a public meeting, officials thereafter have no right to determine which groups may or may not use the building, nor can the government establish conditions censoring what may and may not be said before granting the use of the facility.

> You have not converted a man when you have silenced him.
>
> JOHN, VISCOUNT MORLEY

With regard to the problem of regulating excessive noise, the courts have approved restrictions ranging from an absolute ban in certain zones (such as hospitals and schools), to limitations on the volume of the amplification and the length of time a sound truck may remain in one spot, to regulations on the hours when such broadcasting may be done. However, in applying these regulations, the governmental body must act without discrimination and with no regard for the popularity of the speaker or the message.

Defamation

The right of free speech is further limited when a speaker's remarks injure the reputation of another person. Injurious statements of this kind are known as defamation of character. For many years, a distinction was made between oral defamation, known as slander, and written defamation, or libel. Because of the permanence of the written word, libel was generally considered a more serious offense. However, with the advent of radio and television, the distinction between libel and slander has become extremely hazy. One of the reasons for this is that the spoken word on a broadcast can now reach many more people than a written defamation can; another reason is that writers, as well as speakers, are usually involved in the preparation of broadcast statements that may be defamatory.

Several conditions must exist before one can claim defamation of character. First, the allegedly defamatory statement must have been communicated to a third party; it is impossible to claim defamation of character if only the speaker and the individual claiming to have been slandered participate in the exchange. Second, the speaker's intent clearly must have been defamatory— that is, the words were not meant to be a joke. Third, the person claiming to have been defamed must be clearly identifiable. Statements such as "Some of the members of the Student Council are drug pushers," or "Many of the legislators are in the pay of gangsters," or "One of the ministers in town is having an affair with a high school girl" are not actionable because the subject has not been specifically identified. On the other hand, statements such as "The president of the Student Council is a drug pusher," "All four of the state's representatives are in the pay of gangsters," and "The pastor of the First Presbyterian Church is having an affair with a high school girl" might be slanderous, because even though the individuals are not actually named, they can be clearly identified.

In a case of defamation, a defendant who can prove that what was said was true usually will be acquitted. If, on the other hand, the plaintiff can prove the statement to be false, the defendant *usually* will be held guilty of defamation.

There are exceptions to both of these generalizations. It is possible for a speaker to be guilty of defamation even though the statement was completely true. Such a verdict would probably result only if it could be proved that the speaker had spoken maliciously with the sole intent of creating trouble and that the remarks could not in any way be construed to contribute to the general welfare of the community. For example, let us suppose that Mrs. Jones becomes irritated because Mr. Smith, her next-door neighbor, has erected a fence 10 feet high between their lots. Smith has lived in the community for many years and has a good reputation as a parent, citizen, and church member. Jones, however, discovers that 20 years earlier Smith had served a short prison term for a minor theft. Angry because Smith erected the fence, Jones goes about the neighborhood telling everyone that Smith is an ex-convict. If Smith were to sue for defamation of character, he probably would win the case (even though it was true that he had served a prison term), because Jones's intent was purely malicious; in other words, the dissemination of this information served no useful purpose. On the other hand, had Smith been a candidate for city treasurer and were Jones to reveal the same information, it is almost certain that no case of slander would exist.

A second exception would be the case of a speaker who makes a defamatory statement that is wholly untrue, but the speaker can prove that the allegation was made in good faith and without malicious intent. This once occurred when a priest who had been attacked repeatedly in the press and in speeches by a former parishioner was told by a physician that the woman had been under psychiatric care and had spent several years in a mental hospital. In a sermon, the priest told his congregation to ignore the attacks of the critic because of her history of mental illness. The woman brought suit for slander and at the trial proved that she had never had any mental problems or treatment. The priest, whose defense was that he had had every reason to believe the physician and that he had not spoken maliciously, was acquitted.

Recent rulings by the courts have made it more difficult for public officials and well-known personalities to collect damages for alleged defamation of character. In the case of government officials, both elected and appointed, the court has ruled that because these people have either sought or agreed to serve the people, rigorous scrutiny of their conduct is in the public interest, and so greater latitude should be permitted in discussing their actions than would be allowed if the persons were ordinary citizens. Regarding prominent celebrities, such as actors, entertainers, professional athletes, and other "stars," the court has ruled that because these individuals have chosen careers

When men can freely communicate their thoughts and their sufferings, real or imaginary, their passions spend themselves in air, like gunpowder scattered upon the surface; but pent up by terrors, they work unseen, burst forth in a moment, and destroy everything in their course.

THOMAS ERSKINE

that place them in the public eye—indeed, in which they seek attention—they should be expected to tolerate greater freedom of discussion of their lives and careers than that accorded ordinary citizens. This does not mean, however, that one is free to say anything one wishes about a "celebrity."

Some persons are immune to prosecution for defamation under particular conditions. The statements of legislators while in session and the testimony of judges, witnesses, and lawyers during a trial are regarded as privileged and not subject to defamation proceedings. Critics of plays, movies, books, sports events, concerts, and public performances are generally immune from suits for defamation so long as they do not misrepresent the facts and they restrict themselves to comments on the merits of the work, rather than the private lives of the individuals involved.

Radio and Television

In the very early days of radio, individual broadcasters simply set up their equipment and began transmitting whatever they wanted at any frequency they chose. However, as the number of broadcasters increased and their signals began to interfere with each other, it became apparent that some kind of control was needed. Accordingly, Congress in 1912 enacted legislation providing for regulation of the growing broadcasting industry. Succeeding acts extended the regulatory powers of the government and created the Federal Communications Commission (FCC) to enforce these controls.

The basis of the FCC's authority rests on its right to grant and renew licenses to broadcasters. Since the number of applicants for licenses exceeds the number of frequencies available, from the outset the FCC has insisted that the airwaves belong to the people and that a license will be granted only if the public convenience, interest, or necessity is served. The commission has no authority to censor any broadcast. However, because it is empowered to review how well a broadcaster has served the public when the license comes up for renewal, in a sense it does exercise a form of censorship after the fact. The most important provisions of the code regulating broadcasters concern (1) the presentation of public affairs programs, (2) fairness in dealing with controversial issues, (3) granting equal time to political candidates, and (4) avoidance of offensive material.

Because purely entertaining programs attract larger audiences than public affairs presentations and are more easily sold to sponsors, most commercial broadcasters tend to shy away from programs dealing with public affairs. After all, they are in the business of making money. However, the FCC has insisted that they are obligated to devote time to public affairs—even if they are not as popular as some other programs—because they clearly serve the public interest.

In addition to an obligation to air public affairs programs, for many years broadcasters were required to deal fairly with controversial issues. Thus a licensee who presented a program favoring a particular policy, proposal, or group was obligated to see that the other side had an opportunity to air its views. Or if a station broadcast an editorial, it was required to make time available for opposing ideas. Many broadcasters contended that the requirement that they make time available for conflicting points of view—unlike newspapers and other print media—violated their freedom of expression. Agreeing with these broadcasters, in 1987 the FCC announced that the fairness doctrine would no longer be enforced. Disagreeing with the commission, that same year Congress passed an act requiring broadcasters to observe the fairness doctrine. President Reagan vetoed the bill. Whether Congress will override the veto or the Supreme Court will uphold the fairness doctrine, as it did in 1969, contending that the rule enhanced rather than abridged freedom of speech and press as protected by the First Amendment, remains to be seen.

For years, in political campaigns, broadcasters were also governed by Section 315 of the Federal Communications Act, stating that if licensees made air time available—either free or for a price—to one candidate, they must offer equal use of their facilities to all other candidates for that office. The law applied to candidates at national, state, and local levels and was fair in that it provided all with equal access to the airwaves. It tended to discourage stations from offering free air time for political broadcasts involving the major candidates, since they would have been required to grant equal amounts of time to all aspirants—however obscure—for the office. (In most presidential elections, there are as many as 15 legally qualified candidates, many of them unknown to the general public.) As a result, most broadcasts were paid for by the candidates or their supporters; the less affluent candidates, although legally entitled to equal time, often simply could not afford it. The first nationally televised presidential campaign debates—between John F. Kennedy and Richard Nixon in 1960—it should be noted, were possible only because Congress suspended the equal-time provision that year.

In 1975 the FCC modified the equal-time rule by giving broadcasters the right to provide coverage of "legitimate news events" involving political candidates without automatically requiring them to give equal access to all their opponents. This ruling—not a suspension of Section 315 of the Federal Communications Act—enabled the television networks to broadcast the debates between the Democratic and Republican candidates for president and vice president in 1976, 1980, and 1984. The debates in these campaigns were arranged by organizers other than broadcasters, so the networks under the new ruling could claim they were simply covering legitimate news events.

Finally, another important restriction on radio and television broadcasting is that the stations have a responsibility not to present material that is vulgar, in bad taste, indecent, obscene, or profane. This particular regulation poses awkward problems for broadcasters, because what is regarded as vulgar or obscene by some may be inoffensive to others. In 1978 the FCC issued a directive that under no circumstances could any of seven allegedly "indecent" words be used in any broadcast earlier than 10 PM, when children might presumably still be listening. The Commission labeled the seven words "indecent" rather than "obscene" because of the legal difficulties in determining what is obscene.

While the FCC has additional regulatory powers, and other federal agencies also exercise some control over broadcasting, the four provisions discussed are probably the most important government restrictions on what can be said or done on the air. In addition to these federal controls, however, the networks and individual stations voluntarily regulate themselves with regard to the presentation of certain kinds of material.

Freedom of Speech on the Campus

Because of the university's importance as an institution in which the most searching and critical examination of ideas can take place, freedom of speech is extremely vital on the college campus. Here, if anywhere, is a place where the widest possible latitude in the discussion of ideas should be encouraged. However, it is also here that there is often bitter controversy over what can or should be said. Campus speakers are not exempt from any of the restriction that government places on other speakers. However, the very nature of a college or university seems to lead to disagreement over the limits of free speech. Parents, trustees, and legislators on the one hand often are disturbed about what students hear or are being taught; students and faculty, on the other hand, usually want the greatest freedom possible in discussing all ideas. Campus disputes concerning freedom of speech revolve around the rights of (1) faculty, (2) the students, and (3) the "outside speaker."

RIGHTS OF THE FACULTY. Attempts to limit the freedom of speech of college faculty members are commonplace today and in most of America's history. Teachers who express new or controversial ideas—either inside or outside the classroom—often are subjected to strong public pressure to keep silent or risk dismissal. Although most colleges and universities profess a belief in academic freedom, this provides no legal protection for a faculty member. Legally the constitution guarantees the rights of free speech to a person but does not protect his or her "right" to remain on the faculty. Most college teachers have legal recourse if attacked for advocating an unpopular idea. The American Association of University Professors champions academic freedom but has little power beyond censuring a university and urging teachers to refuse employment at a school. Because no faculty member has a constitutional right to teach at a particular institution, the courts usually will not intervene, or they will uphold the validity of a professor's discharge.

RIGHTS OF THE STUDENT. It wasn't until the 1960s that college students began to show concern over their rights of free speech. Before then colleges and universities exercised tight control over what kinds of student

Progress by dissent . . . is characteristic of human societies. It has been responsible for the growth and success of democracy in the last four hundred years, and the decline and failure of absolute forms of government: For the crucial feature of democracy is not simply that the majority rules, but that *the minority is free to persuade people* to come over to its side and make a new majority. Of course, the minority is abused at first—Socrates was, and so was Charles Darwin. But the strength of democracy is that the dissident minority is not silenced; on the contrary, it is the business of the minority to convert the majority; and this is how a democratic society invigorates and renews itself in change as no totalitarian society can.

J. BRONOWSKI

meetings could be held, what speakers could be invited, and even what subjects students might discuss. It was not uncommon for administrators to ban debates, prohibit speeches on particular subjects, and deny certain groups holding meetings on campus. However, the widespread student revolt against such restrictions, which began at the University of California at Berkeley in 1964 and spread throughout most of the nation in subsequent years, has largely brought to an end most of these restrictions. A large number of schools, either under pressure from dissenting students or faced with the possibility of future disorder if they did not liberalize their policies, eliminated the most restrictive regulations on free speech. Most disputes between colleges and students over free speech never reach the courts. However, one important court decision in 1961 held that students may not be expelled from state colleges or universities for disciplinary reasons without some form of hearing that meets the tests of due process of law.

THE OUTSIDE SPEAKER.   Most disputes over whether a speaker should be permitted to address a student audience involve individuals regarded as extremists (for example, religious cult leaders, spokespersons for unpopular governments or causes, atheists, Ku Klux Klan members, American Nazis). Students and faculty members tend to support a policy that does not prohibit any speaker from appearing on campus. They contend that students come to college to learn and should be exposed to many different points of view. Furthermore, they argue that since no one is required to attend such lectures, students who do not wish to hear the speaker may simply stay away. Parents and the public, however, often oppose the appearance of certain speakers on campus because they believe the ideas of some speakers are so thoroughly discredited, subversive, or repugnant that there is no value in listening to them. They further contend that since their taxes or tuition fees support the school, they have a right to decide what speakers should be permitted on campus. The college administrator usually is caught in the middle, trying to satisfy the demands of the faculty and the student groups and attempting to please the parents and the public.

No speaker has the constitutional right to demand the use of college facilities. While many colleges and universities permit campus groups to invite anyone to speak, most schools exercise some control over the appearance of outside speakers. Regulations may range from a simple rule that speakers be invited by a recognized campus group and that the school be notified, to provisions requiring approval by some committee or official, to an outright ban on speakers belonging to certain groups. In an effort to resolve the question of who may speak on campus, many schools have worked out detailed codes, and some state legislatures have enacted laws prohibiting the appearance of speakers belonging to unpopular or allegedly subversive organizations.

Most battles over who should be allowed to speak on campus are waged between students who insist that controversial speakers should be allowed to appear and administrators or citizen's groups who regard such persons as dangerous and wish to ban them. At most colleges and universities the battle in recent years has been won by the student who demanded the right to hear controversial speakers. However, more recently the conflict has taken a different turn. Perhaps buoyed by their success in bringing controversial speakers to campus, some student groups have begun to exert pressure to prevent the appearance of speakers with whose views they disagree. Among those whose invitations to speak have been withdrawn due to fear of "adverse student reaction" or because of possible disruptions were two presidents, a Nobel laureate, a distinguished professor of constitutional law, the chief judge of a United States District Court of Appeals, the United States ambassador to the United Nations, and several officials implicated in the Watergate affair.

Judge Irving R. Kaufman, who was compelled to cancel a commencement address when students threatened to disrupt his speech because he had presided over a controversial trial more than 20 years before, regards this growing spirit of intolerance as disquieting, especially at colleges and universities, the principal purpose of which should be to promote the free interchange of ideas.

We can never be sure that the opinion we are endeavoring to stifle is a false opinion; and if we were sure, stifling it would be an evil still.

JOHN STUART MILL

Explaining his own reasons for believing in complete freedom of speech, Kaufman says:

> I would never be certain of my own reasons for opposing a speaker until I had allowed him to speak. To restrain anyone who opposes a principle to which I adhere carries with it the risk that I will be forever foreclosed from reconsidering my own views, which may have been arrived at initially on the basis of inadequate or mistaken information or defective reasoning. . . . Even in those views we hold most strongly we may be mistaken.

Only in a totalitarian environment are there "right" ideas that are permitted and "wrong" ideas that are suppressed. The basic objection to any restriction on the expression of an idea—whether by a student, faculty member, or outside speaker—on a college or university campus is that when anyone is prohibited from presenting ideas because they are regarded as worthless, dangerous, or incompatible with the aims of the school, that institution automatically endorses the educational value and respectability of the ideas expressed by those who are allowed to address the students. Such a policy is one of indoctrination. Under no circumstances can it be described as "education," "scholarship," "learning," or "intellectual freedom."

SUMMARY

Public address is most important in societies that permit a wide scope in the discussion of ideas and issues. However, if speech is to function as it should in a democracy, the speaker must adhere to certain ethical standards. These include being well-informed, presenting factually accurate material, accepting responsibility for what one says, presenting the message in such a manner that listeners are able to react intelligently and rationally, and permitting opposing viewpoints to be heard. Without these self-imposed ethical standards, speech cannot fulfill its vital role in giving the public the insight and understanding necessary for the efficient functioning of a democratic government.

Even in the freest society, however, some restrictions on speech are necessary. In the United States, these limitations include regulations on time, place, and manner of speaking; defamation of character; advocacy of the forcible overthrow of the government; and speech that violates the law. Because of the nature of broadcasting, radio and television speakers are further restricted by federal regulations. Colleges and universities are governed by the same legal restrictions affecting the populace in general. However, because of the educational function of the university, the question of who should be allowed to address students and what speakers should be permitted to say is often a point of controversy.

> Many have fallen by the edge of the sword; but not so many as have fallen by the tongue.
>
> ECCLESIASTICUS 28:18

STUDY QUESTIONS AND EXERCISES

1. What is the "clear and present danger" test?
2. What is meant by *breach of the peace*?
3. What is obscenity? Is it constitutionally protected?
4. How do time, place, and manner of speaking affect the individual's right to free speech?
5. What is defamation? libel? slander?
6. Is truth always a defense against libel and slander?
7. In the United States, who owns the broadcasting airwaves?
8. Why is Section 315 of the Federal Communications Act important?
9. Do noncampus speakers have a constitutional right to speak at colleges and universities if they wish?
10. What ethical responsibilities must speakers assume if the democratic process is to flourish?
11. What is the equal-time provision? To whom does it apply?
12. What is the fairness doctrine?
13. What is your opinion on each of the following questions:
    a. Should a democratic government allow complete freedom of expression to persons espousing unpopular causes? dangerous causes? antidemocratic viewpoints?
    b. Should there be any legal restraints on public speakers who advocate atheism? communism? fascism?
    c. Can society be trusted to see through the claims of demagogues and subversive speakers?
    d. Should Communists be allowed to address college students?
    e. Should our laws against libel and slander be strengthened?
    f. Do we need federal legislation to prevent profanity and obscenity on the airwaves?
    g. Should college students refrain from publicly criticizing their schools?
    h. Is a speaker justified in promoting discontent, dissension, and demonstrations?
    i. Does a speaker have an ethical responsibility to avoid highly controversial subjects?
    j. Do most college students believe strongly in freedom of speech?
14. Project: Prepare a short questionnaire designed to discover the attitudes of students at your school toward (1) free speech, (2) academic freedom, (3) restrictions on outside speakers appearing on campus, or some other related topic. Administer the questionnaire to 20 students.

FURTHER READINGS

Haiman, Franklyn S., *Freedom of Speech, Issues and Cases* (New York: Random House, 1965).

Haiman, Franklyn S., "How Fares the First Amendment?" *Representative American Speeches, 1984–1985* (New York: H. W. Wilson Company, 1985), pp. 42–58.

Johanneson, Richard L., *Ethics in Human Communication* (Columbus, Ohio: Charles E. Merrill, 1975), p. 11.

Mathias, Charles M., Jr., "The State of Civil Liberties," *Representative American Speeches, 1980–1981* (New York: H. W. Wilson Company, 1981), pp. 203–209.

Mill, John Stuart, "On Liberty of Thought and Discussion," in Nels G. Juleus, *Perspectives on Public Speaking* (New York: American Book Co., 1966), p. 159 ff.

Nilsen, Thomas R., *Ethics of Speech Communication* (Indianapolis: Bobbs-Merrill, 1966).

O'Neil, Robert M., *Free Speech: Responsible Communication Under Law* (Indianapolis: Bobbs-Merrill, 1972).

CREDITS

For permission to use copyrighted materials, grateful acknowledgment is made to the copyright holders whose materials appear on the following pages:

pp. 4, 217–218, 285 Excerpts from *Rules for Radicals* by Saul Alinsky. Used with permission of Random House.

pp. 25–28 Excerpt from "Polarization, Social Facilitation, and Listening." Copyright 1961 by the Western Speech Communication Association. Reprinted by permission.

pp. 259–260 Excerpt from *The LeBaron Secret* by Stephen Birmingham. Copyright 1986 by Stephen Birmingham. By permission of Little, Brown and Company and Brandt & Brandt Literary Agents, Inc.

pp. 126–127 Excerpt from "Dissent, Dissension, and the News," in *The Decline of Radicalism,* used with permission of Random House.

pp. 221–223 "Halley's Comet: Since the Last Time" used with permission of the author, Jerald L. Boykin, Jr.

pp. 329–331 "A Memorial to American Vietnam War Veterans" used with permission of the author, Albert Keller, Jr.

pp. 331–333 "Tribute to John F. Kennedy" used with permission of the author, Thomas J. Scanlon.

pp. 334–336 "The Remarkable Man from Missouri" used with permission of the author, Margaret Truman Daniel.

INDEX